Stone Soup

The First Collection of the Syndicated Cartoon

by
Jan Eliot

Cheers!
Jan Eliot

Andrews and McMeel
A Universal Press Syndicate Company
Kansas City

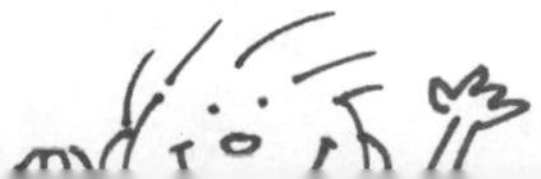

Stone Soup is distributed internationally by Universal Press Syndicate.

Stone Soup copyright © 1997 by Jan Eliot. All rights reserved. Printed in the United States of America. No part of this book may be used or reproduced in any manner whatsoever without written permission except in the case of reprints in the context of reviews. For information write Andrews and McMeel, a Universal Press Syndicate Company, 4520 Main Street, Kansas City, Missouri 64111.

ISBN: 0-8362-2893-6

Library of Congress Catalog Card Number: 96-86593

98 99 00 01   EBA   10 9 8 7 6 5 4 3 2

ATTENTION: SCHOOLS AND BUSINESSES

Andrews and McMeel books are available at quantity discounts with bulk purchase for educational, business, or sales promotional use. For information, write to: Special Sales Department, Andrews and McMeel, 4520 Main Street, Kansas City, Missouri 64111.

To Ted, Jennifer, Johanna, and Val.

Where would I be without you?

Foreword

I confess, I had never heard the expression "Stone Soup" before Jan Eliot's insightful and very funny comic strip appeared in my mailbox awhile ago. "Would you look at this and tell me what you think?" she asked. Which I did.

Recognizing true competition and knowing that, if published, her work would certainly rival mine, I naturally told her that her work was, well . . . excellent. The problem with cartoonists, you see, is that we're far too honest—which is why *Stone Soup* will appeal to everyone so much.

Making soup from a stone is, after all, something parents (especially single parents) are often required to do. In fact, we can make do for our families with just about anything! (Stones require extra spicing.)

Jan Eliot began as a resourceful mother, became a talented cartoonist, and is now a colleague—a welcome friend in this heretofore male-dominated industry. We share many things in common. For example, we know that in this world, it is "survival of the funniest" and I expect Jan and her work to enhance the lives of comics-loving families everywhere for a long, long time!

—Lynn Johnston, creator of
For Better or For Worse

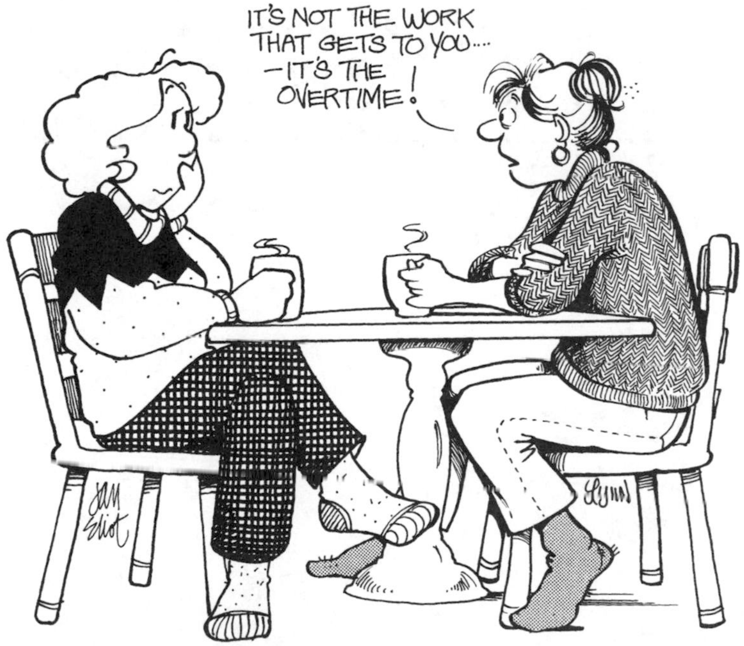
IT'S NOT THE WORK THAT GETS TO YOU.... -IT'S THE OVERTIME!
JAN Eliot
Lynn

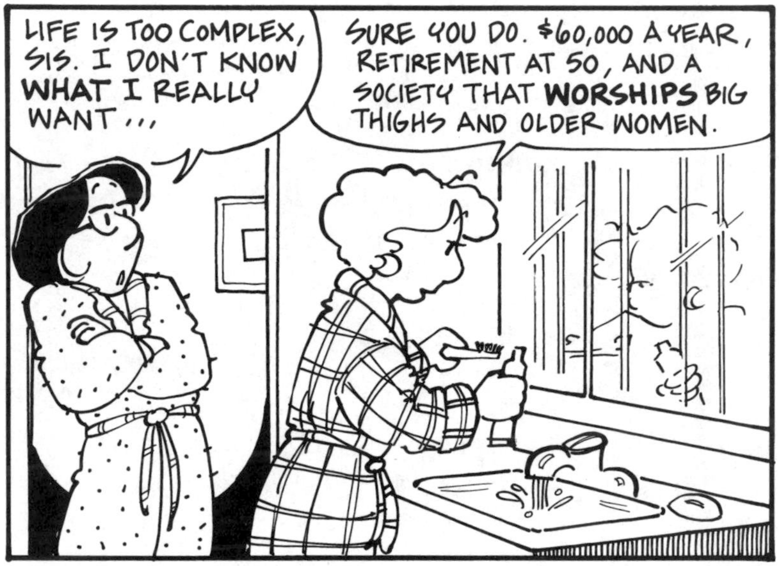
LIFE IS TOO COMPLEX, SIS. I DON'T KNOW **WHAT** I REALLY WANT...
SURE YOU DO. $60,000 A YEAR, RETIREMENT AT 50, AND A SOCIETY THAT **WORSHIPS** BIG THIGHS AND OLDER WOMEN.

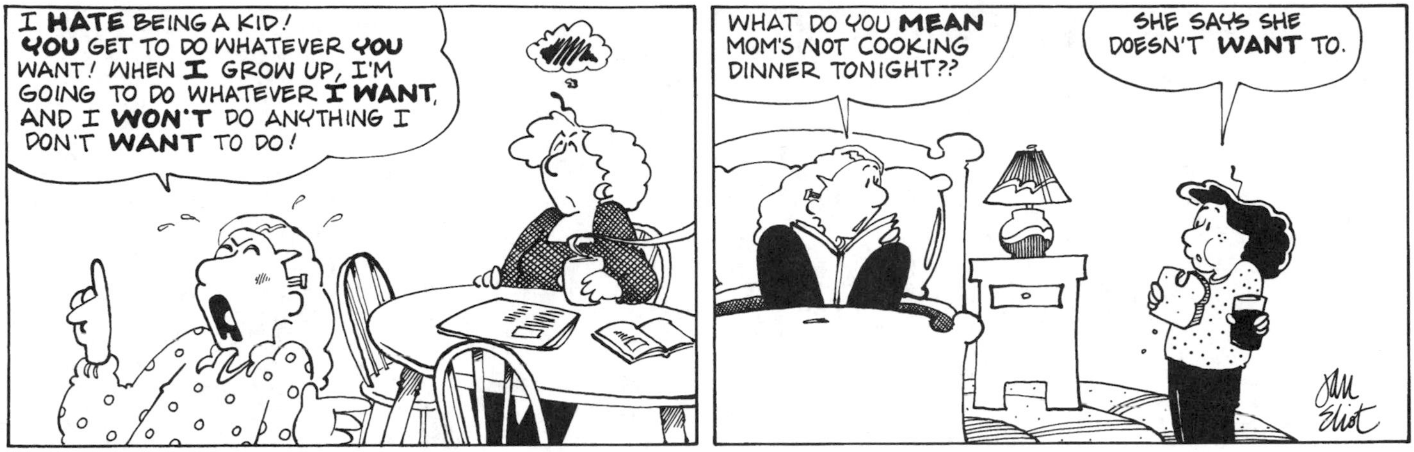
I HATE BEING A KID! YOU GET TO DO WHATEVER YOU WANT! WHEN I GROW UP, I'M GOING TO DO WHATEVER I WANT, AND I WON'T DO ANYTHING I DON'T WANT TO DO!
WHAT DO YOU MEAN MOM'S NOT COOKING DINNER TONIGHT??
SHE SAYS SHE DOESN'T WANT TO.

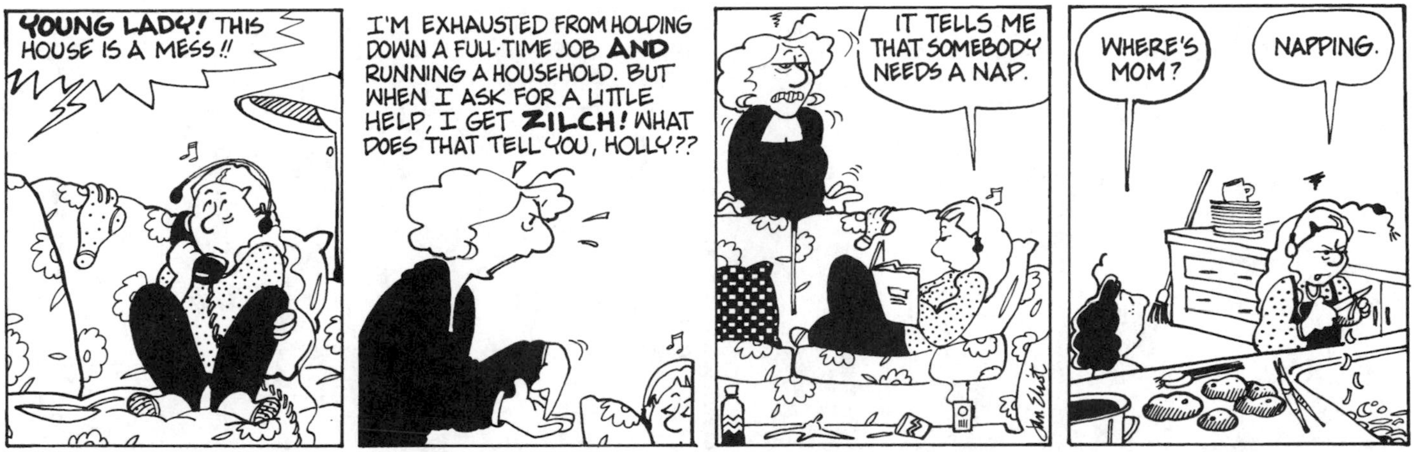
YOUNG LADY! THIS HOUSE IS A MESS!!
I'M EXHAUSTED FROM HOLDING DOWN A FULL-TIME JOB AND RUNNING A HOUSEHOLD. BUT WHEN I ASK FOR A LITTLE HELP, I GET ZILCH! WHAT DOES THAT TELL YOU, HOLLY??
IT TELLS ME THAT SOMEBODY NEEDS A NAP.
WHERE'S MOM?
NAPPING.

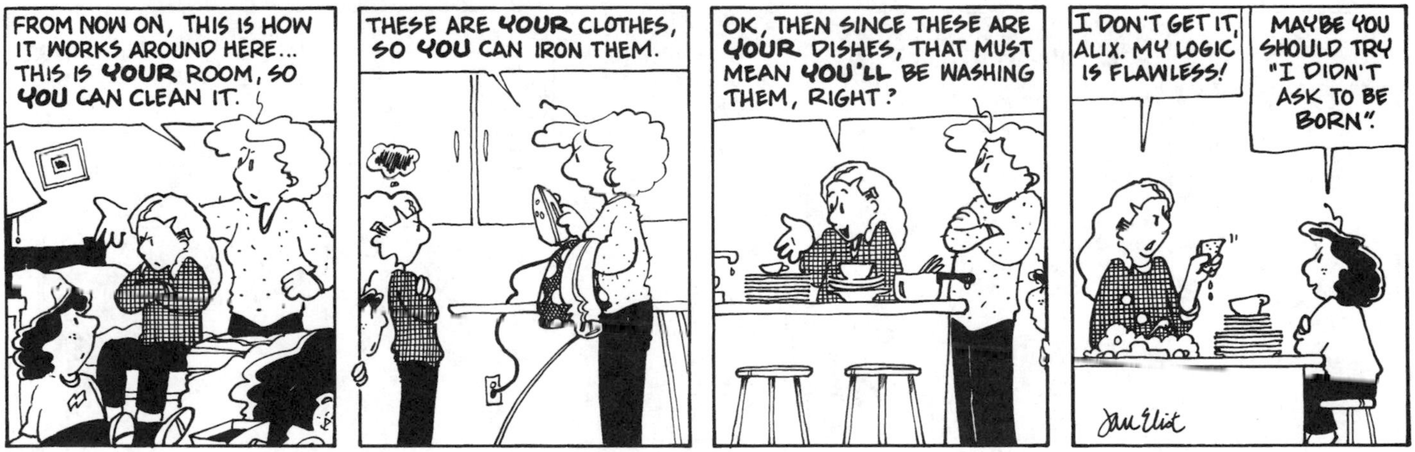
FROM NOW ON, THIS IS HOW IT WORKS AROUND HERE... THIS IS YOUR ROOM, SO YOU CAN CLEAN IT.
THESE ARE YOUR CLOTHES, SO YOU CAN IRON THEM.
OK, THEN SINCE THESE ARE YOUR DISHES, THAT MUST MEAN YOU'LL BE WASHING THEM, RIGHT?
I DON'T GET IT, ALIX. MY LOGIC IS FLAWLESS!
MAYBE YOU SHOULD TRY "I DIDN'T ASK TO BE BORN".

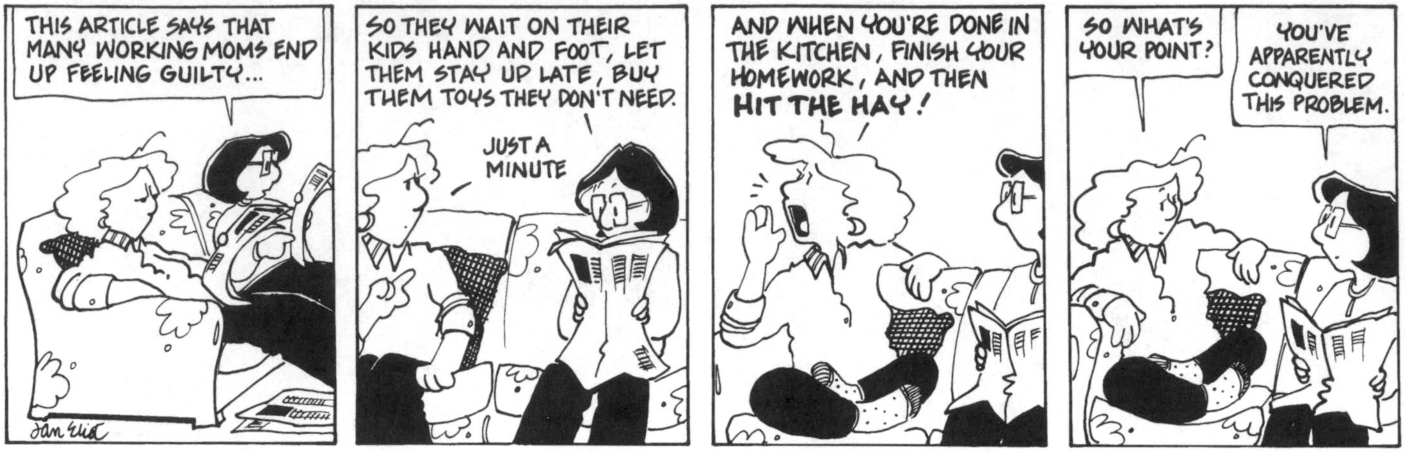
THIS ARTICLE SAYS THAT MANY WORKING MOMS END UP FEELING GUILTY...
SO THEY WAIT ON THEIR KIDS HAND AND FOOT, LET THEM STAY UP LATE, BUY THEM TOYS THEY DON'T NEED.
JUST A MINUTE
AND WHEN YOU'RE DONE IN THE KITCHEN, FINISH YOUR HOMEWORK, AND THEN **HIT THE HAY**!
SO WHAT'S YOUR POINT?
YOU'VE APPARENTLY CONQUERED THIS PROBLEM.

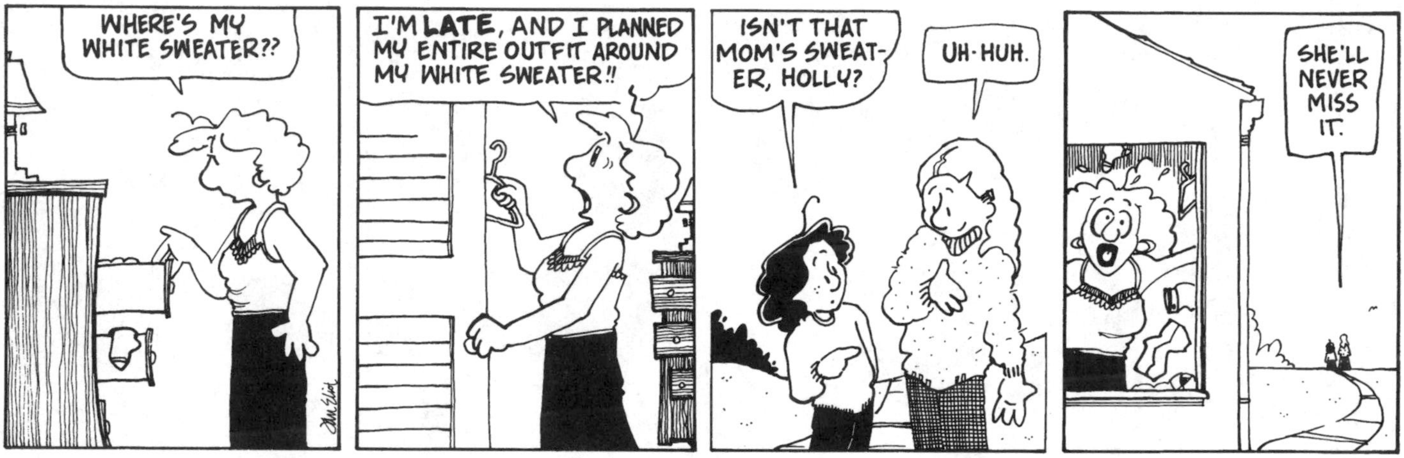
WHERE'S MY WHITE SWEATER??
I'M **LATE**, AND I PLANNED MY ENTIRE OUTFIT AROUND MY WHITE SWEATER!!
ISN'T THAT MOM'S SWEATER, HOLLY?
UH-HUH.
SHE'LL NEVER MISS IT.

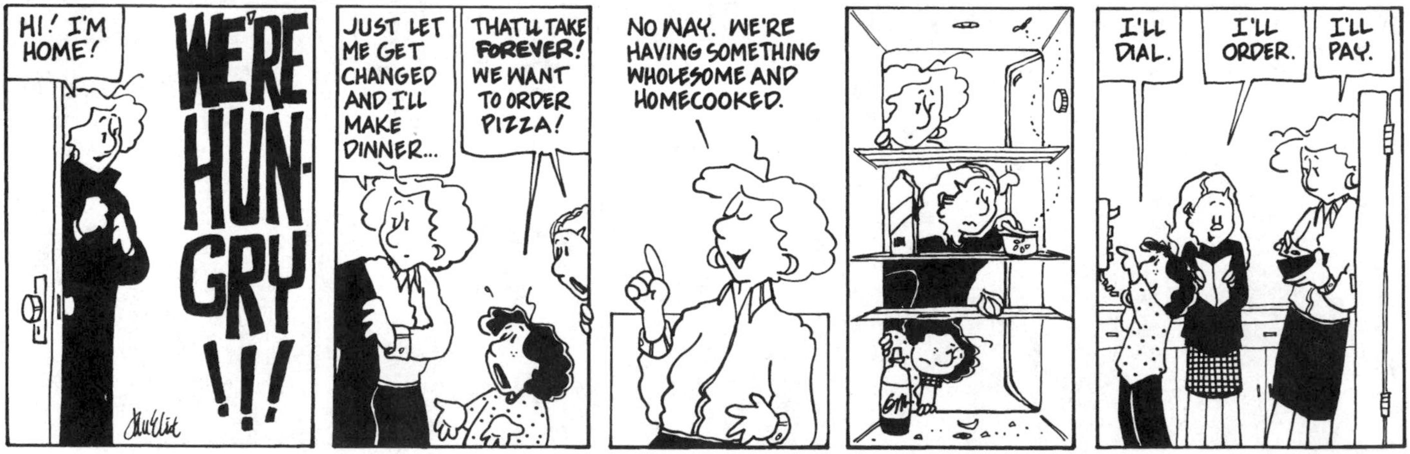
HI! I'M HOME!
WE'RE HUN-GRY!!!
JUST LET ME GET CHANGED AND I'LL MAKE DINNER...
THAT'LL TAKE **FOREVER**! WE WANT TO ORDER PIZZA!
NO WAY. WE'RE HAVING SOMETHING WHOLESOME AND HOMECOOKED.
I'LL DIAL.
I'LL ORDER.
I'LL PAY.

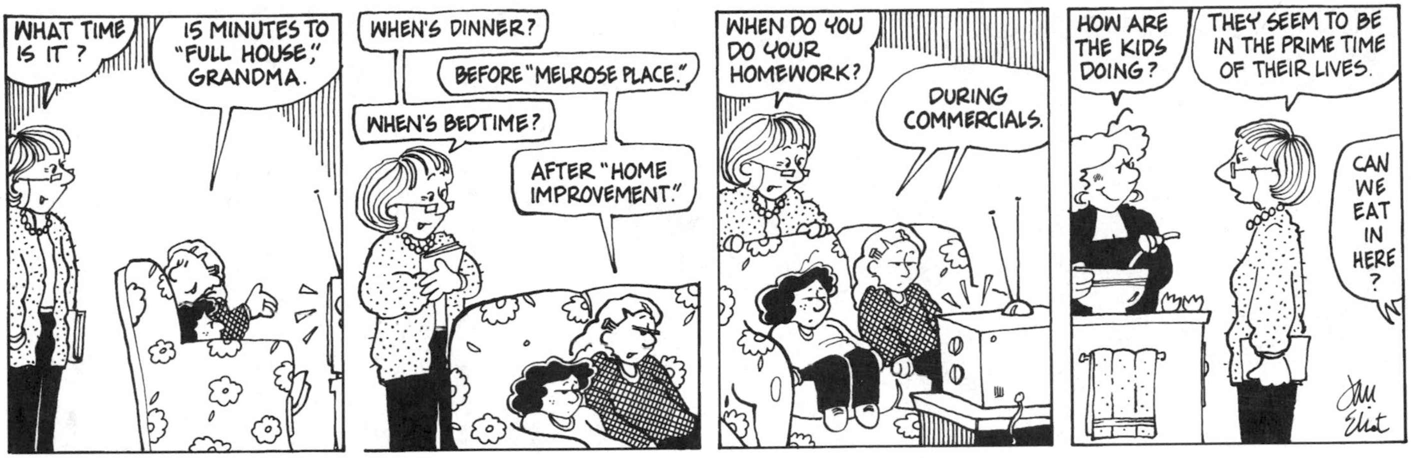
WHAT TIME IS IT ?
15 MINUTES TO "FULL HOUSE," GRANDMA.
WHEN'S DINNER?
BEFORE "MELROSE PLACE."
WHEN'S BEDTIME?
AFTER "HOME IMPROVEMENT."
WHEN DO YOU DO YOUR HOMEWORK?
DURING COMMERCIALS.
HOW ARE THE KIDS DOING?
THEY SEEM TO BE IN THE PRIME TIME OF THEIR LIVES.
CAN WE EAT IN HERE ?

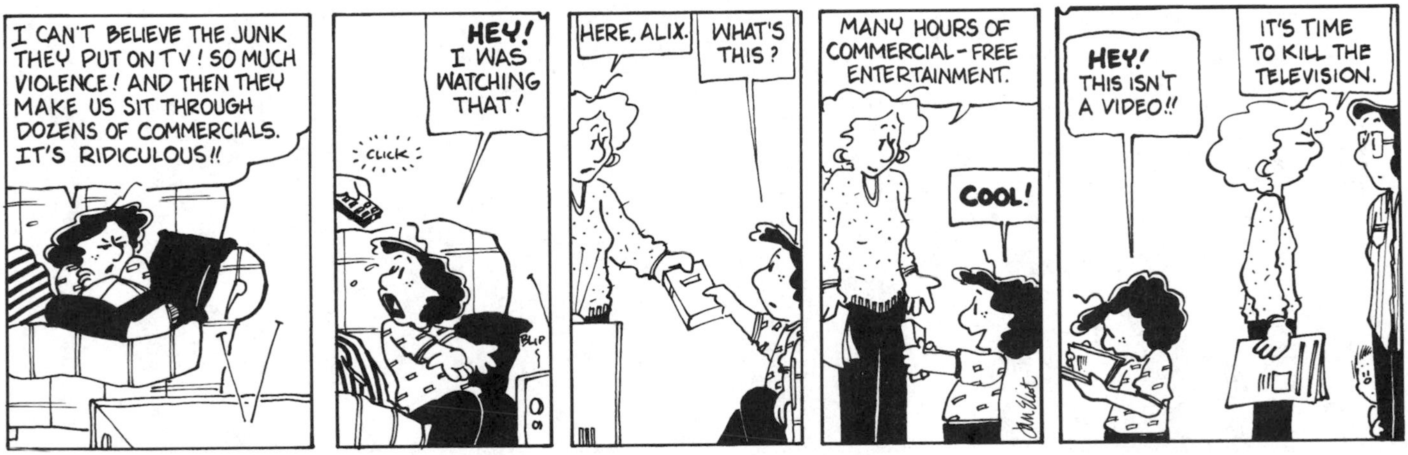
I CAN'T BELIEVE THE JUNK THEY PUT ON TV! SO MUCH VIOLENCE! AND THEN THEY MAKE US SIT THROUGH DOZENS OF COMMERCIALS. IT'S RIDICULOUS!!
CLICK
HEY! I WAS WATCHING THAT!
BLIP
HERE, ALIX.
WHAT'S THIS?
MANY HOURS OF COMMERCIAL-FREE ENTERTAINMENT.
COOL!
HEY! THIS ISN'T A VIDEO!!
IT'S TIME TO KILL THE TELEVISION.

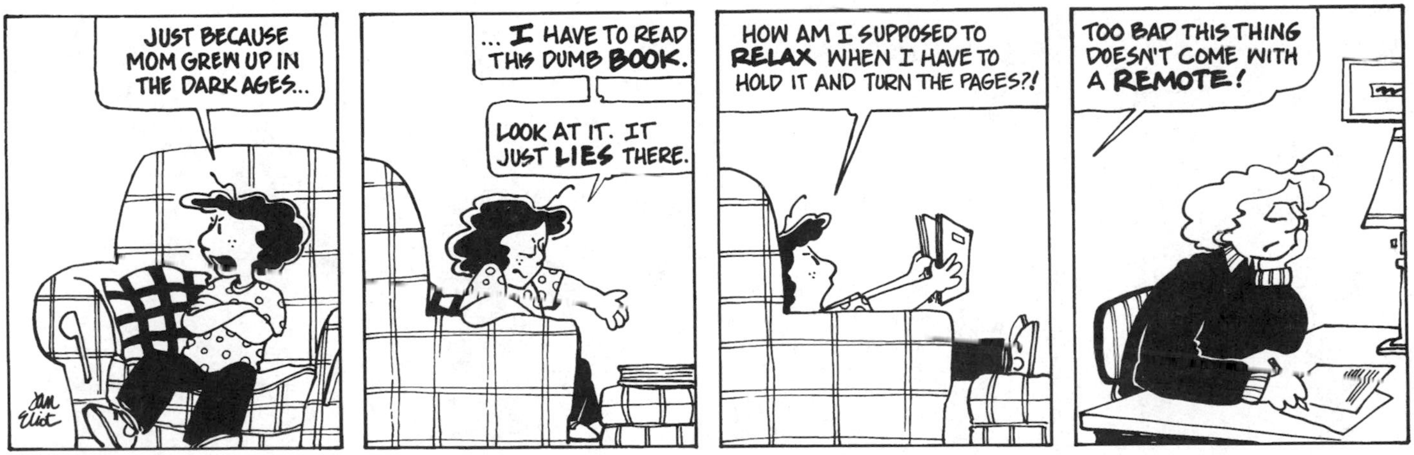
JUST BECAUSE MOM GREW UP IN THE DARK AGES...
... I HAVE TO READ THIS DUMB BOOK.
LOOK AT IT. IT JUST LIES THERE.
HOW AM I SUPPOSED TO RELAX WHEN I HAVE TO HOLD IT AND TURN THE PAGES?!
TOO BAD THIS THING DOESN'T COME WITH A REMOTE!

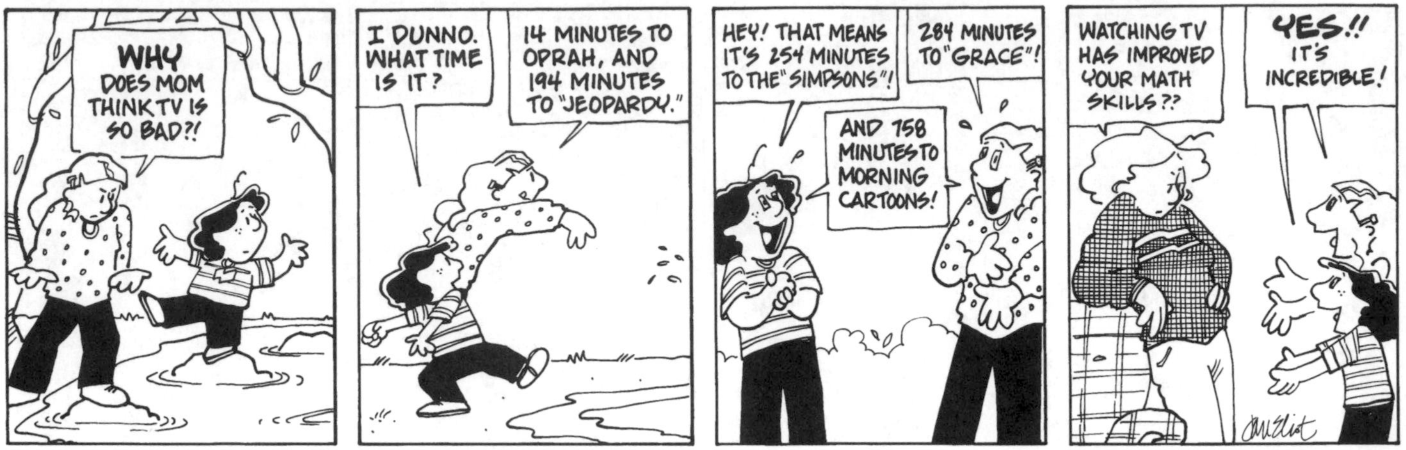
WHY DOES MOM THINK TV IS SO BAD?!
I DUNNO. WHAT TIME IS IT?
14 MINUTES TO OPRAH, AND 194 MINUTES TO "JEOPARDY."
HEY! THAT MEANS IT'S 254 MINUTES TO THE "SIMPSONS"!
284 MINUTES TO "GRACE"!
AND 758 MINUTES TO MORNING CARTOONS!
WATCHING TV HAS IMPROVED YOUR MATH SKILLS??
YES!! IT'S INCREDIBLE!

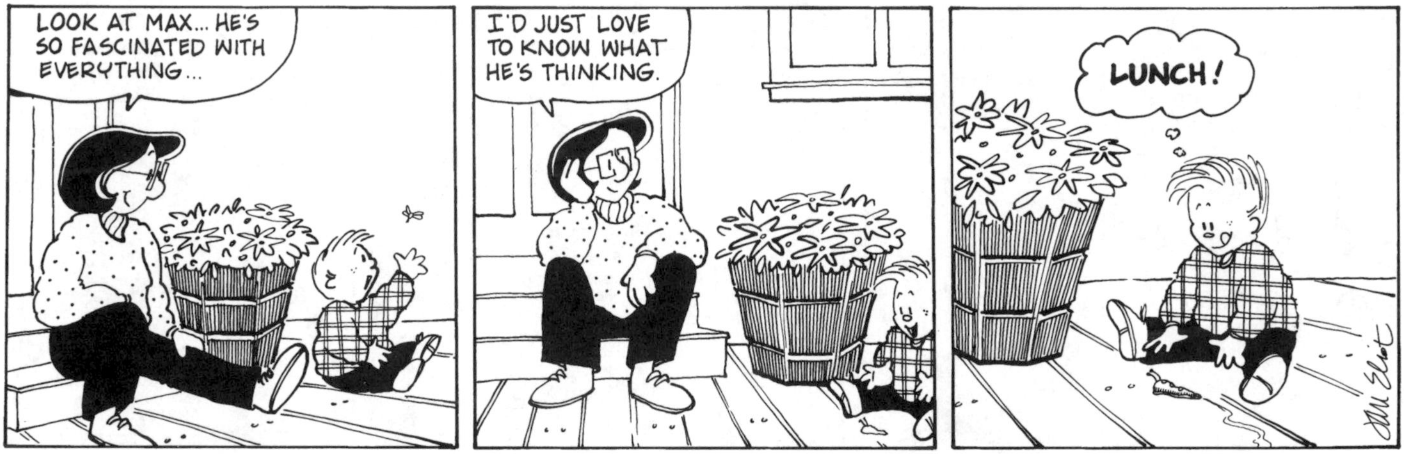
LOOK AT MAX... HE'S SO FASCINATED WITH EVERYTHING...
I'D JUST LOVE TO KNOW WHAT HE'S THINKING.
LUNCH!

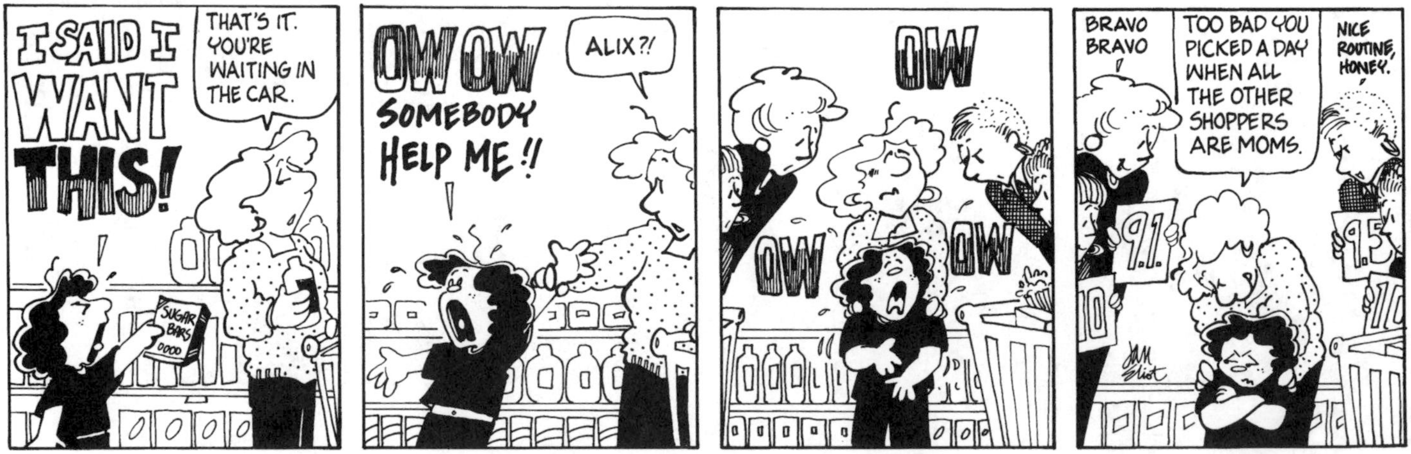
I SAID I WANT THIS!
SUGAR BARS
THAT'S IT. YOU'RE WAITING IN THE CAR.
OW OW SOMEBODY HELP ME!!
ALIX?!
OW
OW
OW
BRAVO BRAVO
TOO BAD YOU PICKED A DAY WHEN ALL THE OTHER SHOPPERS ARE MOMS.
NICE ROUTINE, HONEY.
9.1
10
9.5
10

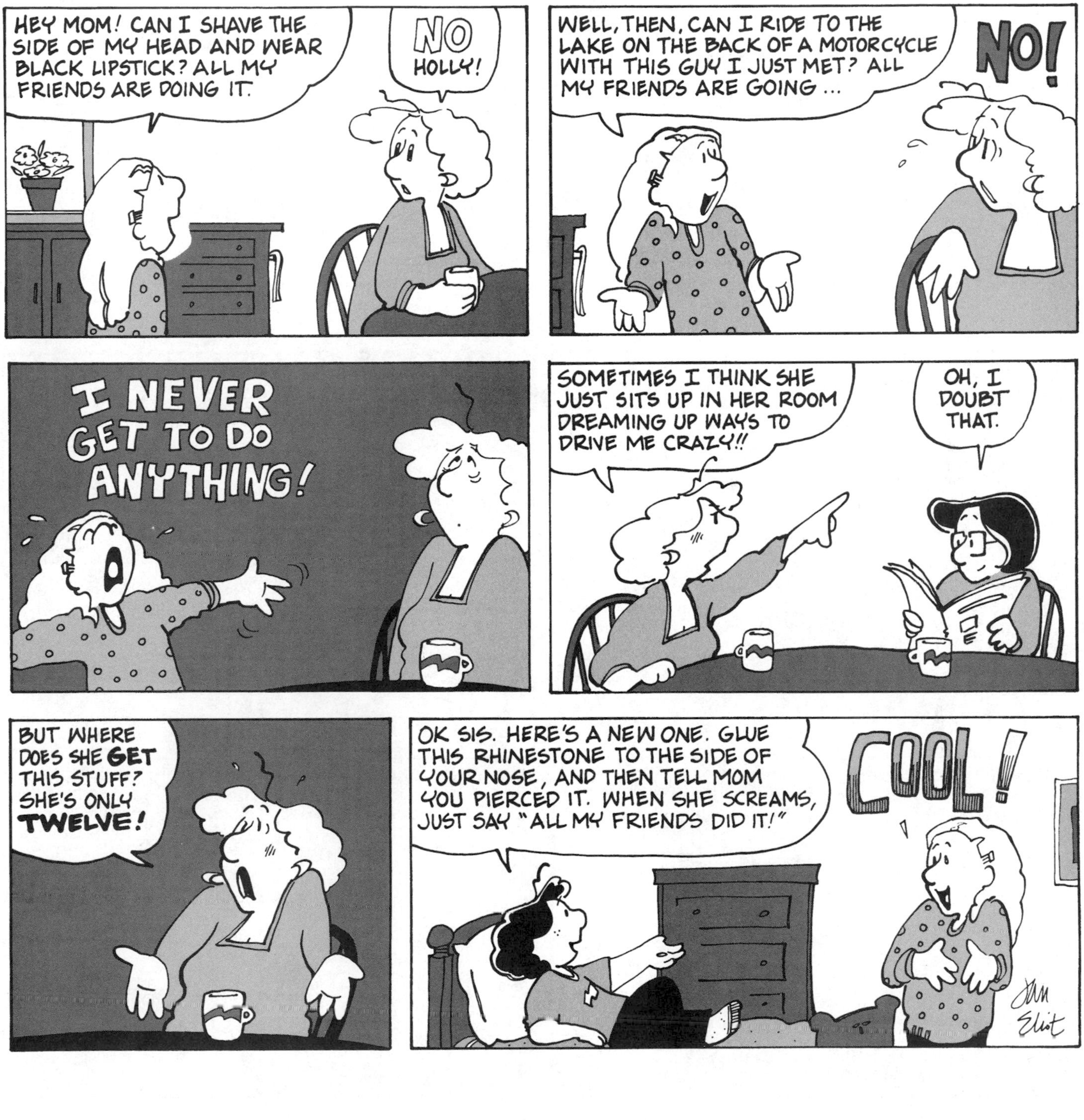
HEY MOM! CAN I SHAVE THE SIDE OF MY HEAD AND WEAR BLACK LIPSTICK? ALL MY FRIENDS ARE DOING IT.
NO HOLLY!
WELL, THEN, CAN I RIDE TO THE LAKE ON THE BACK OF A MOTORCYCLE WITH THIS GUY I JUST MET? ALL MY FRIENDS ARE GOING ...
NO!
I NEVER GET TO DO ANYTHING!
SOMETIMES I THINK SHE JUST SITS UP IN HER ROOM DREAMING UP WAYS TO DRIVE ME CRAZY!!
OH, I DOUBT THAT.
BUT WHERE DOES SHE GET THIS STUFF? SHE'S ONLY TWELVE!
OK SIS. HERE'S A NEW ONE. GLUE THIS RHINESTONE TO THE SIDE OF YOUR NOSE, AND THEN TELL MOM YOU PIERCED IT. WHEN SHE SCREAMS, JUST SAY "ALL MY FRIENDS DID IT!"
COOL!
Jan Eliot

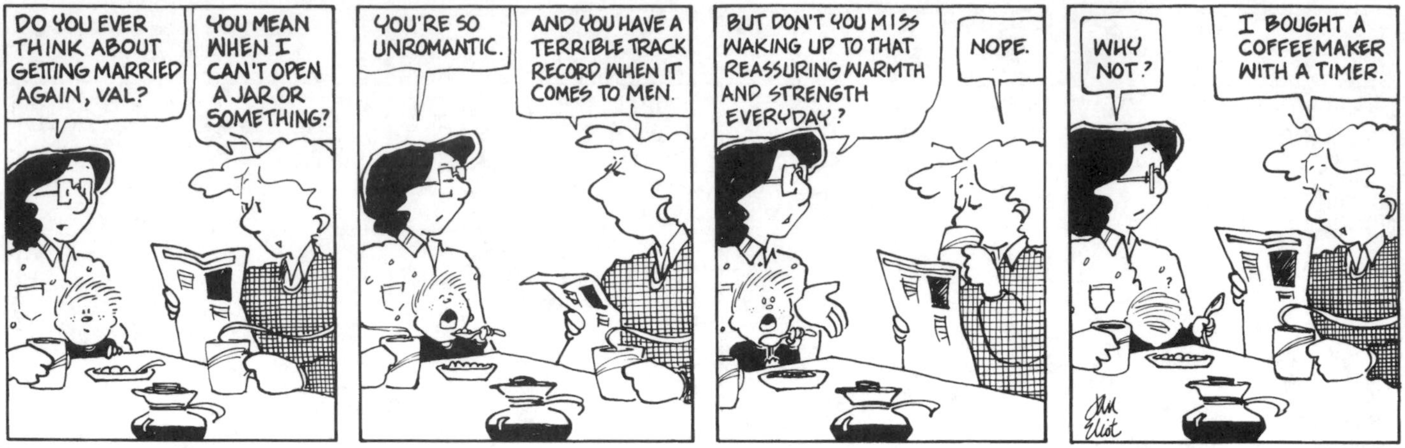
DO YOU EVER THINK ABOUT GETTING MARRIED AGAIN, VAL?
YOU MEAN WHEN I CAN'T OPEN A JAR OR SOMETHING?
YOU'RE SO UNROMANTIC.
AND YOU HAVE A TERRIBLE TRACK RECORD WHEN IT COMES TO MEN.
BUT DON'T YOU MISS WAKING UP TO THAT REASSURING WARMTH AND STRENGTH EVERYDAY?
NOPE.
WHY NOT?
I BOUGHT A COFFEEMAKER WITH A TIMER.

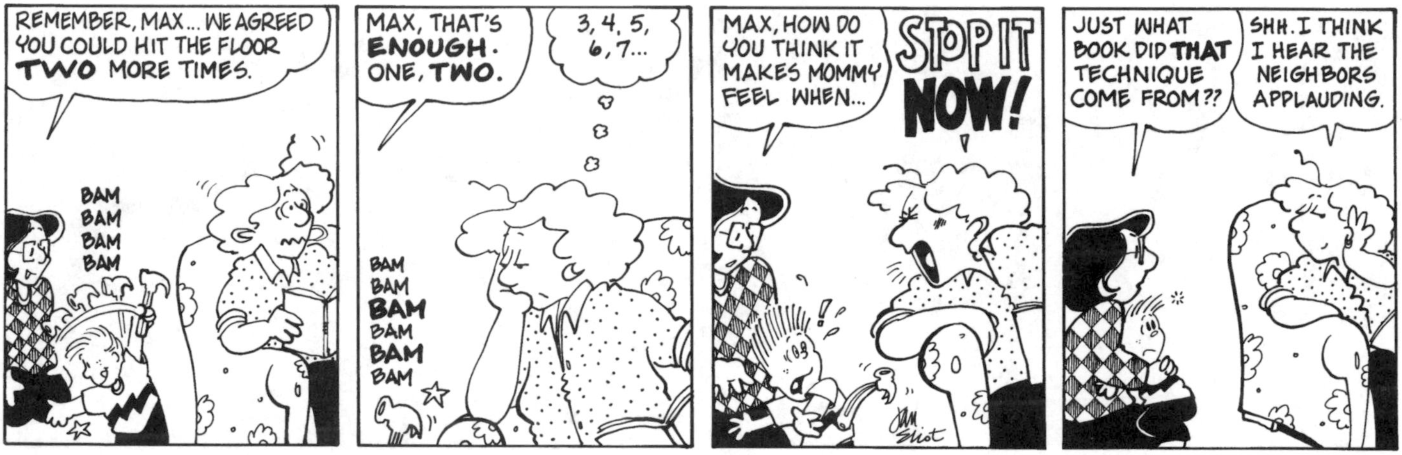
REMEMBER, MAX... WE AGREED YOU COULD HIT THE FLOOR **TWO** MORE TIMES.
BAM BAM BAM BAM
MAX, THAT'S **ENOUGH**. ONE, **TWO**.
3, 4, 5, 6, 7...
BAM BAM **BAM** BAM **BAM** BAM
MAX, HOW DO YOU THINK IT MAKES MOMMY FEEL WHEN...
STOP IT NOW!
JUST WHAT BOOK DID **THAT** TECHNIQUE COME FROM??
SHH. I THINK I HEAR THE NEIGHBORS APPLAUDING.

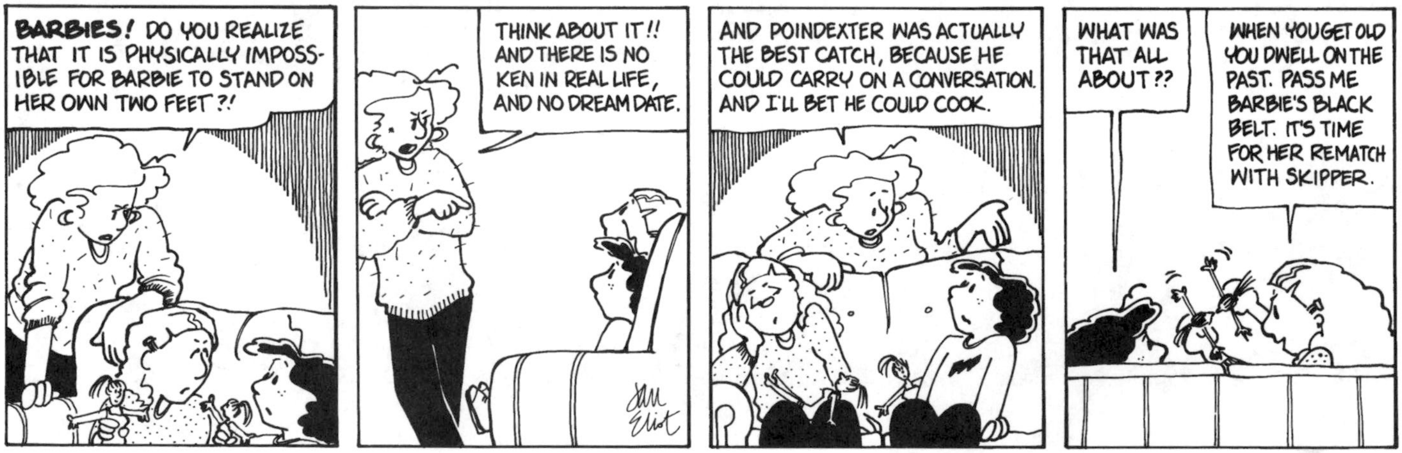
BARBIES! DO YOU REALIZE THAT IT IS PHYSICALLY IMPOSSIBLE FOR BARBIE TO STAND ON HER OWN TWO FEET?!
THINK ABOUT IT!! AND THERE IS NO KEN IN REAL LIFE, AND NO DREAM DATE.
AND POINDEXTER WAS ACTUALLY THE BEST CATCH, BECAUSE HE COULD CARRY ON A CONVERSATION. AND I'LL BET HE COULD COOK.
WHAT WAS THAT ALL ABOUT??
WHEN YOU GET OLD YOU DWELL ON THE PAST. PASS ME BARBIE'S BLACK BELT. IT'S TIME FOR HER REMATCH WITH SKIPPER.

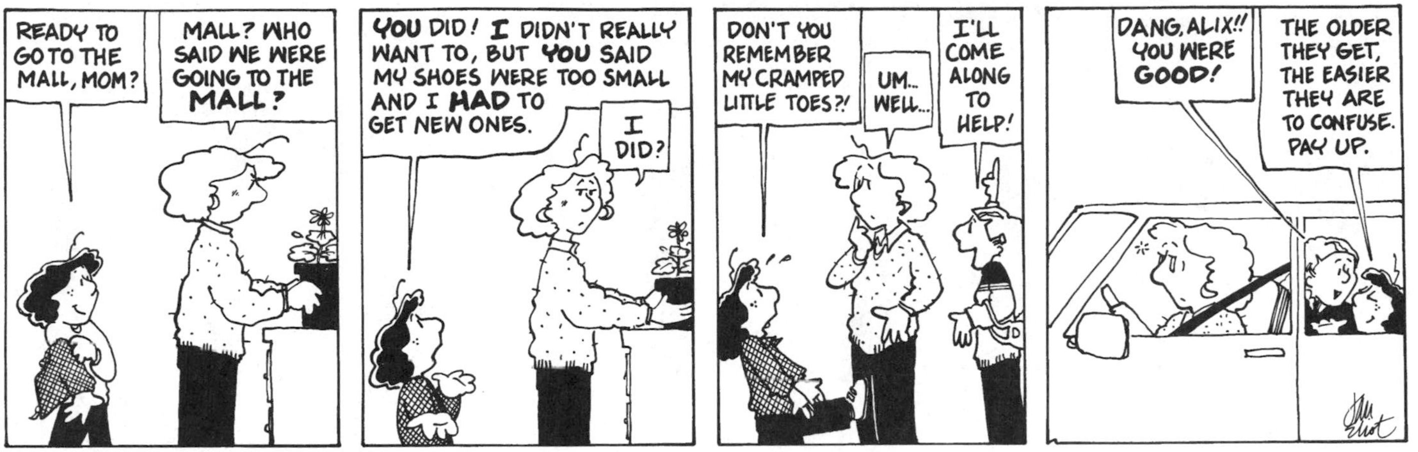
READY TO GO TO THE MALL, MOM?
MALL? WHO SAID WE WERE GOING TO THE **MALL**?
YOU DID! **I** DIDN'T REALLY WANT TO, BUT **YOU** SAID MY SHOES WERE TOO SMALL AND I **HAD** TO GET NEW ONES.
I DID?
DON'T YOU REMEMBER MY CRAMPED LITTLE TOES?!
UM... WELL...
I'LL COME ALONG TO HELP!
DANG, ALIX!! YOU WERE **GOOD**!
THE OLDER THEY GET, THE EASIER THEY ARE TO CONFUSE. PAY UP.

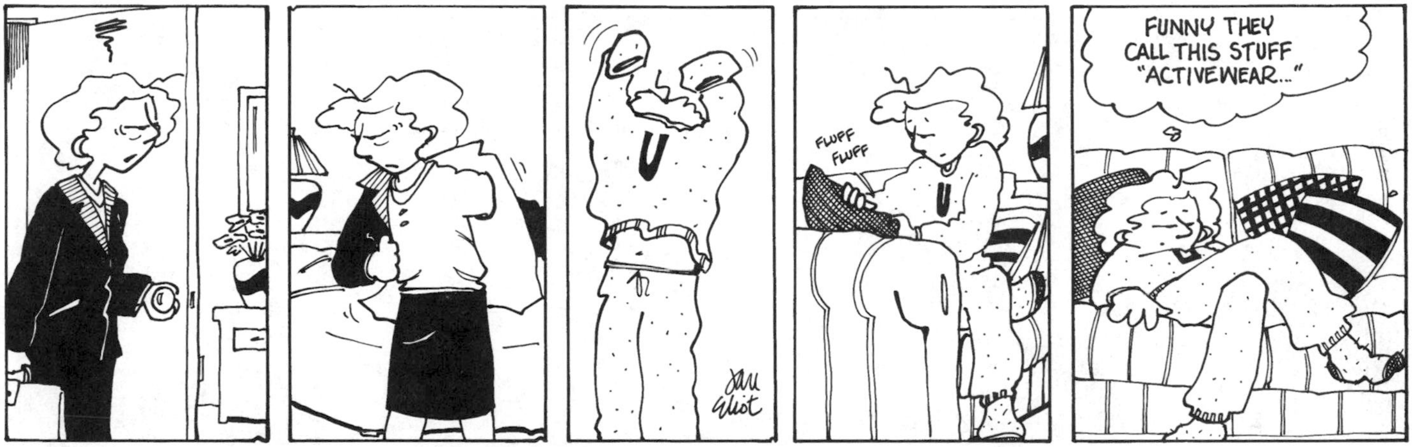
FLUFF FLUFF
FUNNY THEY CALL THIS STUFF "ACTIVEWEAR..."

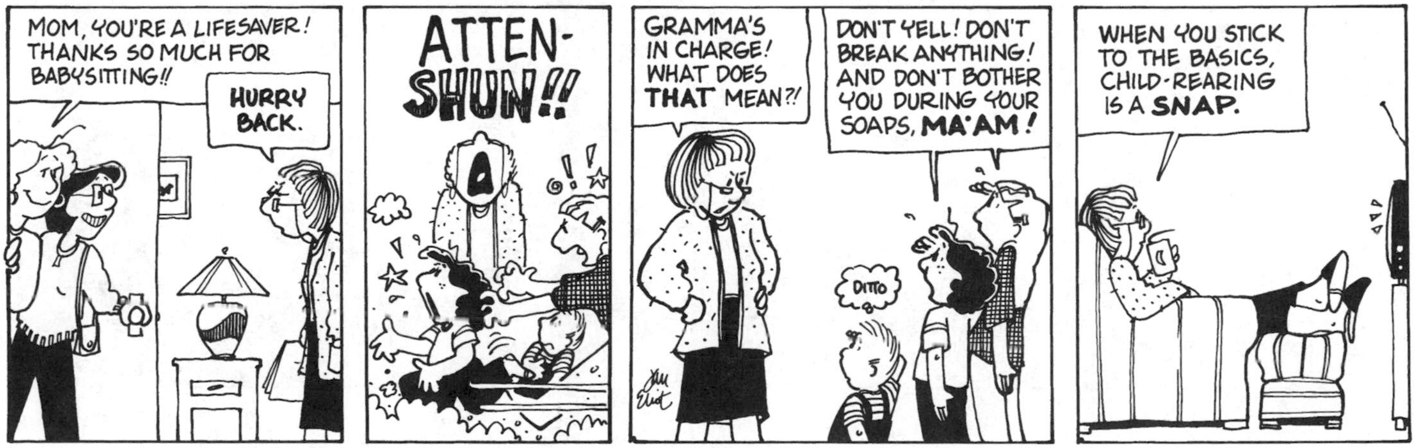
MOM, YOU'RE A LIFESAVER! THANKS SO MUCH FOR BABYSITTING!!
HURRY BACK.
ATTEN-SHUN!!
GRAMMA'S IN CHARGE! WHAT DOES **THAT** MEAN?!
DON'T YELL! DON'T BREAK ANYTHING! AND DON'T BOTHER YOU DURING YOUR SOAPS, **MA'AM**!
DITTO
WHEN YOU STICK TO THE BASICS, CHILD-REARING IS A **SNAP**.

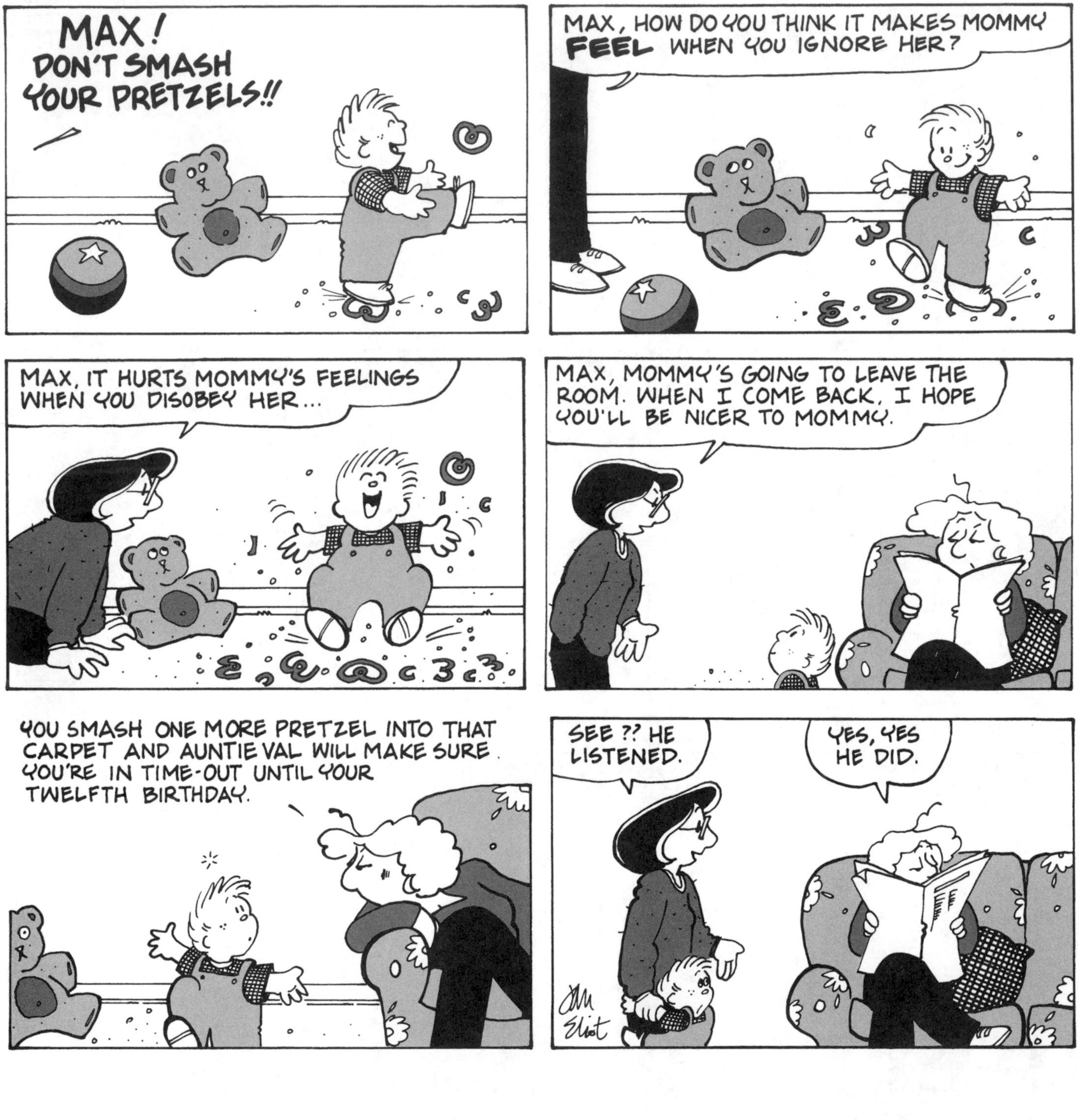
MAX! DON'T SMASH YOUR PRETZELS!!
MAX, HOW DO YOU THINK IT MAKES MOMMY FEEL WHEN YOU IGNORE HER?
MAX, IT HURTS MOMMY'S FEELINGS WHEN YOU DISOBEY HER...
MAX, MOMMY'S GOING TO LEAVE THE ROOM. WHEN I COME BACK, I HOPE YOU'LL BE NICER TO MOMMY.
YOU SMASH ONE MORE PRETZEL INTO THAT CARPET AND AUNTIE VAL WILL MAKE SURE YOU'RE IN TIME-OUT UNTIL YOUR TWELFTH BIRTHDAY.
SEE ?? HE LISTENED.
YES, YES HE DID.

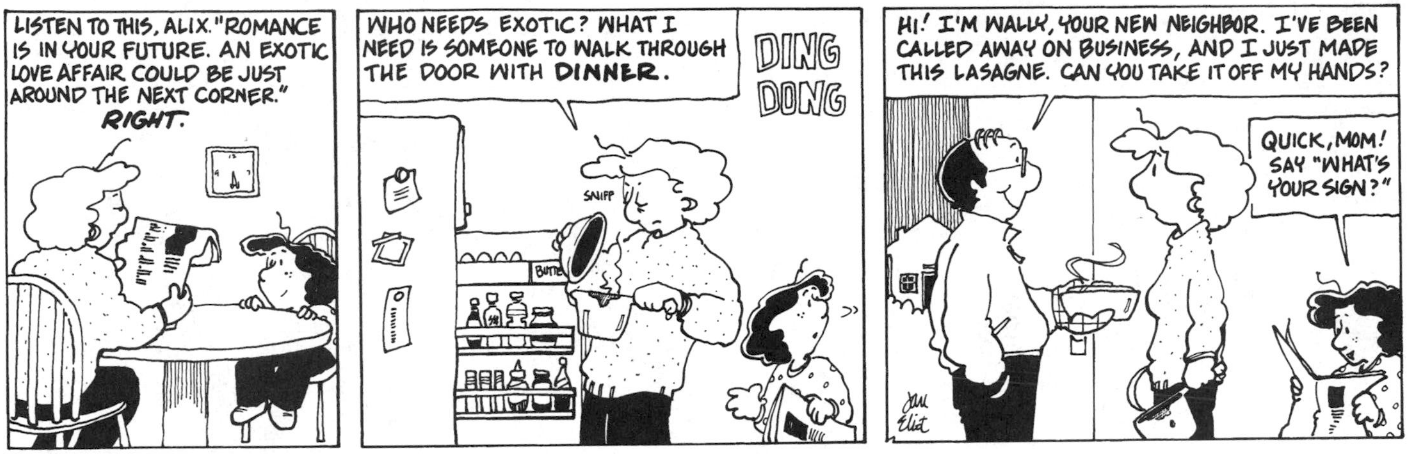
LISTEN TO THIS, ALIX. "ROMANCE IS IN YOUR FUTURE. AN EXOTIC LOVE AFFAIR COULD BE JUST AROUND THE NEXT CORNER." RIGHT.
WHO NEEDS EXOTIC? WHAT I NEED IS SOMEONE TO WALK THROUGH THE DOOR WITH DINNER.
DING DONG
SNIFF
HI! I'M WALLY, YOUR NEW NEIGHBOR. I'VE BEEN CALLED AWAY ON BUSINESS, AND I JUST MADE THIS LASAGNE. CAN YOU TAKE IT OFF MY HANDS?
QUICK, MOM! SAY "WHAT'S YOUR SIGN?"

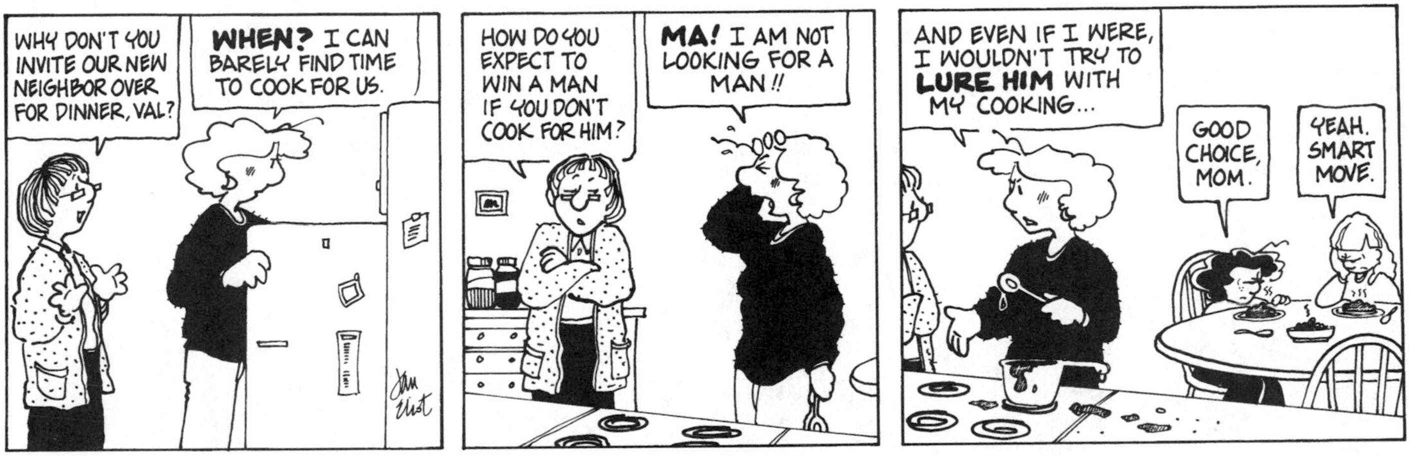
WHY DON'T YOU INVITE OUR NEW NEIGHBOR OVER FOR DINNER, VAL?
WHEN? I CAN BARELY FIND TIME TO COOK FOR US.
HOW DO YOU EXPECT TO WIN A MAN IF YOU DON'T COOK FOR HIM?
MA! I AM NOT LOOKING FOR A MAN!!
AND EVEN IF I WERE, I WOULDN'T TRY TO LURE HIM WITH MY COOKING...
GOOD CHOICE, MOM.
YEAH. SMART MOVE.

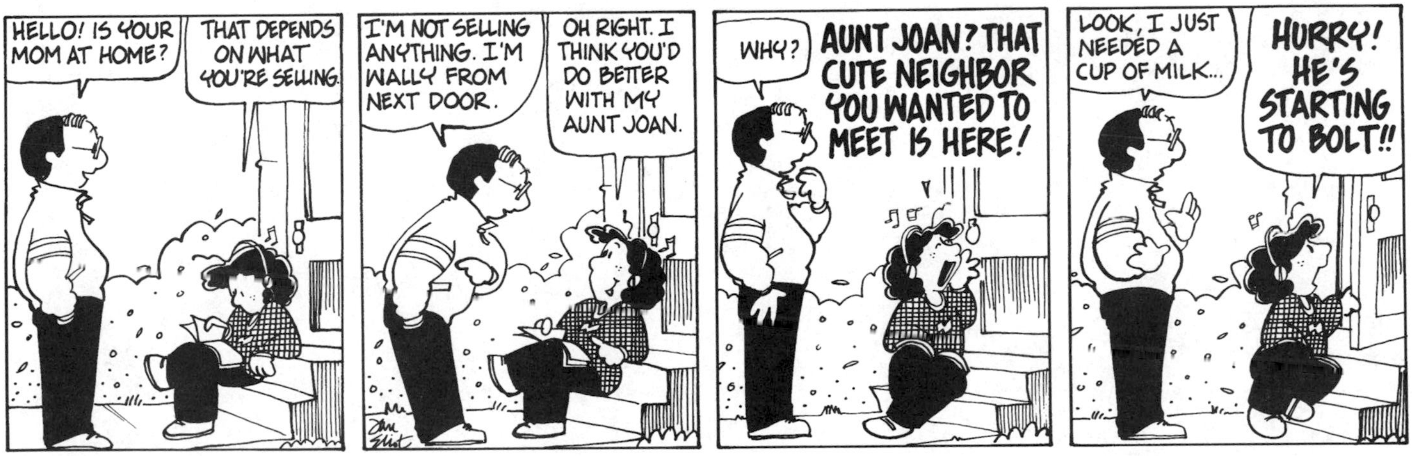
HELLO! IS YOUR MOM AT HOME?
THAT DEPENDS ON WHAT YOU'RE SELLING.
I'M NOT SELLING ANYTHING. I'M WALLY FROM NEXT DOOR.
OH RIGHT. I THINK YOU'D DO BETTER WITH MY AUNT JOAN.
WHY?
AUNT JOAN? THAT CUTE NEIGHBOR YOU WANTED TO MEET IS HERE!
LOOK, I JUST NEEDED A CUP OF MILK...
HURRY! HE'S STARTING TO BOLT!!

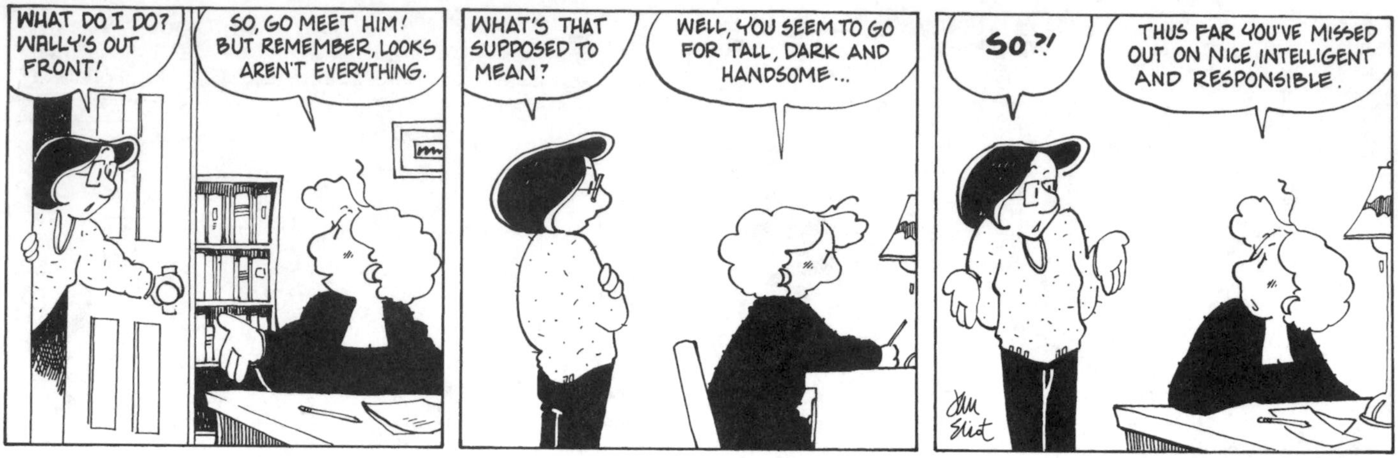
WHAT DO I DO? WALLY'S OUT FRONT!
SO, GO MEET HIM! BUT REMEMBER, LOOKS AREN'T EVERYTHING.
WHAT'S THAT SUPPOSED TO MEAN?
WELL, YOU SEEM TO GO FOR TALL, DARK AND HANDSOME...
SO?!
THUS FAR YOU'VE MISSED OUT ON NICE, INTELLIGENT AND RESPONSIBLE.

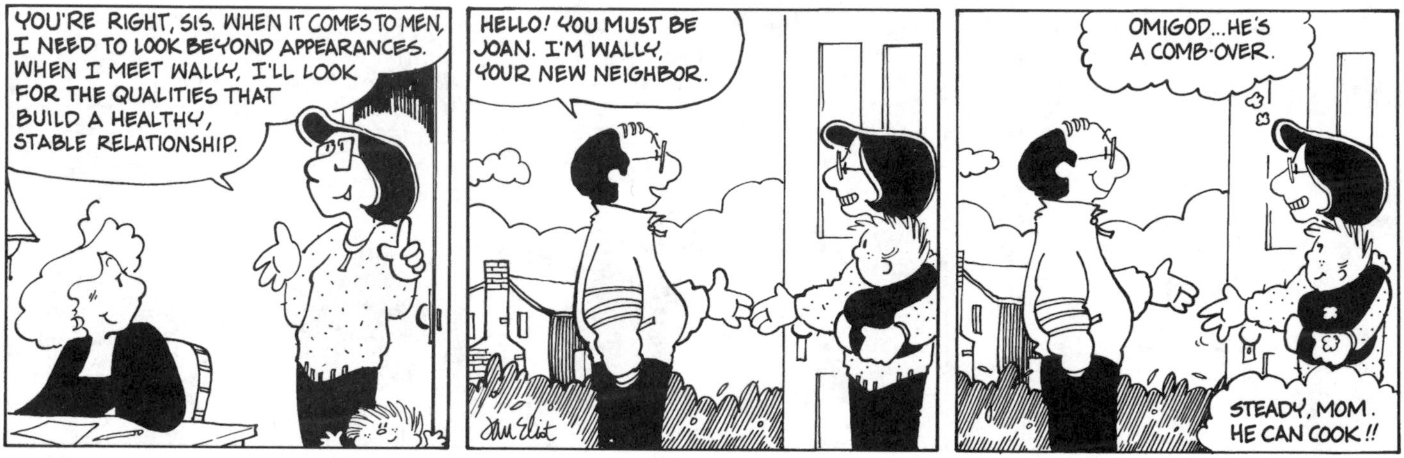
YOU'RE RIGHT, SIS. WHEN IT COMES TO MEN, I NEED TO LOOK BEYOND APPEARANCES. WHEN I MEET WALLY, I'LL LOOK FOR THE QUALITIES THAT BUILD A HEALTHY, STABLE RELATIONSHIP.
HELLO! YOU MUST BE JOAN. I'M WALLY, YOUR NEW NEIGHBOR.
OMIGOD...HE'S A COMB-OVER.
STEADY, MOM. HE CAN COOK!!

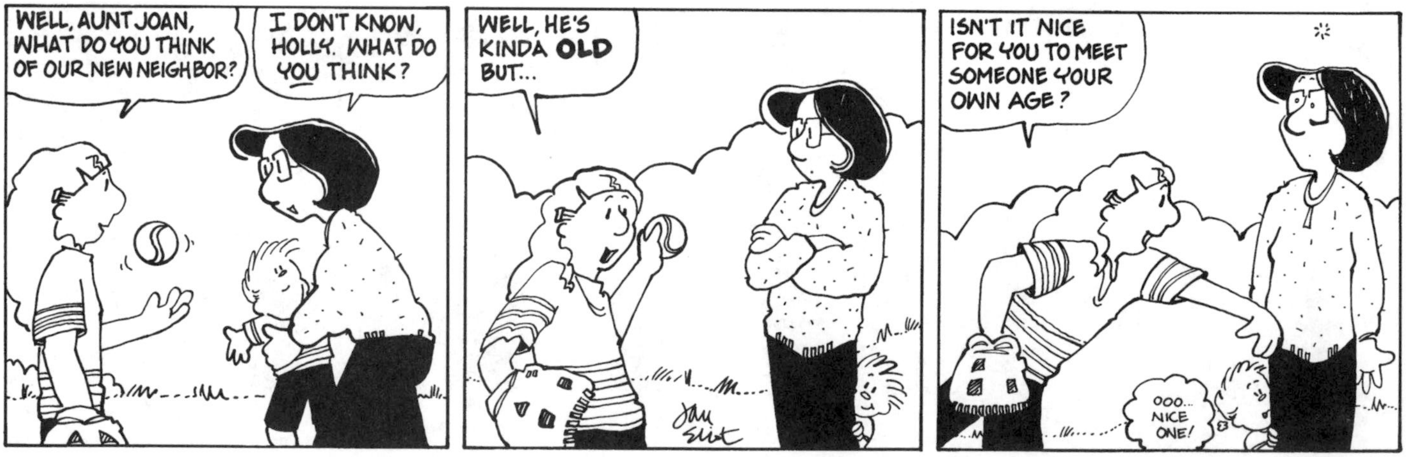
WELL, AUNT JOAN, WHAT DO YOU THINK OF OUR NEW NEIGHBOR?
I DON'T KNOW, HOLLY. WHAT DO YOU THINK?
WELL, HE'S KINDA OLD BUT...
ISN'T IT NICE FOR YOU TO MEET SOMEONE YOUR OWN AGE?
OOO... NICE ONE!

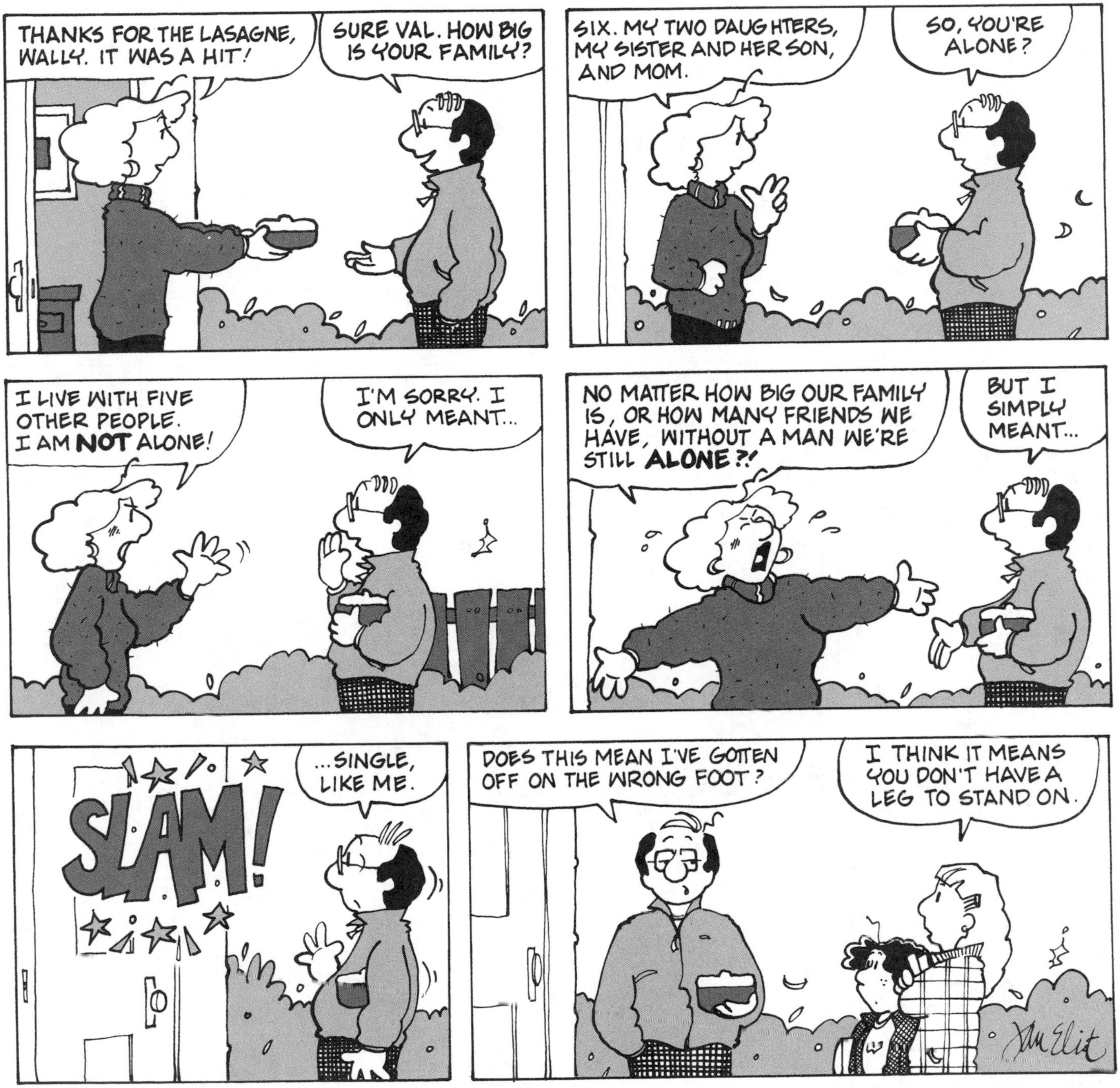
THANKS FOR THE LASAGNE, WALLY. IT WAS A HIT!
SURE VAL. HOW BIG IS YOUR FAMILY?
SIX. MY TWO DAUGHTERS, MY SISTER AND HER SON, AND MOM.
SO, YOU'RE ALONE?
I LIVE WITH FIVE OTHER PEOPLE. I AM **NOT** ALONE!
I'M SORRY. I ONLY MEANT...
NO MATTER HOW BIG OUR FAMILY IS, OR HOW MANY FRIENDS WE HAVE, WITHOUT A MAN WE'RE STILL **ALONE**?!
BUT I SIMPLY MEANT...
SLAM!
...SINGLE, LIKE ME.
DOES THIS MEAN I'VE GOTTEN OFF ON THE WRONG FOOT?
I THINK IT MEANS YOU DON'T HAVE A LEG TO STAND ON.

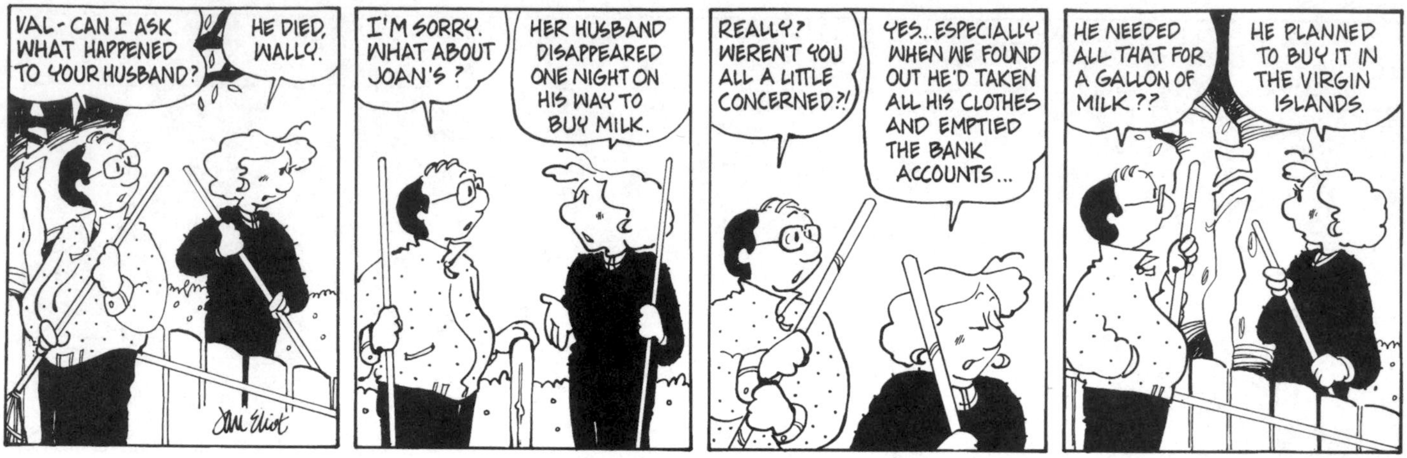
VAL- CAN I ASK WHAT HAPPENED TO YOUR HUSBAND?
HE DIED, WALLY.
I'M SORRY. WHAT ABOUT JOAN'S ?
HER HUSBAND DISAPPEARED ONE NIGHT ON HIS WAY TO BUY MILK.
REALLY? WEREN'T YOU ALL A LITTLE CONCERNED?!
YES...ESPECIALLY WHEN WE FOUND OUT HE'D TAKEN ALL HIS CLOTHES AND EMPTIED THE BANK ACCOUNTS...
HE NEEDED ALL THAT FOR A GALLON OF MILK??
HE PLANNED TO BUY IT IN THE VIRGIN ISLANDS.

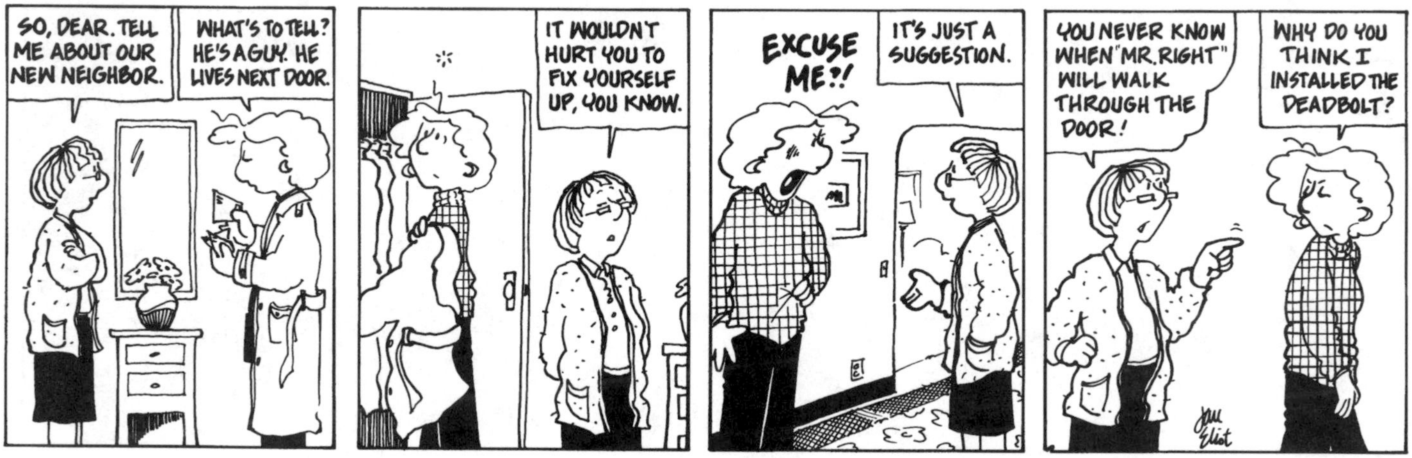
SO, DEAR. TELL ME ABOUT OUR NEW NEIGHBOR.
WHAT'S TO TELL? HE'S A GUY. HE LIVES NEXT DOOR.
IT WOULDN'T HURT YOU TO FIX YOURSELF UP, YOU KNOW.
EXCUSE ME?!
IT'S JUST A SUGGESTION.
YOU NEVER KNOW WHEN "MR. RIGHT" WILL WALK THROUGH THE DOOR!
WHY DO YOU THINK I INSTALLED THE DEADBOLT?

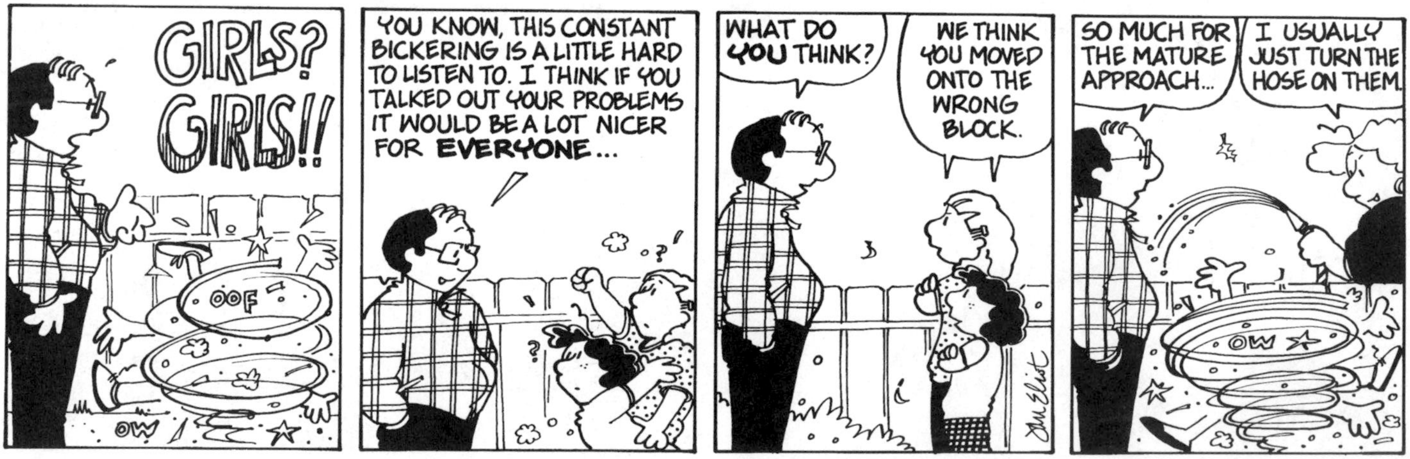
GIRLS? GIRLS!!
OOF
OW
YOU KNOW, THIS CONSTANT BICKERING IS A LITTLE HARD TO LISTEN TO. I THINK IF YOU TALKED OUT YOUR PROBLEMS IT WOULD BE A LOT NICER FOR EVERYONE...
WHAT DO YOU THINK?
WE THINK YOU MOVED ONTO THE WRONG BLOCK.
SO MUCH FOR THE MATURE APPROACH...
I USUALLY JUST TURN THE HOSE ON THEM.
OW

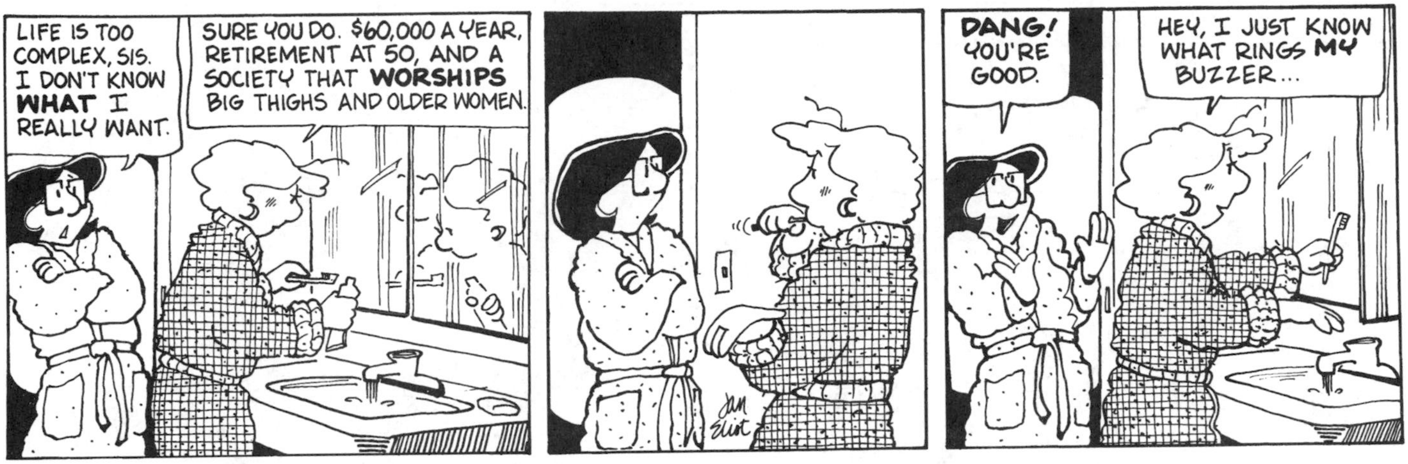
LIFE IS TOO COMPLEX, SIS. I DON'T KNOW **WHAT** I REALLY WANT.
SURE YOU DO. $60,000 A YEAR, RETIREMENT AT 50, AND A SOCIETY THAT **WORSHIPS** BIG THIGHS AND OLDER WOMEN.
DANG! YOU'RE GOOD.
HEY, I JUST KNOW WHAT RINGS **MY** BUZZER...

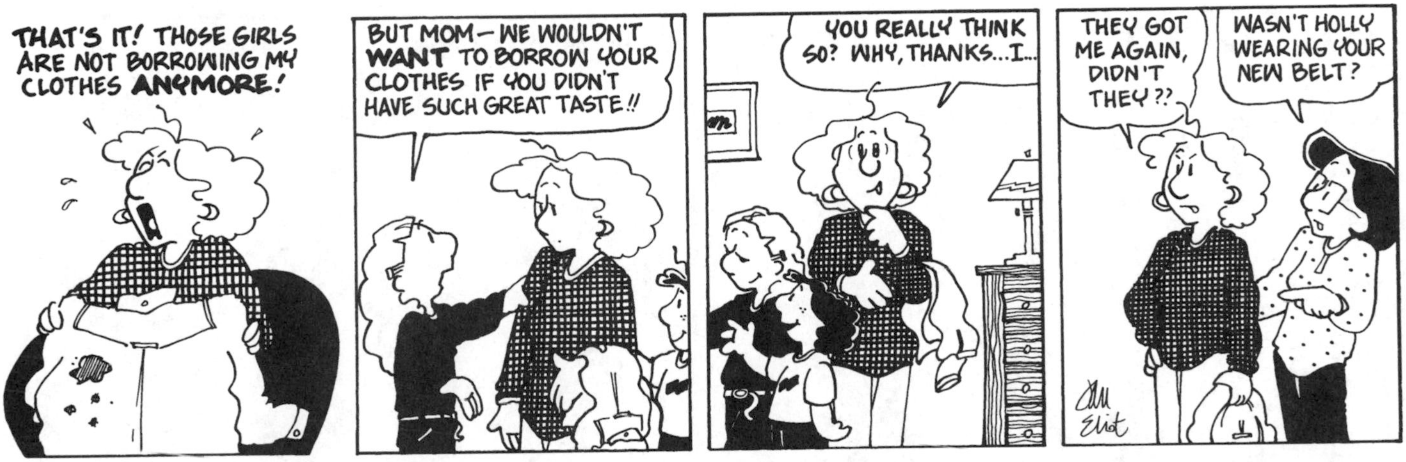
THAT'S IT! THOSE GIRLS ARE NOT BORROWING MY CLOTHES **ANYMORE**!
BUT MOM — WE WOULDN'T **WANT** TO BORROW YOUR CLOTHES IF YOU DIDN'T HAVE SUCH GREAT TASTE!!
YOU REALLY THINK SO? WHY, THANKS...I...
THEY GOT ME AGAIN, DIDN'T THEY??
WASN'T HOLLY WEARING YOUR NEW BELT?

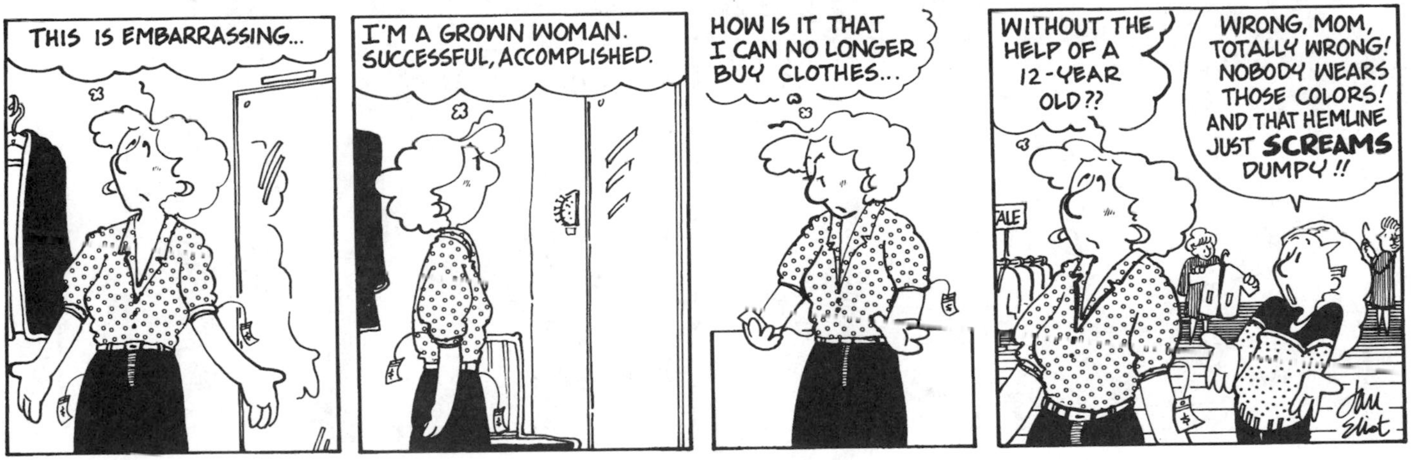
THIS IS EMBARRASSING...
I'M A GROWN WOMAN. SUCCESSFUL, ACCOMPLISHED.
HOW IS IT THAT I CAN NO LONGER BUY CLOTHES...
WITHOUT THE HELP OF A 12-YEAR OLD??
WRONG, MOM, TOTALLY WRONG! NOBODY WEARS THOSE COLORS! AND THAT HEMLINE JUST **SCREAMS** DUMPY!!

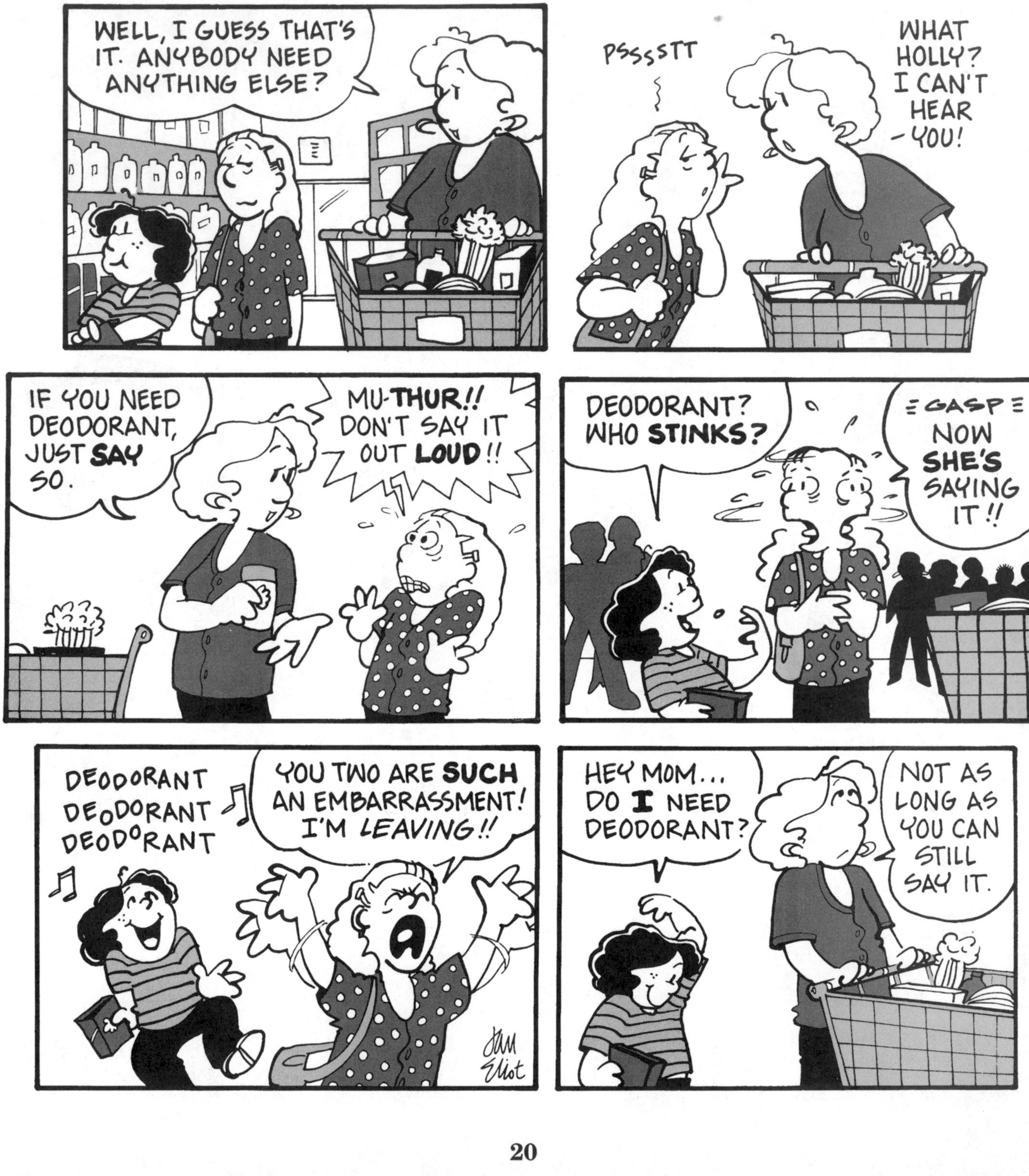
WELL, I GUESS THAT'S IT. ANYBODY NEED ANYTHING ELSE?
PSSSSTT
WHAT HOLLY? I CAN'T HEAR YOU!
IF YOU NEED DEODORANT, JUST **SAY** SO.
MU-**THUR**!! DON'T SAY IT OUT **LOUD**!!
DEODORANT? WHO **STINKS**?
GASP NOW **SHE'S** SAYING IT!!
DEODORANT DEODORANT DEODORANT
YOU TWO ARE **SUCH** AN EMBARRASSMENT! I'M *LEAVING*!!
Jan Eliot
HEY MOM... DO **I** NEED DEODORANT?
NOT AS LONG AS YOU CAN STILL SAY IT.

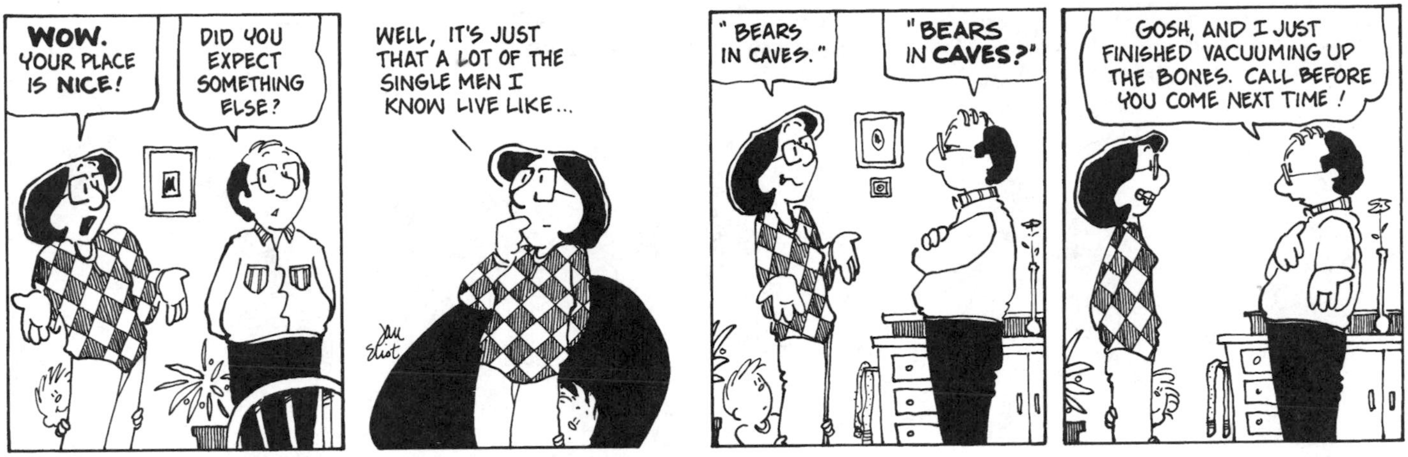
WOW. YOUR PLACE IS NICE!
DID YOU EXPECT SOMETHING ELSE?
WELL, IT'S JUST THAT A LOT OF THE SINGLE MEN I KNOW LIVE LIKE...
"BEARS IN CAVES."
"BEARS IN CAVES?"
GOSH, AND I JUST FINISHED VACUUMING UP THE BONES. CALL BEFORE YOU COME NEXT TIME!

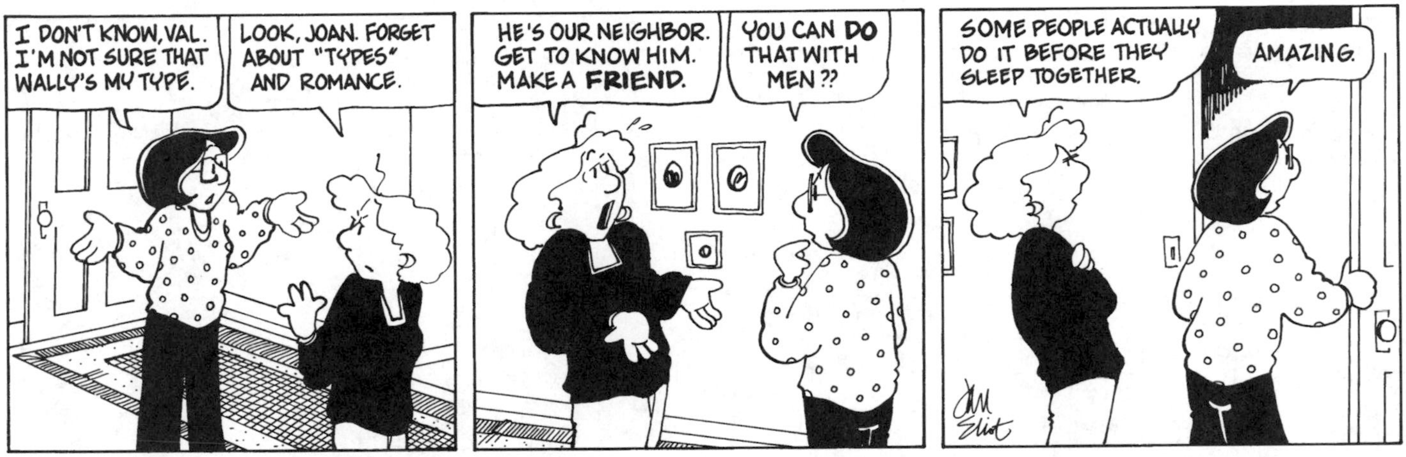
I DON'T KNOW, VAL. I'M NOT SURE THAT WALLY'S MY TYPE.
LOOK, JOAN. FORGET ABOUT "TYPES" AND ROMANCE.
HE'S OUR NEIGHBOR. GET TO KNOW HIM. MAKE A FRIEND.
YOU CAN DO THAT WITH MEN??
SOME PEOPLE ACTUALLY DO IT BEFORE THEY SLEEP TOGETHER.
AMAZING.

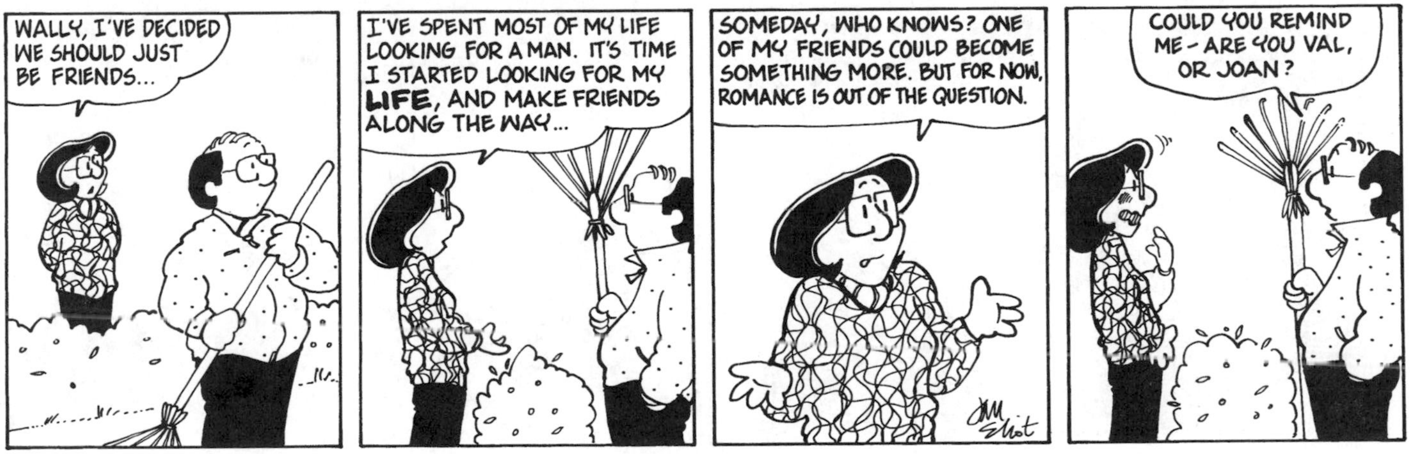
WALLY, I'VE DECIDED WE SHOULD JUST BE FRIENDS...
I'VE SPENT MOST OF MY LIFE LOOKING FOR A MAN. IT'S TIME I STARTED LOOKING FOR MY LIFE, AND MAKE FRIENDS ALONG THE WAY...
SOMEDAY, WHO KNOWS? ONE OF MY FRIENDS COULD BECOME SOMETHING MORE. BUT FOR NOW, ROMANCE IS OUT OF THE QUESTION.
COULD YOU REMIND ME - ARE YOU VAL, OR JOAN?

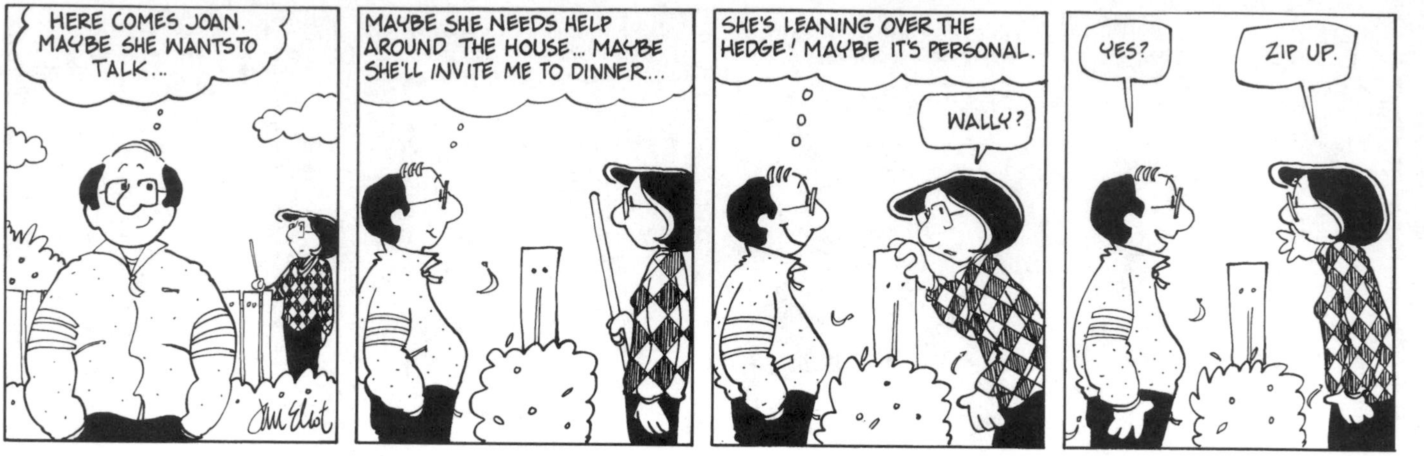
HERE COMES JOAN. MAYBE SHE WANTS TO TALK...
MAYBE SHE NEEDS HELP AROUND THE HOUSE... MAYBE SHE'LL INVITE ME TO DINNER...
SHE'S LEANING OVER THE HEDGE! MAYBE IT'S PERSONAL.
WALLY?
YES?
ZIP UP.

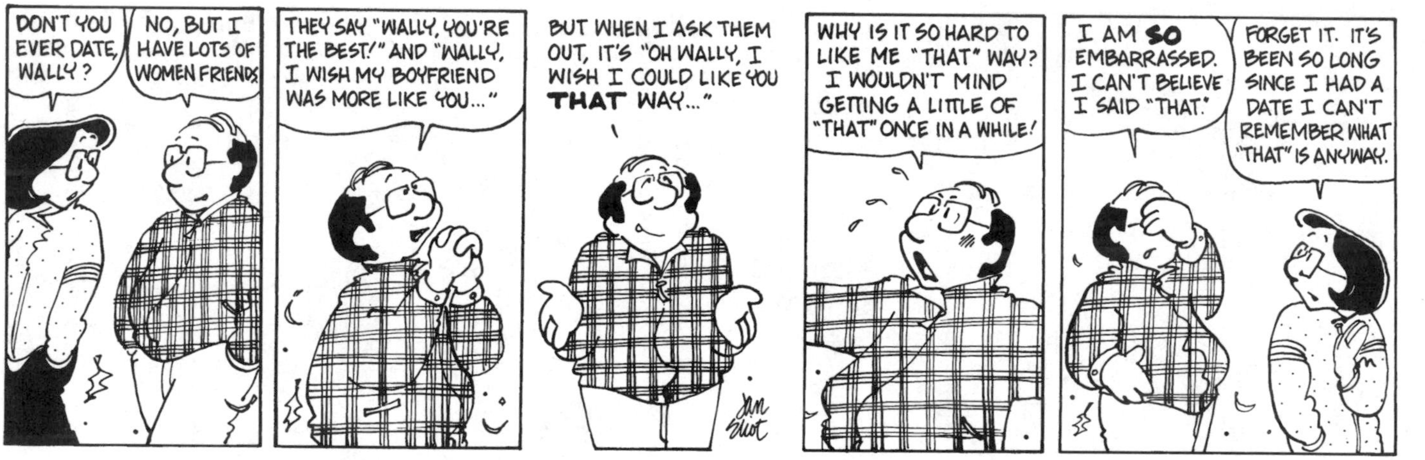
DON'T YOU EVER DATE, WALLY?
NO, BUT I HAVE LOTS OF WOMEN FRIENDS.
THEY SAY "WALLY, YOU'RE THE BEST!" AND "WALLY, I WISH MY BOYFRIEND WAS MORE LIKE YOU..."
BUT WHEN I ASK THEM OUT, IT'S "OH WALLY, I WISH I COULD LIKE YOU THAT WAY..."
WHY IS IT SO HARD TO LIKE ME "THAT" WAY? I WOULDN'T MIND GETTING A LITTLE OF "THAT" ONCE IN A WHILE!
I AM SO EMBARRASSED. I CAN'T BELIEVE I SAID "THAT."
FORGET IT. IT'S BEEN SO LONG SINCE I HAD A DATE I CAN'T REMEMBER WHAT "THAT" IS ANYWAY.

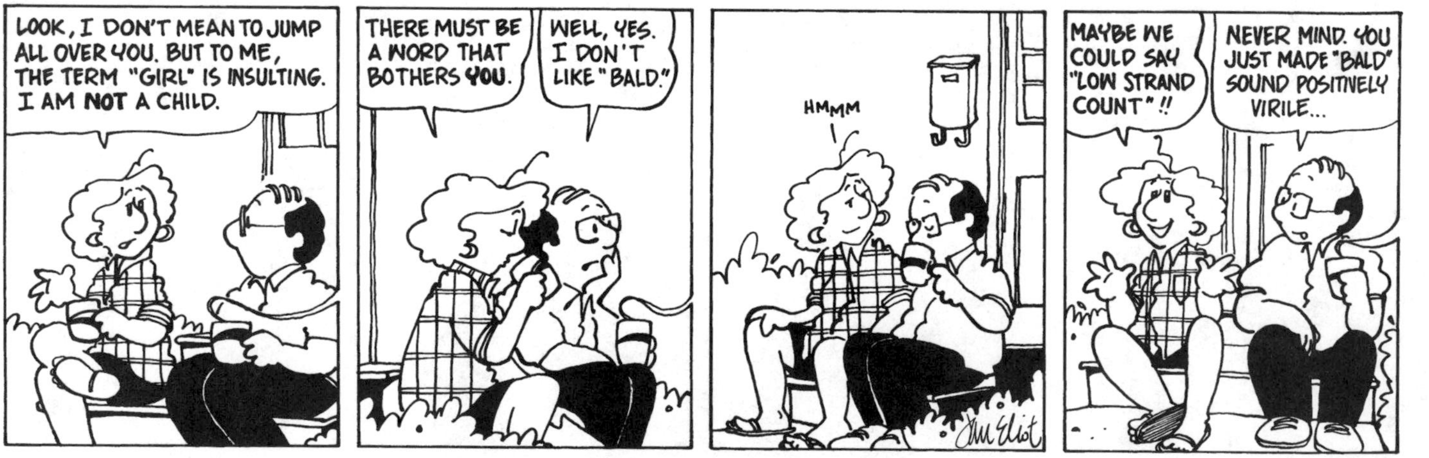
LOOK, I DON'T MEAN TO JUMP ALL OVER YOU. BUT TO ME, THE TERM "GIRL" IS INSULTING. I AM NOT A CHILD.
THERE MUST BE A WORD THAT BOTHERS YOU.
WELL, YES. I DON'T LIKE "BALD."
HMMM
MAYBE WE COULD SAY "LOW STRAND COUNT"!!
NEVER MIND. YOU JUST MADE "BALD" SOUND POSITIVELY VIRILE...

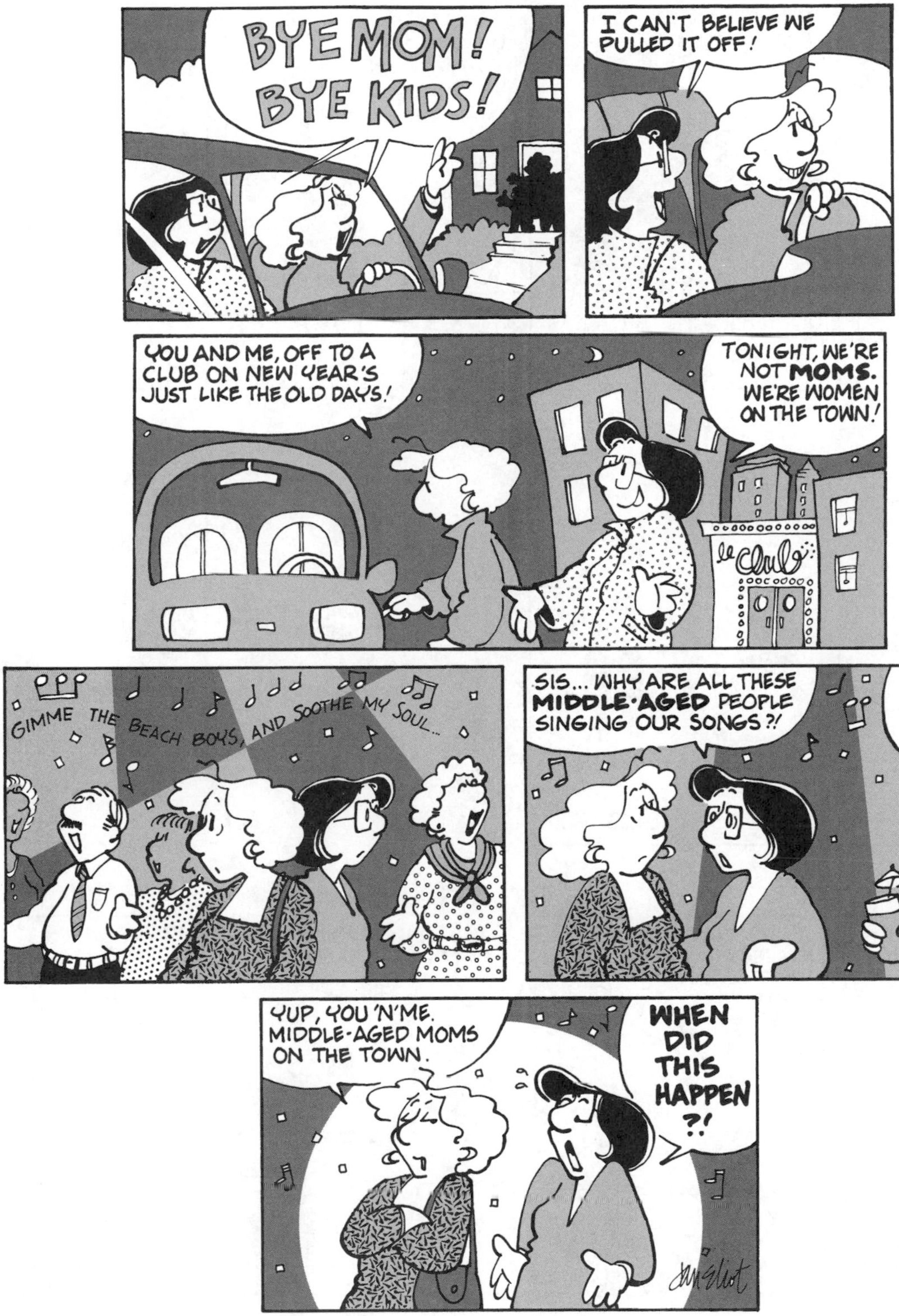

BYE MOM! BYE KIDS!
I CAN'T BELIEVE WE PULLED IT OFF!
YOU AND ME, OFF TO A CLUB ON NEW YEAR'S JUST LIKE THE OLD DAYS!
TONIGHT, WE'RE NOT **MOMS.** WE'RE WOMEN ON THE TOWN!
le Club
GIMME THE BEACH BOYS, AND SOOTHE MY SOUL...
SIS... WHY ARE ALL THESE **MIDDLE-AGED** PEOPLE SINGING OUR SONGS?!
HEY **HEY!** YOU TWO HERE ALL ALONE?
YUP, YOU 'N' ME. MIDDLE-AGED MOMS ON THE TOWN.
WHEN DID THIS HAPPEN ?!
Jan Eliot

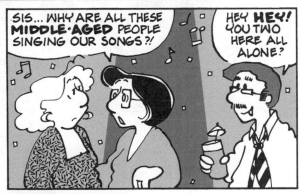

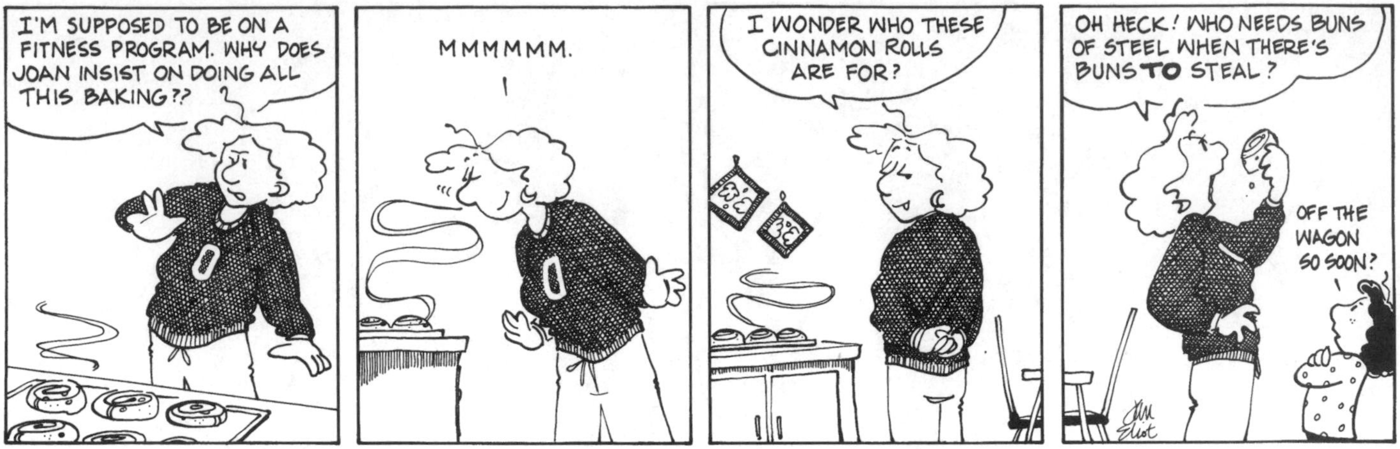
I'M SUPPOSED TO BE ON A FITNESS PROGRAM. WHY DOES JOAN INSIST ON DOING ALL THIS BAKING??
MMMMMM.
I WONDER WHO THESE CINNAMON ROLLS ARE FOR?
OH HECK! WHO NEEDS BUNS OF STEEL WHEN THERE'S BUNS TO STEAL?
OFF THE WAGON SO SOON?

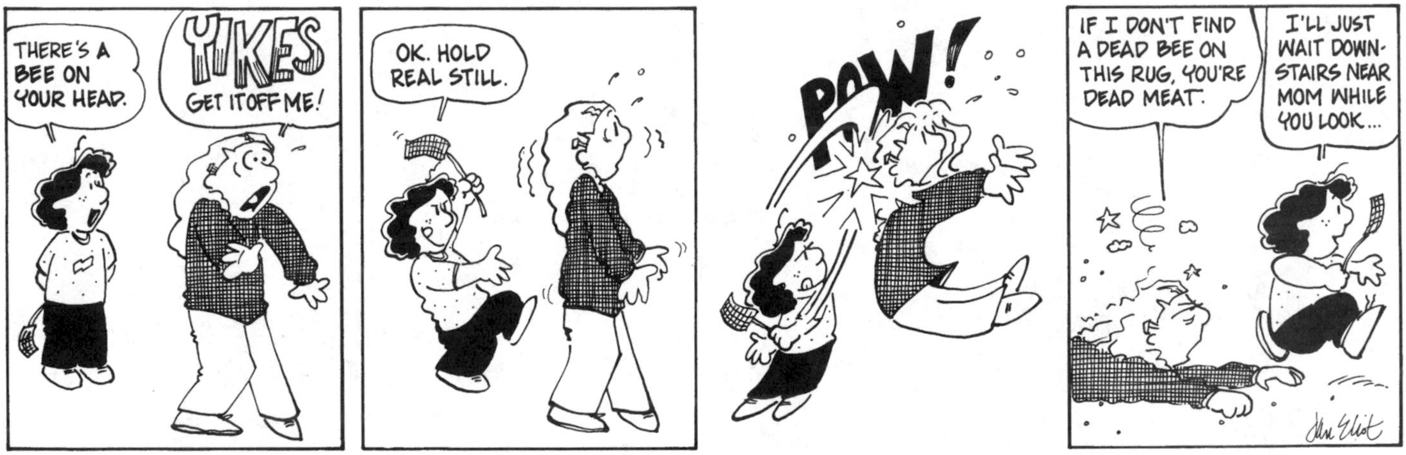
THERE'S A BEE ON YOUR HEAD.
YIKES
GET IT OFF ME!
OK. HOLD REAL STILL.
POW!
IF I DON'T FIND A DEAD BEE ON THIS RUG, YOU'RE DEAD MEAT.
I'LL JUST WAIT DOWN-STAIRS NEAR MOM WHILE YOU LOOK...

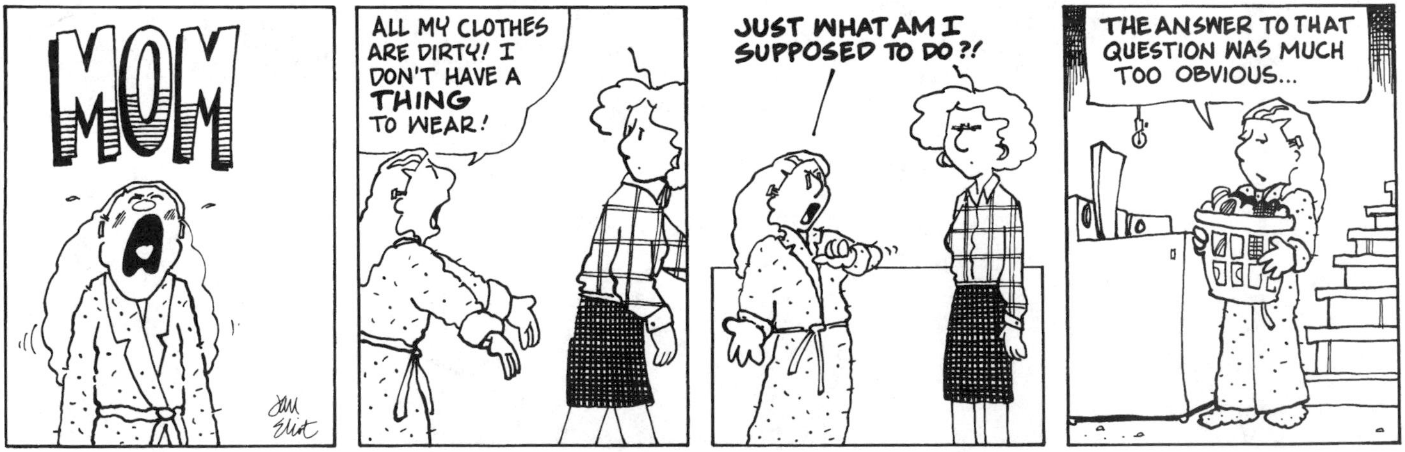
MOM
ALL MY CLOTHES ARE DIRTY! I DON'T HAVE A THING TO WEAR!
JUST WHAT AM I SUPPOSED TO DO?!
THE ANSWER TO THAT QUESTION WAS MUCH TOO OBVIOUS...

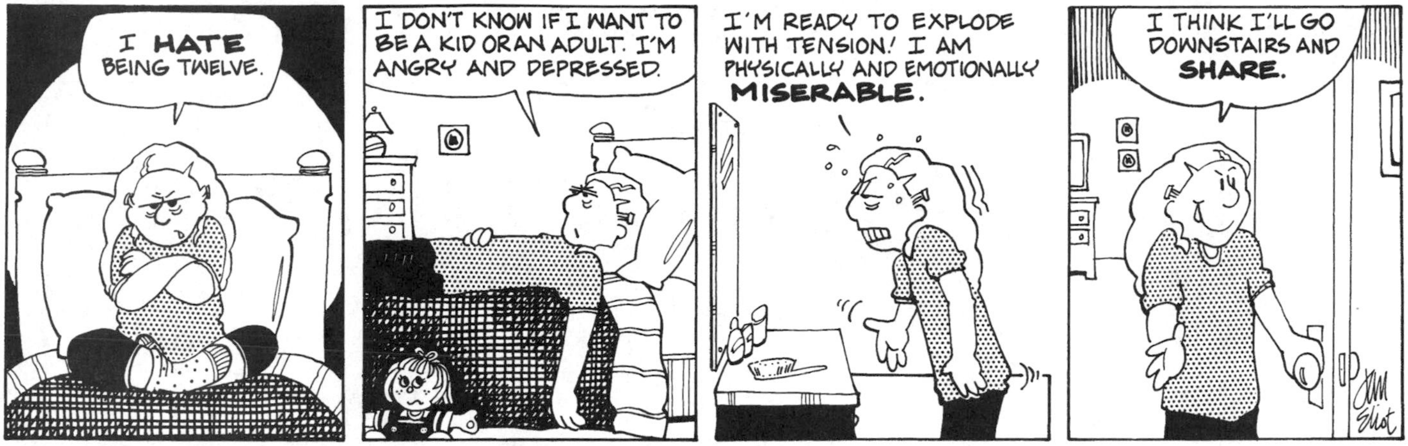
I **HATE** BEING TWELVE.
I DON'T KNOW IF I WANT TO BE A KID OR AN ADULT. I'M ANGRY AND DEPRESSED.
I'M READY TO EXPLODE WITH TENSION! I AM PHYSICALLY AND EMOTIONALLY **MISERABLE**.
I THINK I'LL GO DOWNSTAIRS AND **SHARE**.

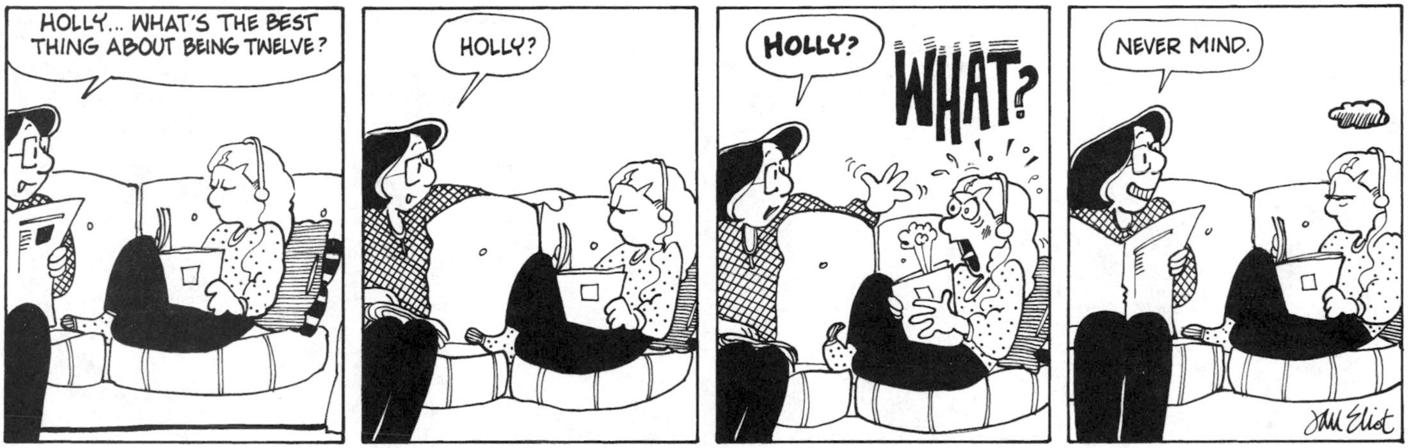
HOLLY... WHAT'S THE BEST THING ABOUT BEING TWELVE?
HOLLY?
HOLLY?
WHAT?
NEVER MIND.

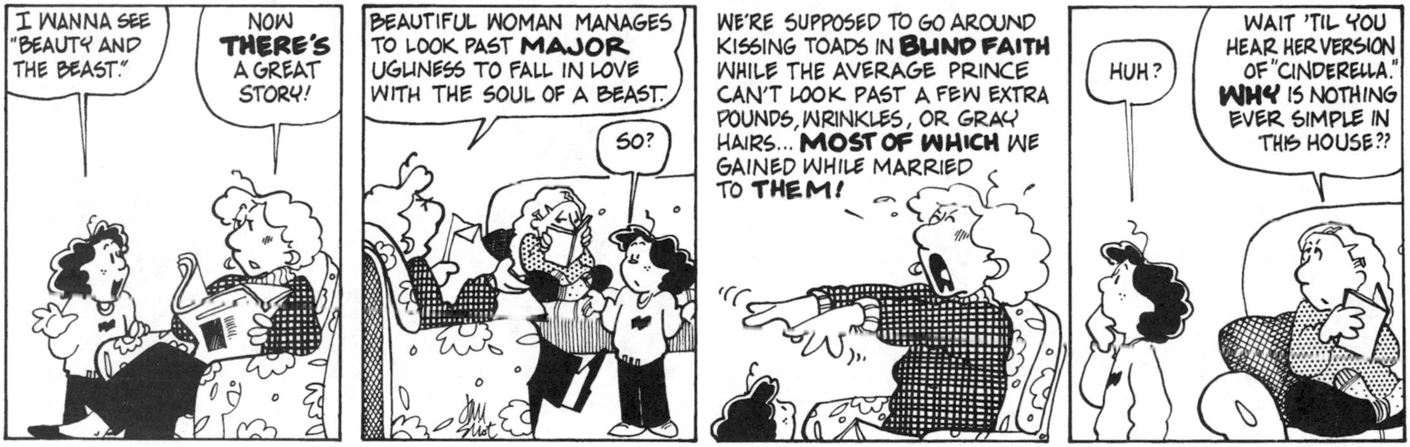
I WANNA SEE "BEAUTY AND THE BEAST."
NOW **THERE'S** A GREAT STORY!
BEAUTIFUL WOMAN MANAGES TO LOOK PAST **MAJOR** UGLINESS TO FALL IN LOVE WITH THE SOUL OF A BEAST.
SO?
WE'RE SUPPOSED TO GO AROUND KISSING TOADS IN **BLIND FAITH** WHILE THE AVERAGE PRINCE CAN'T LOOK PAST A FEW EXTRA POUNDS, WRINKLES, OR GRAY HAIRS... **MOST OF WHICH** WE GAINED WHILE MARRIED TO **THEM!**
HUH?
WAIT 'TIL YOU HEAR HER VERSION OF "CINDERELLA." **WHY** IS NOTHING EVER SIMPLE IN THIS HOUSE??

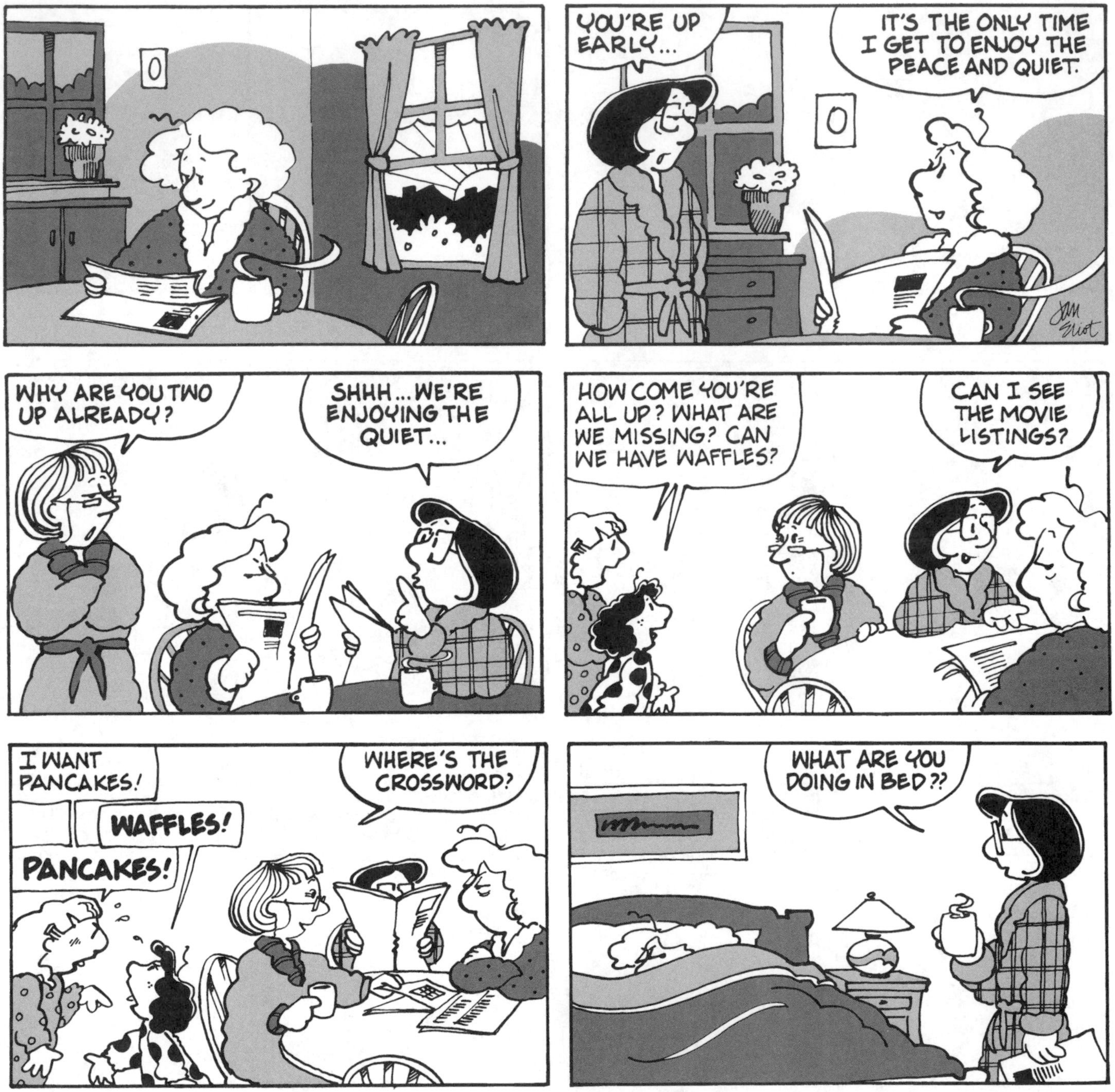
YOU'RE UP EARLY...
IT'S THE ONLY TIME I GET TO ENJOY THE PEACE AND QUIET.
WHY ARE YOU TWO UP ALREADY?
SHHH... WE'RE ENJOYING THE QUIET...
HOW COME YOU'RE ALL UP? WHAT ARE WE MISSING? CAN WE HAVE WAFFLES?
CAN I SEE THE MOVIE LISTINGS?
I WANT PANCAKES!
WAFFLES!
PANCAKES!
WHERE'S THE CROSSWORD?
WHAT ARE YOU DOING IN BED??

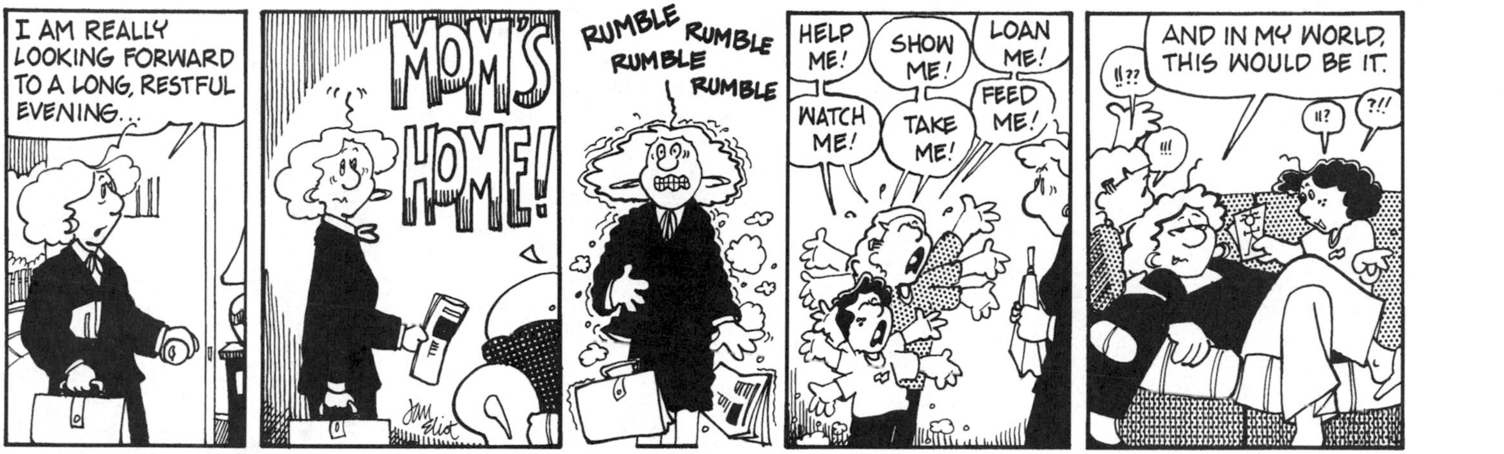
I AM REALLY LOOKING FORWARD TO A LONG, RESTFUL EVENING...
MOM'S HOME!
RUMBLE RUMBLE RUMBLE RUMBLE
HELP ME!
SHOW ME!
LOAN ME!
WATCH ME!
TAKE ME!
FEED ME!
AND IN MY WORLD, THIS WOULD BE IT.
!!??
!!!
!!?
?!!

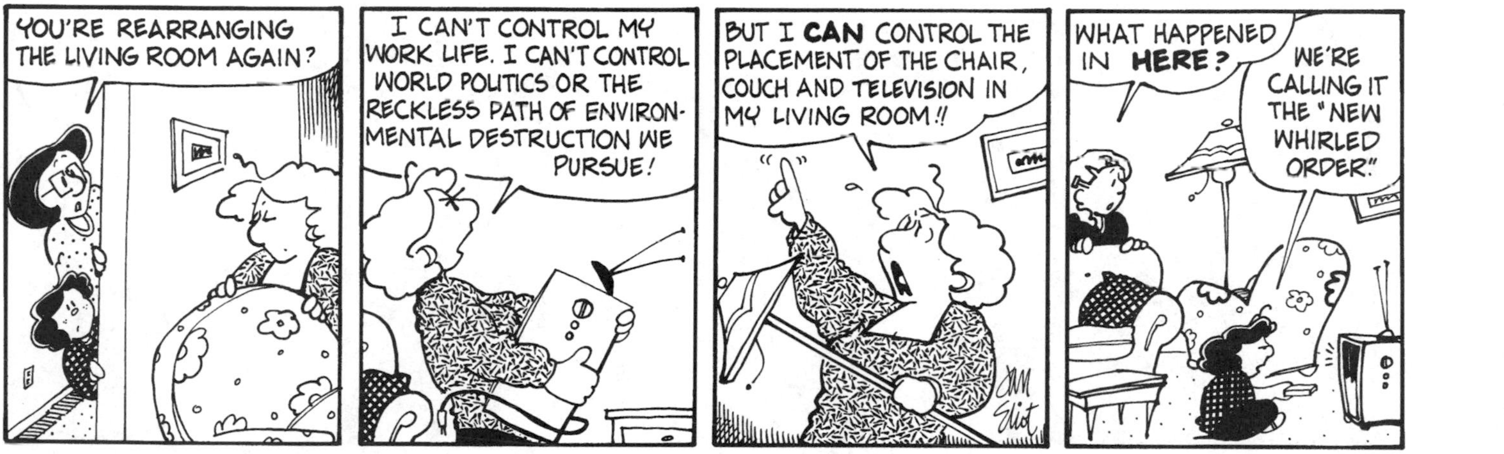
YOU'RE REARRANGING THE LIVING ROOM AGAIN?
I CAN'T CONTROL MY WORK LIFE. I CAN'T CONTROL WORLD POLITICS OR THE RECKLESS PATH OF ENVIRONMENTAL DESTRUCTION WE PURSUE!
BUT I CAN CONTROL THE PLACEMENT OF THE CHAIR, COUCH AND TELEVISION IN MY LIVING ROOM!!
WHAT HAPPENED IN HERE?
WE'RE CALLING IT THE "NEW WHIRLED ORDER."

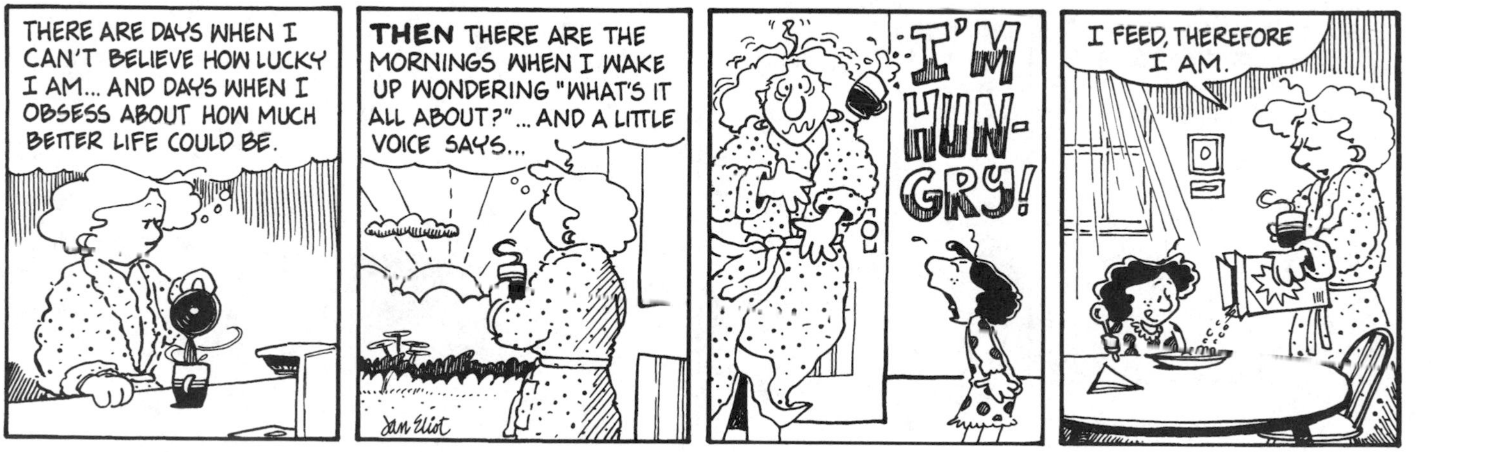
THERE ARE DAYS WHEN I CAN'T BELIEVE HOW LUCKY I AM... AND DAYS WHEN I OBSESS ABOUT HOW MUCH BETTER LIFE COULD BE.
THEN THERE ARE THE MORNINGS WHEN I WAKE UP WONDERING "WHAT'S IT ALL ABOUT?" ... AND A LITTLE VOICE SAYS...
I'M HUNGRY!
I FEED, THEREFORE I AM.

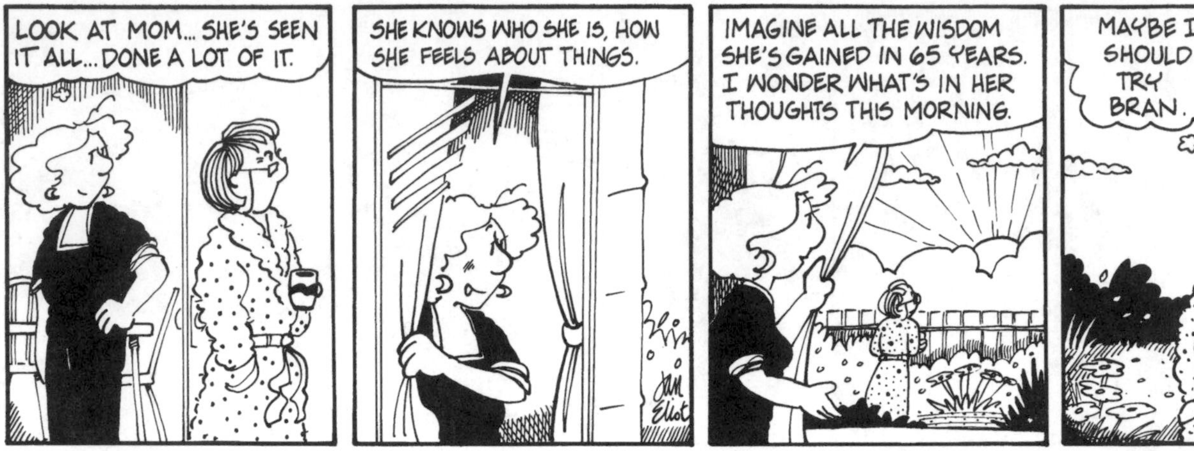
LOOK AT MOM... SHE'S SEEN IT ALL... DONE A LOT OF IT.
SHE KNOWS WHO SHE IS, HOW SHE FEELS ABOUT THINGS.
IMAGINE ALL THE WISDOM SHE'S GAINED IN 65 YEARS. I WONDER WHAT'S IN HER THOUGHTS THIS MORNING.
MAYBE I SHOULD TRY BRAN.

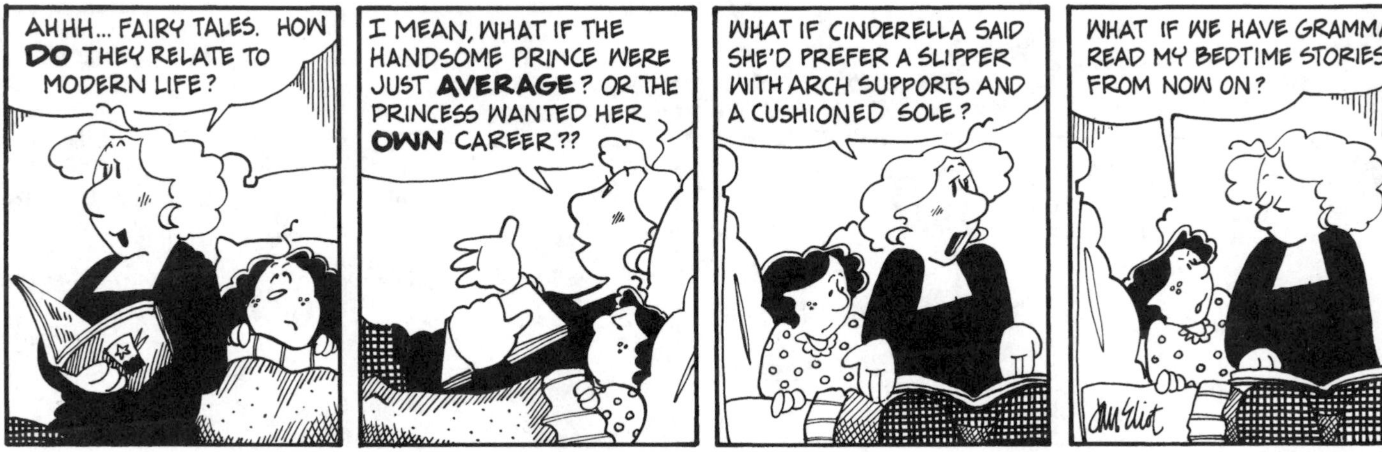
AHHH... FAIRY TALES. HOW DO THEY RELATE TO MODERN LIFE?
I MEAN, WHAT IF THE HANDSOME PRINCE WERE JUST AVERAGE? OR THE PRINCESS WANTED HER OWN CAREER??
WHAT IF CINDERELLA SAID SHE'D PREFER A SLIPPER WITH ARCH SUPPORTS AND A CUSHIONED SOLE?
WHAT IF WE HAVE GRAMMA READ MY BEDTIME STORIES FROM NOW ON?

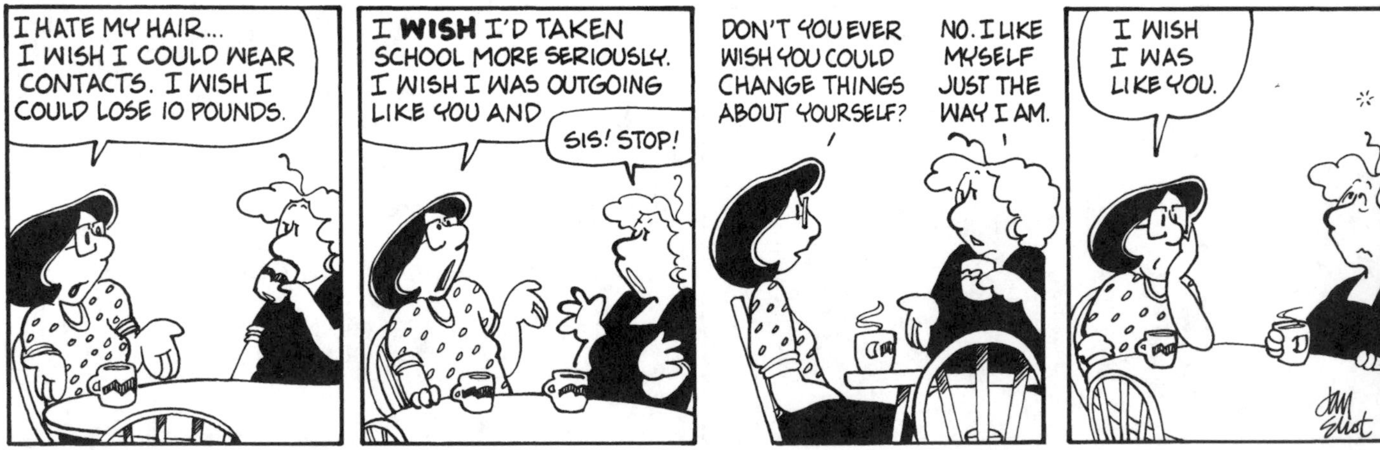
I HATE MY HAIR... I WISH I COULD WEAR CONTACTS. I WISH I COULD LOSE 10 POUNDS.
I WISH I'D TAKEN SCHOOL MORE SERIOUSLY. I WISH I WAS OUTGOING LIKE YOU AND
SIS! STOP!
DON'T YOU EVER WISH YOU COULD CHANGE THINGS ABOUT YOURSELF?
NO. I LIKE MYSELF JUST THE WAY I AM.
I WISH I WAS LIKE YOU.

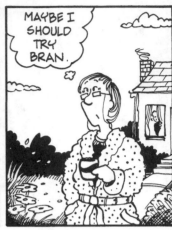

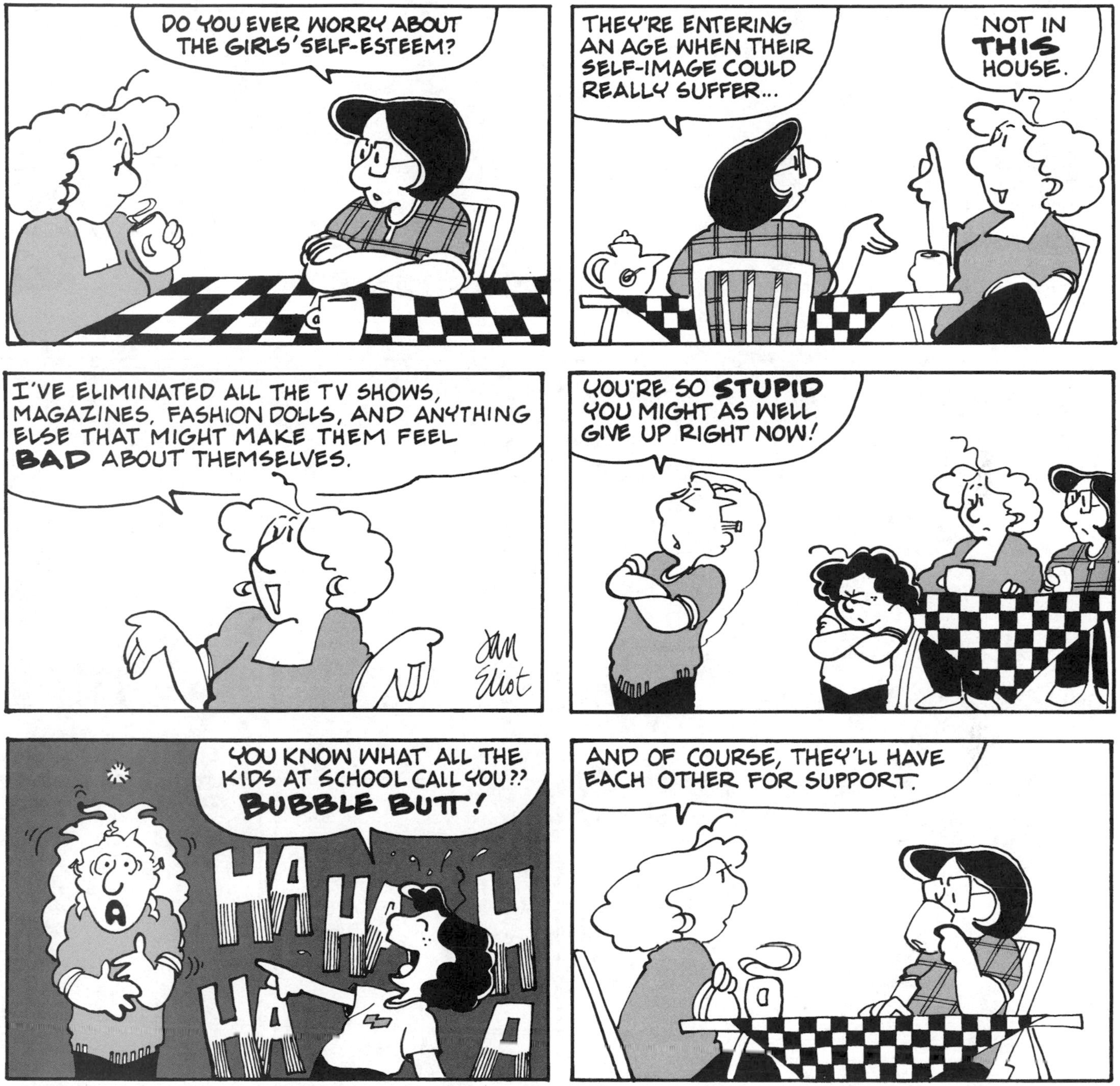
DO YOU EVER WORRY ABOUT THE GIRLS' SELF-ESTEEM?
THEY'RE ENTERING AN AGE WHEN THEIR SELF-IMAGE COULD REALLY SUFFER...
NOT IN **THIS** HOUSE.
I'VE ELIMINATED ALL THE TV SHOWS, MAGAZINES, FASHION DOLLS, AND ANYTHING ELSE THAT MIGHT MAKE THEM FEEL **BAD** ABOUT THEMSELVES.
Jan Eliot
YOU'RE SO **STUPID** YOU MIGHT AS WELL GIVE UP RIGHT NOW!
YOU KNOW WHAT ALL THE KIDS AT SCHOOL CALL YOU?? **BUBBLE BUTT!**
HA HA HA HA HA
AND OF COURSE, THEY'LL HAVE EACH OTHER FOR SUPPORT.

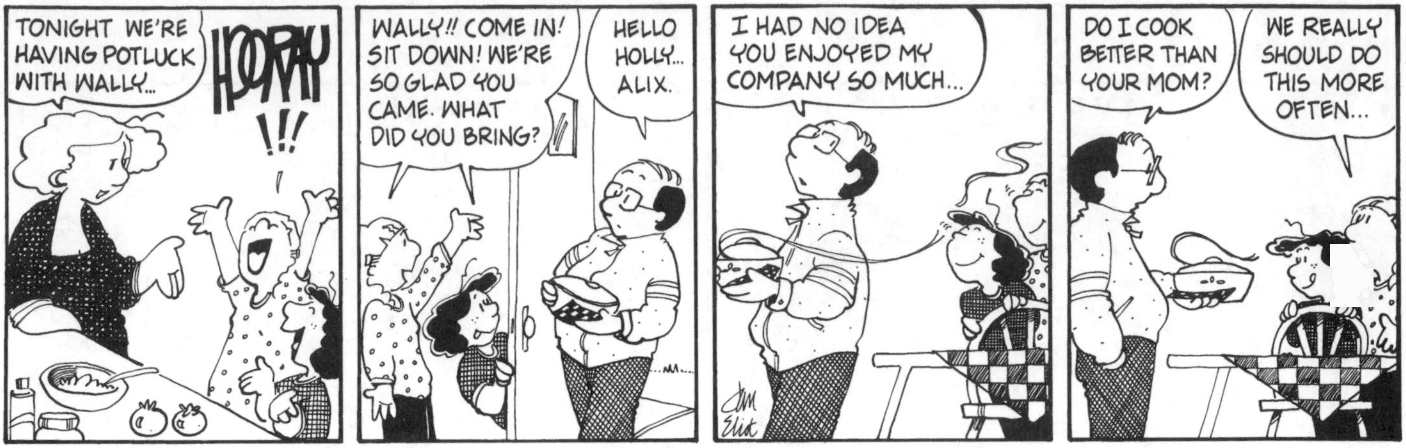
TONIGHT WE'RE HAVING POTLUCK WITH WALLY...
HOORAY
!!!
WALLY!! COME IN! SIT DOWN! WE'RE SO GLAD YOU CAME. WHAT DID YOU BRING?
HELLO HOLLY... ALIX.
I HAD NO IDEA YOU ENJOYED MY COMPANY SO MUCH...
DO I COOK BETTER THAN YOUR MOM?
WE REALLY SHOULD DO THIS MORE OFTEN...

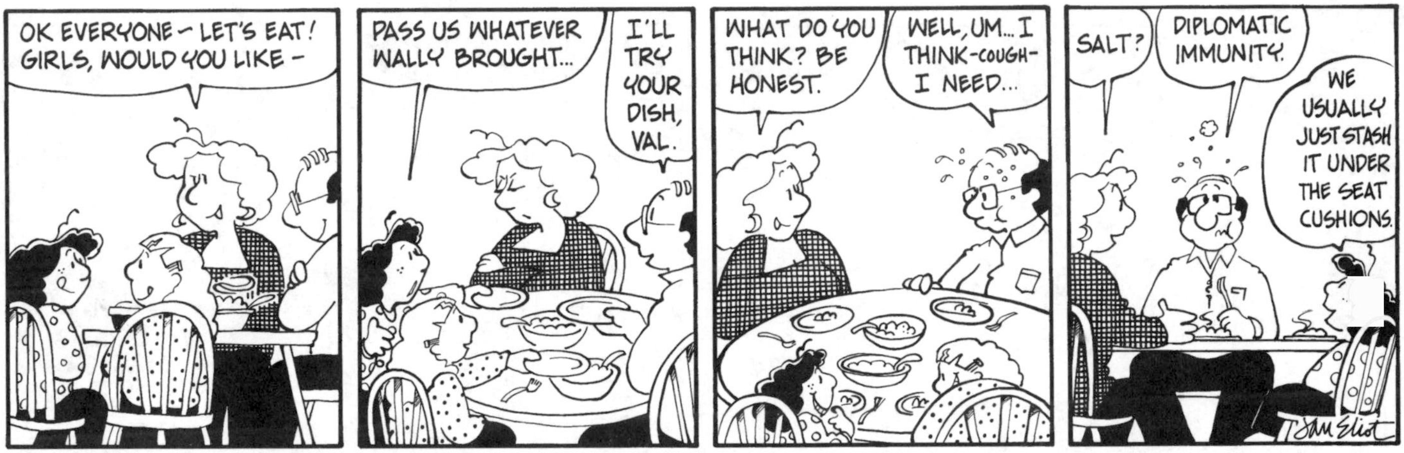
OK EVERYONE – LET'S EAT! GIRLS, WOULD YOU LIKE –
PASS US WHATEVER WALLY BROUGHT...
I'LL TRY YOUR DISH, VAL.
WHAT DO YOU THINK? BE HONEST.
WELL, UM... I THINK-cough- I NEED...
SALT?
DIPLOMATIC IMMUNITY.
WE USUALLY JUST STASH IT UNDER THE SEAT CUSHIONS.

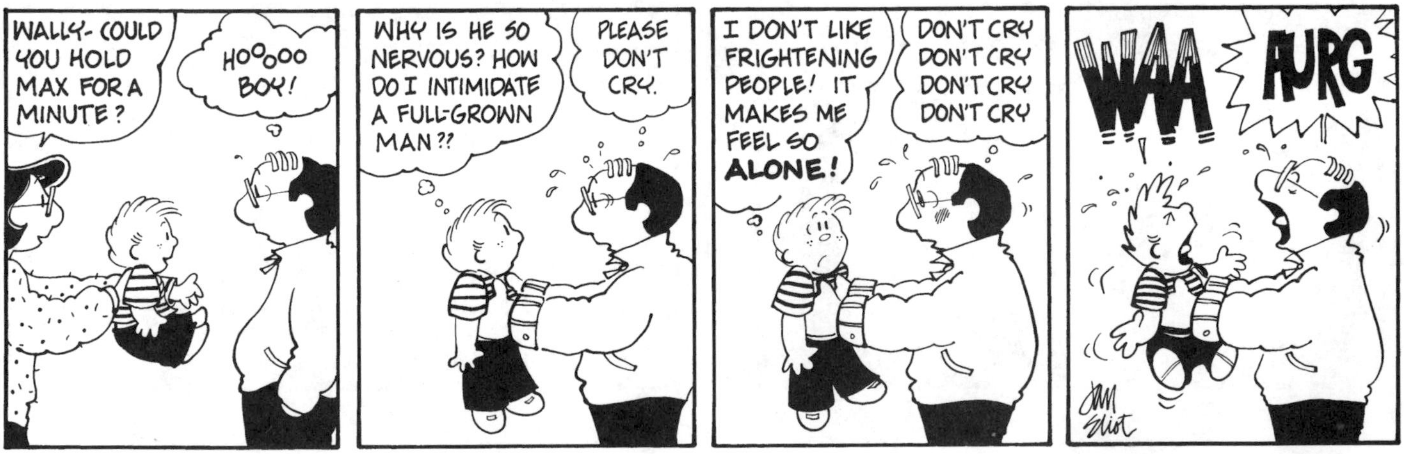
WALLY- COULD YOU HOLD MAX FOR A MINUTE?
HOoooo BOY!
WHY IS HE SO NERVOUS? HOW DO I INTIMIDATE A FULL-GROWN MAN??
PLEASE DON'T CRY.
I DON'T LIKE FRIGHTENING PEOPLE! IT MAKES ME FEEL SO ALONE!
DON'T CRY DON'T CRY DON'T CRY DON'T CRY
WAA
AURG

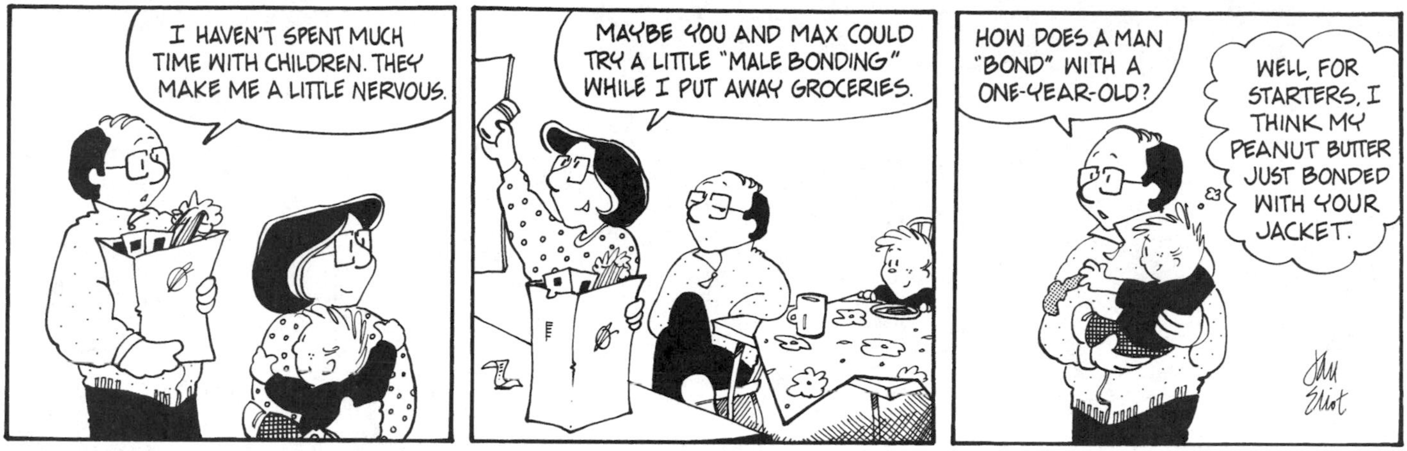
I HAVEN'T SPENT MUCH TIME WITH CHILDREN. THEY MAKE ME A LITTLE NERVOUS.
MAYBE YOU AND MAX COULD TRY A LITTLE "MALE BONDING" WHILE I PUT AWAY GROCERIES.
HOW DOES A MAN "BOND" WITH A ONE-YEAR-OLD?
WELL, FOR STARTERS, I THINK MY PEANUT BUTTER JUST BONDED WITH YOUR JACKET.

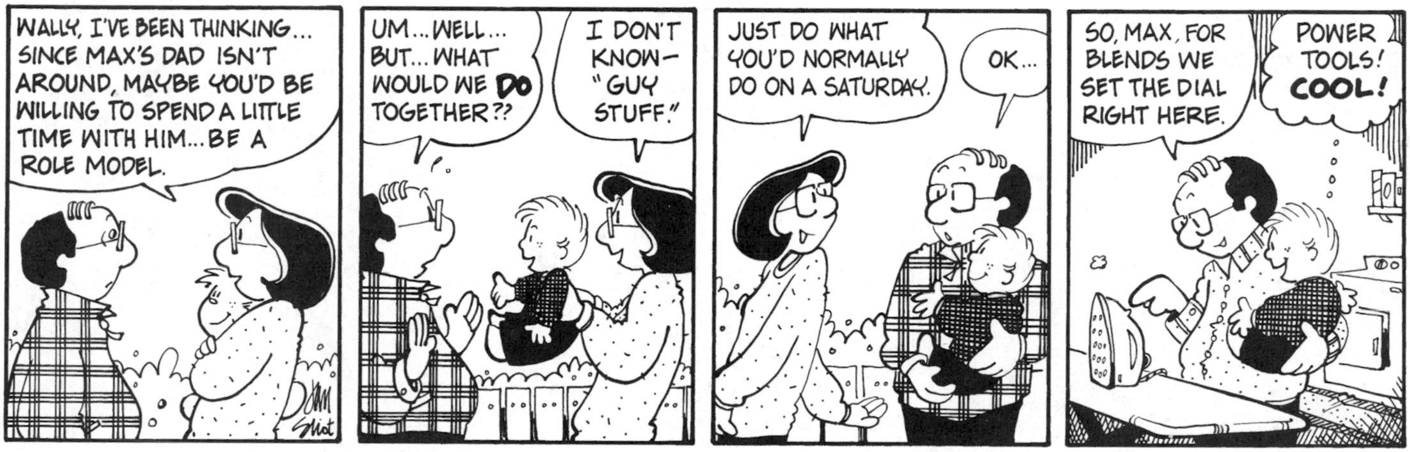
WALLY, I'VE BEEN THINKING... SINCE MAX'S DAD ISN'T AROUND, MAYBE YOU'D BE WILLING TO SPEND A LITTLE TIME WITH HIM... BE A ROLE MODEL.
UM... WELL... BUT... WHAT WOULD WE DO TOGETHER??
I DON'T KNOW– "GUY STUFF."
JUST DO WHAT YOU'D NORMALLY DO ON A SATURDAY.
OK...
SO, MAX, FOR BLENDS WE SET THE DIAL RIGHT HERE.
POWER TOOLS! COOL!

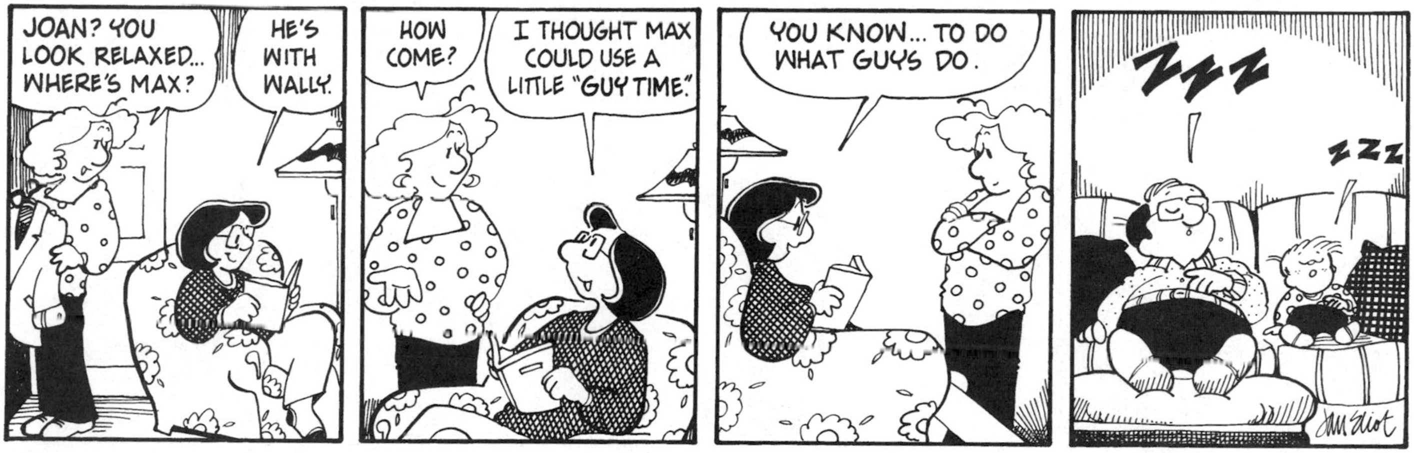
JOAN? YOU LOOK RELAXED... WHERE'S MAX?
HE'S WITH WALLY.
HOW COME?
I THOUGHT MAX COULD USE A LITTLE "GUY TIME."
YOU KNOW... TO DO WHAT GUYS DO.
ZZZ
ZZZ

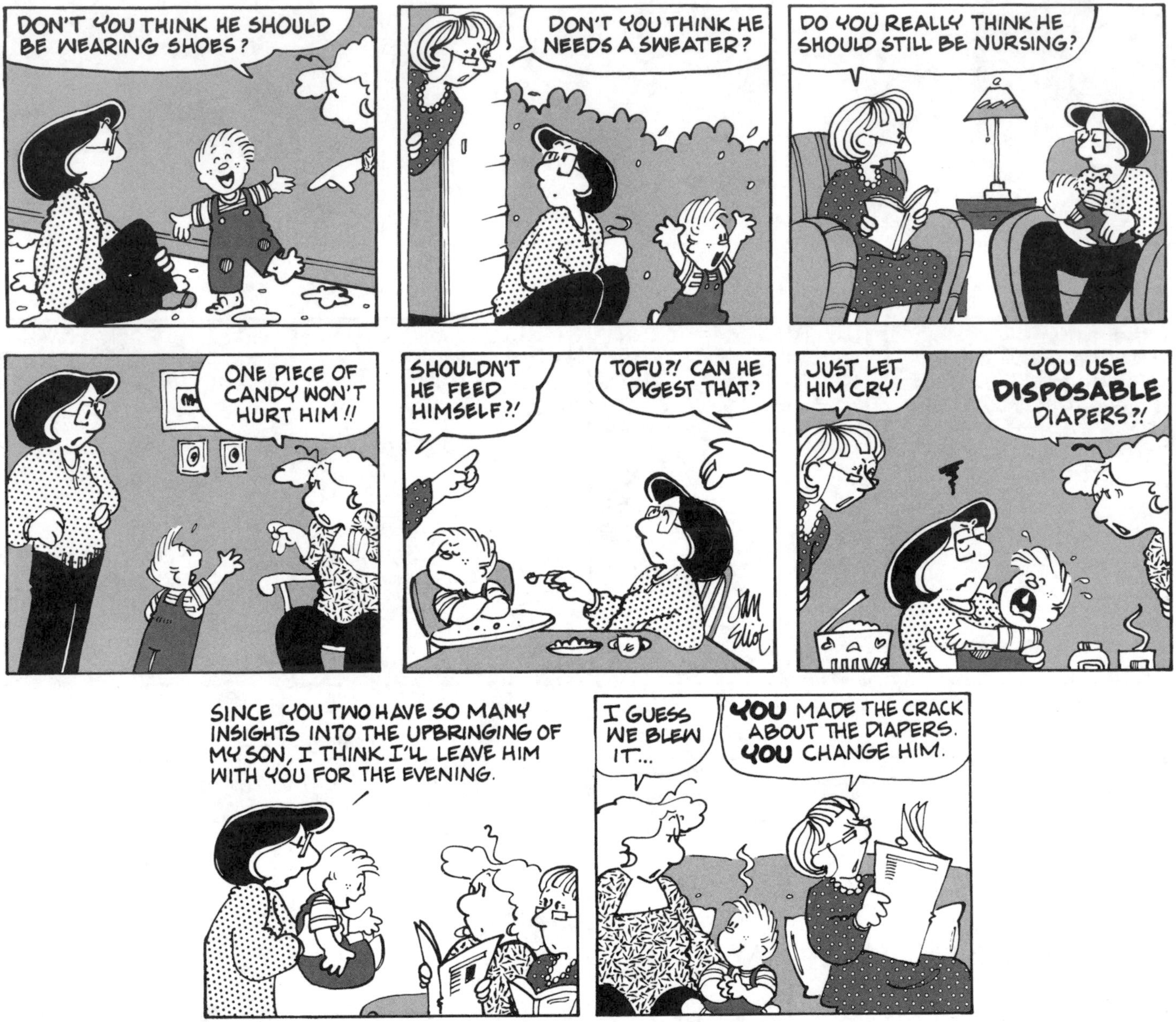
DON'T YOU THINK HE SHOULD BE WEARING SHOES?
DON'T YOU THINK HE NEEDS A SWEATER?
DO YOU REALLY THINK HE SHOULD STILL BE NURSING?
ONE PIECE OF CANDY WON'T HURT HIM!!
SHOULDN'T HE FEED HIMSELF?!
TOFU?! CAN HE DIGEST THAT?
JUST LET HIM CRY!
YOU USE DISPOSABLE DIAPERS?!
SINCE YOU TWO HAVE SO MANY INSIGHTS INTO THE UPBRINGING OF MY SON, I THINK I'LL LEAVE HIM WITH YOU FOR THE EVENING.
I GUESS WE BLEW IT...
YOU MADE THE CRACK ABOUT THE DIAPERS. YOU CHANGE HIM.

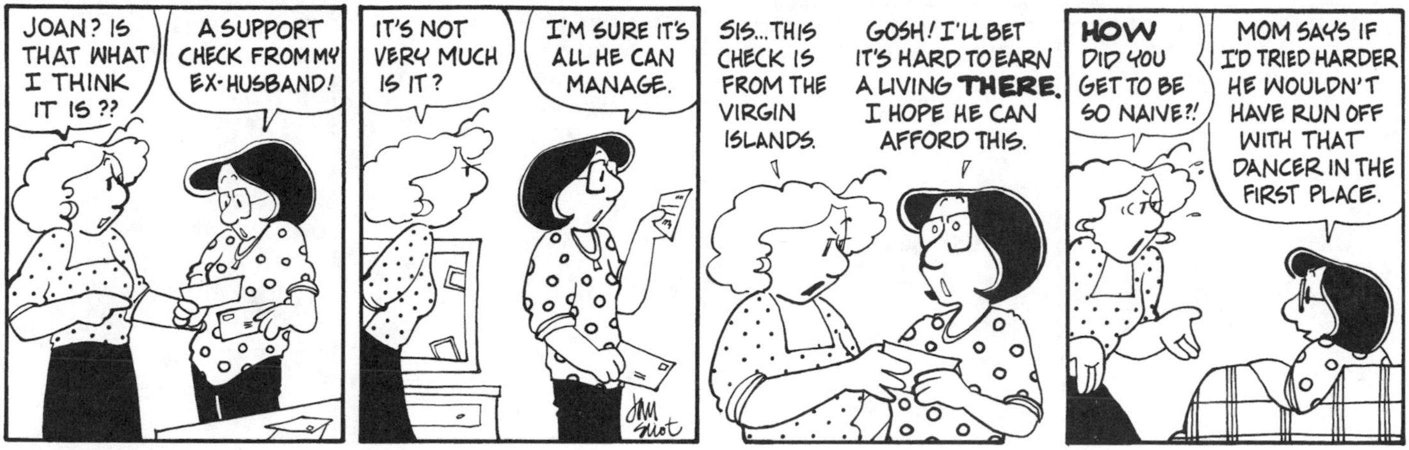
JOAN? IS THAT WHAT I THINK IT IS??
A SUPPORT CHECK FROM MY EX-HUSBAND!
IT'S NOT VERY MUCH IS IT?
I'M SURE IT'S ALL HE CAN MANAGE.
SIS...THIS CHECK IS FROM THE VIRGIN ISLANDS.
GOSH! I'LL BET IT'S HARD TO EARN A LIVING THERE. I HOPE HE CAN AFFORD THIS.
HOW DID YOU GET TO BE SO NAIVE?!
MOM SAYS IF I'D TRIED HARDER HE WOULDN'T HAVE RUN OFF WITH THAT DANCER IN THE FIRST PLACE.

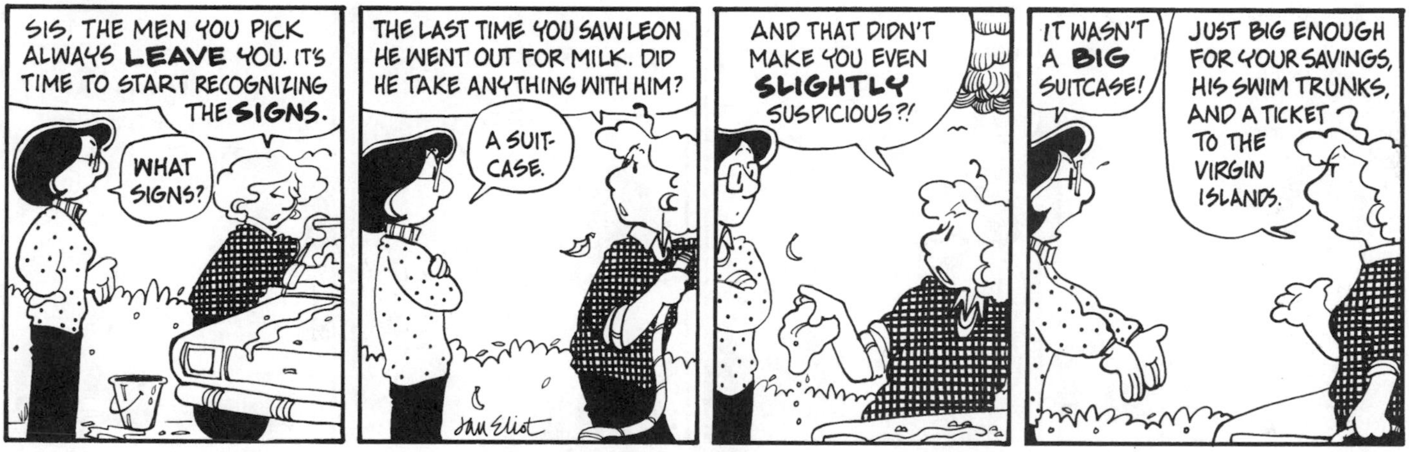
SIS, THE MEN YOU PICK ALWAYS LEAVE YOU. IT'S TIME TO START RECOGNIZING THE SIGNS.
WHAT SIGNS?
THE LAST TIME YOU SAW LEON HE WENT OUT FOR MILK. DID HE TAKE ANYTHING WITH HIM?
A SUIT-CASE.
AND THAT DIDN'T MAKE YOU EVEN SLIGHTLY SUSPICIOUS?!
IT WASN'T A BIG SUITCASE!
JUST BIG ENOUGH FOR YOUR SAVINGS, HIS SWIM TRUNKS, AND A TICKET TO THE VIRGIN ISLANDS.

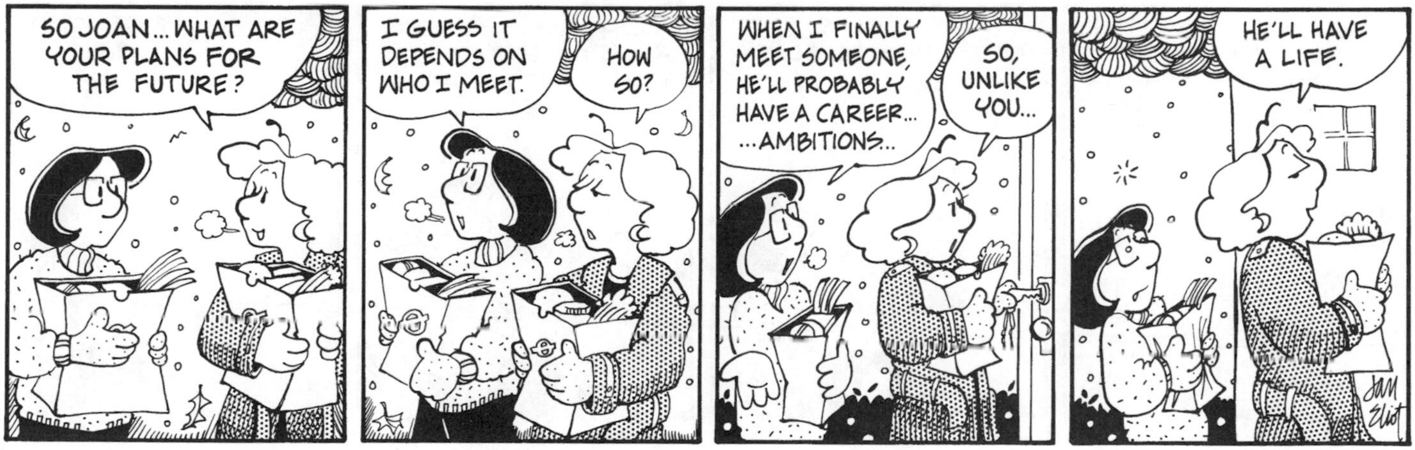
SO JOAN... WHAT ARE YOUR PLANS FOR THE FUTURE?
I GUESS IT DEPENDS ON WHO I MEET.
HOW SO?
WHEN I FINALLY MEET SOMEONE, HE'LL PROBABLY HAVE A CAREER... ...AMBITIONS...
SO, UNLIKE YOU...
HE'LL HAVE A LIFE.

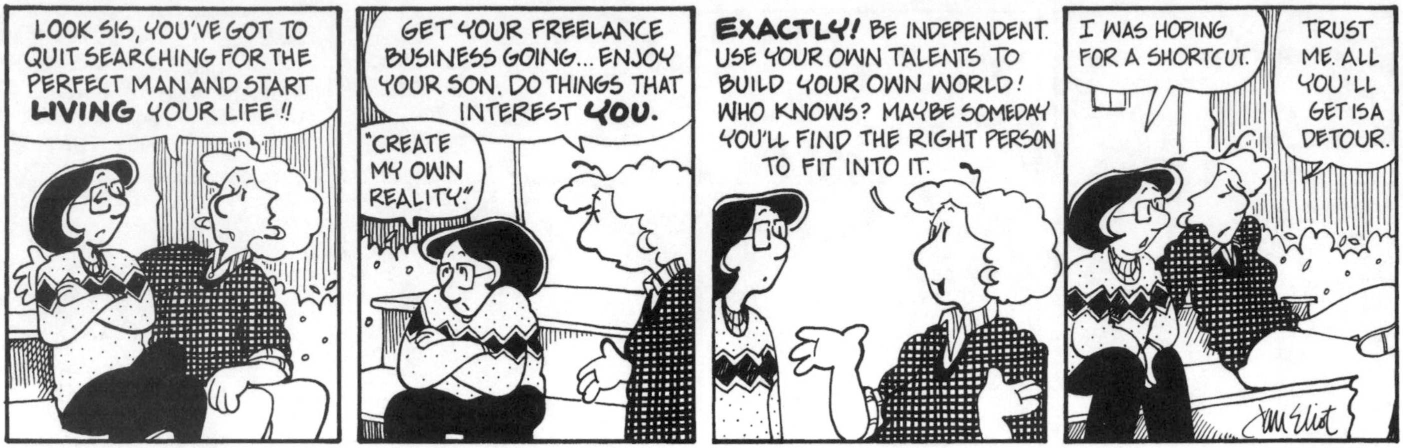
LOOK SIS, YOU'VE GOT TO QUIT SEARCHING FOR THE PERFECT MAN AND START **LIVING** YOUR LIFE!!
GET YOUR FREELANCE BUSINESS GOING... ENJOY YOUR SON. DO THINGS THAT INTEREST **YOU.**
"CREATE MY OWN REALITY."
EXACTLY! BE INDEPENDENT. USE YOUR OWN TALENTS TO BUILD YOUR OWN WORLD! WHO KNOWS? MAYBE SOMEDAY YOU'LL FIND THE RIGHT PERSON TO FIT INTO IT.
I WAS HOPING FOR A SHORTCUT.
TRUST ME. ALL YOU'LL GET IS A DETOUR.

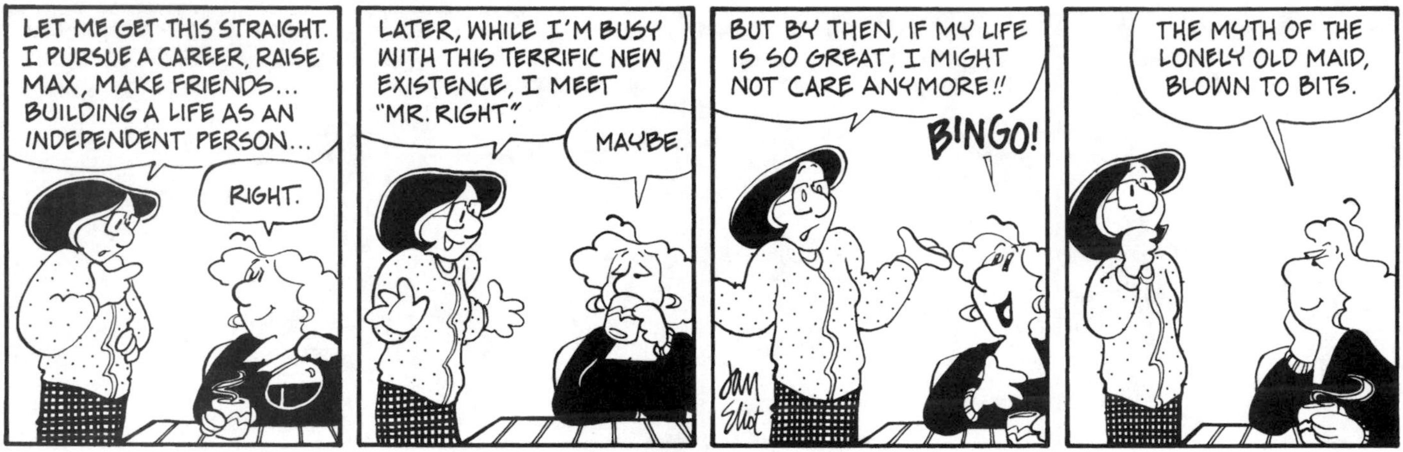
LET ME GET THIS STRAIGHT. I PURSUE A CAREER, RAISE MAX, MAKE FRIENDS... BUILDING A LIFE AS AN INDEPENDENT PERSON...
RIGHT.
LATER, WHILE I'M BUSY WITH THIS TERRIFIC NEW EXISTENCE, I MEET "MR. RIGHT."
MAYBE.
BUT BY THEN, IF MY LIFE IS SO GREAT, I MIGHT NOT CARE ANYMORE!!
BINGO!
THE MYTH OF THE LONELY OLD MAID, BLOWN TO BITS.

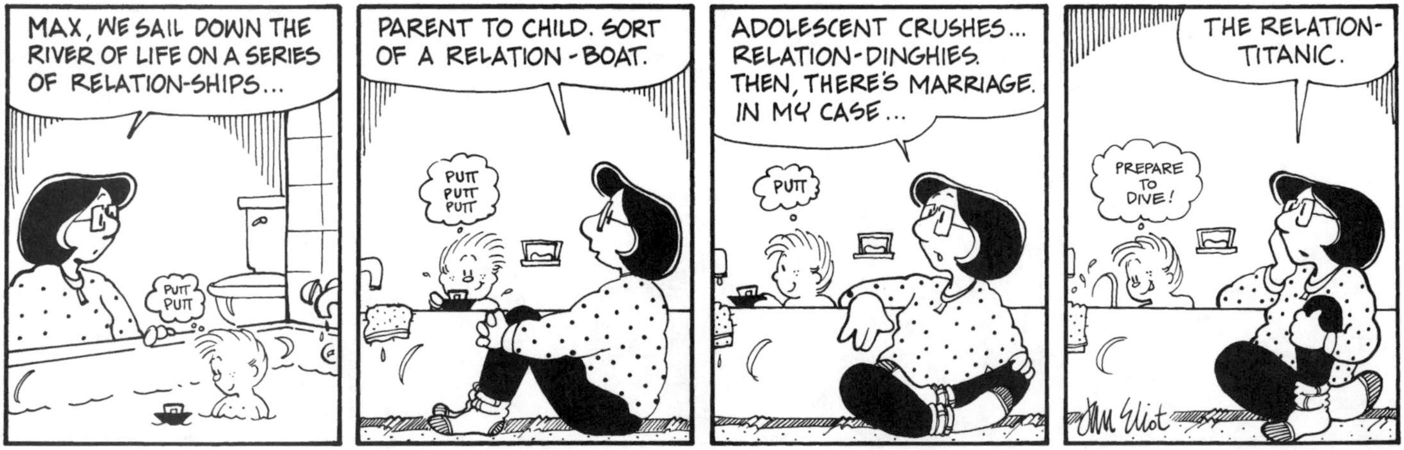
MAX, WE SAIL DOWN THE RIVER OF LIFE ON A SERIES OF RELATION-SHIPS...
PUTT PUTT
PARENT TO CHILD. SORT OF A RELATION-BOAT.
PUTT PUTT PUTT
ADOLESCENT CRUSHES... RELATION-DINGHIES. THEN, THERE'S MARRIAGE. IN MY CASE...
PUTT
THE RELATION-TITANIC.
PREPARE TO DIVE!

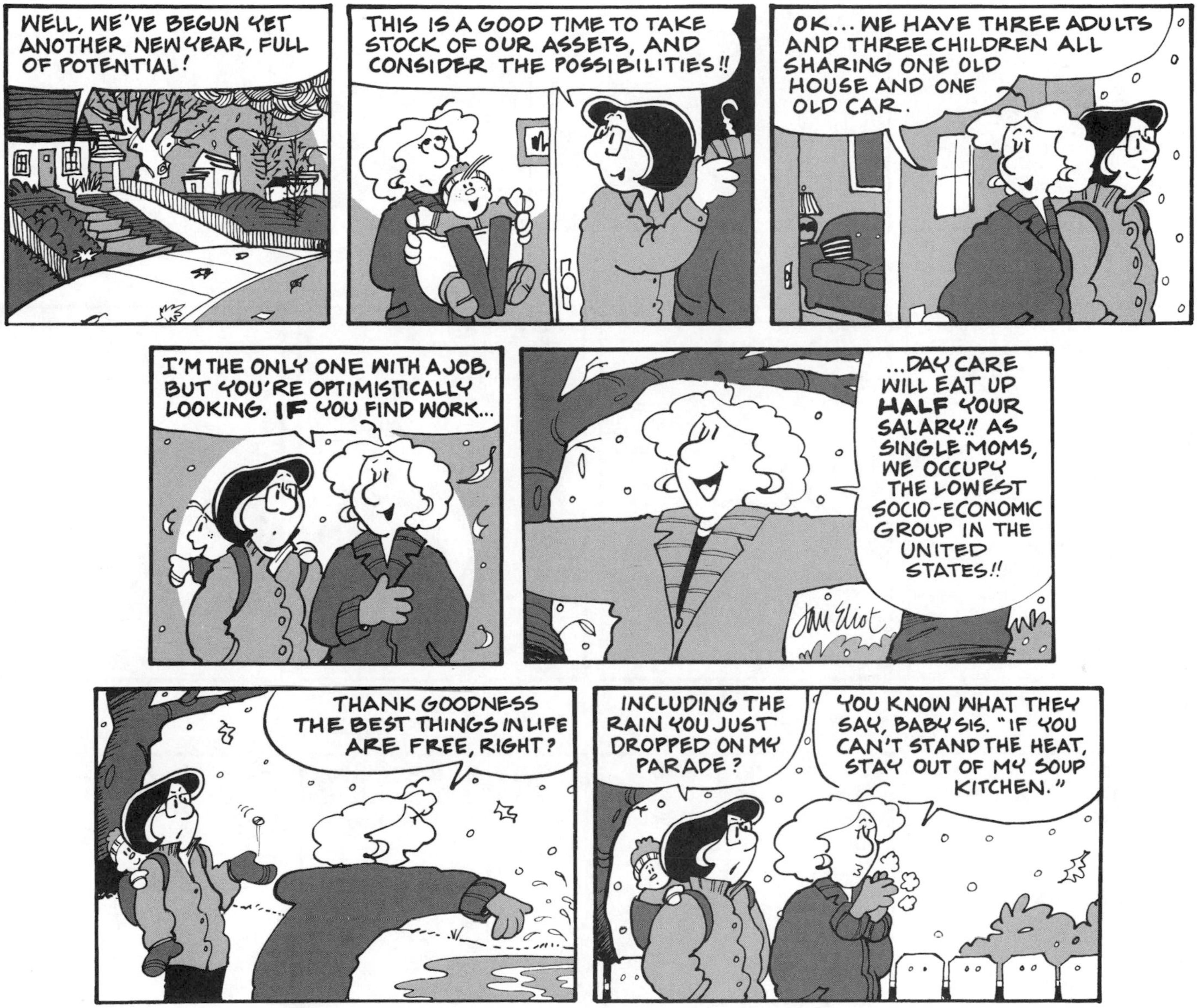
WELL, WE'VE BEGUN YET ANOTHER NEW YEAR, FULL OF POTENTIAL!
THIS IS A GOOD TIME TO TAKE STOCK OF OUR ASSETS, AND CONSIDER THE POSSIBILITIES!!
OK... WE HAVE THREE ADULTS AND THREE CHILDREN ALL SHARING ONE OLD HOUSE AND ONE OLD CAR.
I'M THE ONLY ONE WITH A JOB, BUT YOU'RE OPTIMISTICALLY LOOKING. IF YOU FIND WORK...
...DAY CARE WILL EAT UP HALF YOUR SALARY!! AS SINGLE MOMS, WE OCCUPY THE LOWEST SOCIO-ECONOMIC GROUP IN THE UNITED STATES!!
Jan Eliot
THANK GOODNESS THE BEST THINGS IN LIFE ARE FREE, RIGHT?
INCLUDING THE RAIN YOU JUST DROPPED ON MY PARADE?
YOU KNOW WHAT THEY SAY, BABY SIS. "IF YOU CAN'T STAND THE HEAT, STAY OUT OF MY SOUP KITCHEN."

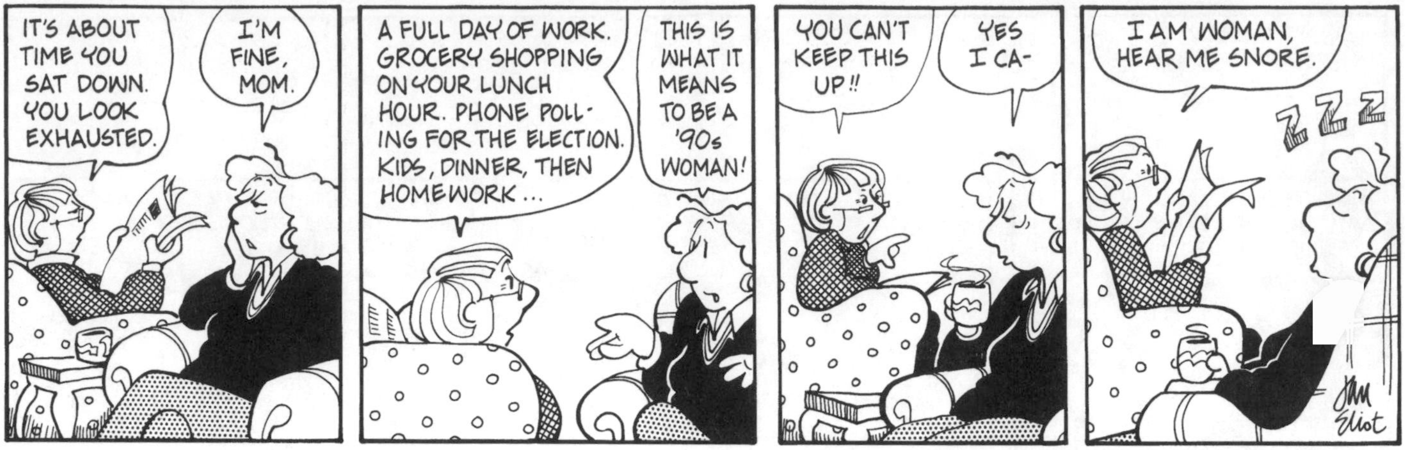
IT'S ABOUT TIME YOU SAT DOWN. YOU LOOK EXHAUSTED.
I'M FINE, MOM.
A FULL DAY OF WORK. GROCERY SHOPPING ON YOUR LUNCH HOUR. PHONE POLLING FOR THE ELECTION. KIDS, DINNER, THEN HOMEWORK...
THIS IS WHAT IT MEANS TO BE A '90s WOMAN!
YOU CAN'T KEEP THIS UP!!
YES I CA-
I AM WOMAN, HEAR ME SNORE.
ZZZ

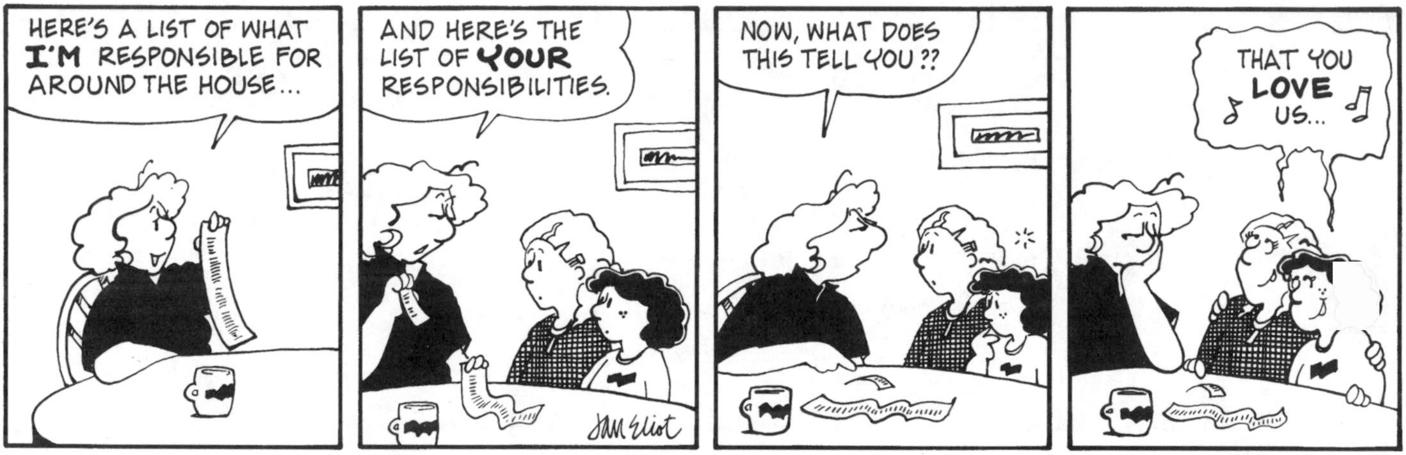
HERE'S A LIST OF WHAT I'M RESPONSIBLE FOR AROUND THE HOUSE...
AND HERE'S THE LIST OF YOUR RESPONSIBILITIES.
NOW, WHAT DOES THIS TELL YOU??
THAT YOU LOVE US...

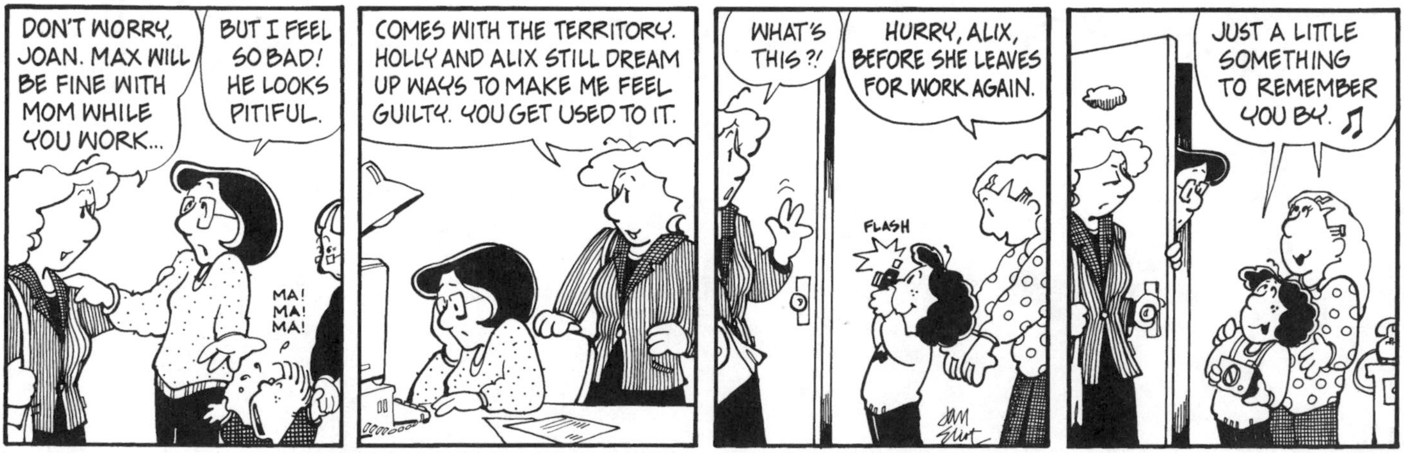
DON'T WORRY, JOAN. MAX WILL BE FINE WITH MOM WHILE YOU WORK...
BUT I FEEL SO BAD! HE LOOKS PITIFUL.
MA! MA! MA!
COMES WITH THE TERRITORY. HOLLY AND ALIX STILL DREAM UP WAYS TO MAKE ME FEEL GUILTY. YOU GET USED TO IT.
WHAT'S THIS?!
HURRY, ALIX, BEFORE SHE LEAVES FOR WORK AGAIN.
FLASH
JUST A LITTLE SOMETHING TO REMEMBER YOU BY.

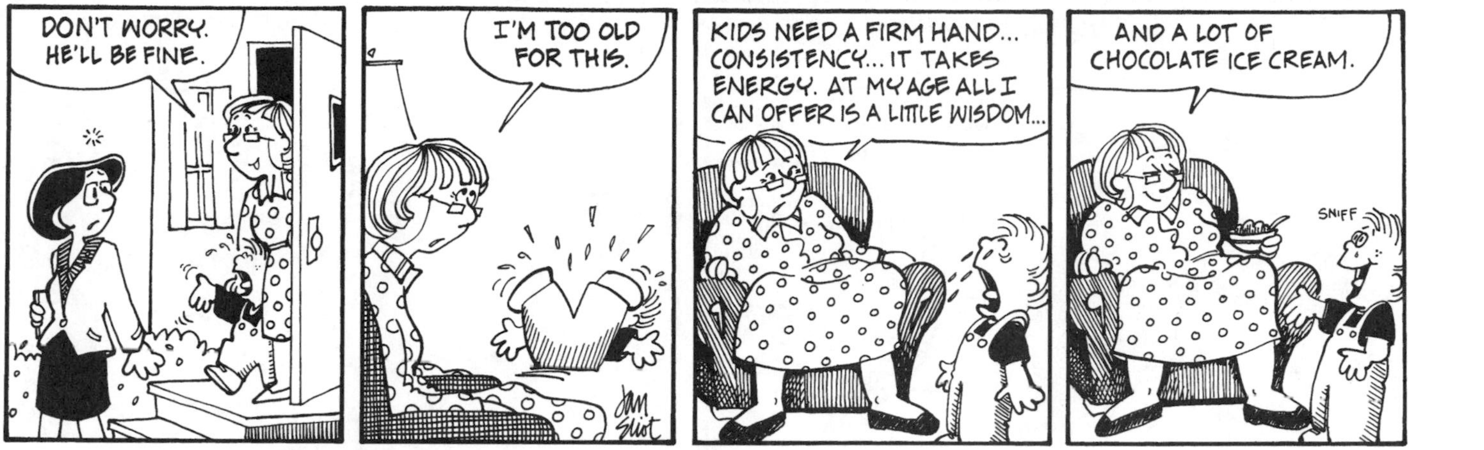
DON'T WORRY. HE'LL BE FINE.
I'M TOO OLD FOR THIS.
KIDS NEED A FIRM HAND... CONSISTENCY... IT TAKES ENERGY. AT MY AGE ALL I CAN OFFER IS A LITTLE WISDOM...
AND A LOT OF CHOCOLATE ICE CREAM.
SNIFF

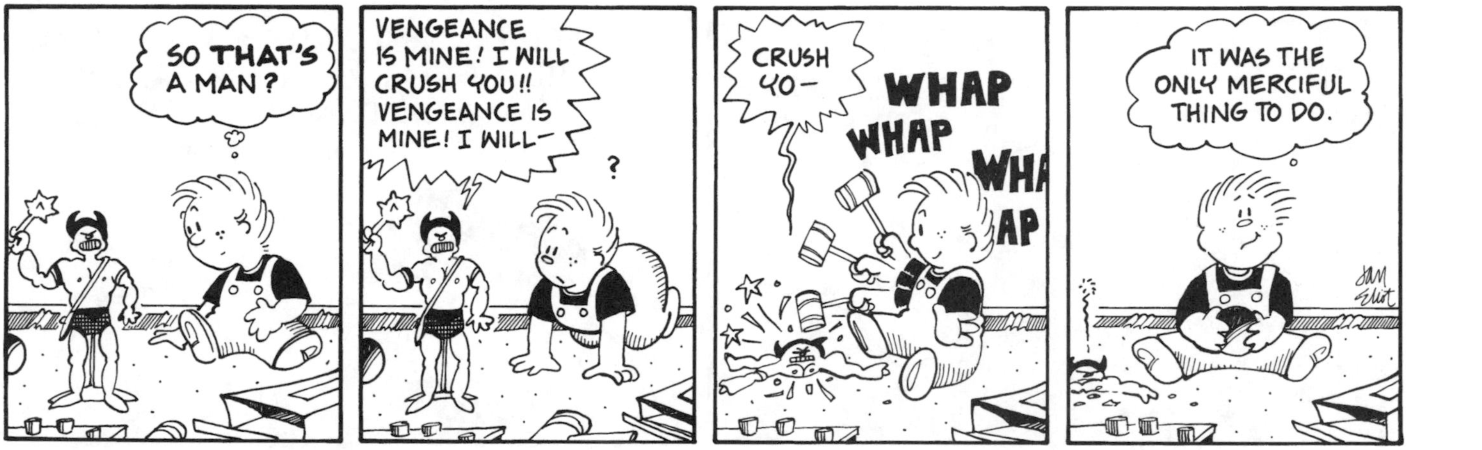
SO THAT'S A MAN?
VENGEANCE IS MINE! I WILL CRUSH YOU!! VENGEANCE IS MINE! I WILL—
?
CRUSH YO—
WHAP
WHAP
WHA
AP
IT WAS THE ONLY MERCIFUL THING TO DO.

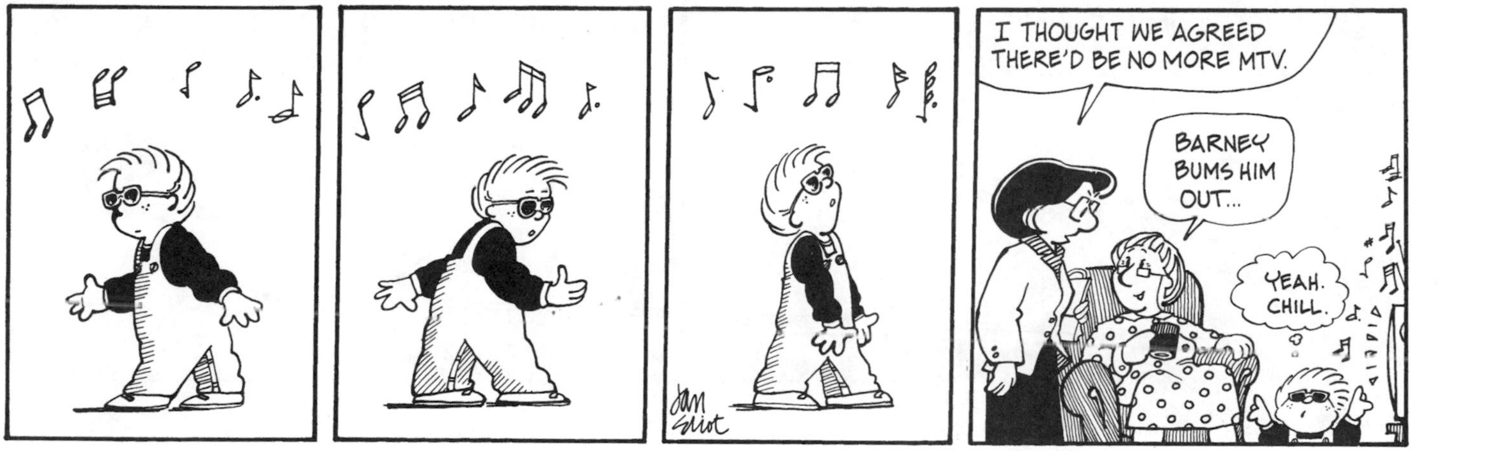
I THOUGHT WE AGREED THERE'D BE NO MORE MTV.
BARNEY BUMS HIM OUT...
YEAH. CHILL.

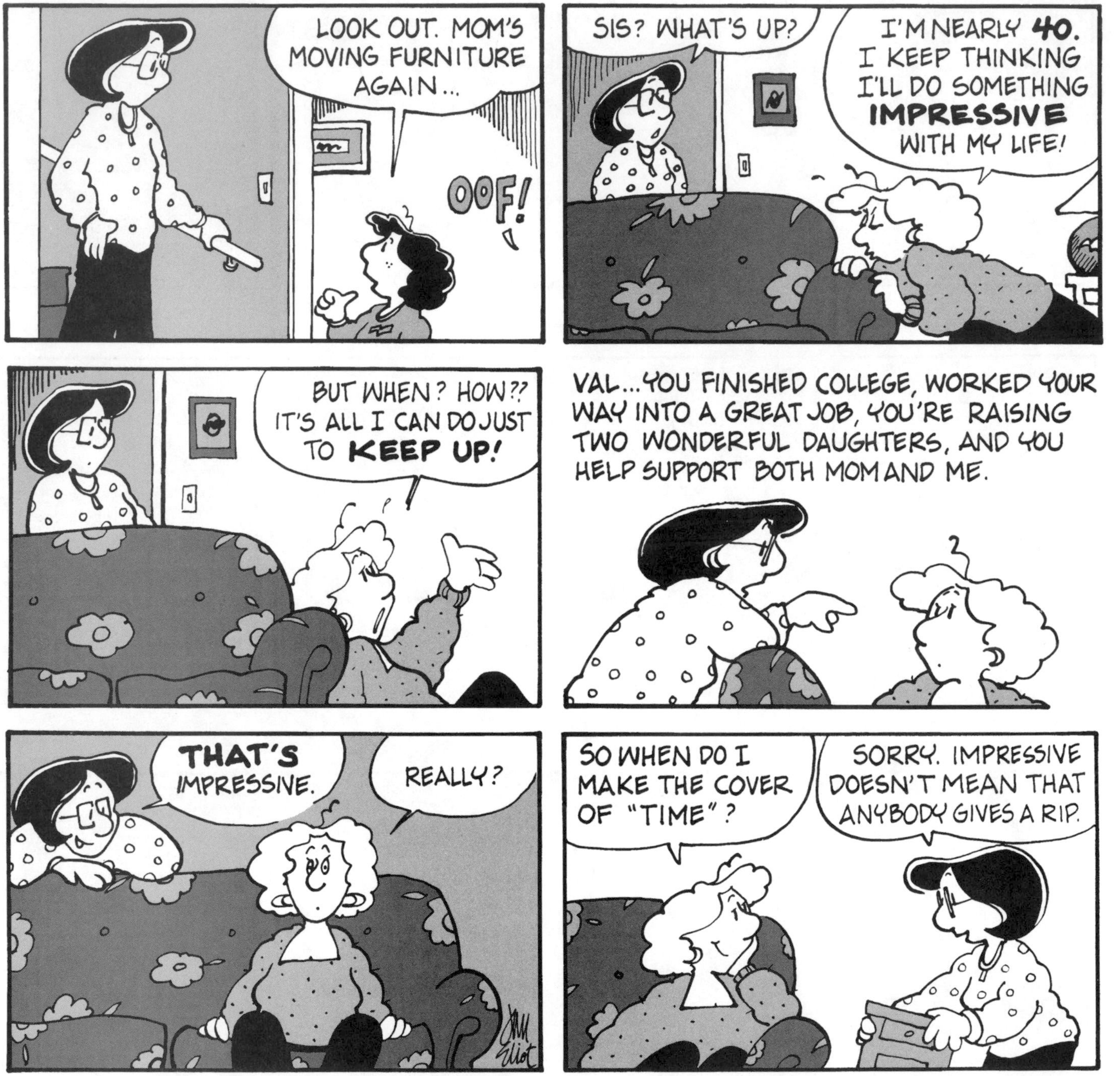
LOOK OUT. MOM'S MOVING FURNITURE AGAIN...
OOF!
SIS? WHAT'S UP?
I'M NEARLY 40. I KEEP THINKING I'LL DO SOMETHING IMPRESSIVE WITH MY LIFE!
BUT WHEN? HOW?? IT'S ALL I CAN DO JUST TO KEEP UP!
VAL... YOU FINISHED COLLEGE, WORKED YOUR WAY INTO A GREAT JOB, YOU'RE RAISING TWO WONDERFUL DAUGHTERS, AND YOU HELP SUPPORT BOTH MOM AND ME.
THAT'S IMPRESSIVE.
REALLY?
SO WHEN DO I MAKE THE COVER OF "TIME"?
SORRY. IMPRESSIVE DOESN'T MEAN THAT ANYBODY GIVES A RIP.

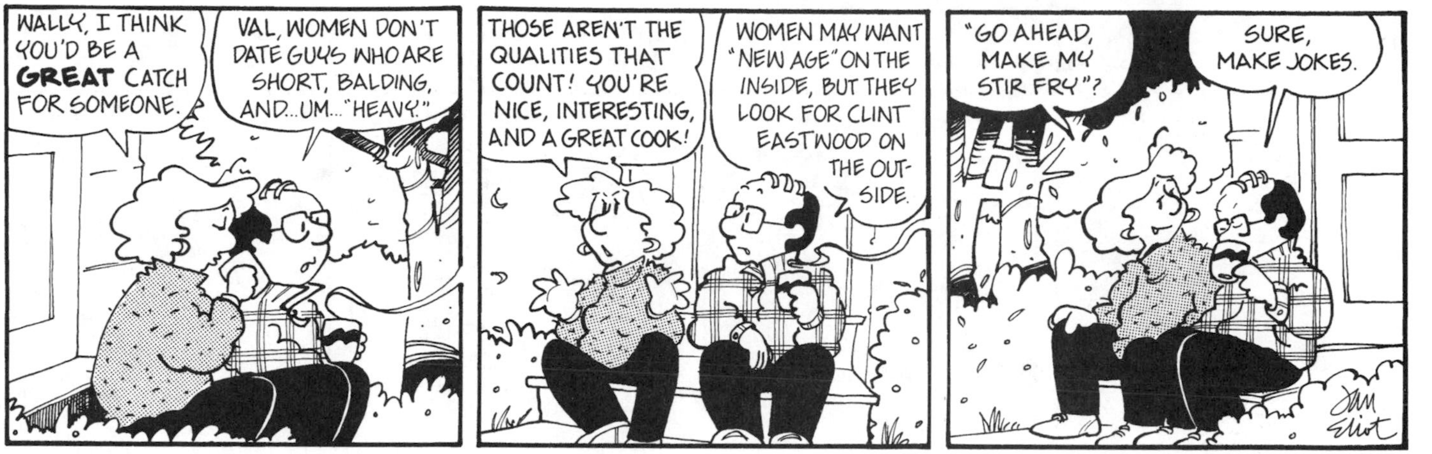
WALLY, I THINK YOU'D BE A GREAT CATCH FOR SOMEONE.
VAL, WOMEN DON'T DATE GUYS WHO ARE SHORT, BALDING, AND...UM..."HEAVY."
THOSE AREN'T THE QUALITIES THAT COUNT! YOU'RE NICE, INTERESTING, AND A GREAT COOK!
WOMEN MAY WANT "NEW AGE" ON THE INSIDE, BUT THEY LOOK FOR CLINT EASTWOOD ON THE OUT-SIDE.
"GO AHEAD, MAKE MY STIR FRY"?
SURE, MAKE JOKES.

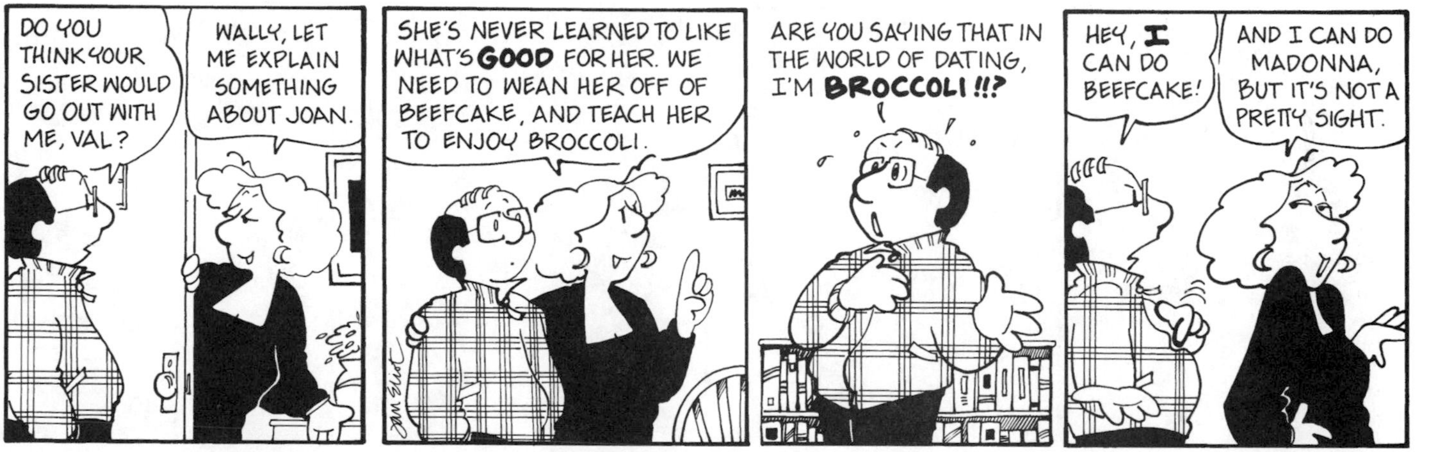
DO YOU THINK YOUR SISTER WOULD GO OUT WITH ME, VAL?
WALLY, LET ME EXPLAIN SOMETHING ABOUT JOAN.
SHE'S NEVER LEARNED TO LIKE WHAT'S GOOD FOR HER. WE NEED TO WEAN HER OFF OF BEEFCAKE, AND TEACH HER TO ENJOY BROCCOLI.
ARE YOU SAYING THAT IN THE WORLD OF DATING, I'M BROCCOLI!!?
HEY, I CAN DO BEEFCAKE!
AND I CAN DO MADONNA, BUT IT'S NOT A PRETTY SIGHT.

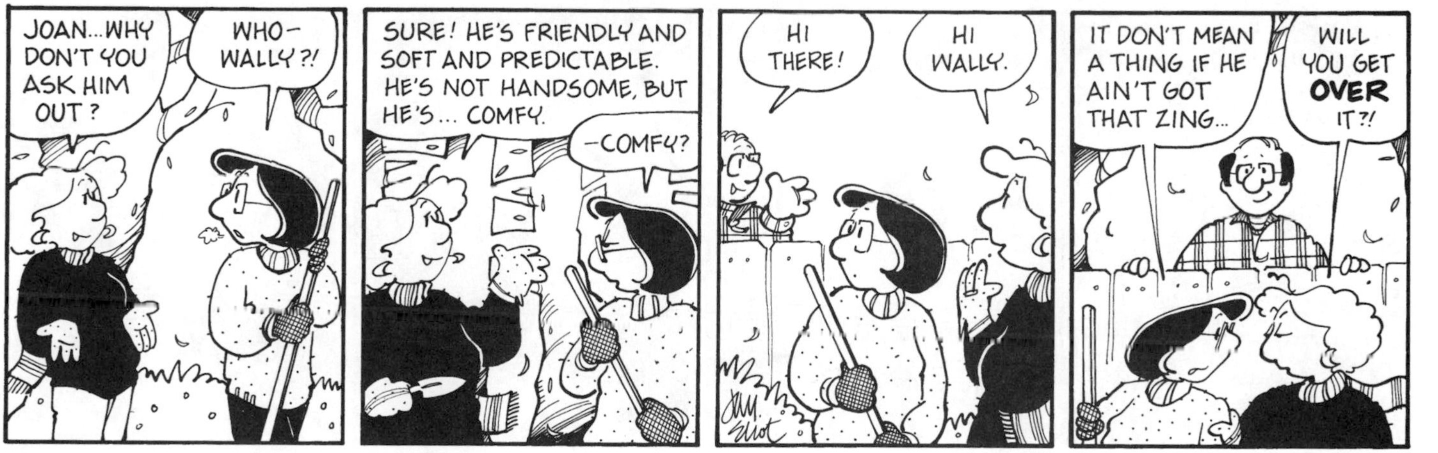
JOAN...WHY DON'T YOU ASK HIM OUT?
WHO-WALLY?!
SURE! HE'S FRIENDLY AND SOFT AND PREDICTABLE. HE'S NOT HANDSOME, BUT HE'S... COMFY.
-COMFY?
HI THERE!
HI WALLY.
IT DON'T MEAN A THING IF HE AIN'T GOT THAT ZING...
WILL YOU GET OVER IT?!

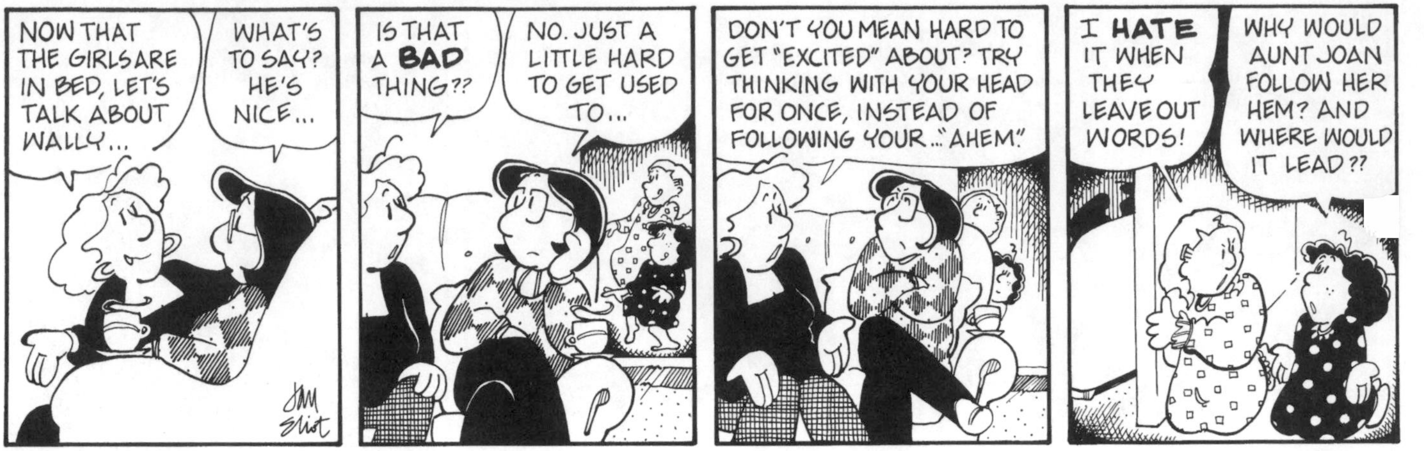
NOW THAT THE GIRLS ARE IN BED, LET'S TALK ABOUT WALLY...
WHAT'S TO SAY? HE'S NICE...
IS THAT A **BAD** THING??
NO. JUST A LITTLE HARD TO GET USED TO...
DON'T YOU MEAN HARD TO GET "EXCITED" ABOUT? TRY THINKING WITH YOUR HEAD FOR ONCE, INSTEAD OF FOLLOWING YOUR..."AHEM."
I **HATE** IT WHEN THEY LEAVE OUT WORDS!
WHY WOULD AUNT JOAN FOLLOW HER HEM? AND WHERE WOULD IT LEAD??

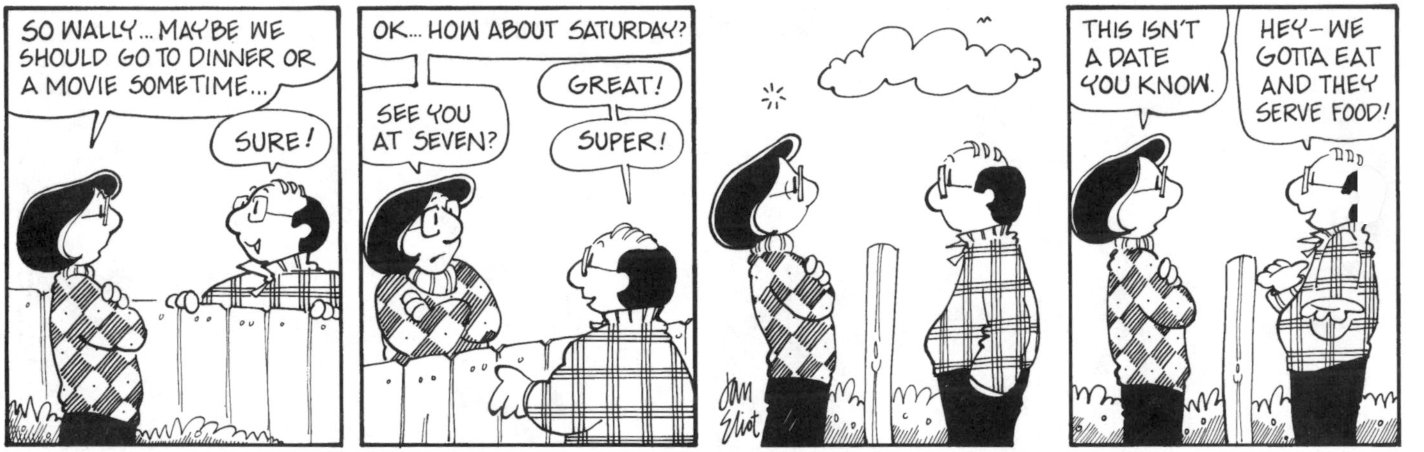
SO WALLY... MAYBE WE SHOULD GO TO DINNER OR A MOVIE SOMETIME...
SURE!
OK... HOW ABOUT SATURDAY?
GREAT!
SEE YOU AT SEVEN?
SUPER!
THIS ISN'T A DATE YOU KNOW.
HEY—WE GOTTA EAT AND THEY SERVE FOOD!

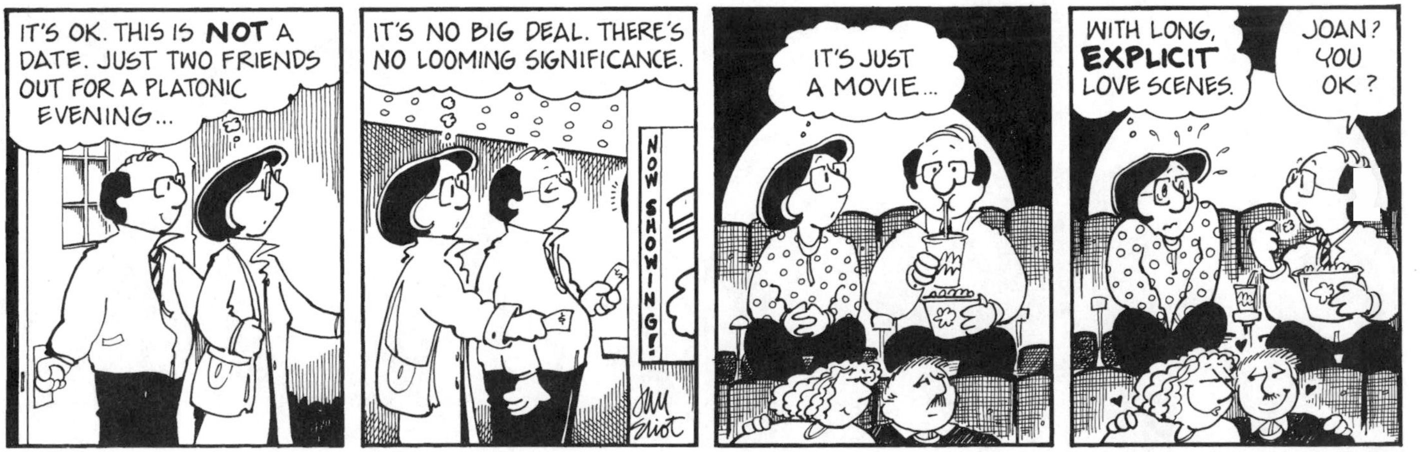
IT'S OK. THIS IS **NOT** A DATE. JUST TWO FRIENDS OUT FOR A PLATONIC EVENING...
IT'S NO BIG DEAL. THERE'S NO LOOMING SIGNIFICANCE.
NOW SHOWING!
IT'S JUST A MOVIE...
WITH LONG, **EXPLICIT** LOVE SCENES.
JOAN? YOU OK?

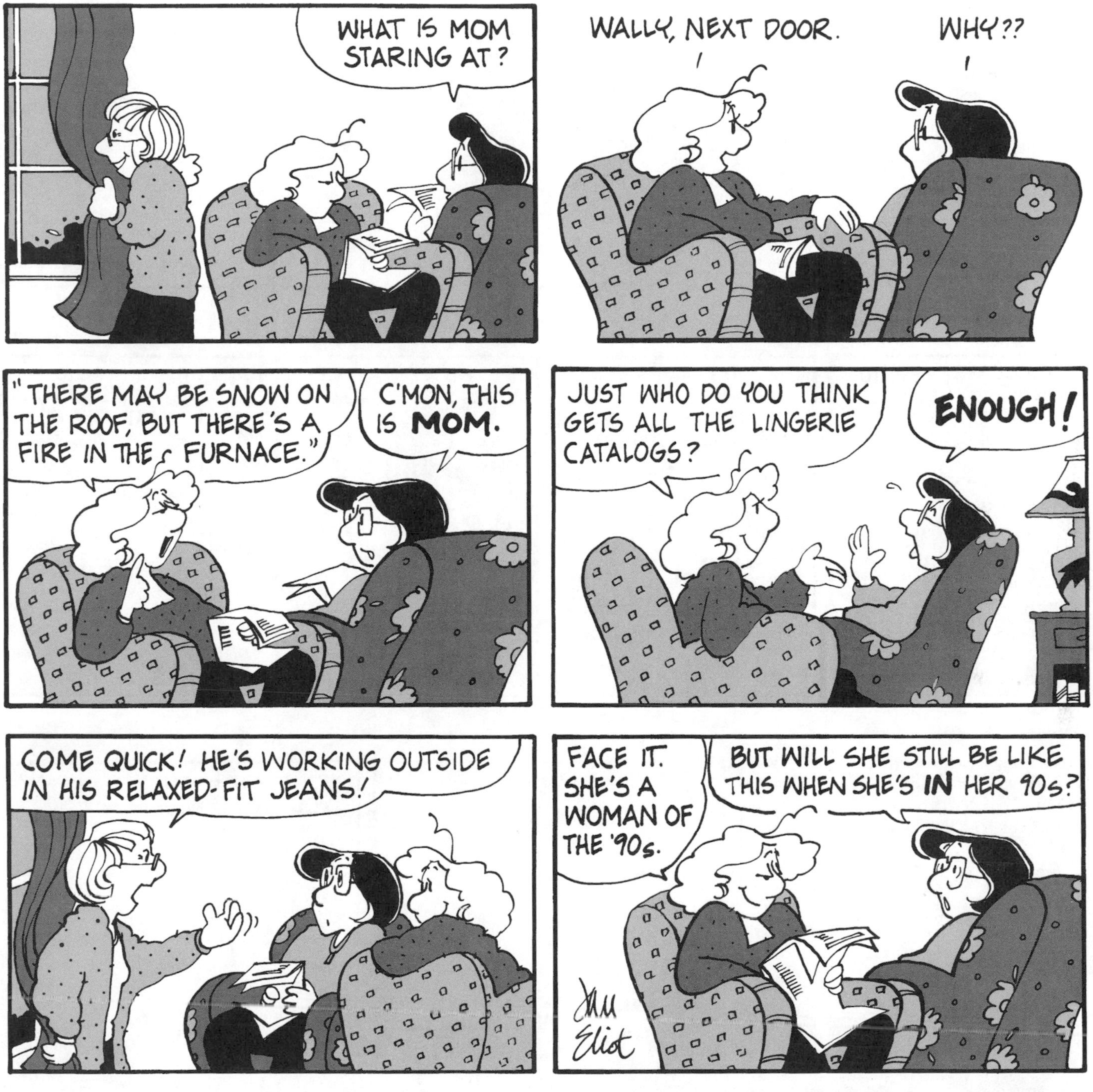
WHAT IS MOM STARING AT?
WALLY, NEXT DOOR.
WHY??
"THERE MAY BE SNOW ON THE ROOF, BUT THERE'S A FIRE IN THE FURNACE."
C'MON, THIS IS **MOM.**
JUST WHO DO YOU THINK GETS ALL THE LINGERIE CATALOGS?
ENOUGH!
COME QUICK! HE'S WORKING OUTSIDE IN HIS RELAXED-FIT JEANS!
FACE IT. SHE'S A WOMAN OF THE '90s.
BUT WILL SHE STILL BE LIKE THIS WHEN SHE'S **IN** HER 90s?
Jan Eliot

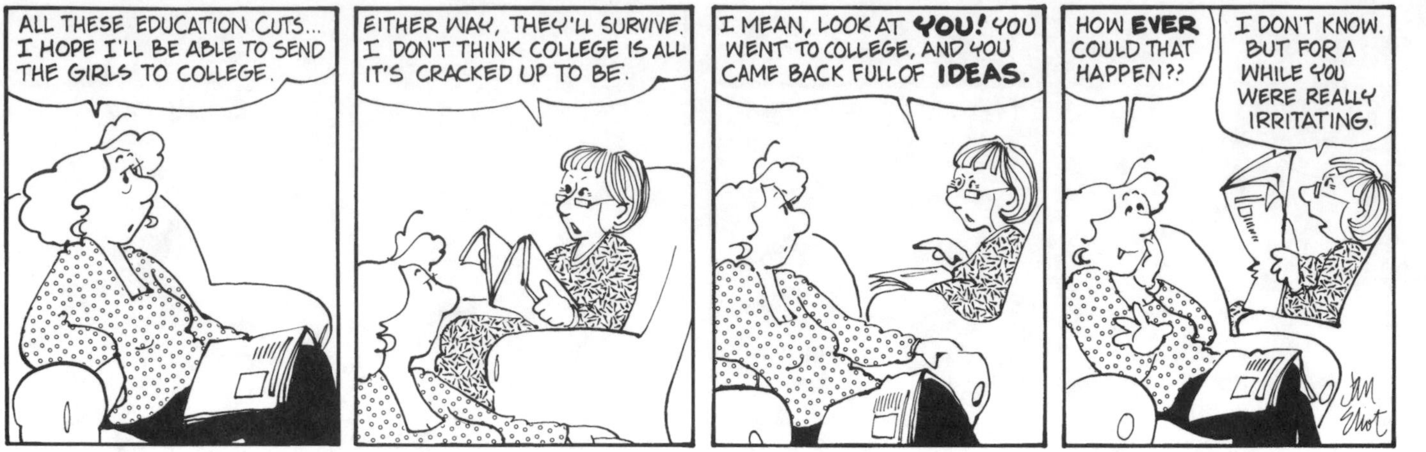
ALL THESE EDUCATION CUTS... I HOPE I'LL BE ABLE TO SEND THE GIRLS TO COLLEGE.
EITHER WAY, THEY'LL SURVIVE. I DON'T THINK COLLEGE IS ALL IT'S CRACKED UP TO BE.
I MEAN, LOOK AT YOU! YOU WENT TO COLLEGE, AND YOU CAME BACK FULL OF IDEAS.
HOW EVER COULD THAT HAPPEN??
I DON'T KNOW. BUT FOR A WHILE YOU WERE REALLY IRRITATING.

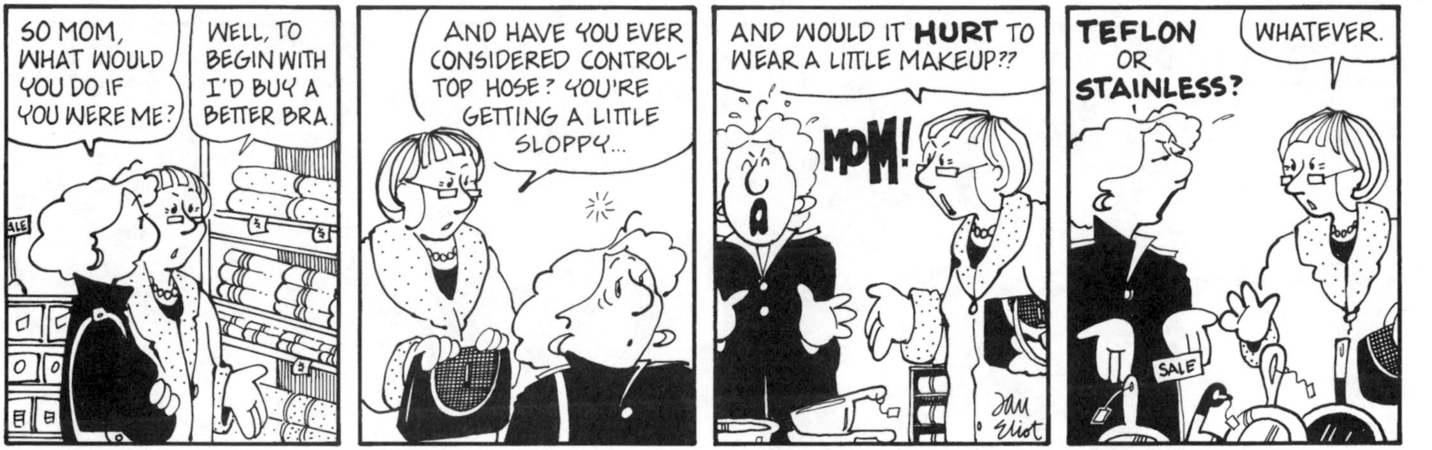
SO MOM, WHAT WOULD YOU DO IF YOU WERE ME?
WELL, TO BEGIN WITH I'D BUY A BETTER BRA.
SALE
AND HAVE YOU EVER CONSIDERED CONTROL-TOP HOSE? YOU'RE GETTING A LITTLE SLOPPY...
AND WOULD IT HURT TO WEAR A LITTLE MAKEUP??
MOM!
TEFLON OR STAINLESS?
WHATEVER.
SALE

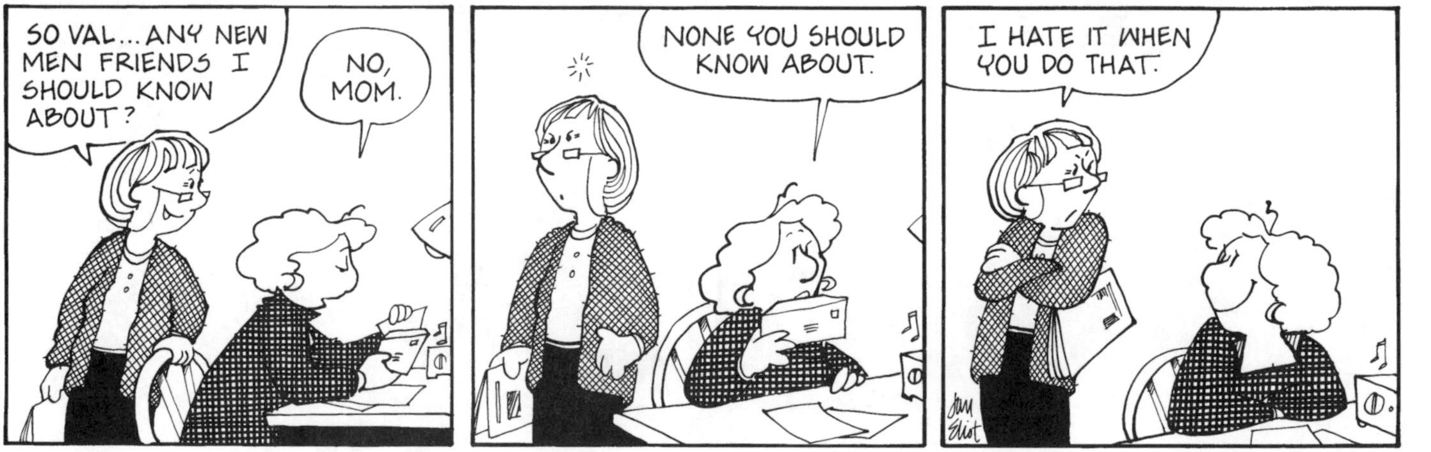
SO VAL... ANY NEW MEN FRIENDS I SHOULD KNOW ABOUT?
NO, MOM.
NONE YOU SHOULD KNOW ABOUT.
I HATE IT WHEN YOU DO THAT.

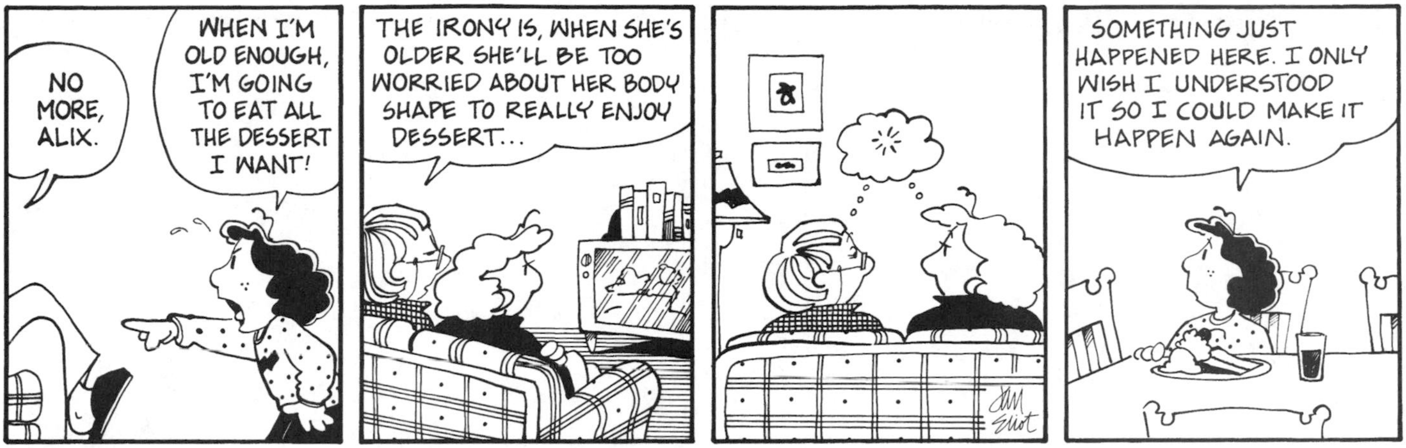
NO MORE, ALIX.
WHEN I'M OLD ENOUGH, I'M GOING TO EAT ALL THE DESSERT I WANT!
THE IRONY IS, WHEN SHE'S OLDER SHE'LL BE TOO WORRIED ABOUT HER BODY SHAPE TO REALLY ENJOY DESSERT...
SOMETHING JUST HAPPENED HERE. I ONLY WISH I UNDERSTOOD IT SO I COULD MAKE IT HAPPEN AGAIN.
JAN Eliot

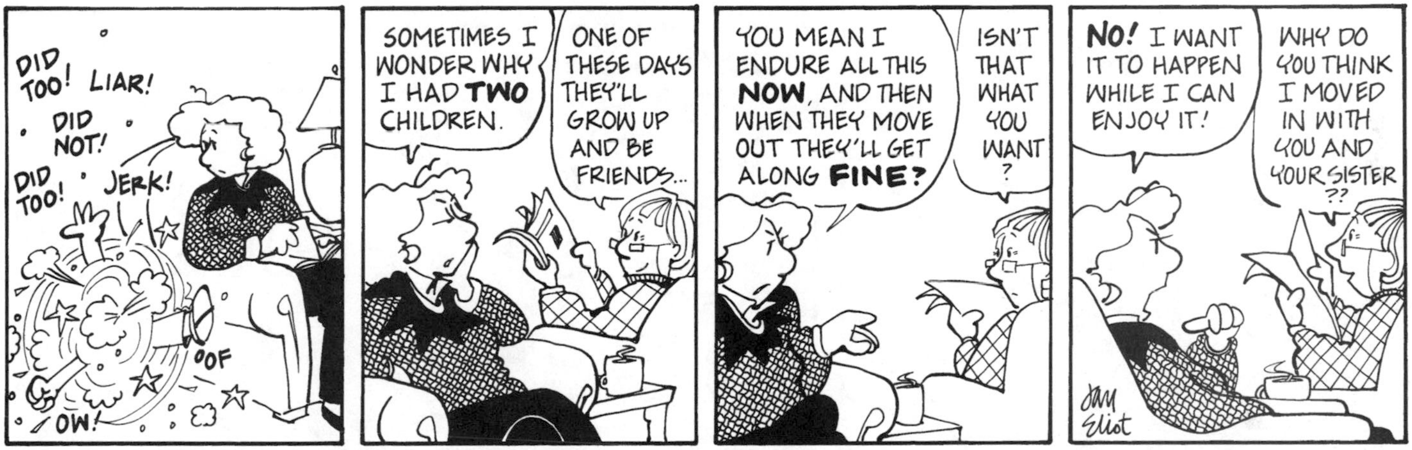
DID TOO! LIAR!
DID NOT!
DID TOO! JERK!
OOF
OW!
SOMETIMES I WONDER WHY I HAD **TWO** CHILDREN.
ONE OF THESE DAYS THEY'LL GROW UP AND BE FRIENDS...
YOU MEAN I ENDURE ALL THIS **NOW**, AND THEN WHEN THEY MOVE OUT THEY'LL GET ALONG **FINE?**
ISN'T THAT WHAT YOU WANT?
NO! I WANT IT TO HAPPEN WHILE I CAN ENJOY IT!
WHY DO YOU THINK I MOVED IN WITH YOU AND YOUR SISTER??
JAN Eliot

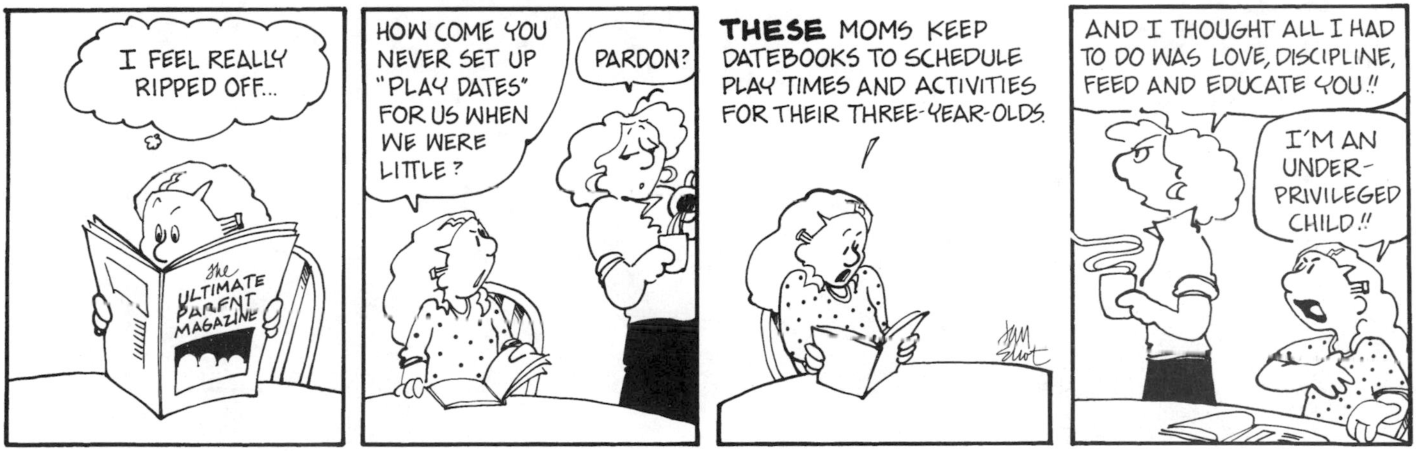
I FEEL REALLY RIPPED OFF...
The ULTIMATE PARENT MAGAZINE
HOW COME YOU NEVER SET UP "PLAY DATES" FOR US WHEN WE WERE LITTLE?
PARDON?
THESE MOMS KEEP DATEBOOKS TO SCHEDULE PLAY TIMES AND ACTIVITIES FOR THEIR THREE-YEAR-OLDS.
JAN Eliot
AND I THOUGHT ALL I HAD TO DO WAS LOVE, DISCIPLINE, FEED AND EDUCATE YOU!!
I'M AN UNDER-PRIVILEGED CHILD!!

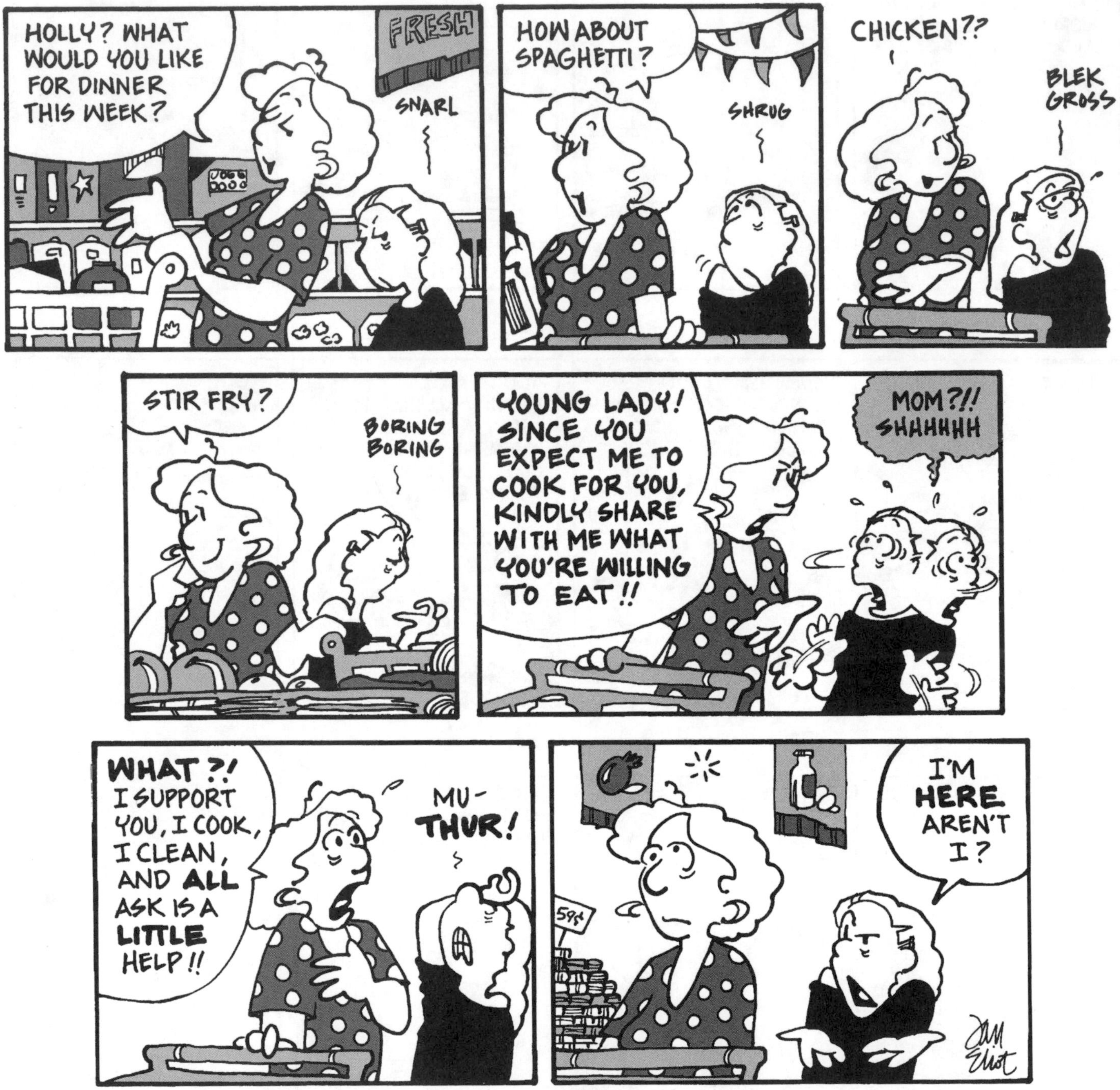
FRESH
HOLLY? WHAT WOULD YOU LIKE FOR DINNER THIS WEEK?
SNARL
HOW ABOUT SPAGHETTI?
SHRUG
CHICKEN??
BLEK GROSS
STIR FRY?
BORING BORING
YOUNG LADY! SINCE YOU EXPECT ME TO COOK FOR YOU, KINDLY SHARE WITH ME WHAT YOU'RE WILLING TO EAT!!
MOM?!! SHHHHHH
WHAT?! I SUPPORT YOU, I COOK, I CLEAN, AND ALL ASK IS A LITTLE HELP!!
MU-THUR!
59¢
I'M HERE AREN'T I?

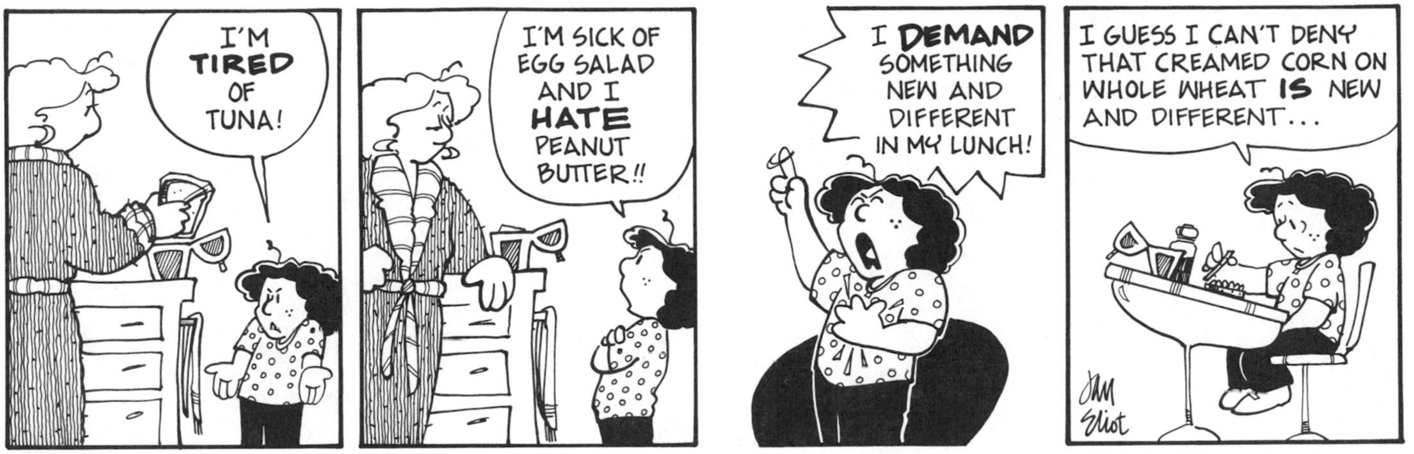
I'M TIRED OF TUNA!
I'M SICK OF EGG SALAD AND I HATE PEANUT BUTTER!!
I DEMAND SOMETHING NEW AND DIFFERENT IN MY LUNCH!
I GUESS I CAN'T DENY THAT CREAMED CORN ON WHOLE WHEAT IS NEW AND DIFFERENT...
JAN Eliot

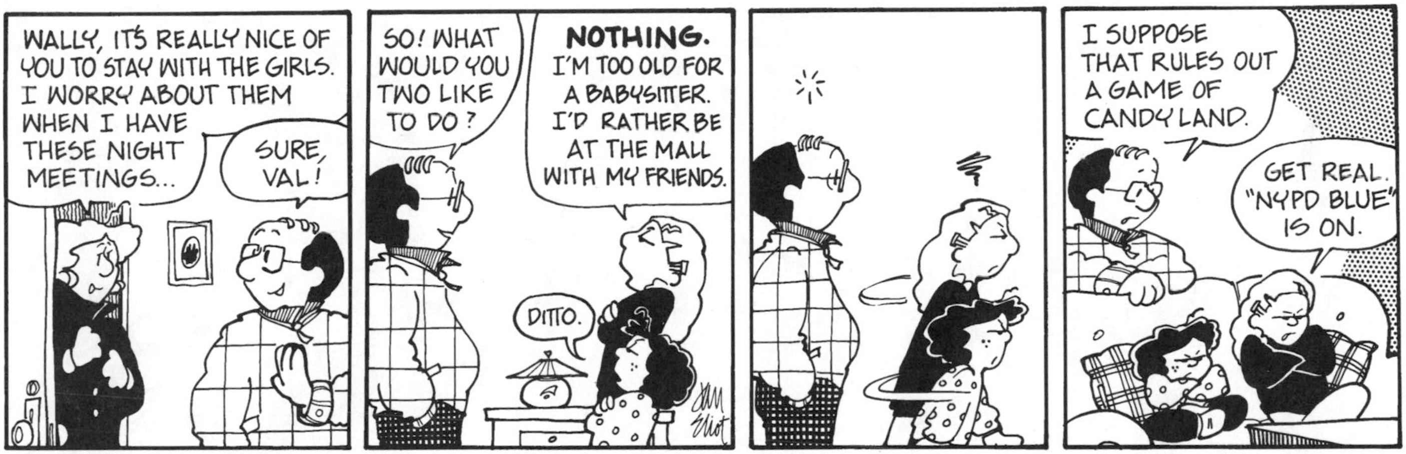
WALLY, IT'S REALLY NICE OF YOU TO STAY WITH THE GIRLS. I WORRY ABOUT THEM WHEN I HAVE THESE NIGHT MEETINGS...
SURE, VAL!
SO! WHAT WOULD YOU TWO LIKE TO DO?
NOTHING. I'M TOO OLD FOR A BABYSITTER. I'D RATHER BE AT THE MALL WITH MY FRIENDS.
DITTO.
JAN Eliot
I SUPPOSE THAT RULES OUT A GAME OF CANDY LAND.
GET REAL. "NYPD BLUE" IS ON.

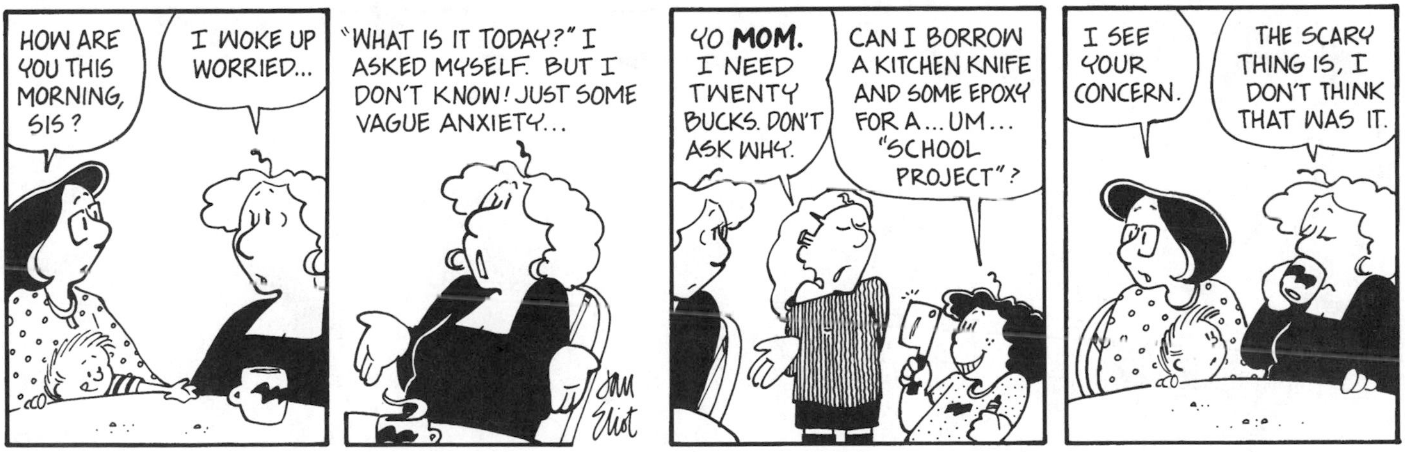
HOW ARE YOU THIS MORNING, SIS?
I WOKE UP WORRIED...
"WHAT IS IT TODAY?" I ASKED MYSELF. BUT I DON'T KNOW! JUST SOME VAGUE ANXIETY...
JAN Eliot
YO MOM. I NEED TWENTY BUCKS. DON'T ASK WHY.
CAN I BORROW A KITCHEN KNIFE AND SOME EPOXY FOR A... UM... "SCHOOL PROJECT"?
I SEE YOUR CONCERN.
THE SCARY THING IS, I DON'T THINK THAT WAS IT.

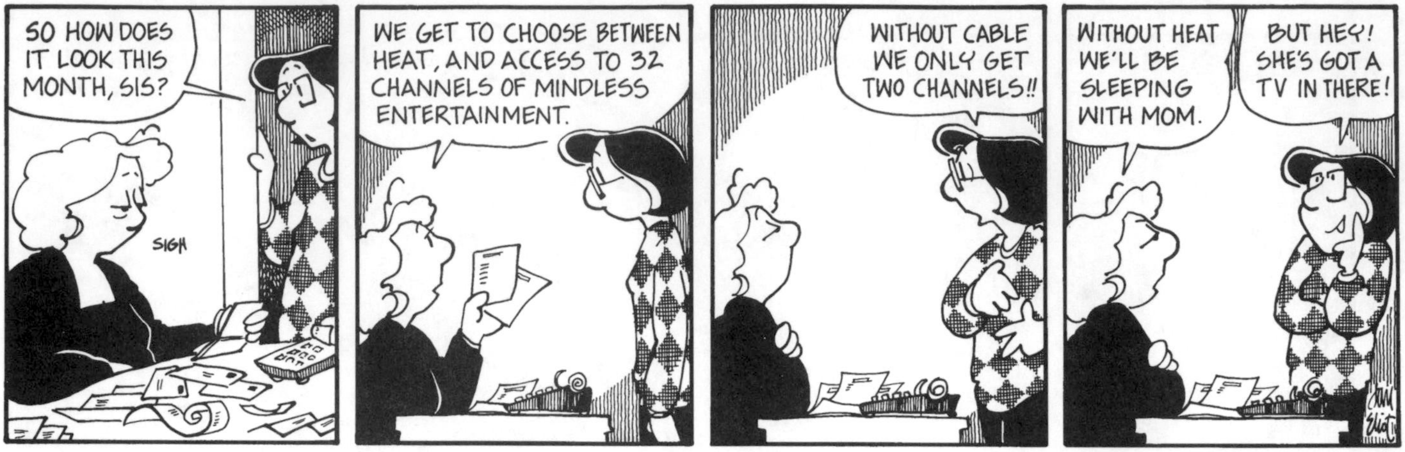
SO HOW DOES IT LOOK THIS MONTH, SIS?
SIGH
WE GET TO CHOOSE BETWEEN HEAT, AND ACCESS TO 32 CHANNELS OF MINDLESS ENTERTAINMENT.
WITHOUT CABLE WE ONLY GET TWO CHANNELS!!
WITHOUT HEAT WE'LL BE SLEEPING WITH MOM.
BUT HEY! SHE'S GOT A TV IN THERE!

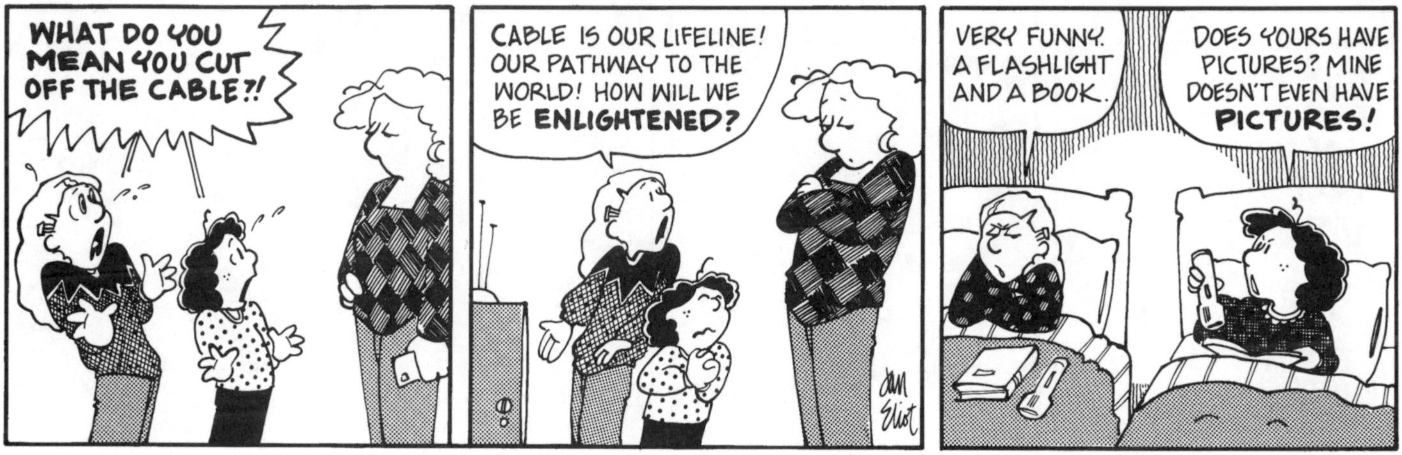
WHAT DO YOU MEAN YOU CUT OFF THE CABLE?!
CABLE IS OUR LIFELINE! OUR PATHWAY TO THE WORLD! HOW WILL WE BE ENLIGHTENED?
VERY FUNNY. A FLASHLIGHT AND A BOOK.
DOES YOURS HAVE PICTURES? MINE DOESN'T EVEN HAVE PICTURES!

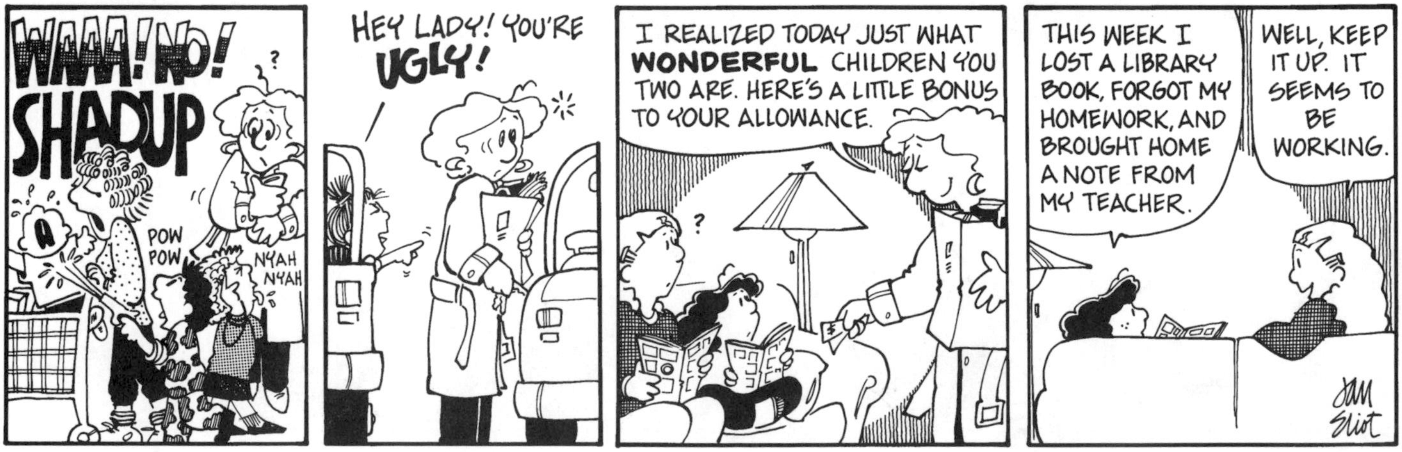
WAAA! NO! SHADUP
POW POW
NYAH NYAH
HEY LADY! YOU'RE UGLY!
I REALIZED TODAY JUST WHAT WONDERFUL CHILDREN YOU TWO ARE. HERE'S A LITTLE BONUS TO YOUR ALLOWANCE.
THIS WEEK I LOST A LIBRARY BOOK, FORGOT MY HOMEWORK, AND BROUGHT HOME A NOTE FROM MY TEACHER.
WELL, KEEP IT UP. IT SEEMS TO BE WORKING.

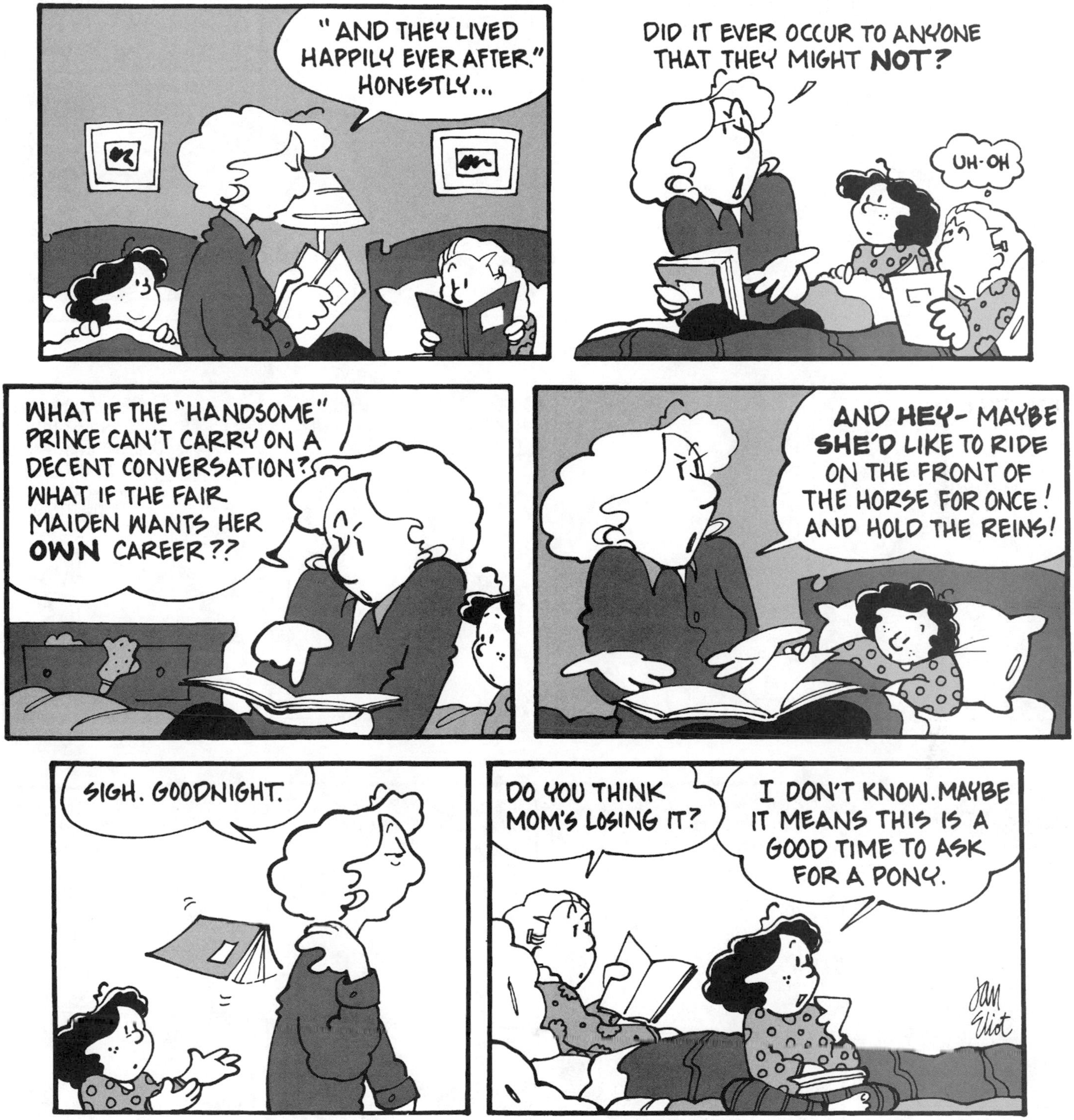
"AND THEY LIVED HAPPILY EVER AFTER." HONESTLY...
DID IT EVER OCCUR TO ANYONE THAT THEY MIGHT **NOT**?
UH-OH
WHAT IF THE "HANDSOME" PRINCE CAN'T CARRY ON A DECENT CONVERSATION? WHAT IF THE FAIR MAIDEN WANTS HER **OWN** CAREER??
AND **HEY**- MAYBE **SHE'D** LIKE TO RIDE ON THE FRONT OF THE HORSE FOR ONCE! AND HOLD THE REINS!
SIGH. GOODNIGHT.
DO YOU THINK MOM'S LOSING IT?
I DON'T KNOW. MAYBE IT MEANS THIS IS A GOOD TIME TO ASK FOR A PONY.
Jan Eliot

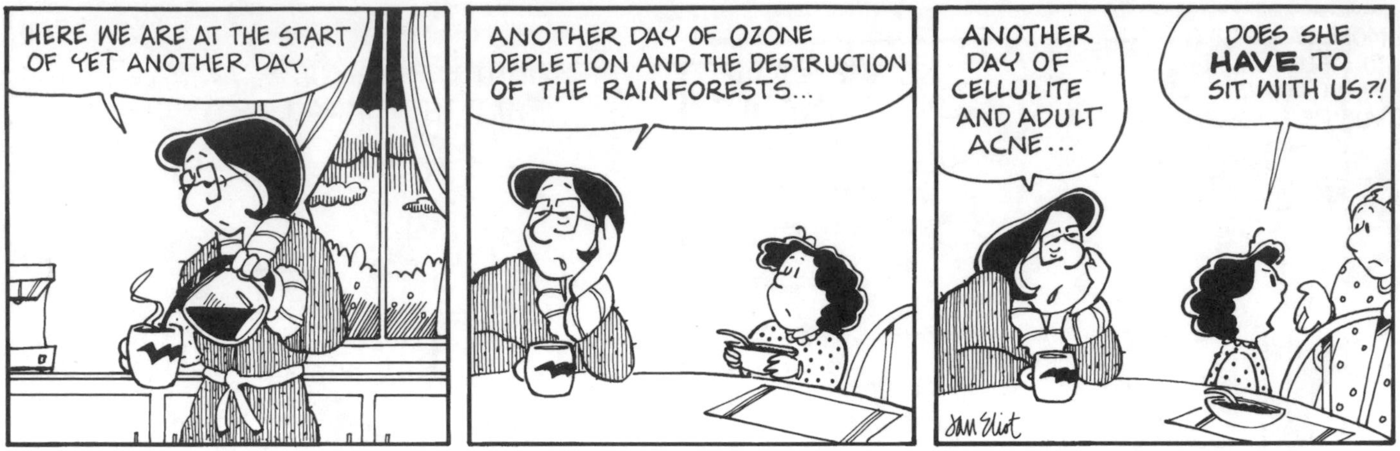
HERE WE ARE AT THE START OF YET ANOTHER DAY.
ANOTHER DAY OF OZONE DEPLETION AND THE DESTRUCTION OF THE RAINFORESTS...
ANOTHER DAY OF CELLULITE AND ADULT ACNE...
DOES SHE **HAVE** TO SIT WITH US?!

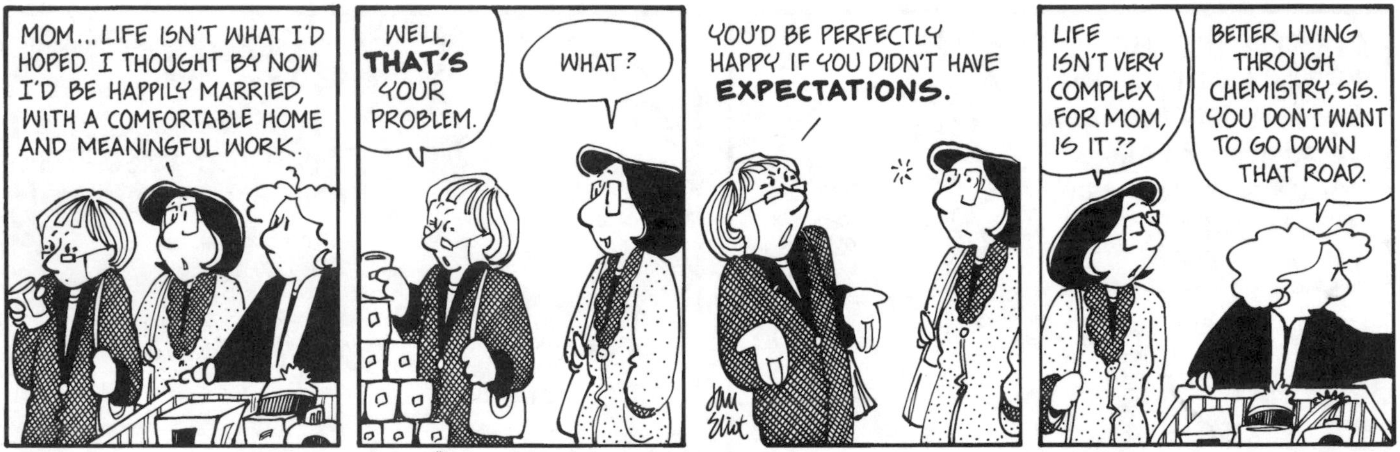
MOM... LIFE ISN'T WHAT I'D HOPED. I THOUGHT BY NOW I'D BE HAPPILY MARRIED, WITH A COMFORTABLE HOME AND MEANINGFUL WORK.
WELL, **THAT'S** YOUR PROBLEM.
WHAT?
YOU'D BE PERFECTLY HAPPY IF YOU DIDN'T HAVE **EXPECTATIONS.**
LIFE ISN'T VERY COMPLEX FOR MOM, IS IT??
BETTER LIVING THROUGH CHEMISTRY, SIS. YOU DON'T WANT TO GO DOWN THAT ROAD.

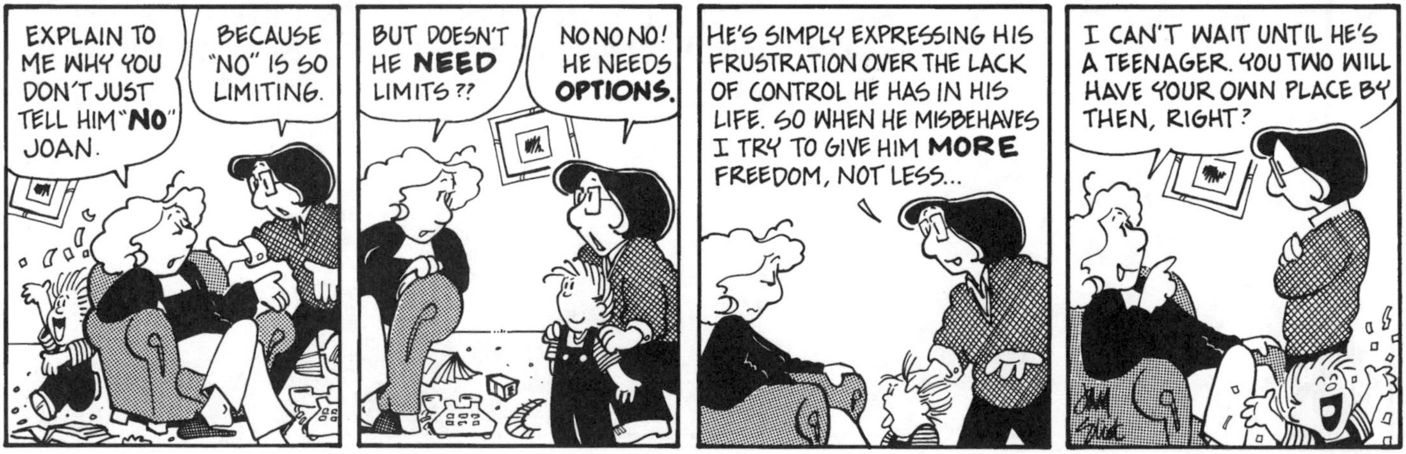
EXPLAIN TO ME WHY YOU DON'T JUST TELL HIM "**NO**" JOAN.
BECAUSE "NO" IS SO LIMITING.
BUT DOESN'T HE **NEED** LIMITS??
NO NO NO! HE NEEDS **OPTIONS.**
HE'S SIMPLY EXPRESSING HIS FRUSTRATION OVER THE LACK OF CONTROL HE HAS IN HIS LIFE. SO WHEN HE MISBEHAVES I TRY TO GIVE HIM **MORE** FREEDOM, NOT LESS...
I CAN'T WAIT UNTIL HE'S A TEENAGER. YOU TWO WILL HAVE YOUR OWN PLACE BY THEN, RIGHT?

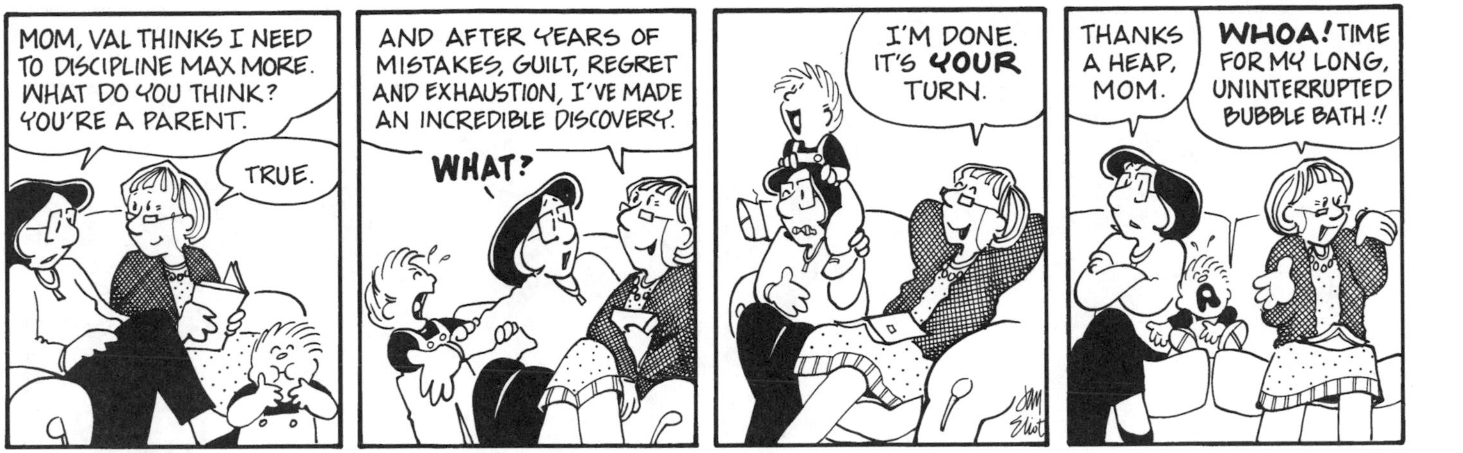
MOM, VAL THINKS I NEED TO DISCIPLINE MAX MORE. WHAT DO YOU THINK? YOU'RE A PARENT.
TRUE.
AND AFTER YEARS OF MISTAKES, GUILT, REGRET AND EXHAUSTION, I'VE MADE AN INCREDIBLE DISCOVERY.
WHAT?
I'M DONE. IT'S YOUR TURN.
THANKS A HEAP, MOM.
WHOA! TIME FOR MY LONG, UNINTERRUPTED BUBBLE BATH!!

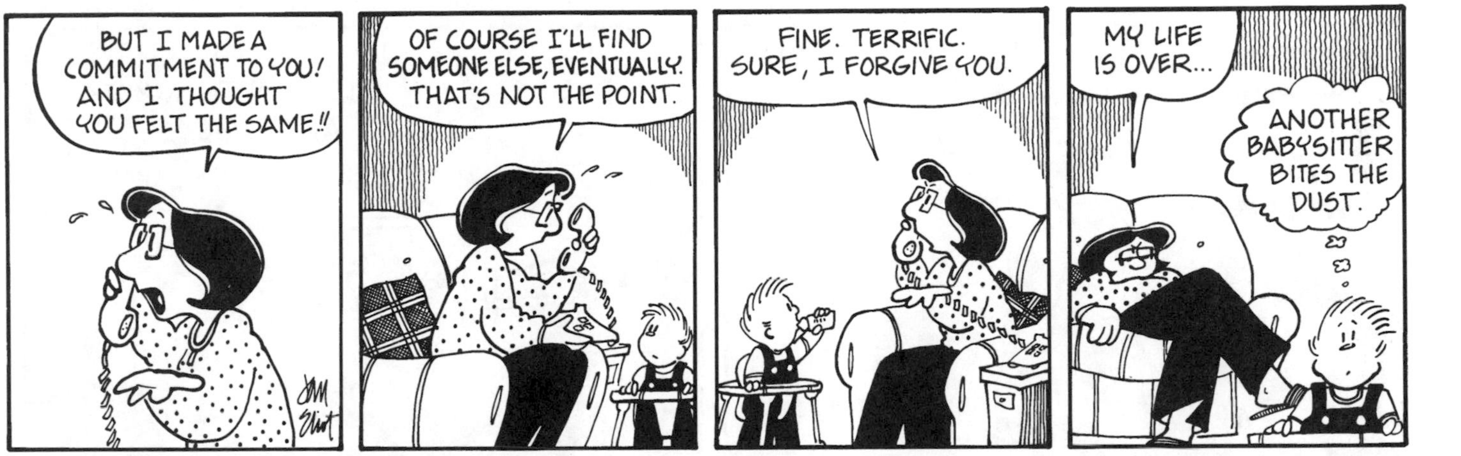
BUT I MADE A COMMITMENT TO YOU! AND I THOUGHT YOU FELT THE SAME!!
OF COURSE I'LL FIND SOMEONE ELSE, EVENTUALLY. THAT'S NOT THE POINT.
FINE. TERRIFIC. SURE, I FORGIVE YOU.
MY LIFE IS OVER...
ANOTHER BABYSITTER BITES THE DUST.

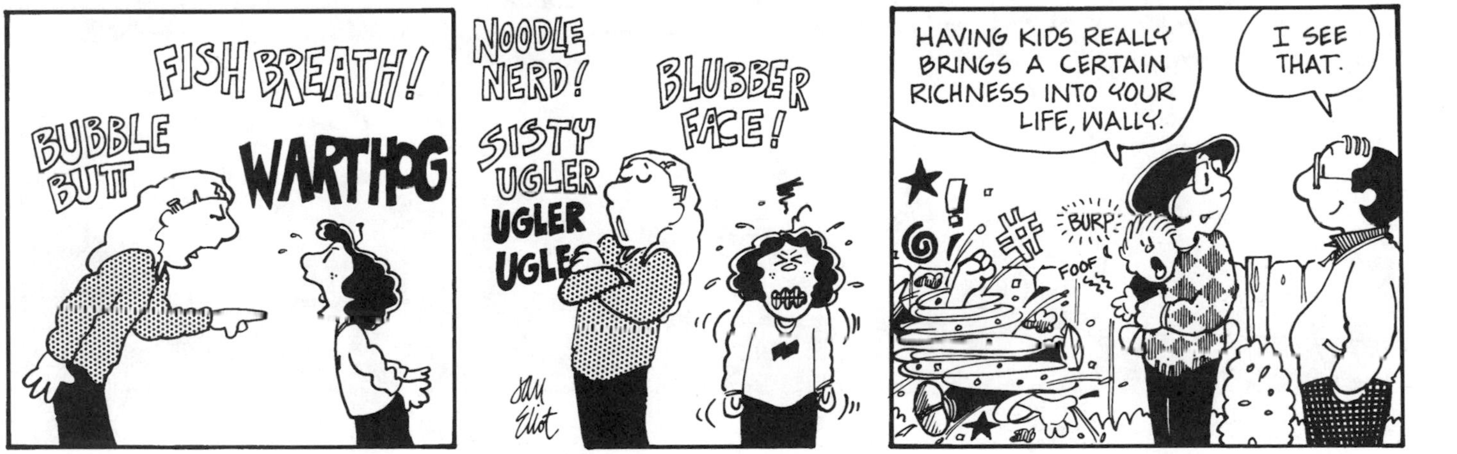
FISH BREATH!
BUBBLE BUTT
WARTHOG
NOODLE NERD!
SISTY UGLER
UGLER
UGLE
BLUBBER FACE!
HAVING KIDS REALLY BRINGS A CERTAIN RICHNESS INTO YOUR LIFE, WALLY.
I SEE THAT.
BURP
FOOF

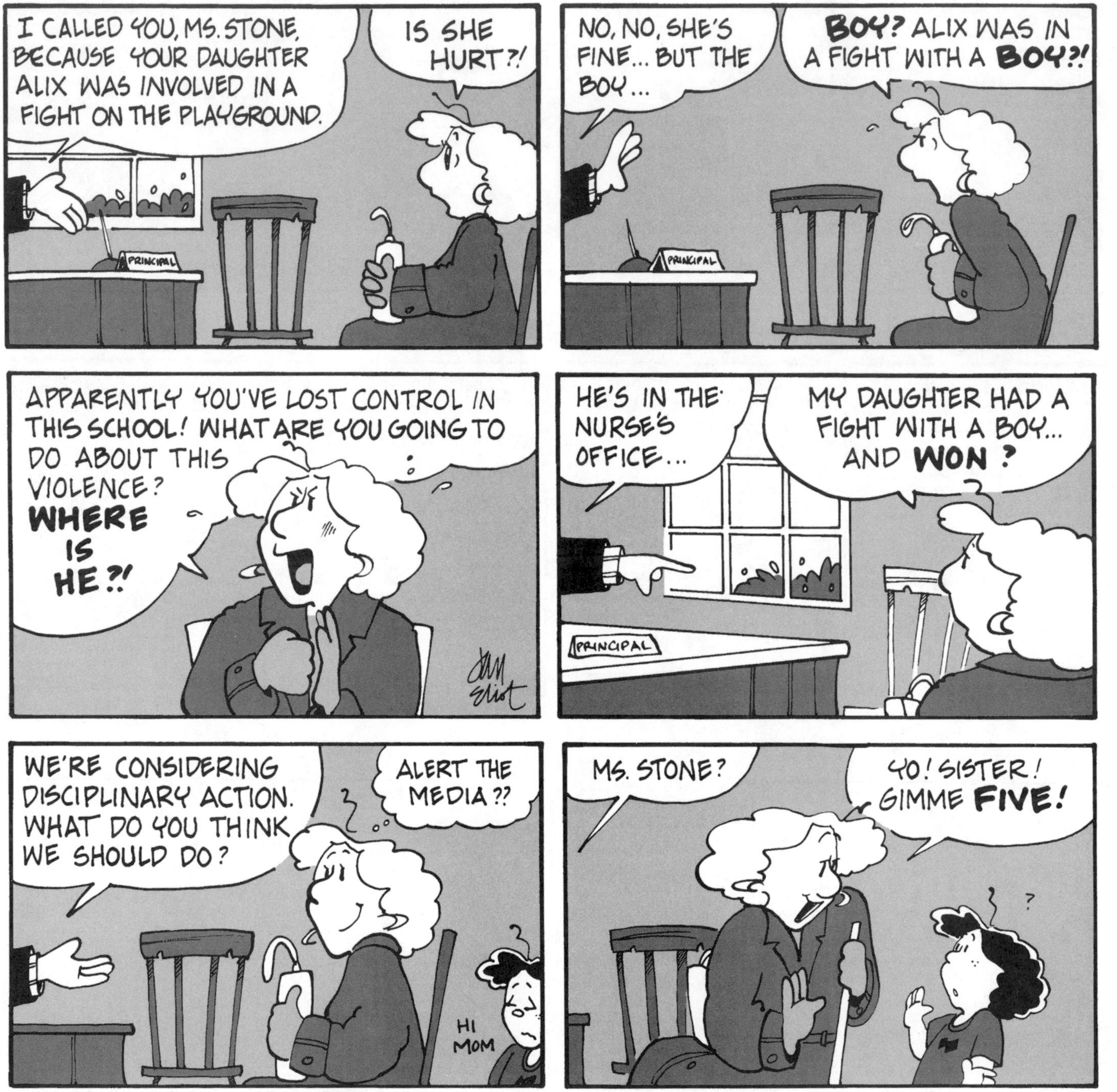
I CALLED YOU, MS. STONE, BECAUSE YOUR DAUGHTER ALIX WAS INVOLVED IN A FIGHT ON THE PLAYGROUND.
IS SHE HURT?!
PRINCIPAL
NO, NO, SHE'S FINE... BUT THE BOY...
BOY? ALIX WAS IN A FIGHT WITH A BOY?!
PRINCIPAL
APPARENTLY YOU'VE LOST CONTROL IN THIS SCHOOL! WHAT ARE YOU GOING TO DO ABOUT THIS VIOLENCE? WHERE IS HE?!
HE'S IN THE NURSE'S OFFICE...
MY DAUGHTER HAD A FIGHT WITH A BOY... AND WON?
PRINCIPAL
WE'RE CONSIDERING DISCIPLINARY ACTION. WHAT DO YOU THINK WE SHOULD DO?
ALERT THE MEDIA??
HI MOM
MS. STONE?
YO! SISTER! GIMME FIVE!

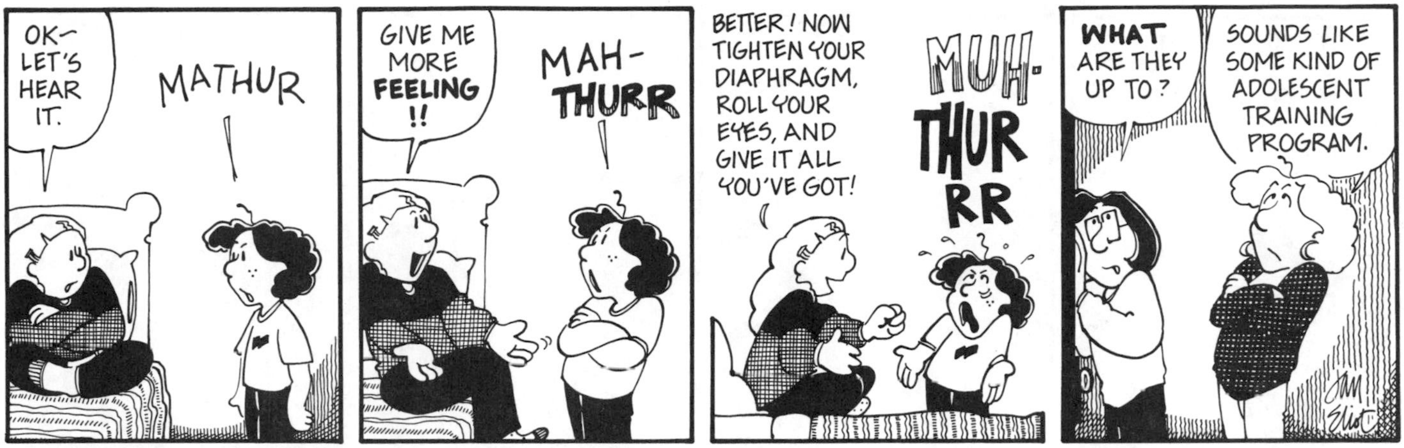
OK— LET'S HEAR IT.
MATHUR
GIVE ME MORE **FEELING** !!
MAH-THURR
BETTER! NOW TIGHTEN YOUR DIAPHRAGM, ROLL YOUR EYES, AND GIVE IT ALL YOU'VE GOT!
MUH-THUR RR
WHAT ARE THEY UP TO?
SOUNDS LIKE SOME KIND OF ADOLESCENT TRAINING PROGRAM.

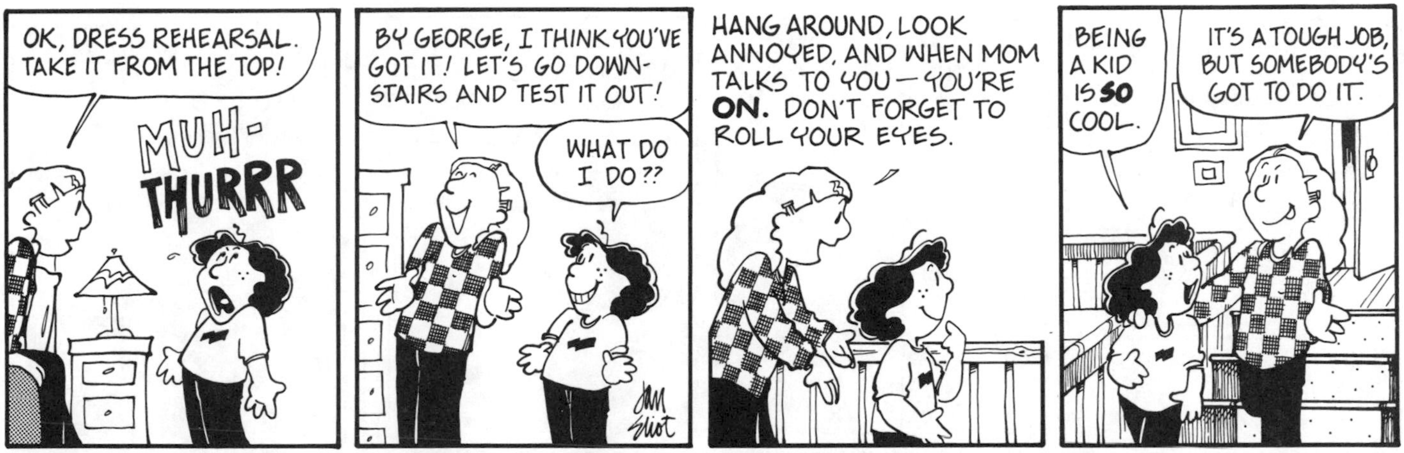
OK, DRESS REHEARSAL. TAKE IT FROM THE TOP!
MUH-THURRR
BY GEORGE, I THINK YOU'VE GOT IT! LET'S GO DOWNSTAIRS AND TEST IT OUT!
WHAT DO I DO??
HANG AROUND, LOOK ANNOYED, AND WHEN MOM TALKS TO YOU — YOU'RE **ON.** DON'T FORGET TO ROLL YOUR EYES.
BEING A KID IS **SO** COOL.
IT'S A TOUGH JOB, BUT SOMEBODY'S GOT TO DO IT.

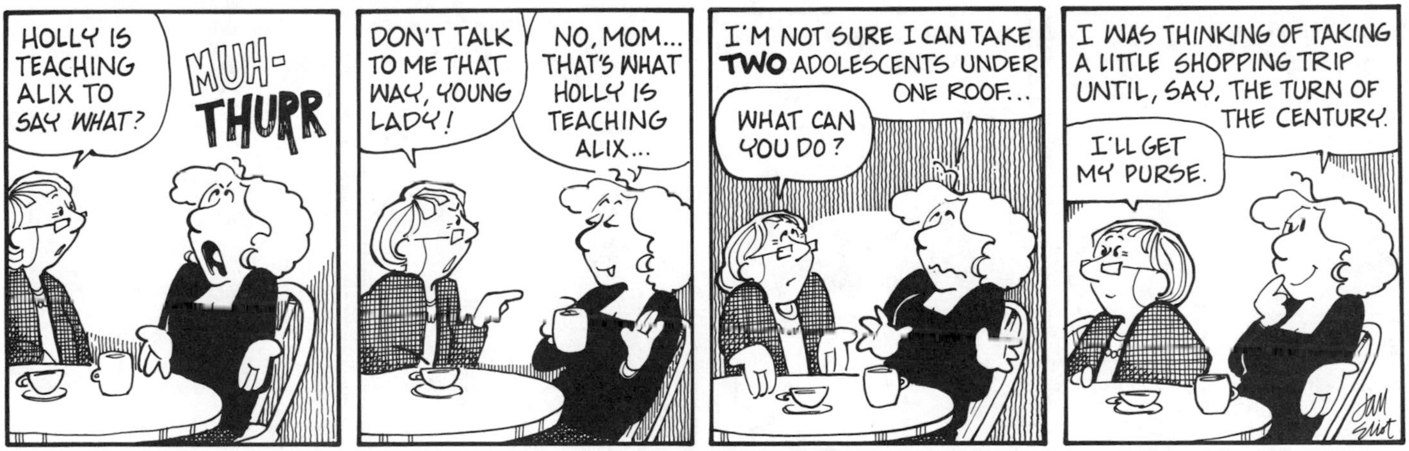
HOLLY IS TEACHING ALIX TO SAY *WHAT*?
MUH-THURR
DON'T TALK TO ME THAT WAY, YOUNG LADY!
NO, MOM... THAT'S WHAT HOLLY IS TEACHING ALIX...
I'M NOT SURE I CAN TAKE **TWO** ADOLESCENTS UNDER ONE ROOF...
WHAT CAN YOU DO?
I WAS THINKING OF TAKING A LITTLE SHOPPING TRIP UNTIL, SAY, THE TURN OF THE CENTURY.
I'LL GET MY PURSE.

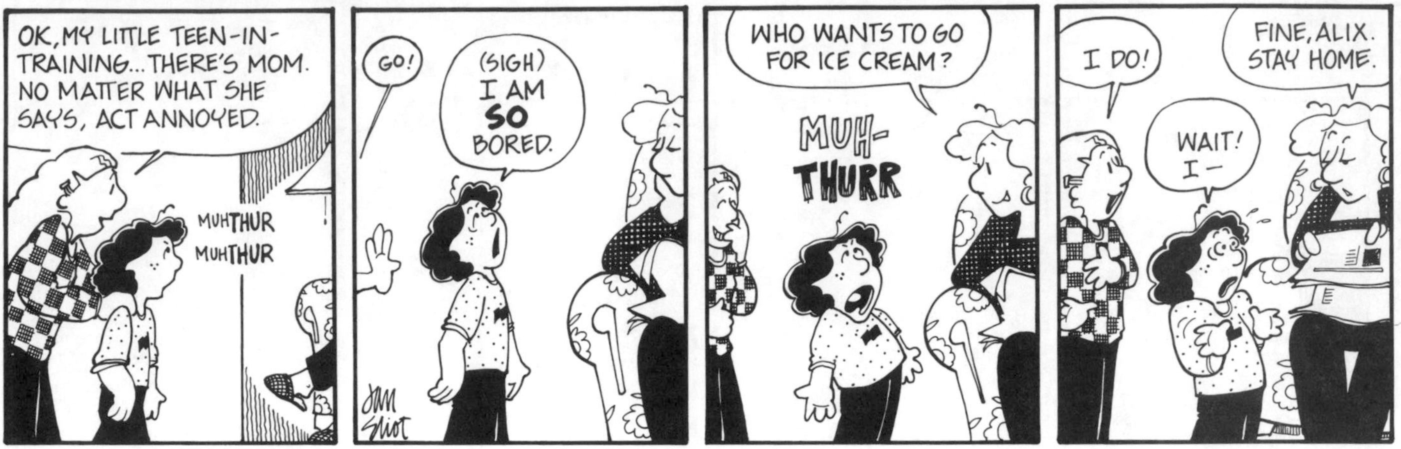
OK, MY LITTLE TEEN-IN-TRAINING... THERE'S MOM. NO MATTER WHAT SHE SAYS, ACT ANNOYED.
MUHTHUR
MUHTHUR
GO!
(SIGH) I AM **SO** BORED.
WHO WANTS TO GO FOR ICE CREAM?
MUH-THURR
I DO!
FINE, ALIX. STAY HOME.
WAIT! I —

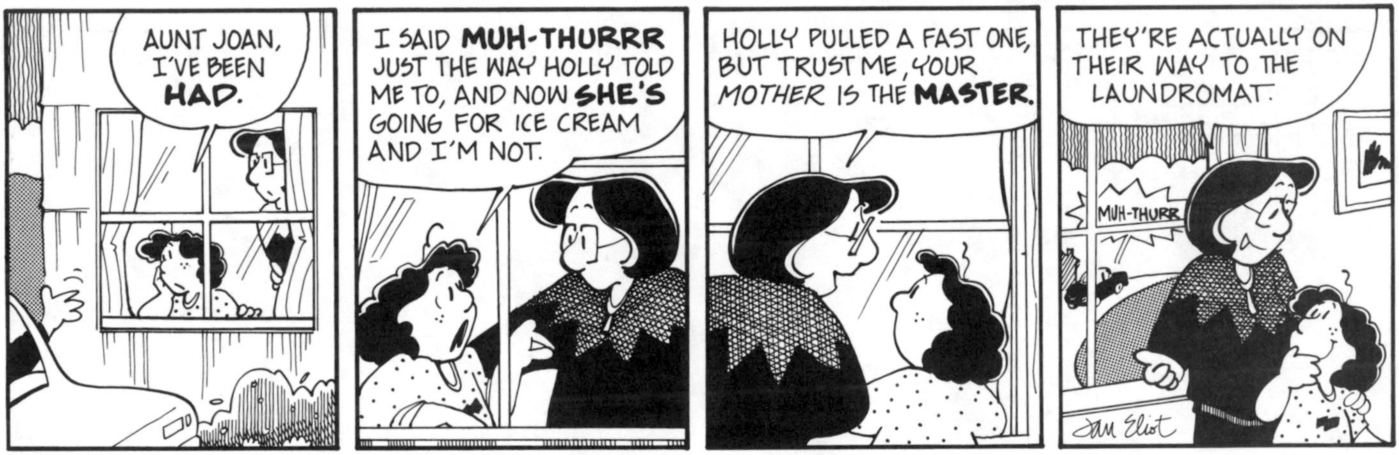
AUNT JOAN, I'VE BEEN **HAD.**
I SAID **MUH-THURRR** JUST THE WAY HOLLY TOLD ME TO, AND NOW **SHE'S** GOING FOR ICE CREAM AND I'M NOT.
HOLLY PULLED A FAST ONE, BUT TRUST ME, YOUR *MOTHER* IS THE **MASTER.**
THEY'RE ACTUALLY ON THEIR WAY TO THE LAUNDROMAT.
MUH-THURR

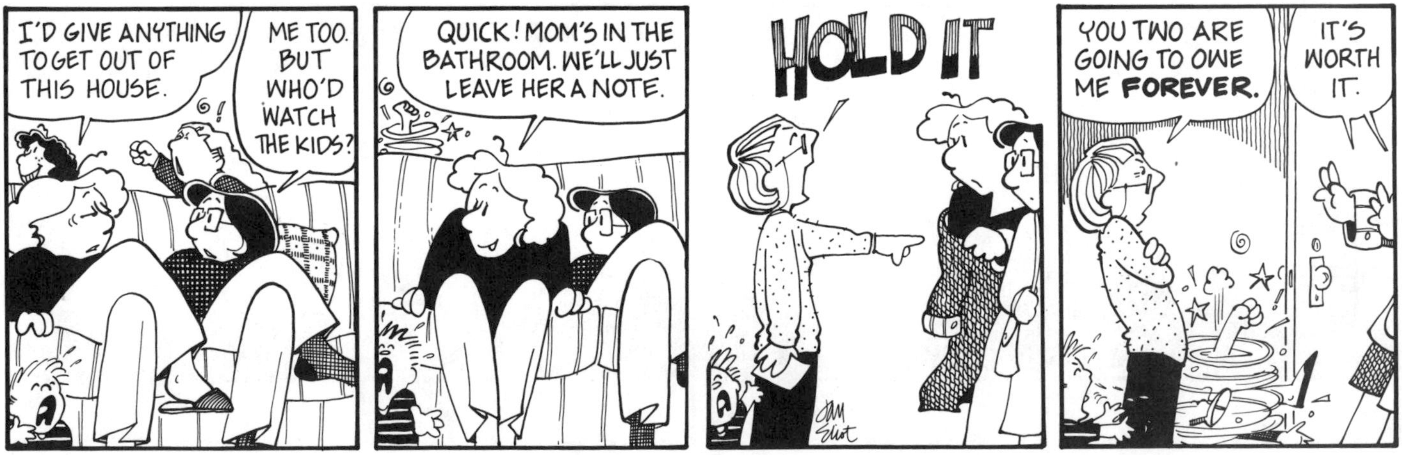
I'D GIVE ANYTHING TO GET OUT OF THIS HOUSE.
ME TOO. BUT WHO'D WATCH THE KIDS?
QUICK! MOM'S IN THE BATHROOM. WE'LL JUST LEAVE HER A NOTE.
HOLD IT
YOU TWO ARE GOING TO OWE ME **FOREVER.**
IT'S WORTH IT.

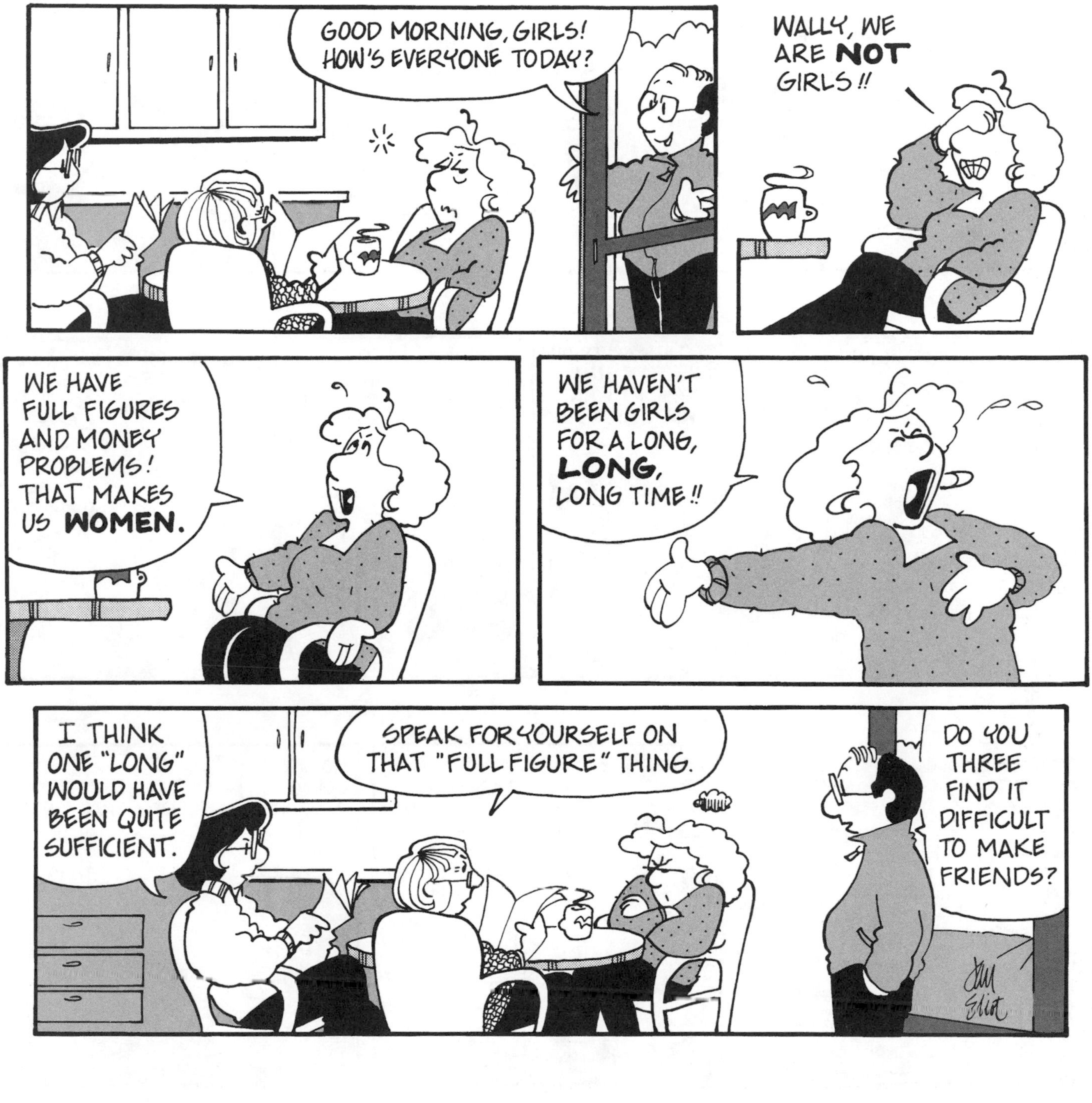
GOOD MORNING, GIRLS! HOW'S EVERYONE TODAY?
WALLY, WE ARE **NOT** GIRLS!!
WE HAVE FULL FIGURES AND MONEY PROBLEMS! THAT MAKES US **WOMEN.**
WE HAVEN'T BEEN GIRLS FOR A LONG, **LONG,** LONG TIME!!
I THINK ONE "LONG" WOULD HAVE BEEN QUITE SUFFICIENT.
SPEAK FOR YOURSELF ON THAT "FULL FIGURE" THING.
DO YOU THREE FIND IT DIFFICULT TO MAKE FRIENDS?

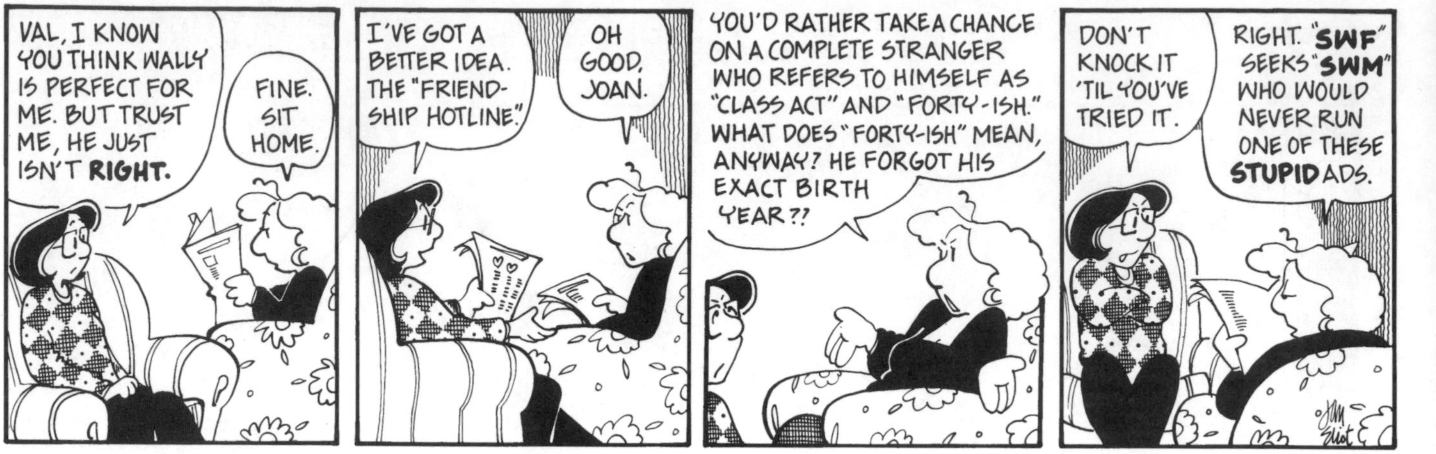
VAL, I KNOW YOU THINK WALLY IS PERFECT FOR ME. BUT TRUST ME, HE JUST ISN'T **RIGHT.**
FINE. SIT HOME.
I'VE GOT A BETTER IDEA. THE "FRIENDSHIP HOTLINE."
OH GOOD, JOAN.
YOU'D RATHER TAKE A CHANCE ON A COMPLETE STRANGER WHO REFERS TO HIMSELF AS "CLASS ACT" AND "FORTY-ISH." WHAT DOES "FORTY-ISH" MEAN, ANYWAY? HE FORGOT HIS EXACT BIRTH YEAR??
DON'T KNOCK IT 'TIL YOU'VE TRIED IT.
RIGHT. "**SWF**" SEEKS "**SWM**" WHO WOULD NEVER RUN ONE OF THESE **STUPID** ADS.

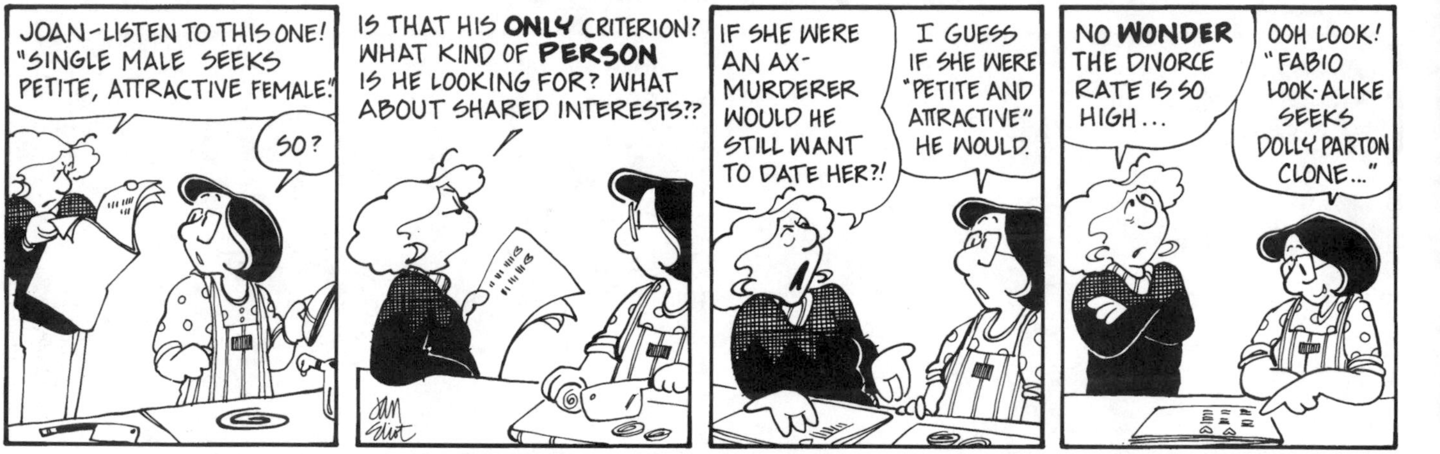
JOAN-LISTEN TO THIS ONE! "SINGLE MALE SEEKS PETITE, ATTRACTIVE FEMALE."
SO?
IS THAT HIS **ONLY** CRITERION? WHAT KIND OF **PERSON** IS HE LOOKING FOR? WHAT ABOUT SHARED INTERESTS??
IF SHE WERE AN AX-MURDERER WOULD HE STILL WANT TO DATE HER?!
I GUESS IF SHE WERE "PETITE AND ATTRACTIVE" HE WOULD.
NO **WONDER** THE DIVORCE RATE IS SO HIGH...
OOH LOOK! "FABIO LOOK-ALIKE SEEKS DOLLY PARTON CLONE..."

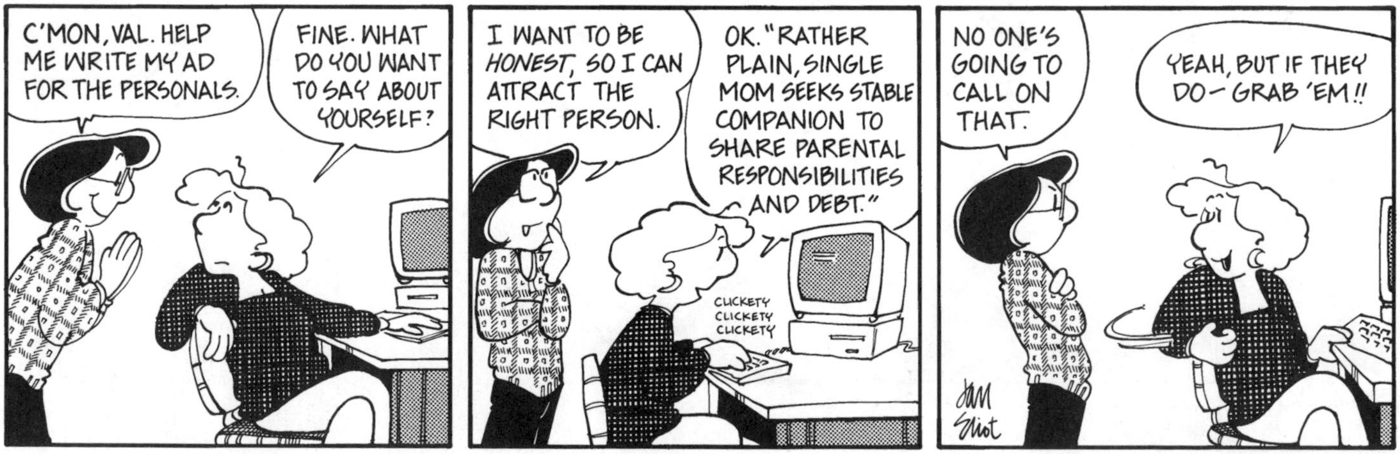
C'MON, VAL. HELP ME WRITE MY AD FOR THE PERSONALS.
FINE. WHAT DO YOU WANT TO SAY ABOUT YOURSELF?
I WANT TO BE *HONEST*, SO I CAN ATTRACT THE RIGHT PERSON.
OK. "RATHER PLAIN, SINGLE MOM SEEKS STABLE COMPANION TO SHARE PARENTAL RESPONSIBILITIES AND DEBT."
CLICKETY CLICKETY CLICKETY
NO ONE'S GOING TO CALL ON THAT.
YEAH, BUT IF THEY DO-GRAB 'EM!!

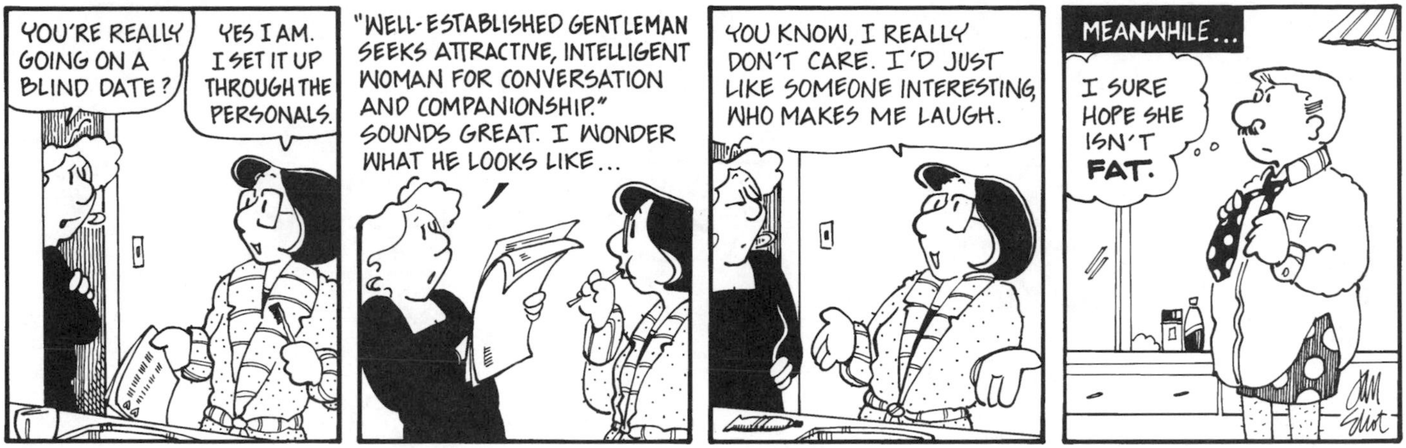
YOU'RE REALLY GOING ON A BLIND DATE?
YES I AM. I SET IT UP THROUGH THE PERSONALS.
"WELL-ESTABLISHED GENTLEMAN SEEKS ATTRACTIVE, INTELLIGENT WOMAN FOR CONVERSATION AND COMPANIONSHIP." SOUNDS GREAT. I WONDER WHAT HE LOOKS LIKE...
YOU KNOW, I REALLY DON'T CARE. I'D JUST LIKE SOMEONE INTERESTING, WHO MAKES ME LAUGH.
MEANWHILE...
I SURE HOPE SHE ISN'T **FAT.**

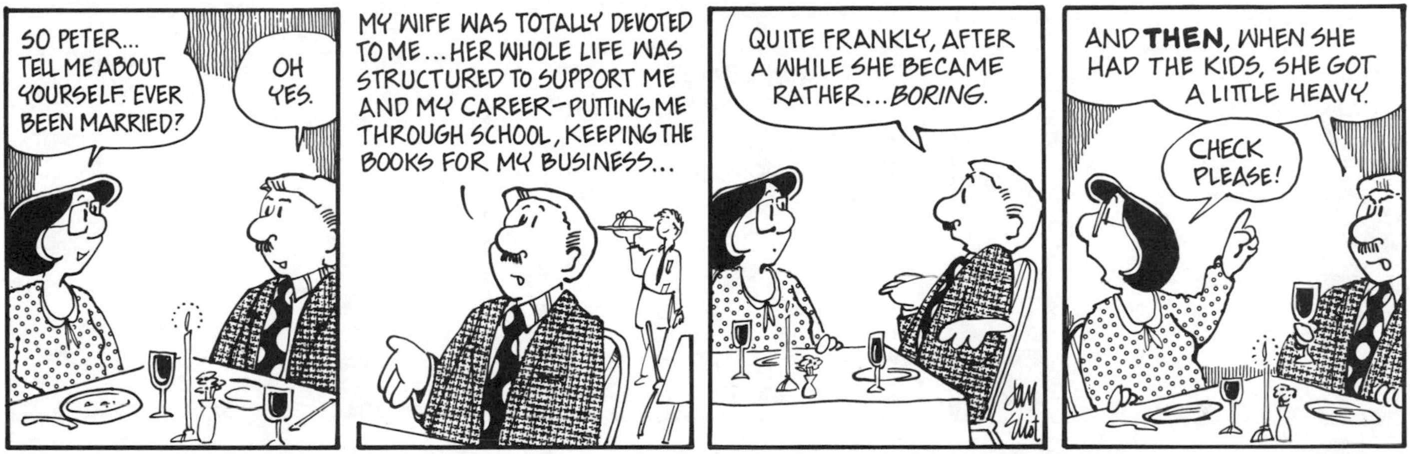
SO PETER... TELL ME ABOUT YOURSELF. EVER BEEN MARRIED?
OH YES.
MY WIFE WAS TOTALLY DEVOTED TO ME... HER WHOLE LIFE WAS STRUCTURED TO SUPPORT ME AND MY CAREER–PUTTING ME THROUGH SCHOOL, KEEPING THE BOOKS FOR MY BUSINESS...
QUITE FRANKLY, AFTER A WHILE SHE BECAME RATHER... *BORING*.
AND **THEN**, WHEN SHE HAD THE KIDS, SHE GOT A LITTLE HEAVY.
CHECK PLEASE!

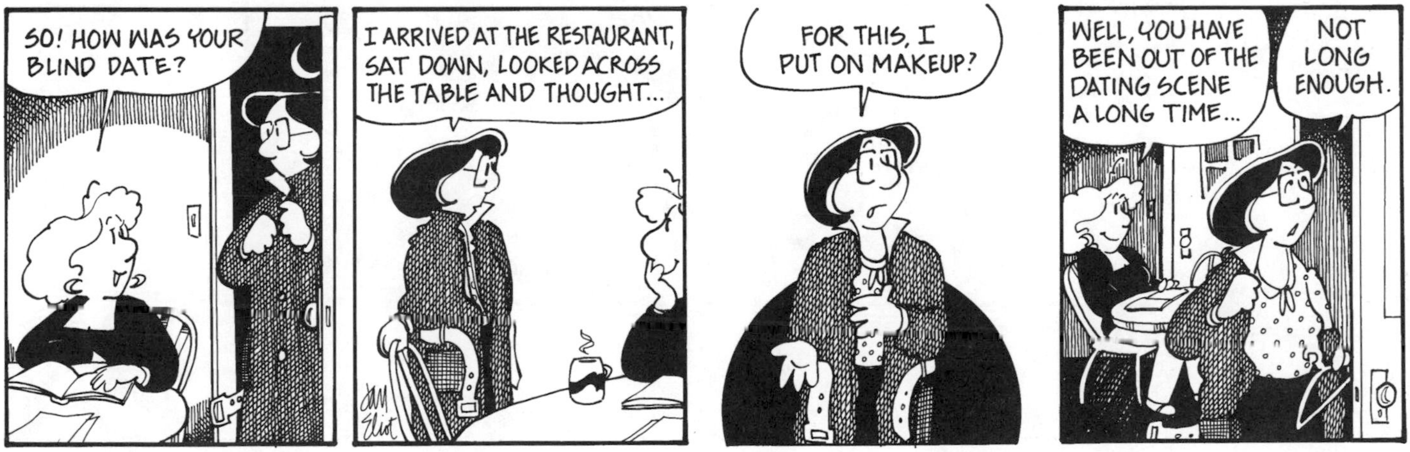
SO! HOW WAS YOUR BLIND DATE?
I ARRIVED AT THE RESTAURANT, SAT DOWN, LOOKED ACROSS THE TABLE AND THOUGHT...
FOR THIS, I PUT ON MAKEUP?
WELL, YOU HAVE BEEN OUT OF THE DATING SCENE A LONG TIME...
NOT LONG ENOUGH.

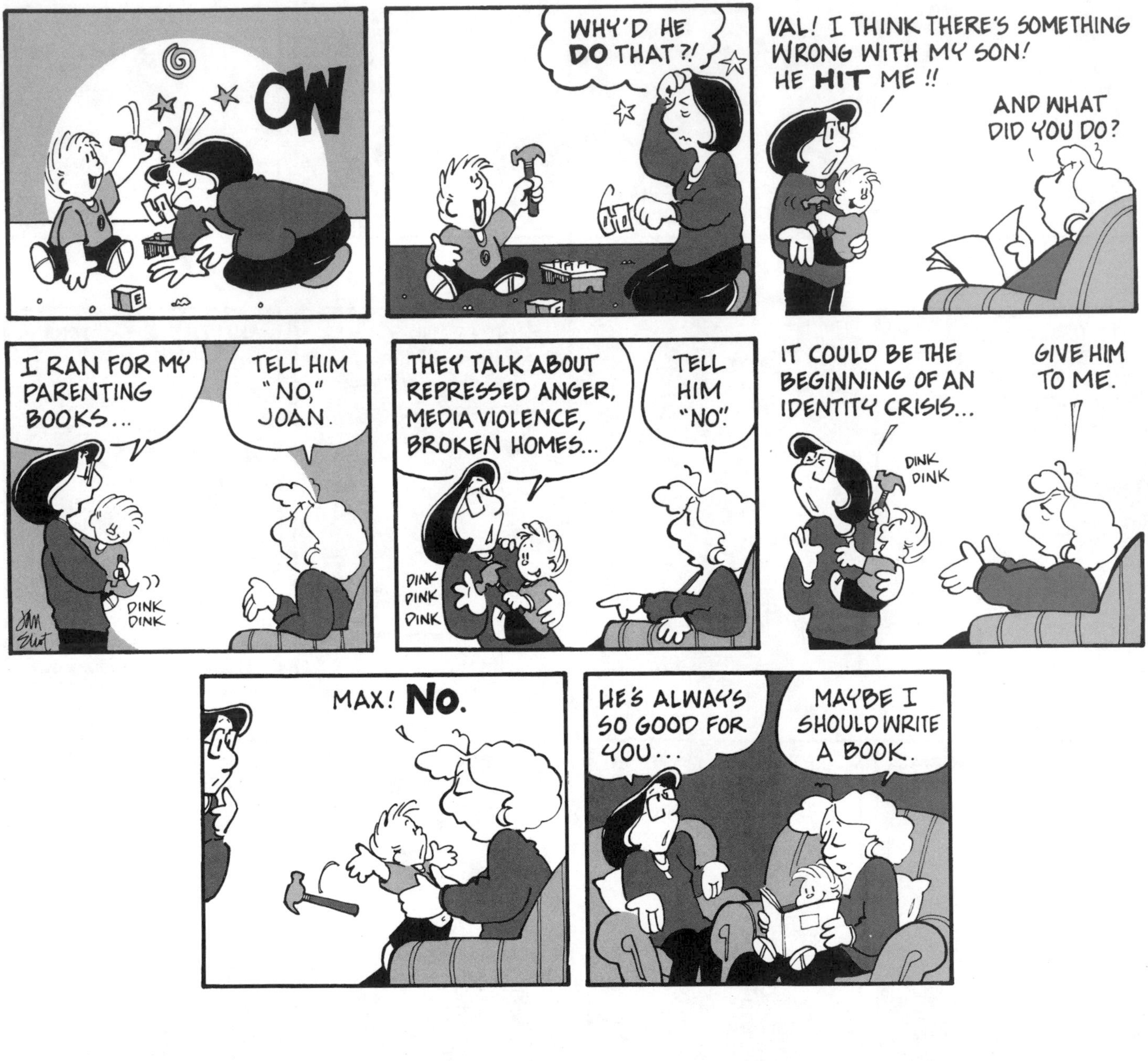
OW
WHY'D HE DO THAT?!
VAL! I THINK THERE'S SOMETHING WRONG WITH MY SON! HE HIT ME !!
AND WHAT DID YOU DO?
I RAN FOR MY PARENTING BOOKS...
TELL HIM "NO," JOAN.
DINK DINK
THEY TALK ABOUT REPRESSED ANGER, MEDIA VIOLENCE, BROKEN HOMES...
TELL HIM "NO".
DINK DINK DINK
IT COULD BE THE BEGINNING OF AN IDENTITY CRISIS...
DINK DINK
GIVE HIM TO ME.
MAX! NO.
HE'S ALWAYS SO GOOD FOR YOU...
MAYBE I SHOULD WRITE A BOOK.

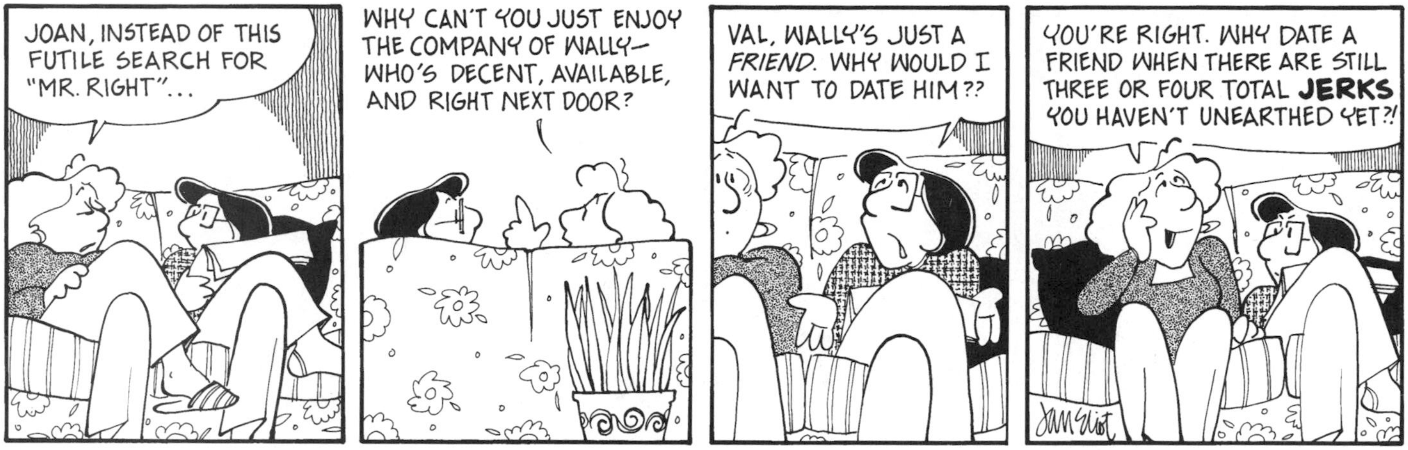
JOAN, INSTEAD OF THIS FUTILE SEARCH FOR "MR. RIGHT"...
WHY CAN'T YOU JUST ENJOY THE COMPANY OF WALLY— WHO'S DECENT, AVAILABLE, AND RIGHT NEXT DOOR?
VAL, WALLY'S JUST A *FRIEND*. WHY WOULD I WANT TO DATE HIM??
YOU'RE RIGHT. WHY DATE A FRIEND WHEN THERE ARE STILL THREE OR FOUR TOTAL **JERKS** YOU HAVEN'T UNEARTHED YET?!

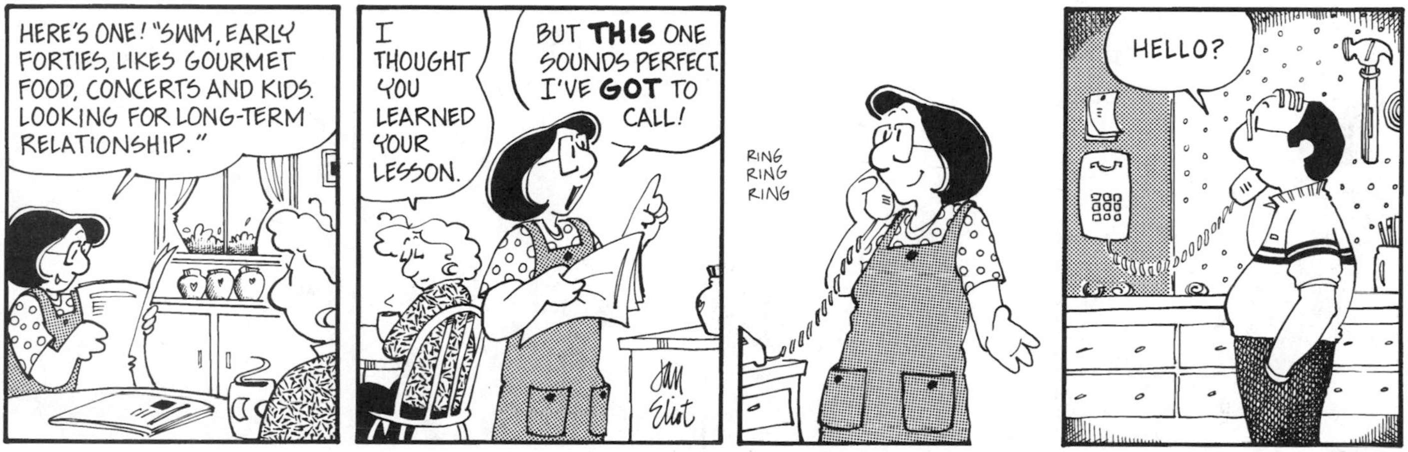
HERE'S ONE! "SWM, EARLY FORTIES, LIKES GOURMET FOOD, CONCERTS AND KIDS. LOOKING FOR LONG-TERM RELATIONSHIP."
I THOUGHT YOU LEARNED YOUR LESSON.
BUT **THIS** ONE SOUNDS PERFECT. I'VE **GOT** TO CALL!
RING RING RING
HELLO?

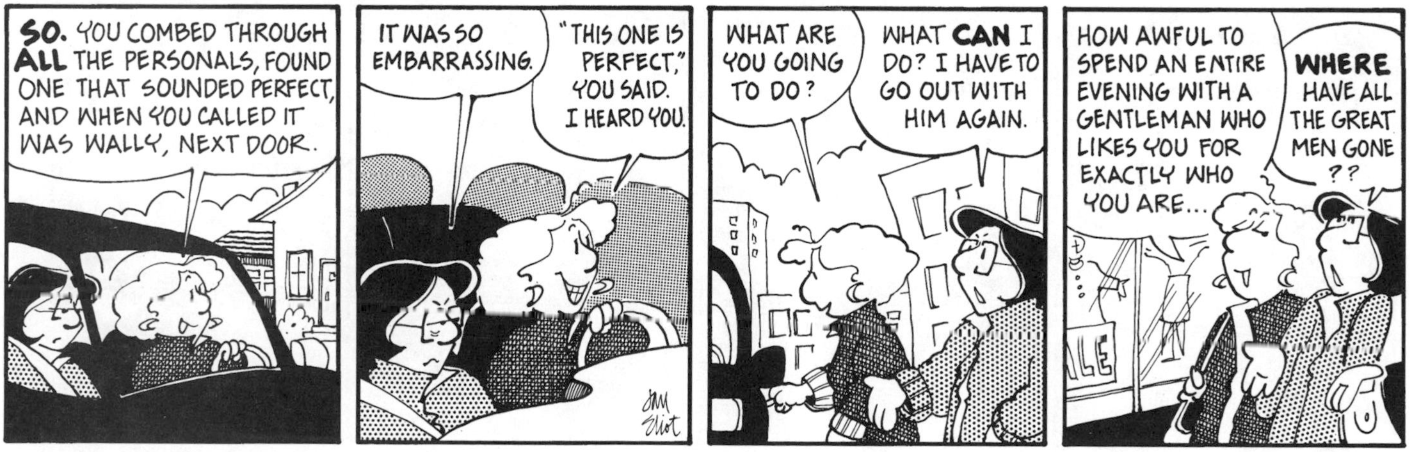
SO. YOU COMBED THROUGH **ALL** THE PERSONALS, FOUND ONE THAT SOUNDED PERFECT, AND WHEN YOU CALLED IT WAS WALLY, NEXT DOOR.
IT WAS SO EMBARRASSING.
"THIS ONE IS PERFECT," YOU SAID. I HEARD YOU.
WHAT ARE YOU GOING TO DO?
WHAT **CAN** I DO? I HAVE TO GO OUT WITH HIM AGAIN.
HOW AWFUL TO SPEND AN ENTIRE EVENING WITH A GENTLEMAN WHO LIKES YOU FOR EXACTLY WHO YOU ARE...
WHERE HAVE ALL THE GREAT MEN GONE??

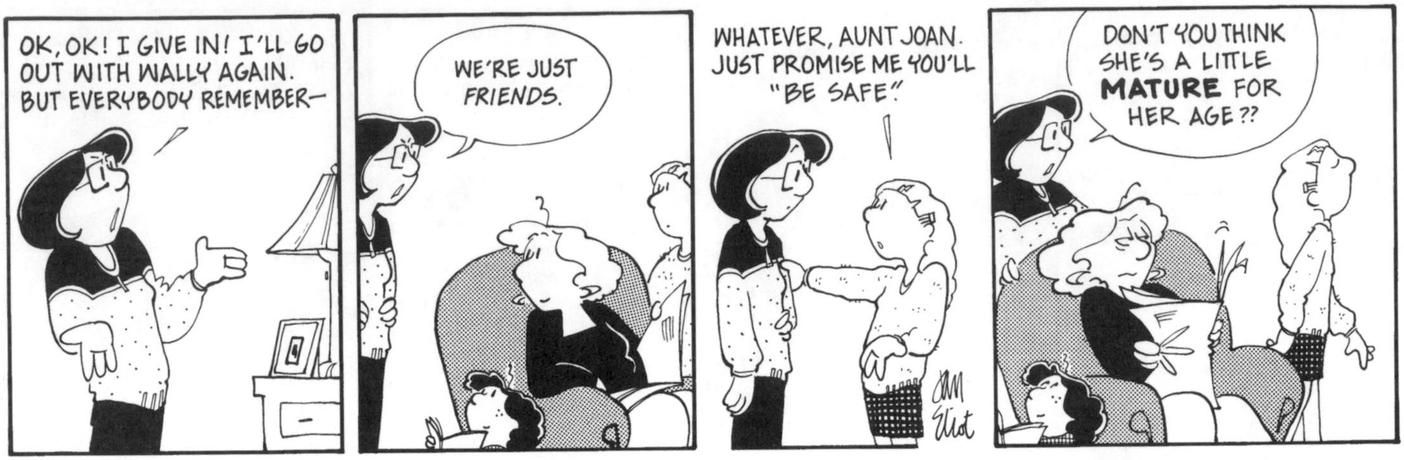
OK, OK! I GIVE IN! I'LL GO OUT WITH WALLY AGAIN. BUT EVERYBODY REMEMBER—
WE'RE JUST FRIENDS.
WHATEVER, AUNT JOAN. JUST PROMISE ME YOU'LL "BE SAFE."
DON'T YOU THINK SHE'S A LITTLE **MATURE** FOR HER AGE??

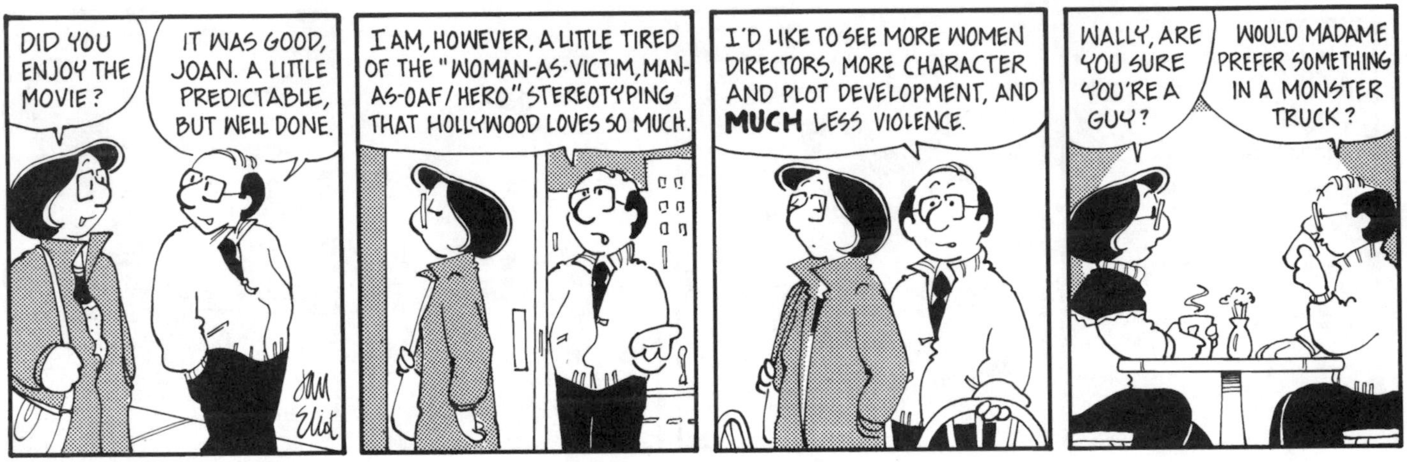
DID YOU ENJOY THE MOVIE?
IT WAS GOOD, JOAN. A LITTLE PREDICTABLE, BUT WELL DONE.
I AM, HOWEVER, A LITTLE TIRED OF THE "WOMAN-AS-VICTIM, MAN-AS-OAF/HERO" STEREOTYPING THAT HOLLYWOOD LOVES SO MUCH.
I'D LIKE TO SEE MORE WOMEN DIRECTORS, MORE CHARACTER AND PLOT DEVELOPMENT, AND **MUCH** LESS VIOLENCE.
WALLY, ARE YOU SURE YOU'RE A GUY?
WOULD MADAME PREFER SOMETHING IN A MONSTER TRUCK?

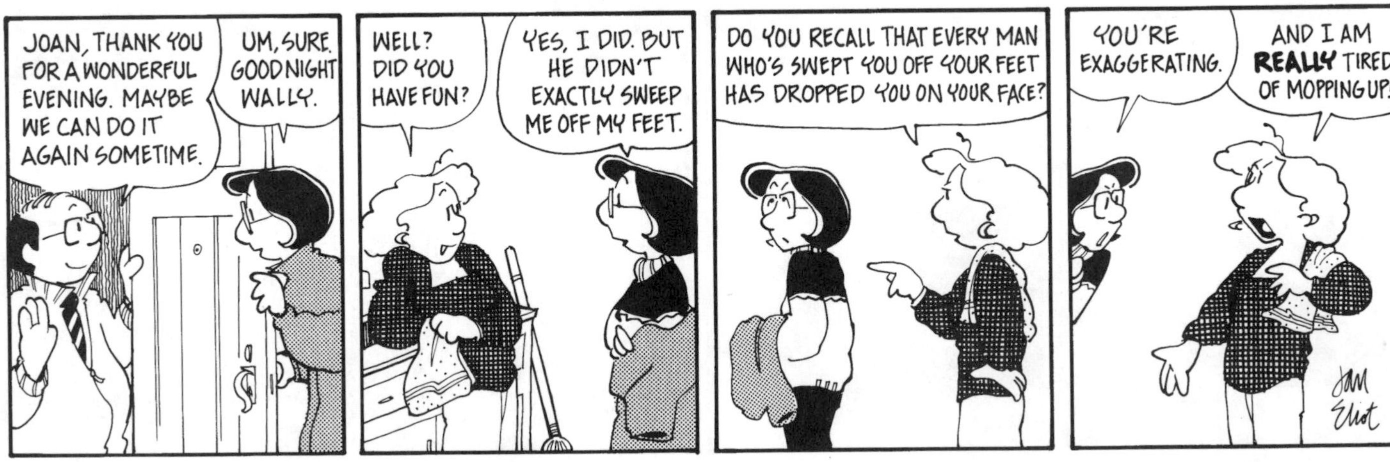
JOAN, THANK YOU FOR A WONDERFUL EVENING. MAYBE WE CAN DO IT AGAIN SOMETIME.
UM, SURE. GOODNIGHT WALLY.
WELL? DID YOU HAVE FUN?
YES, I DID. BUT HE DIDN'T EXACTLY SWEEP ME OFF MY FEET.
DO YOU RECALL THAT EVERY MAN WHO'S SWEPT YOU OFF YOUR FEET HAS DROPPED YOU ON YOUR FACE?
YOU'RE EXAGGERATING.
AND I AM **REALLY** TIRED OF MOPPING UP!

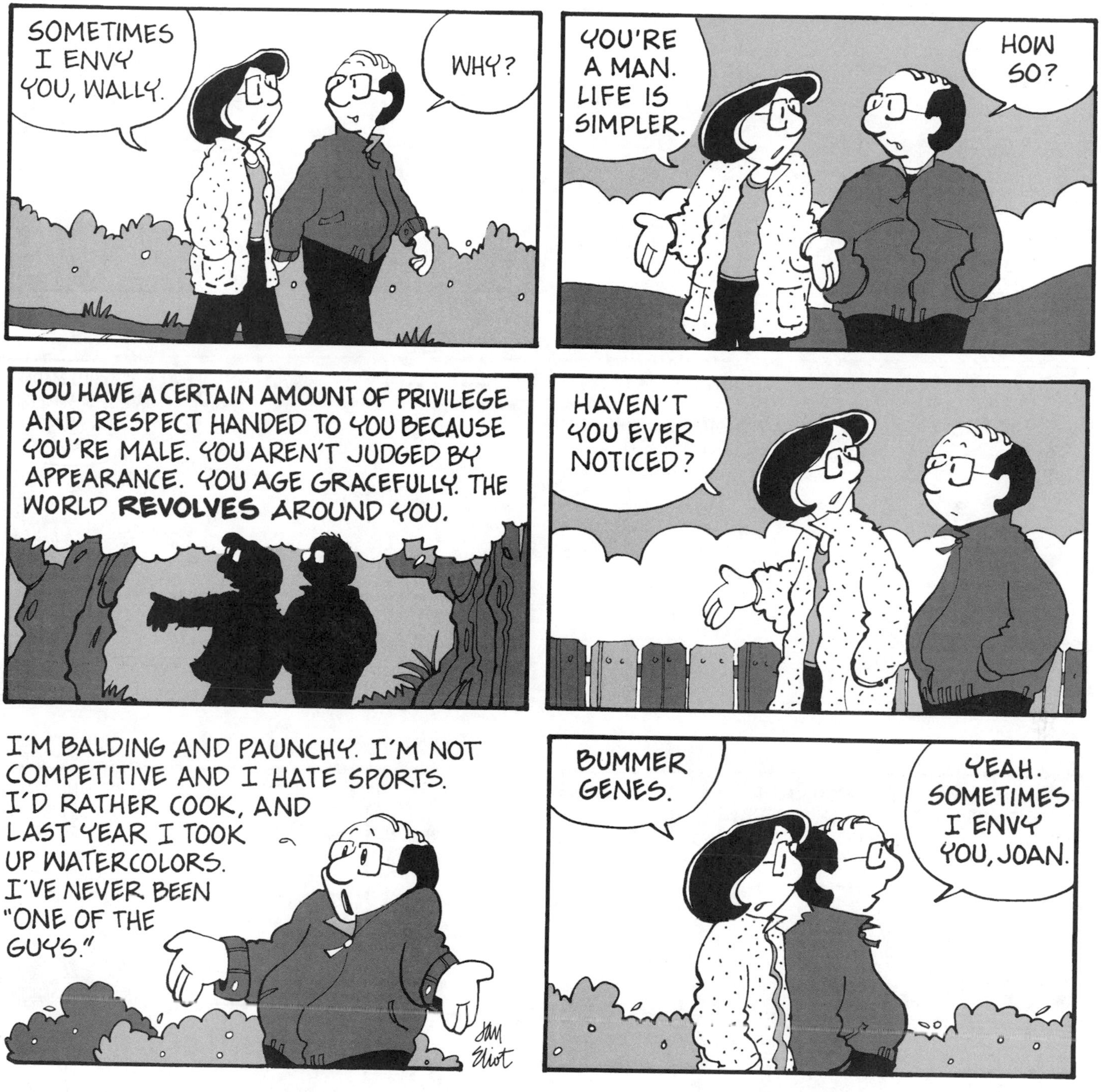
SOMETIMES I ENVY YOU, WALLY.
WHY?
YOU'RE A MAN. LIFE IS SIMPLER.
HOW SO?
YOU HAVE A CERTAIN AMOUNT OF PRIVILEGE AND RESPECT HANDED TO YOU BECAUSE YOU'RE MALE. YOU AREN'T JUDGED BY APPEARANCE. YOU AGE GRACEFULLY. THE WORLD **REVOLVES** AROUND YOU.
HAVEN'T YOU EVER NOTICED?
I'M BALDING AND PAUNCHY. I'M NOT COMPETITIVE AND I HATE SPORTS. I'D RATHER COOK, AND LAST YEAR I TOOK UP WATERCOLORS. I'VE NEVER BEEN "ONE OF THE GUYS."
Jan Eliot
BUMMER GENES.
YEAH. SOMETIMES I ENVY YOU, JOAN.

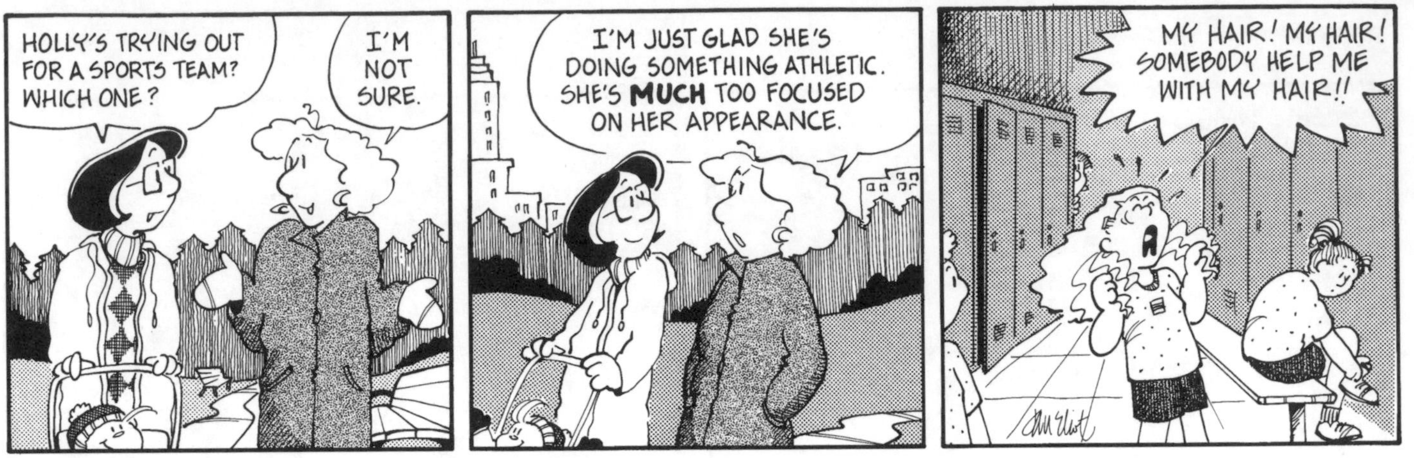
HOLLY'S TRYING OUT FOR A SPORTS TEAM? WHICH ONE?
I'M NOT SURE.
I'M JUST GLAD SHE'S DOING SOMETHING ATHLETIC. SHE'S **MUCH** TOO FOCUSED ON HER APPEARANCE.
MY HAIR! MY HAIR! SOMEBODY HELP ME WITH MY HAIR!!

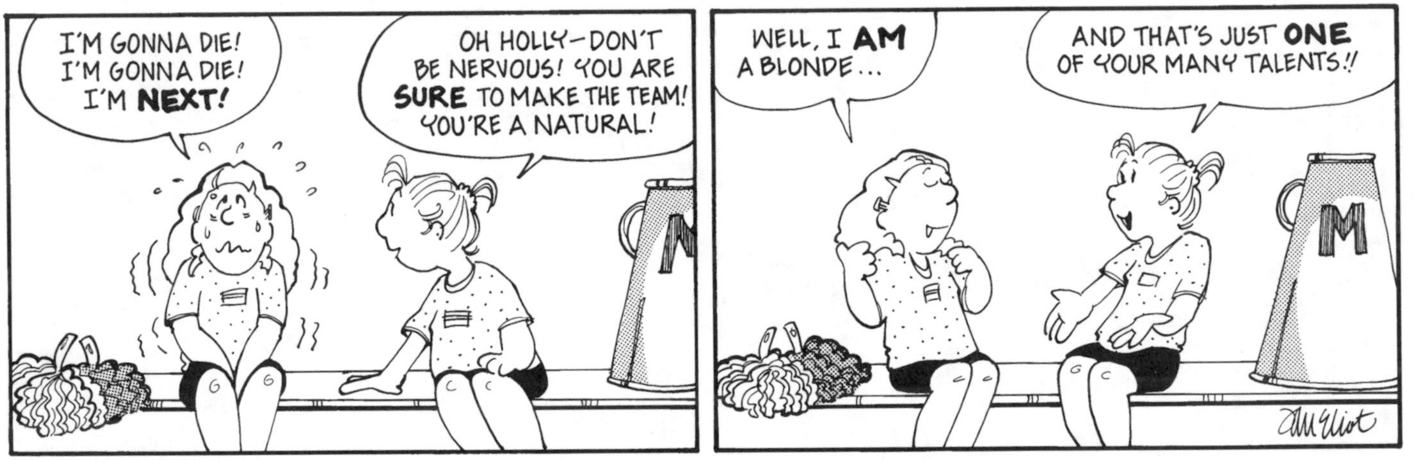
I'M GONNA DIE! I'M GONNA DIE! I'M **NEXT!**
OH HOLLY—DON'T BE NERVOUS! YOU ARE **SURE** TO MAKE THE TEAM! YOU'RE A NATURAL!
WELL, I **AM** A BLONDE...
AND THAT'S JUST **ONE** OF YOUR MANY TALENTS!!
M

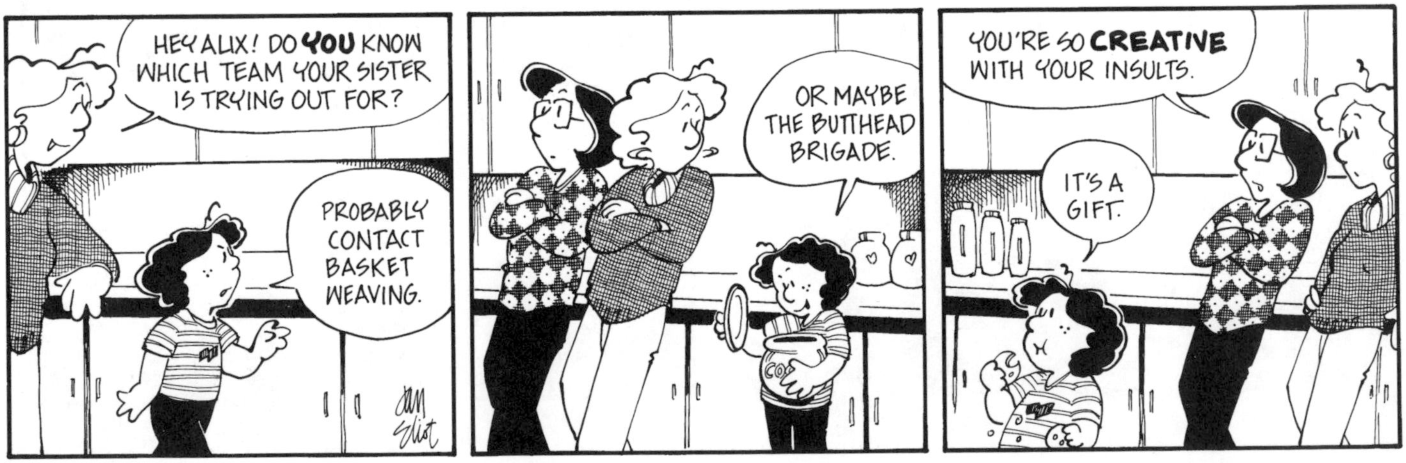
HEY ALIX! DO **YOU** KNOW WHICH TEAM YOUR SISTER IS TRYING OUT FOR?
PROBABLY CONTACT BASKET WEAVING.
OR MAYBE THE BUTTHEAD BRIGADE.
YOU'RE SO **CREATIVE** WITH YOUR INSULTS.
IT'S A GIFT.

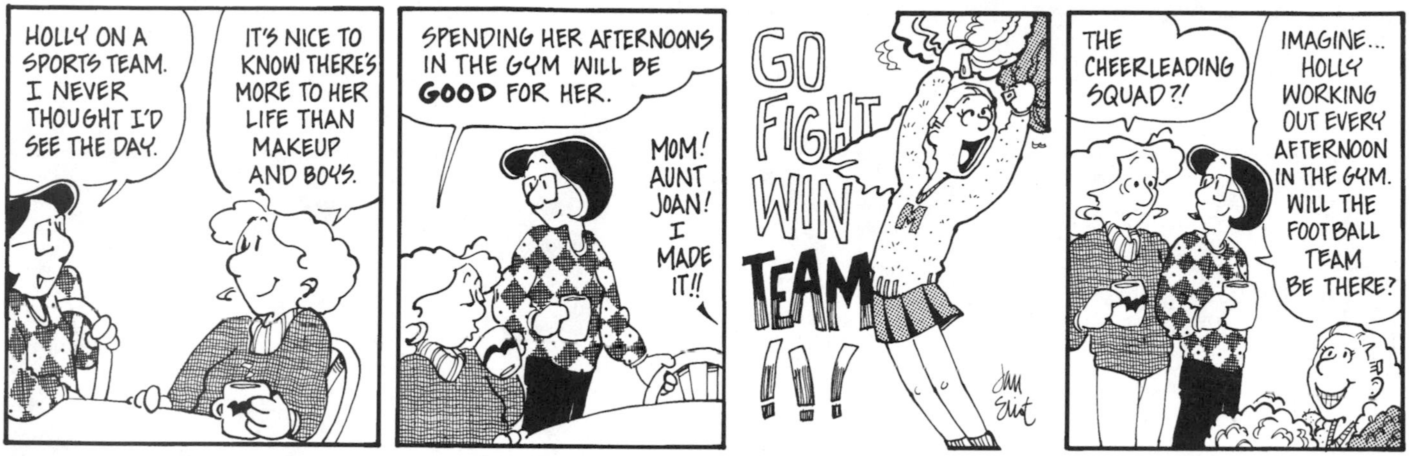
HOLLY ON A SPORTS TEAM. I NEVER THOUGHT I'D SEE THE DAY.
IT'S NICE TO KNOW THERE'S MORE TO HER LIFE THAN MAKEUP AND BOYS.
SPENDING HER AFTERNOONS IN THE GYM WILL BE **GOOD** FOR HER.
MOM! AUNT JOAN! I MADE IT!!
GO FIGHT WIN TEAM!!!
THE CHEERLEADING SQUAD?!
IMAGINE... HOLLY WORKING OUT EVERY AFTERNOON IN THE GYM. WILL THE FOOTBALL TEAM BE THERE?

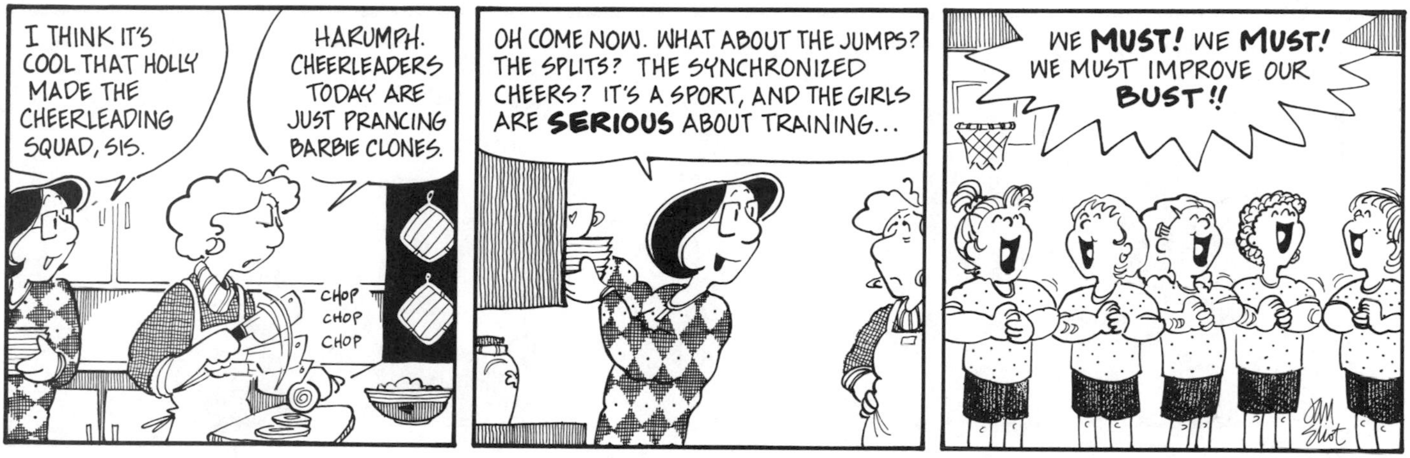
I THINK IT'S COOL THAT HOLLY MADE THE CHEERLEADING SQUAD, SIS.
HARUMPH. CHEERLEADERS TODAY ARE JUST PRANCING BARBIE CLONES.
CHOP CHOP CHOP
OH COME NOW. WHAT ABOUT THE JUMPS? THE SPLITS? THE SYNCHRONIZED CHEERS? IT'S A SPORT, AND THE GIRLS ARE **SERIOUS** ABOUT TRAINING...
WE **MUST!** WE **MUST!** WE MUST IMPROVE OUR **BUST**!!

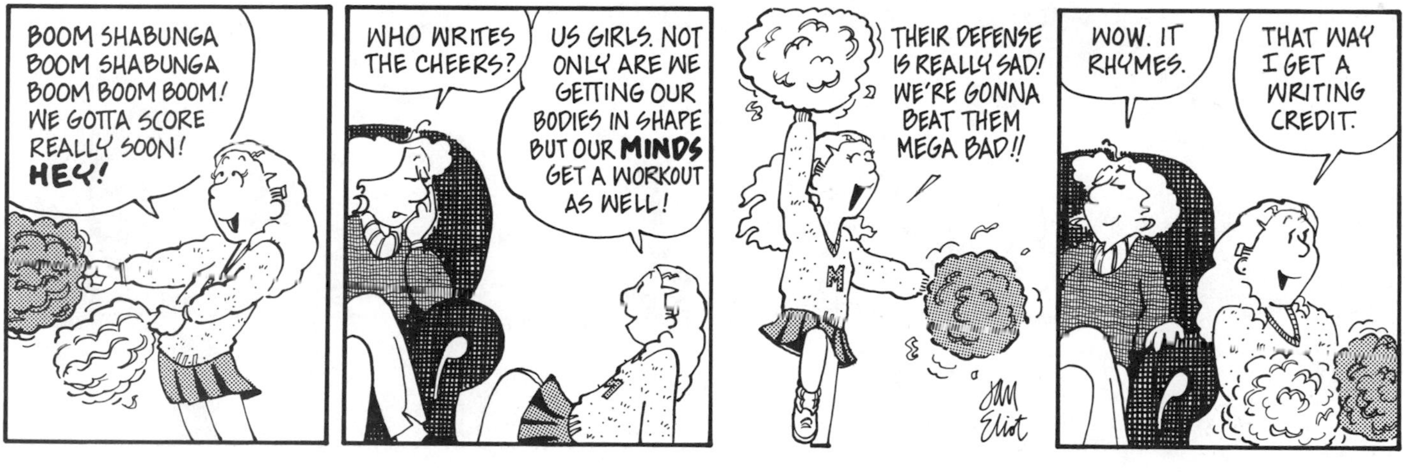
BOOM SHABUNGA BOOM SHABUNGA BOOM BOOM BOOM! WE GOTTA SCORE REALLY SOON! **HEY!**
WHO WRITES THE CHEERS?
US GIRLS. NOT ONLY ARE WE GETTING OUR BODIES IN SHAPE BUT OUR **MINDS** GET A WORKOUT AS WELL!
THEIR DEFENSE IS REALLY SAD! WE'RE GONNA BEAT THEM MEGA BAD!!
WOW. IT RHYMES.
THAT WAY I GET A WRITING CREDIT.

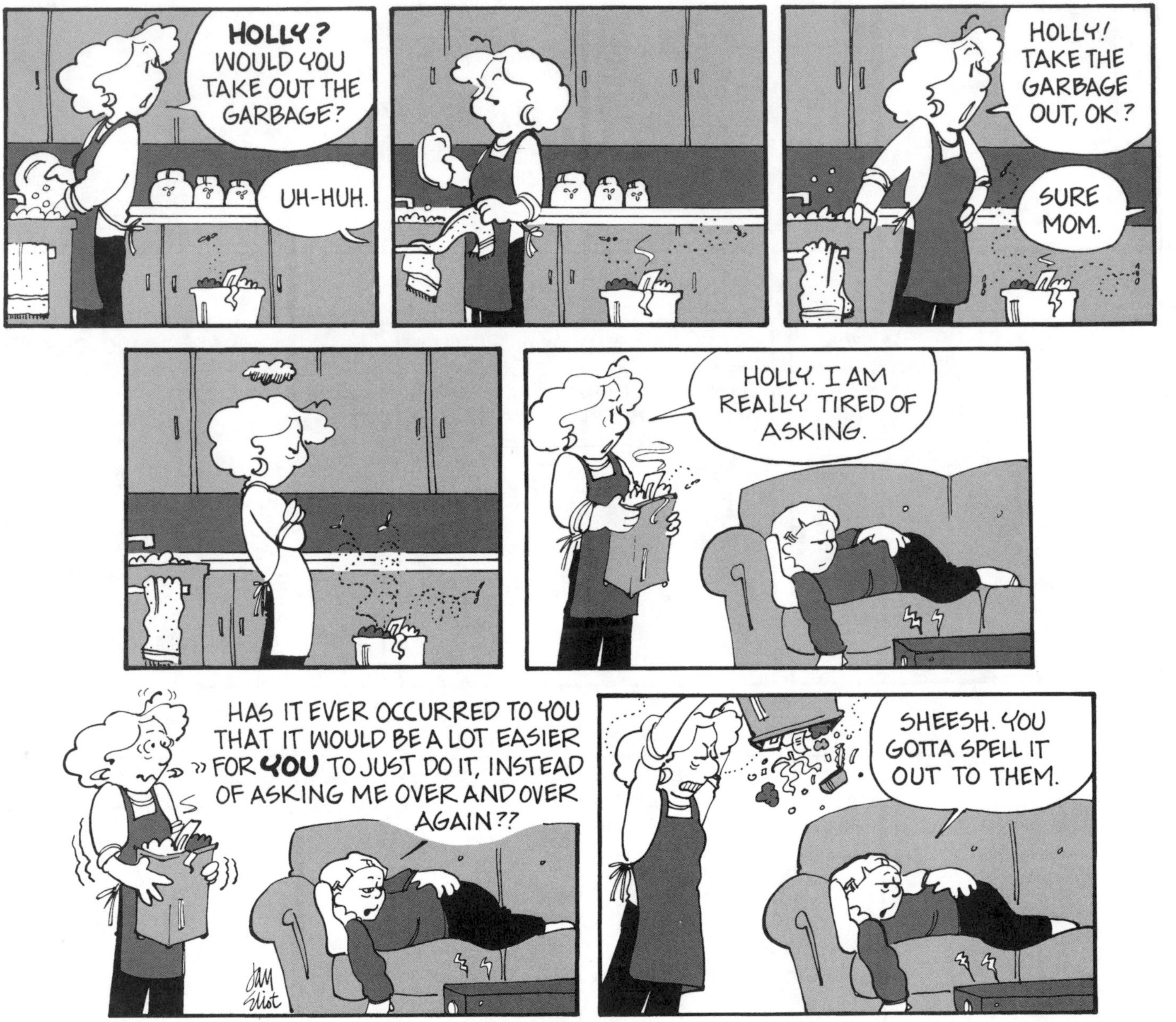
HOLLY? WOULD YOU TAKE OUT THE GARBAGE?
UH-HUH.
HOLLY! TAKE THE GARBAGE OUT, OK?
SURE MOM.
HOLLY. I AM REALLY TIRED OF ASKING.
HAS IT EVER OCCURRED TO YOU THAT IT WOULD BE A LOT EASIER FOR YOU TO JUST DO IT, INSTEAD OF ASKING ME OVER AND OVER AGAIN??
SHEESH. YOU GOTTA SPELL IT OUT TO THEM.

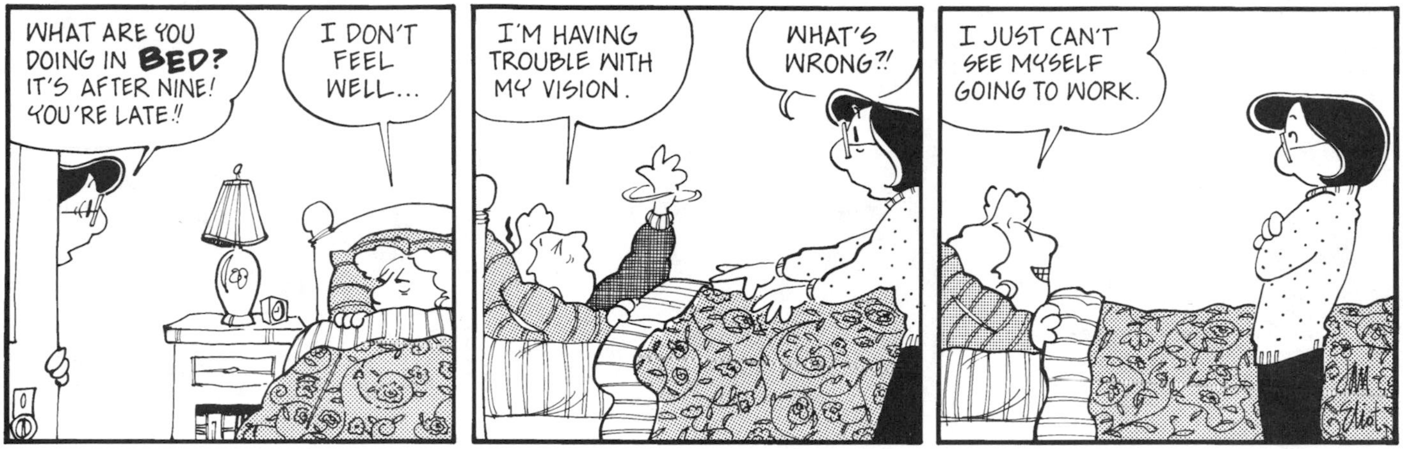
WHAT ARE YOU DOING IN BED? IT'S AFTER NINE! YOU'RE LATE!!
I DON'T FEEL WELL...
I'M HAVING TROUBLE WITH MY VISION.
WHAT'S WRONG?!
I JUST CAN'T SEE MYSELF GOING TO WORK.

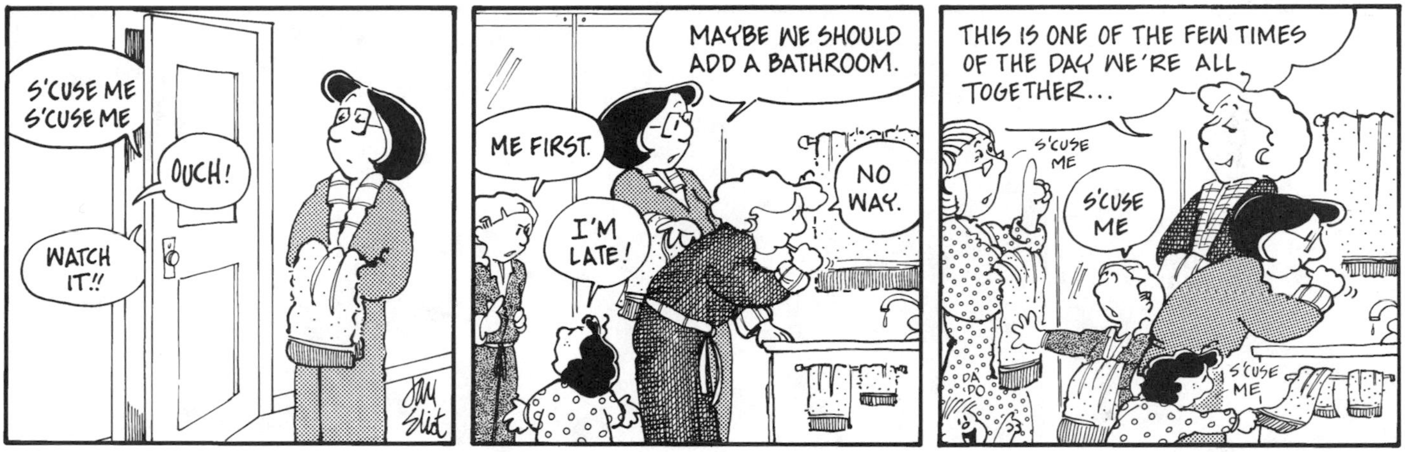
S'CUSE ME S'CUSE ME
OUCH!
WATCH IT!!
MAYBE WE SHOULD ADD A BATHROOM.
ME FIRST.
NO WAY.
I'M LATE!
THIS IS ONE OF THE FEW TIMES OF THE DAY WE'RE ALL TOGETHER...
S'CUSE ME
S'CUSE ME
S'CUSE ME!

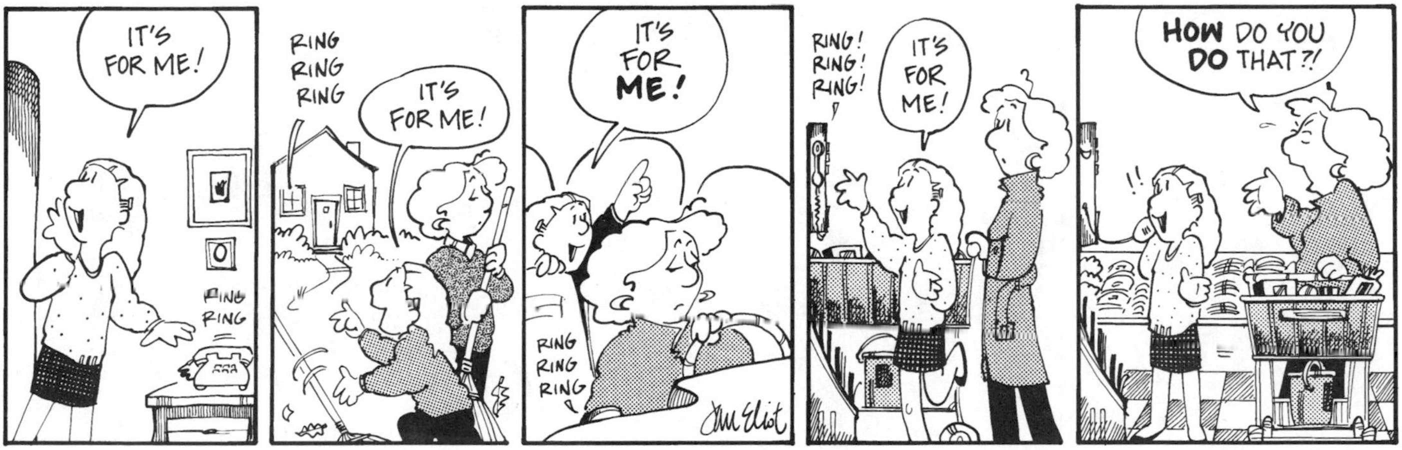
IT'S FOR ME!
RING RING
RING RING RING
IT'S FOR ME!
IT'S FOR ME!
RING RING RING
RING! RING! RING!
IT'S FOR ME!
HOW DO YOU DO THAT?!
!!

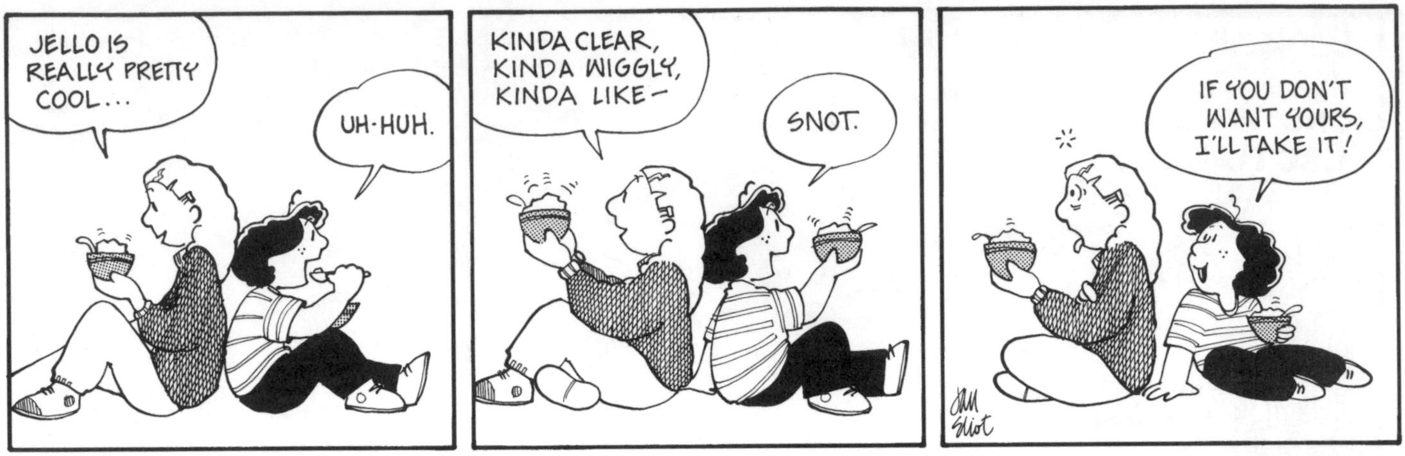
JELLO IS REALLY PRETTY COOL...
UH-HUH.
KINDA CLEAR, KINDA WIGGLY, KINDA LIKE—
SNOT.
IF YOU DON'T WANT YOURS, I'LL TAKE IT!

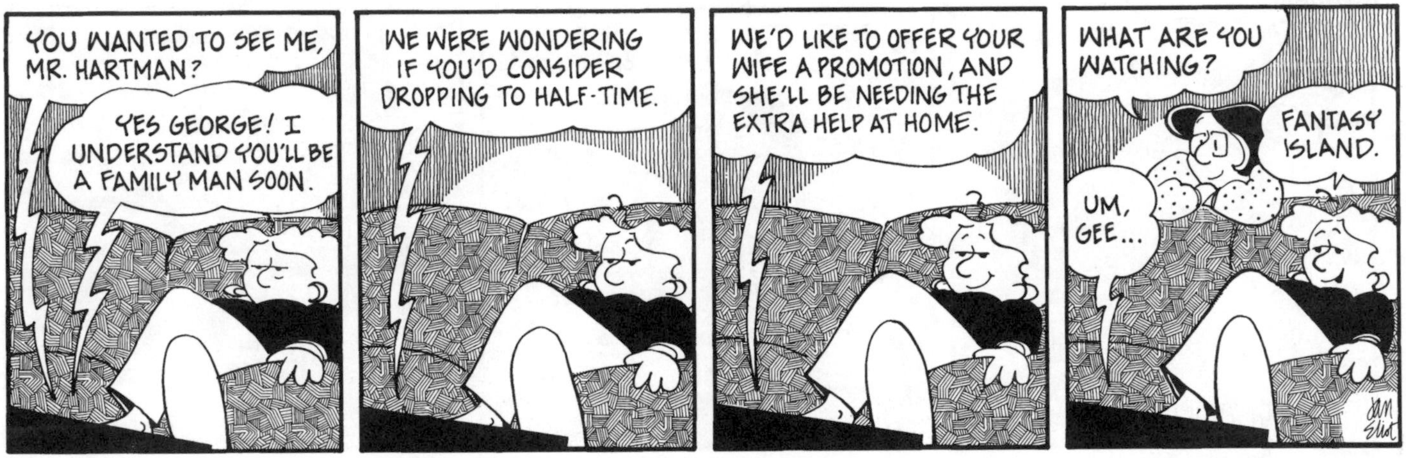
YOU WANTED TO SEE ME, MR. HARTMAN?
YES GEORGE! I UNDERSTAND YOU'LL BE A FAMILY MAN SOON.
WE WERE WONDERING IF YOU'D CONSIDER DROPPING TO HALF-TIME.
WE'D LIKE TO OFFER YOUR WIFE A PROMOTION, AND SHE'LL BE NEEDING THE EXTRA HELP AT HOME.
WHAT ARE YOU WATCHING?
FANTASY ISLAND.
UM, GEE...

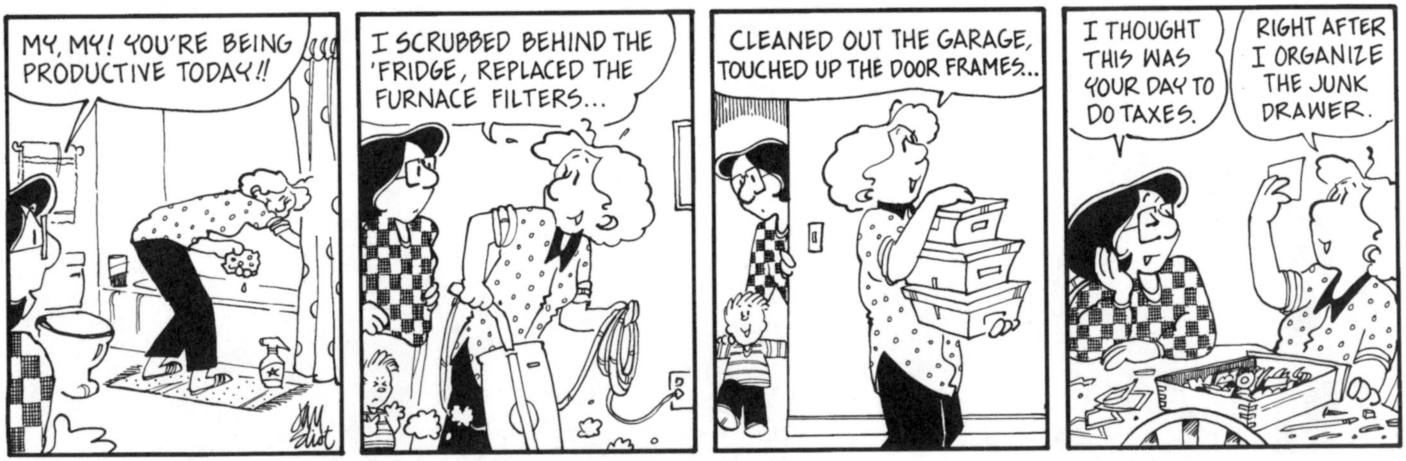
MY, MY! YOU'RE BEING PRODUCTIVE TODAY!!
I SCRUBBED BEHIND THE 'FRIDGE, REPLACED THE FURNACE FILTERS...
CLEANED OUT THE GARAGE, TOUCHED UP THE DOOR FRAMES...
I THOUGHT THIS WAS YOUR DAY TO DO TAXES.
RIGHT AFTER I ORGANIZE THE JUNK DRAWER.

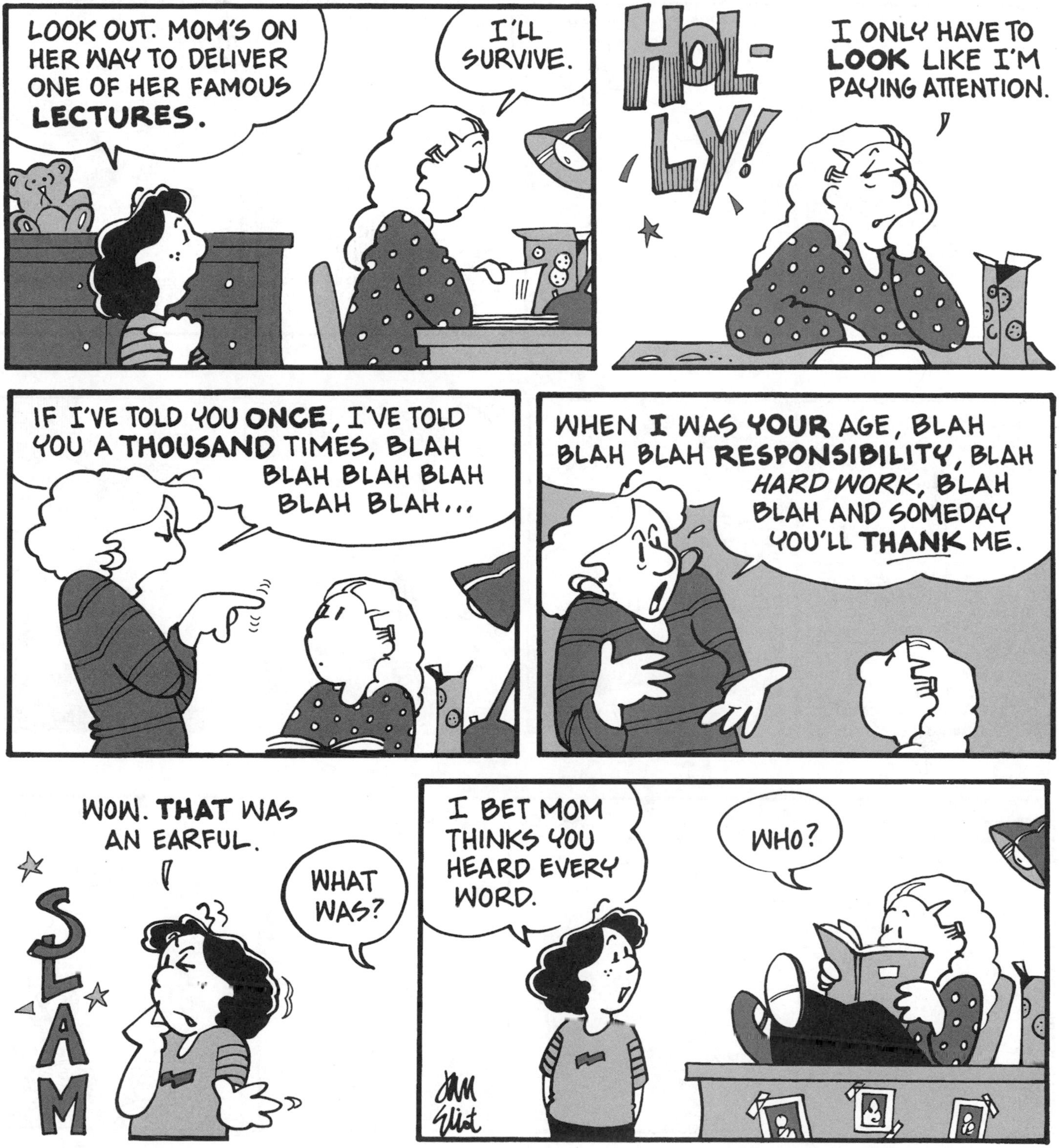
LOOK OUT. MOM'S ON HER WAY TO DELIVER ONE OF HER FAMOUS LECTURES.
I'LL SURVIVE.
HOL-LY!
I ONLY HAVE TO LOOK LIKE I'M PAYING ATTENTION.
IF I'VE TOLD YOU ONCE, I'VE TOLD YOU A THOUSAND TIMES, BLAH BLAH BLAH BLAH BLAH BLAH...
WHEN I WAS YOUR AGE, BLAH BLAH BLAH RESPONSIBILITY, BLAH HARD WORK, BLAH BLAH AND SOMEDAY YOU'LL THANK ME.
SLAM
WOW. THAT WAS AN EARFUL.
WHAT WAS?
I BET MOM THINKS YOU HEARD EVERY WORD.
WHO?

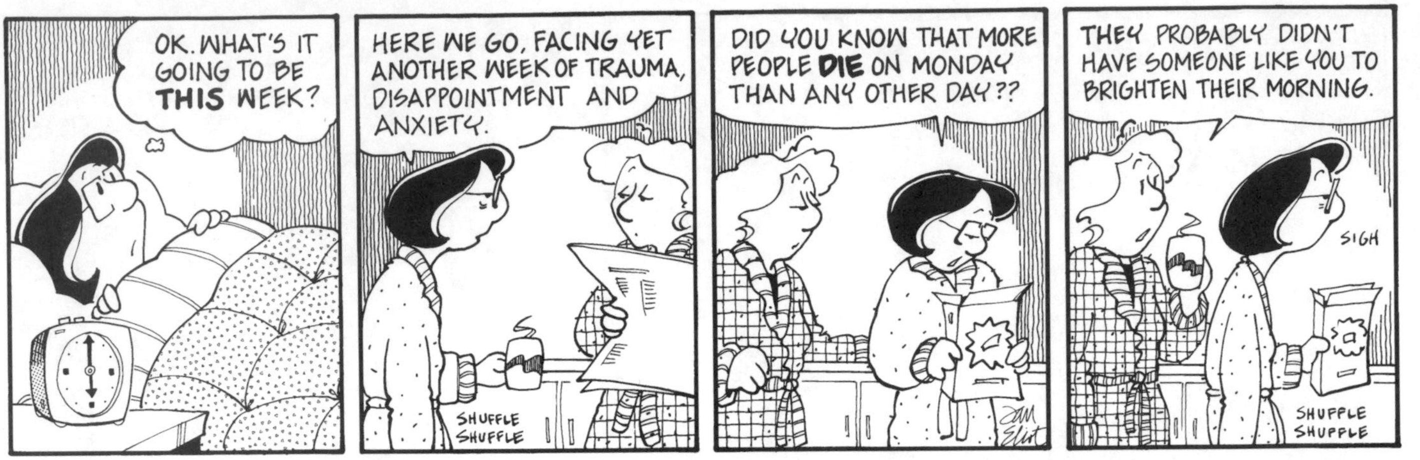
OK. WHAT'S IT GOING TO BE THIS WEEK?
HERE WE GO, FACING YET ANOTHER WEEK OF TRAUMA, DISAPPOINTMENT AND ANXIETY.
SHUFFLE SHUFFLE
DID YOU KNOW THAT MORE PEOPLE DIE ON MONDAY THAN ANY OTHER DAY??
THEY PROBABLY DIDN'T HAVE SOMEONE LIKE YOU TO BRIGHTEN THEIR MORNING.
SIGH
SHUFFLE SHUFFLE

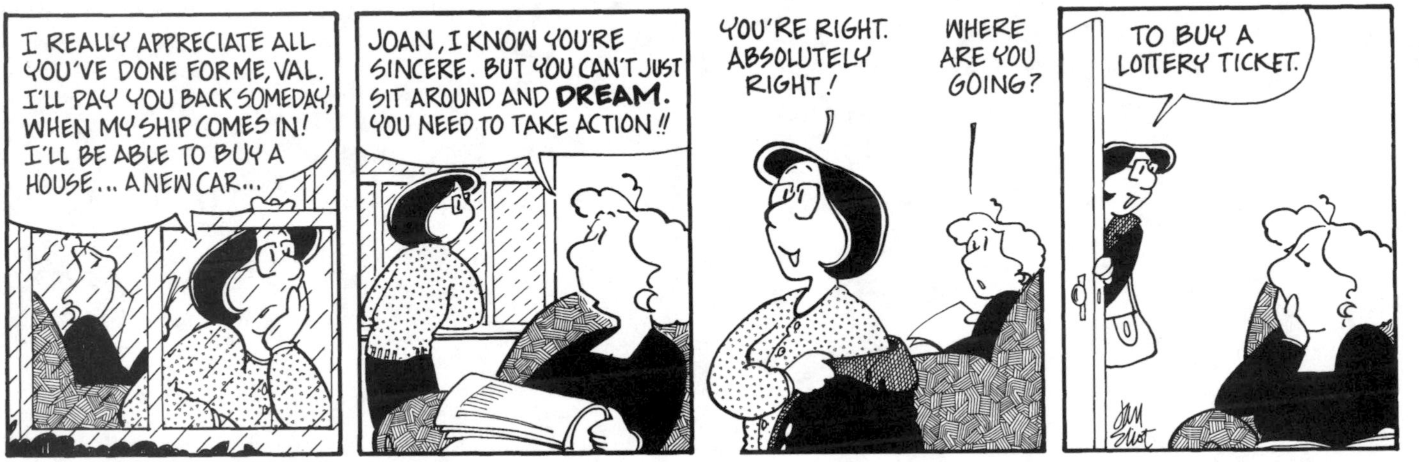
I REALLY APPRECIATE ALL YOU'VE DONE FOR ME, VAL. I'LL PAY YOU BACK SOMEDAY, WHEN MY SHIP COMES IN! I'LL BE ABLE TO BUY A HOUSE... A NEW CAR...
JOAN, I KNOW YOU'RE SINCERE. BUT YOU CAN'T JUST SIT AROUND AND DREAM. YOU NEED TO TAKE ACTION!!
YOU'RE RIGHT. ABSOLUTELY RIGHT!
WHERE ARE YOU GOING?
TO BUY A LOTTERY TICKET.

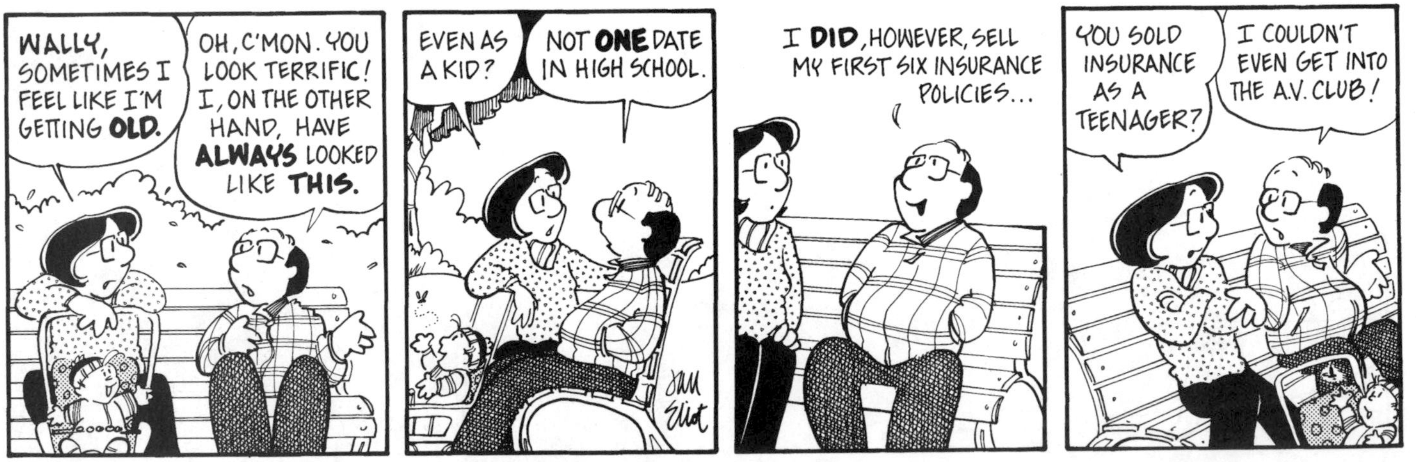
WALLY, SOMETIMES I FEEL LIKE I'M GETTING OLD.
OH, C'MON. YOU LOOK TERRIFIC! I, ON THE OTHER HAND, HAVE ALWAYS LOOKED LIKE THIS.
EVEN AS A KID?
NOT ONE DATE IN HIGH SCHOOL.
I DID, HOWEVER, SELL MY FIRST SIX INSURANCE POLICIES...
YOU SOLD INSURANCE AS A TEENAGER?
I COULDN'T EVEN GET INTO THE A.V. CLUB!

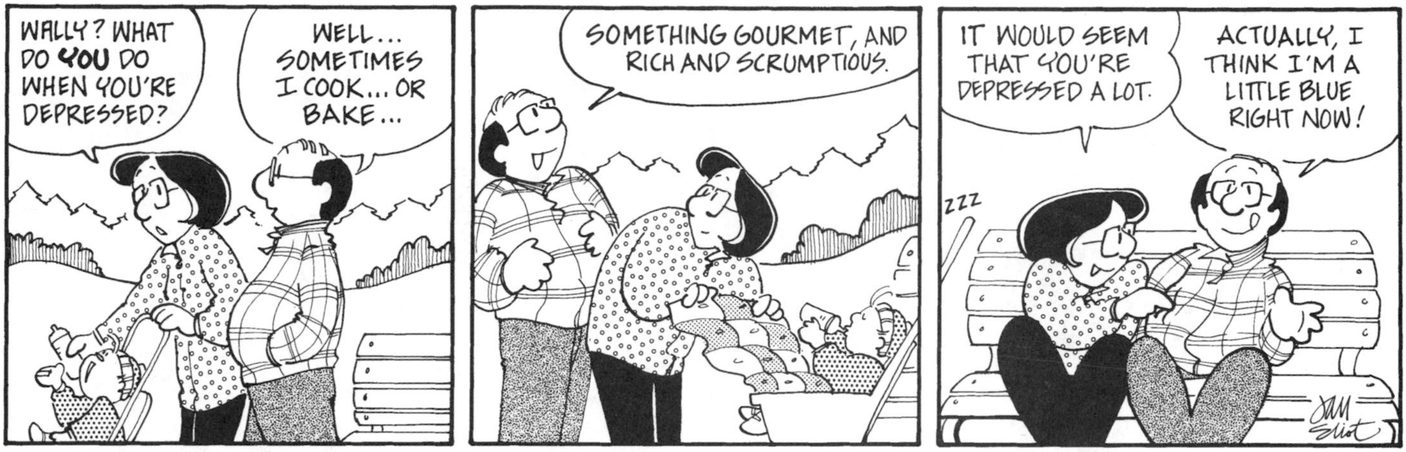
WALLY? WHAT DO YOU DO WHEN YOU'RE DEPRESSED?
WELL... SOMETIMES I COOK... OR BAKE...
SOMETHING GOURMET, AND RICH AND SCRUMPTIOUS.
ZZZ
IT WOULD SEEM THAT YOU'RE DEPRESSED A LOT.
ACTUALLY, I THINK I'M A LITTLE BLUE RIGHT NOW!

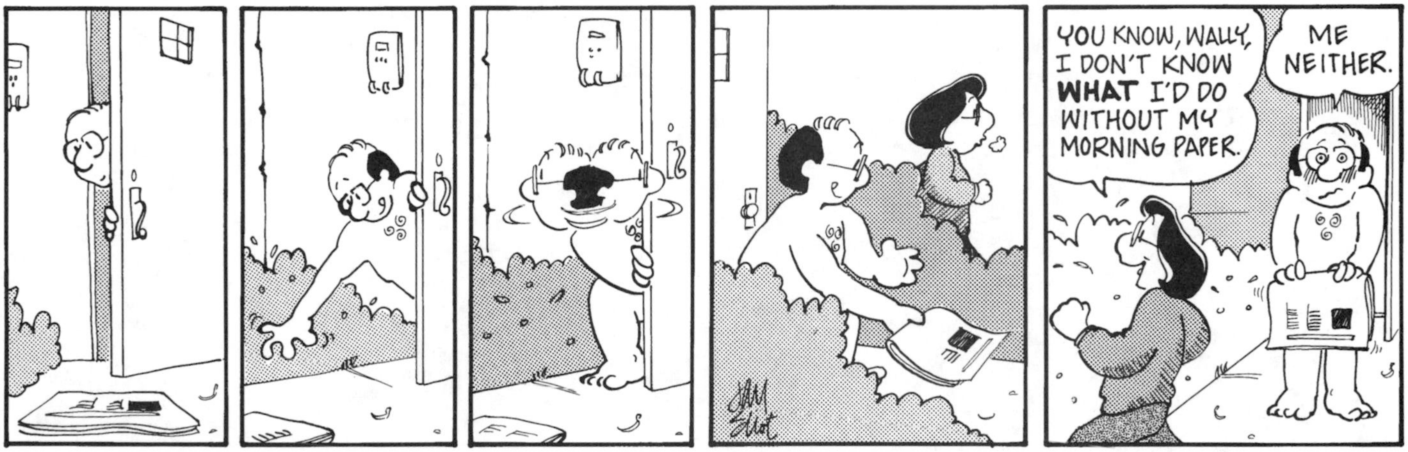
YOU KNOW, WALLY, I DON'T KNOW WHAT I'D DO WITHOUT MY MORNING PAPER.
ME NEITHER.

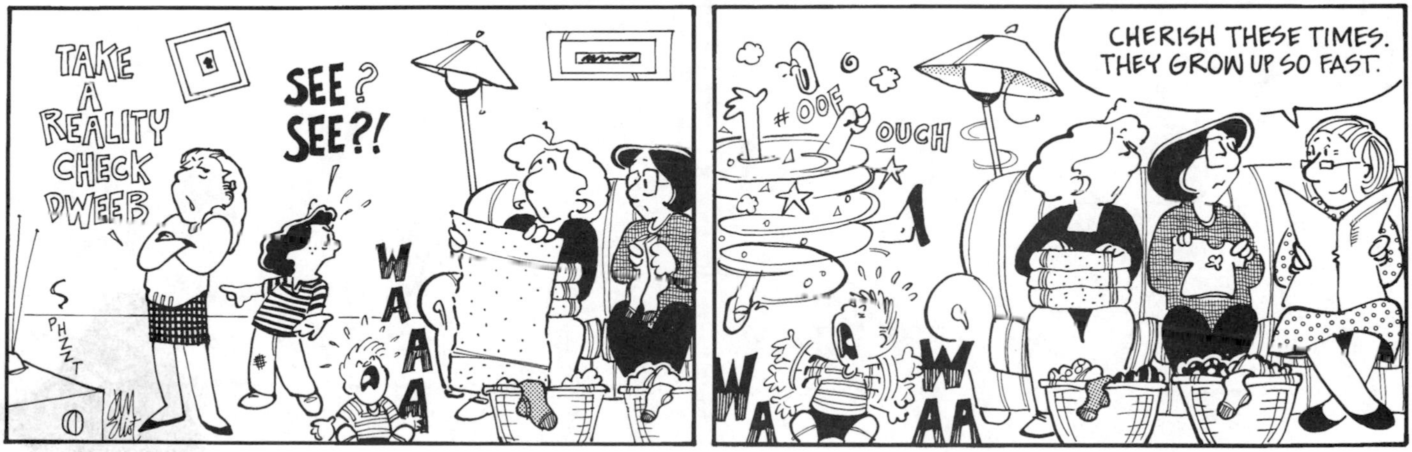
TAKE A REALITY CHECK DWEEB
SEE? SEE?!
PHZZT
WAAAA
OOF
OUCH
CHERISH THESE TIMES. THEY GROW UP SO FAST.
WA
WAA

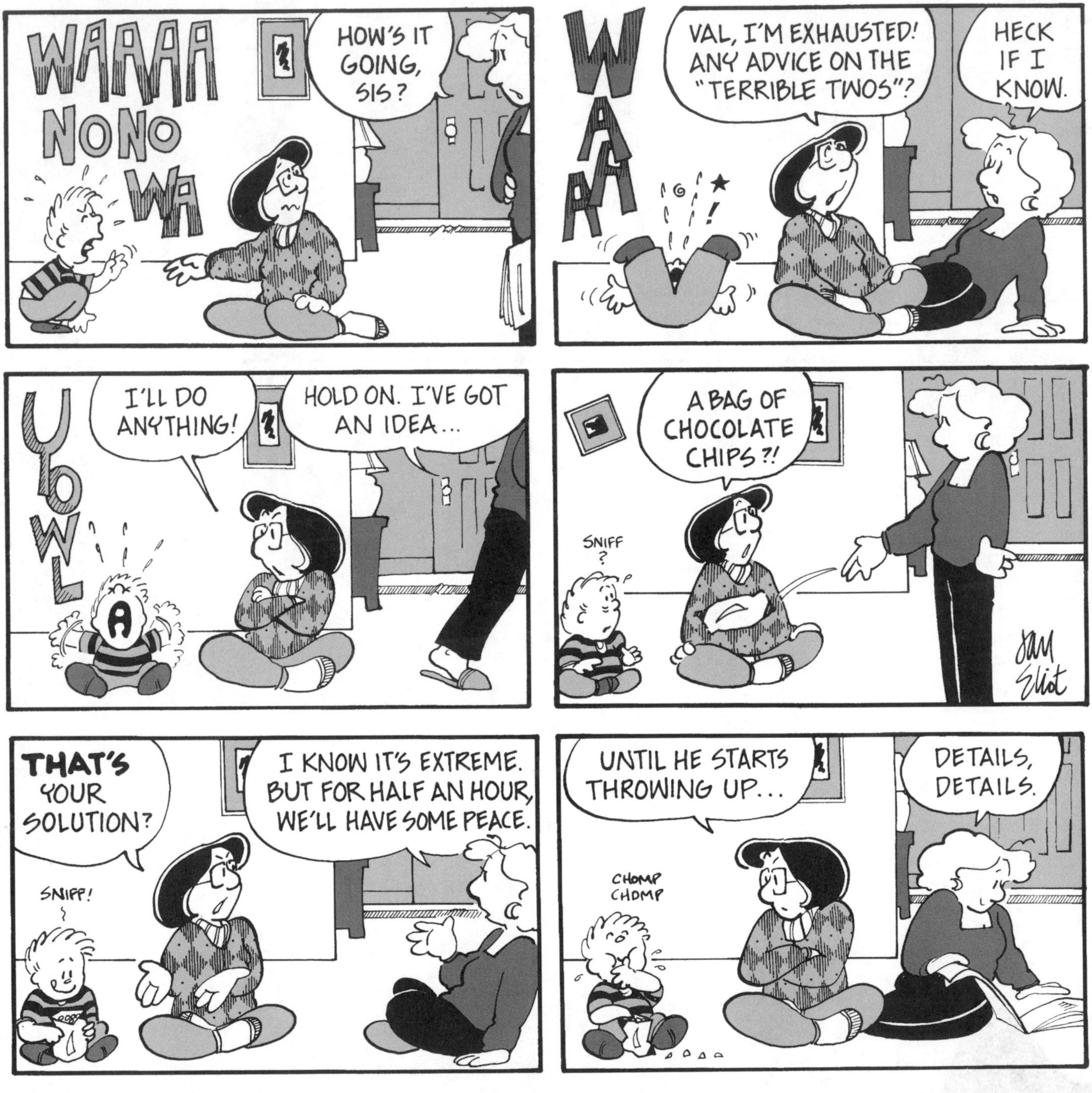
WAAAA
NONO
WA
HOW'S IT GOING, SIS?
WAAA
VAL, I'M EXHAUSTED! ANY ADVICE ON THE "TERRIBLE TWOS"?
HECK IF I KNOW.
YOWL
I'LL DO ANYTHING!
HOLD ON. I'VE GOT AN IDEA...
A BAG OF CHOCOLATE CHIPS?!
SNIFF ?
THAT'S YOUR SOLUTION?
I KNOW IT'S EXTREME. BUT FOR HALF AN HOUR, WE'LL HAVE SOME PEACE.
SNIFF!
UNTIL HE STARTS THROWING UP...
DETAILS, DETAILS.
CHOMP CHOMP

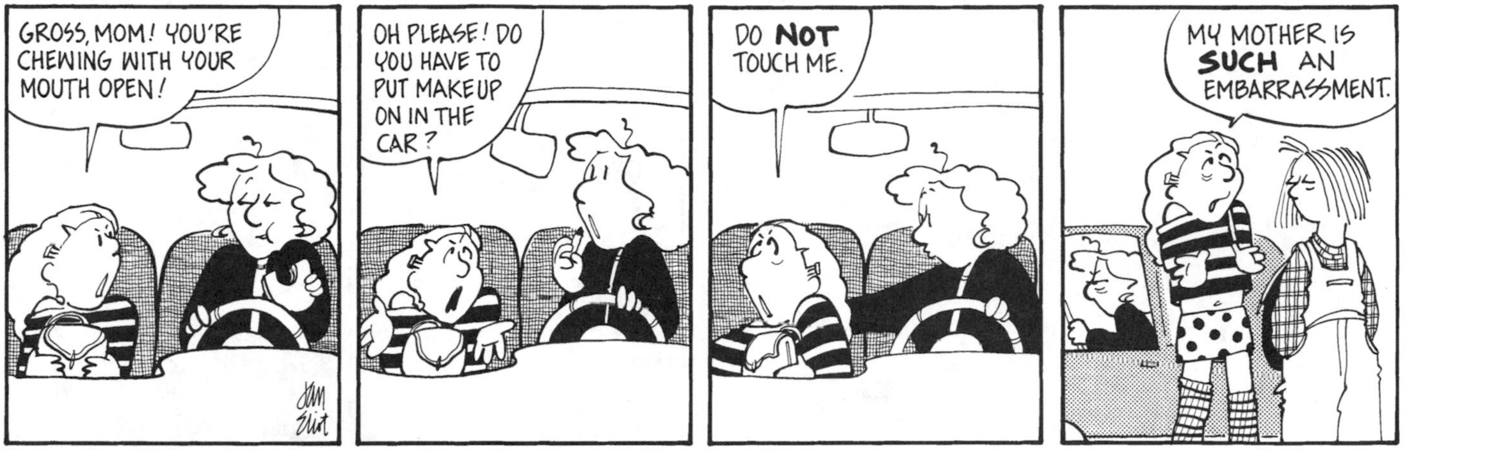
GROSS, MOM! YOU'RE CHEWING WITH YOUR MOUTH OPEN!
OH PLEASE! DO YOU HAVE TO PUT MAKEUP ON IN THE CAR?
DO **NOT** TOUCH ME.
MY MOTHER IS **SUCH** AN EMBARRASSMENT.

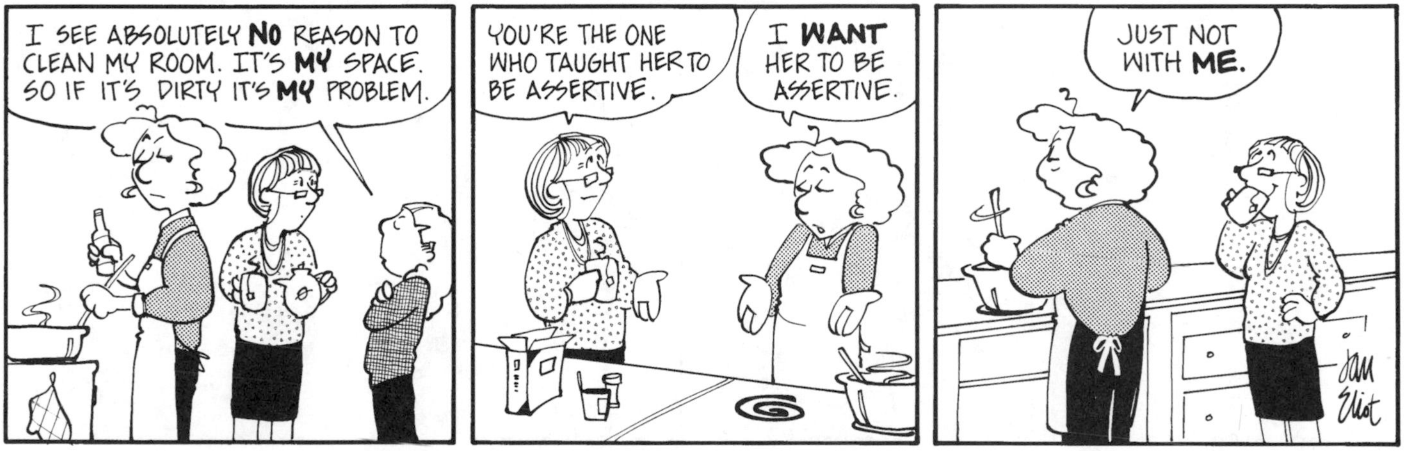
I SEE ABSOLUTELY **NO** REASON TO CLEAN MY ROOM. IT'S **MY** SPACE. SO IF IT'S DIRTY IT'S **MY** PROBLEM.
YOU'RE THE ONE WHO TAUGHT HER TO BE ASSERTIVE.
I **WANT** HER TO BE ASSERTIVE.
JUST NOT WITH **ME.**

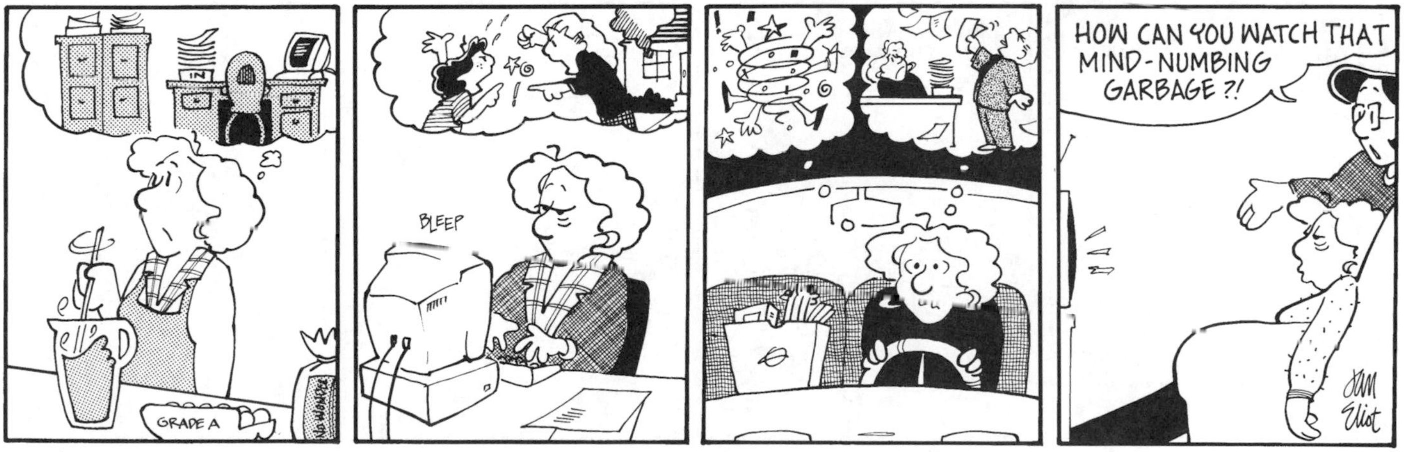
IN
GRADE A
BLEEP
HOW CAN YOU WATCH THAT MIND-NUMBING GARBAGE?!

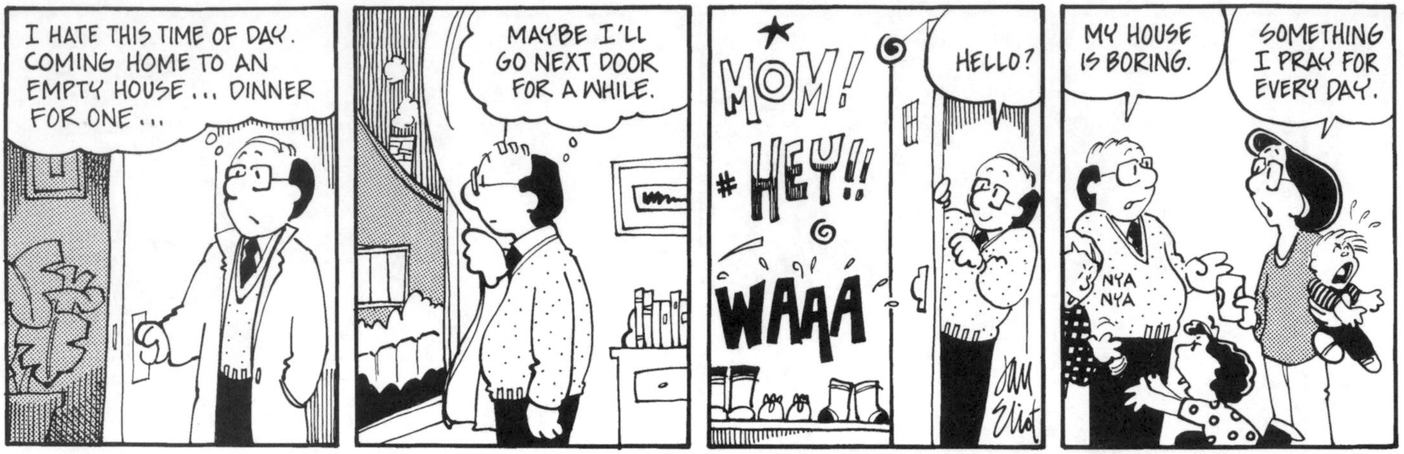
I HATE THIS TIME OF DAY. COMING HOME TO AN EMPTY HOUSE... DINNER FOR ONE...
MAYBE I'LL GO NEXT DOOR FOR A WHILE.
MOM!
HEY!!
WAAA
HELLO?
MY HOUSE IS BORING.
SOMETHING I PRAY FOR EVERY DAY.
NYA NYA

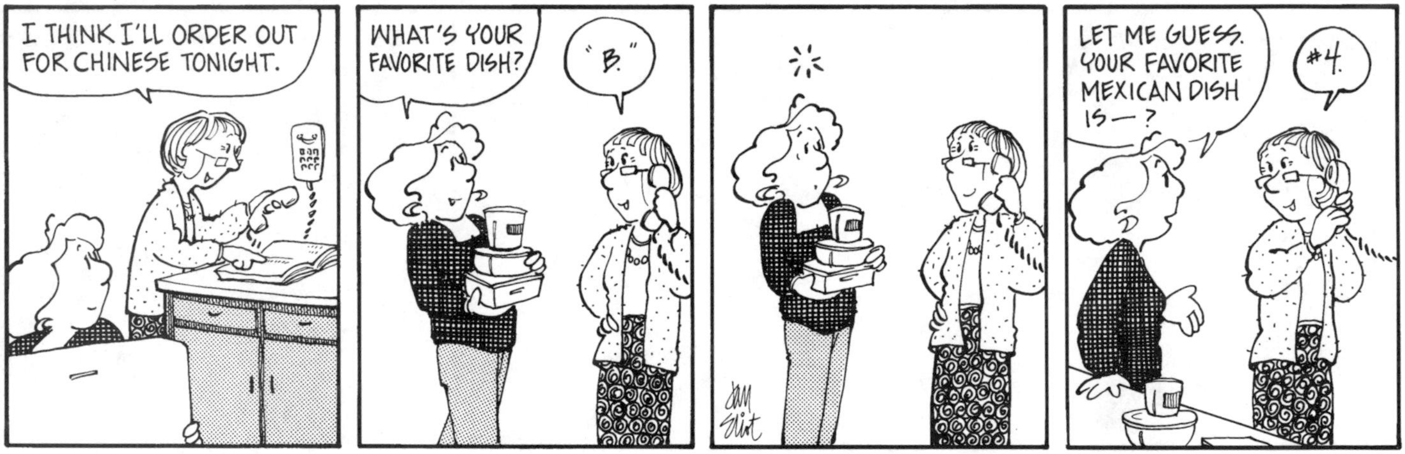
I THINK I'LL ORDER OUT FOR CHINESE TONIGHT.
WHAT'S YOUR FAVORITE DISH?
"B."
LET ME GUESS. YOUR FAVORITE MEXICAN DISH IS—?
#4.

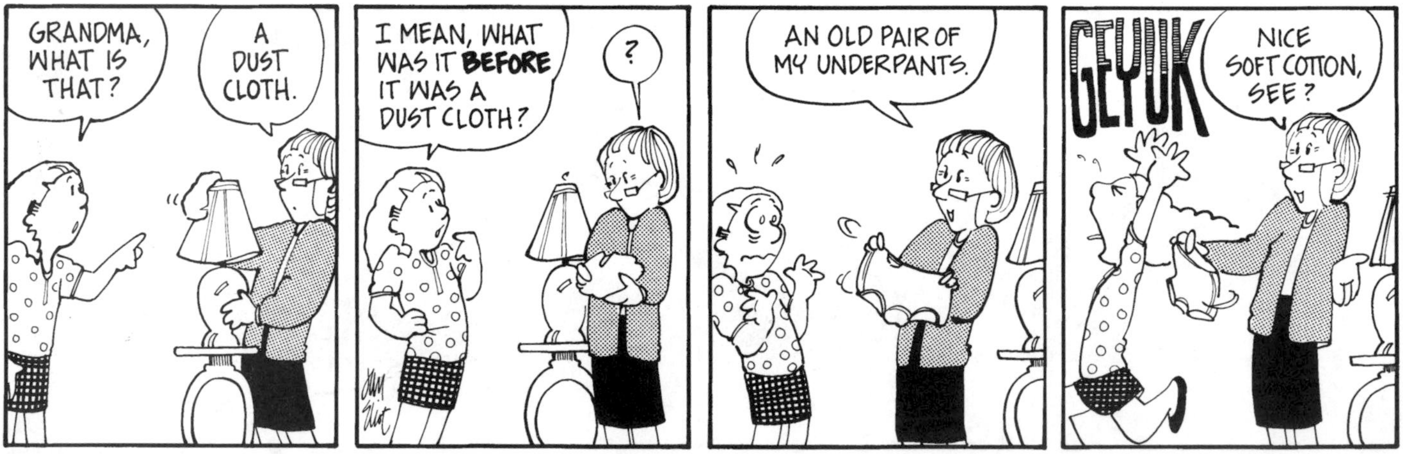
GRANDMA, WHAT IS THAT?
A DUST CLOTH.
I MEAN, WHAT WAS IT **BEFORE** IT WAS A DUST CLOTH?
?
AN OLD PAIR OF MY UNDERPANTS.
GEYUK
NICE SOFT COTTON, SEE?

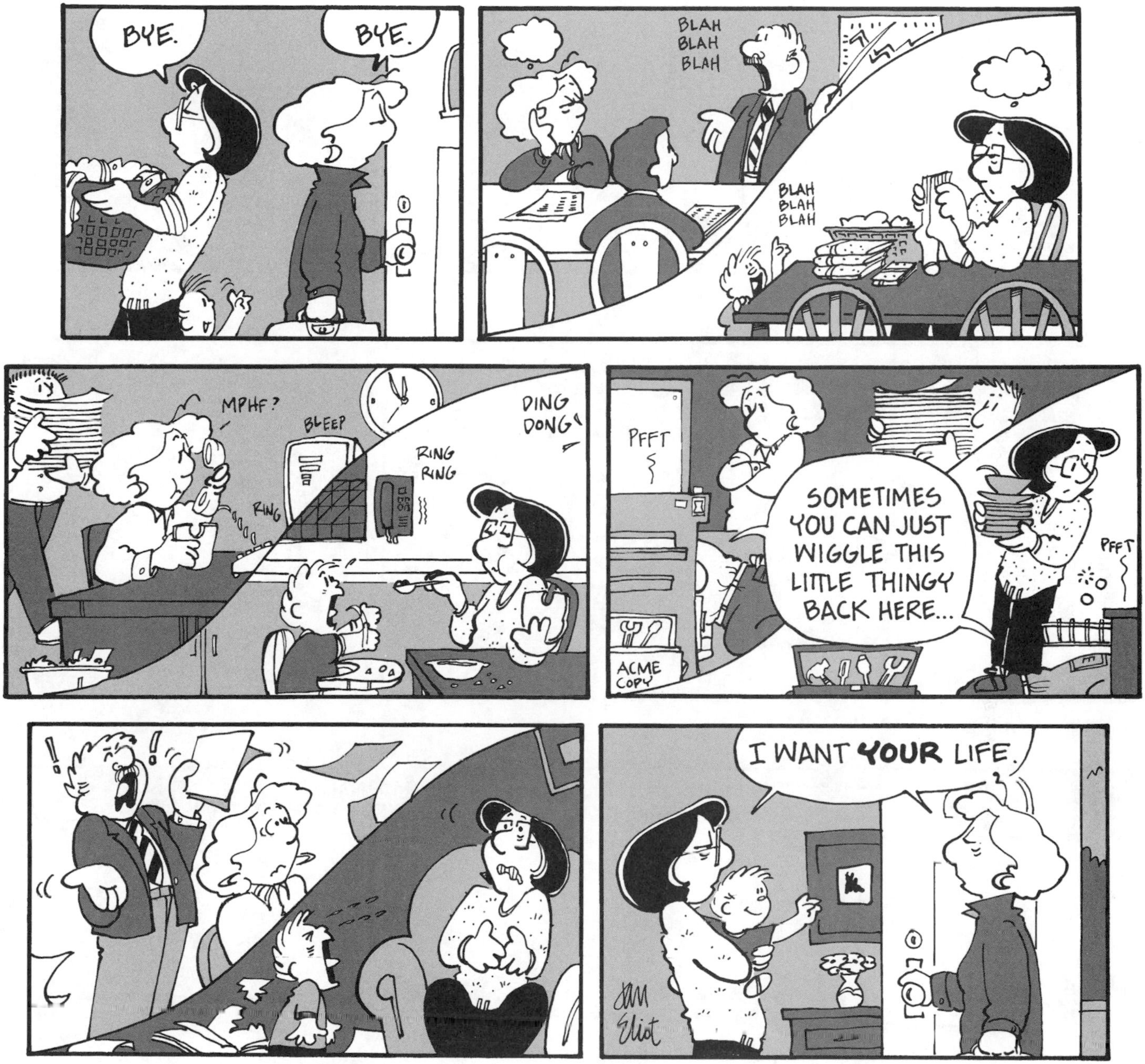
BYE.
BYE.
BLAH
BLAH
BLAH
BLAH
BLAH
BLAH
MPHF?
BLEEP
RING
DING
DONG
RING
RING
PFFT
SOMETIMES YOU CAN JUST WIGGLE THIS LITTLE THINGY BACK HERE...
PFFT
ACME
COPY
I WANT **YOUR** LIFE.
Jan Eliot

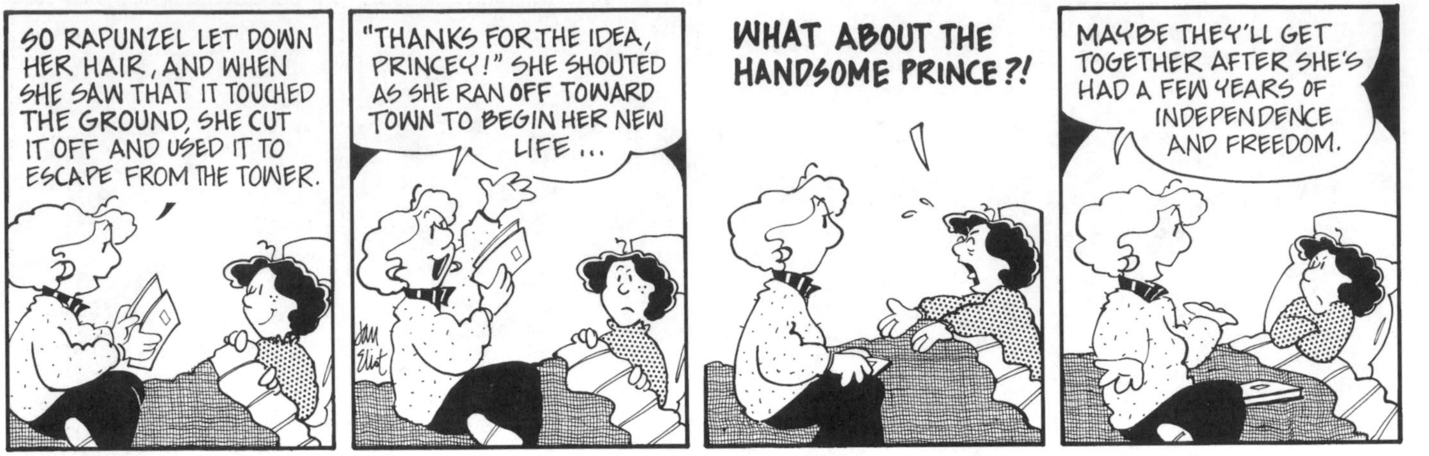
SO RAPUNZEL LET DOWN HER HAIR, AND WHEN SHE SAW THAT IT TOUCHED THE GROUND, SHE CUT IT OFF AND USED IT TO ESCAPE FROM THE TOWER.
"THANKS FOR THE IDEA, PRINCEY!" SHE SHOUTED AS SHE RAN OFF TOWARD TOWN TO BEGIN HER NEW LIFE ...
WHAT ABOUT THE HANDSOME PRINCE?!
MAYBE THEY'LL GET TOGETHER AFTER SHE'S HAD A FEW YEARS OF INDEPENDENCE AND FREEDOM.

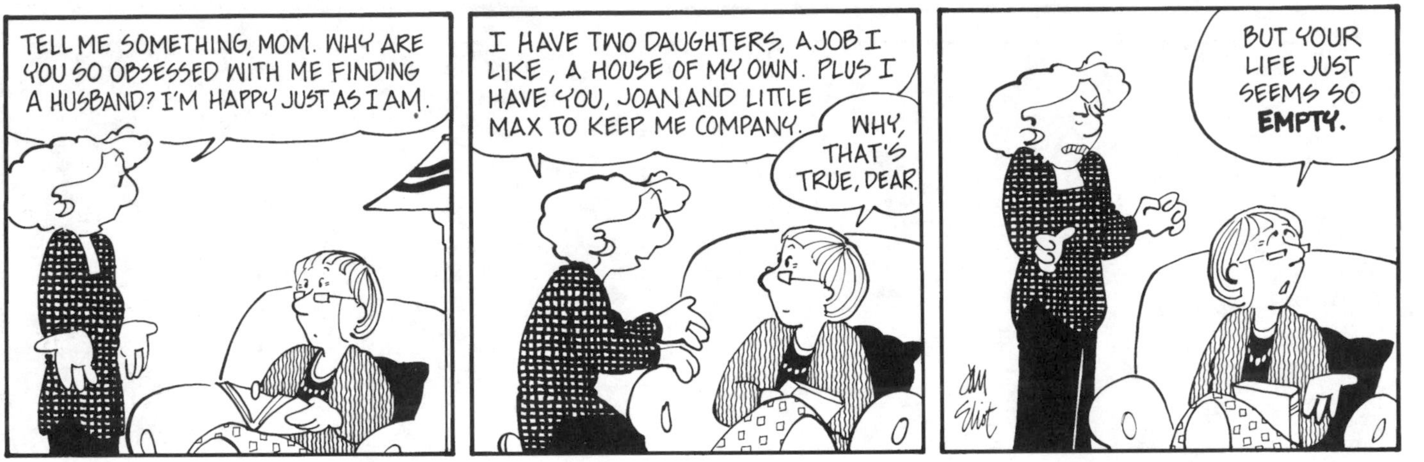
TELL ME SOMETHING, MOM. WHY ARE YOU SO OBSESSED WITH ME FINDING A HUSBAND? I'M HAPPY JUST AS I AM.
I HAVE TWO DAUGHTERS, A JOB I LIKE, A HOUSE OF MY OWN. PLUS I HAVE YOU, JOAN AND LITTLE MAX TO KEEP ME COMPANY.
WHY, THAT'S TRUE, DEAR.
BUT YOUR LIFE JUST SEEMS SO EMPTY.

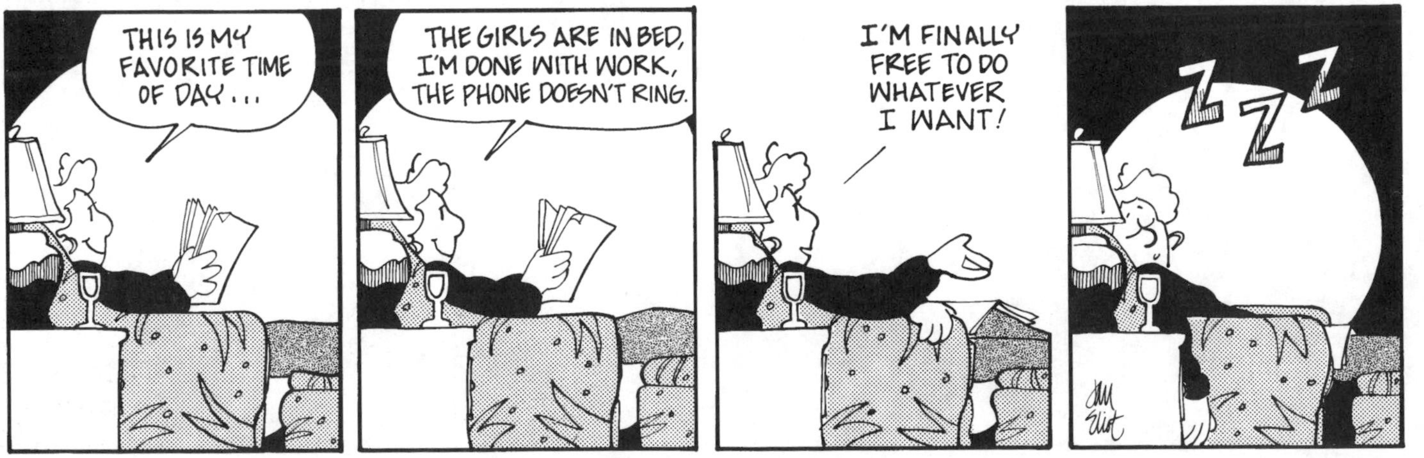
THIS IS MY FAVORITE TIME OF DAY...
THE GIRLS ARE IN BED, I'M DONE WITH WORK, THE PHONE DOESN'T RING.
I'M FINALLY FREE TO DO WHATEVER I WANT!
ZZZ

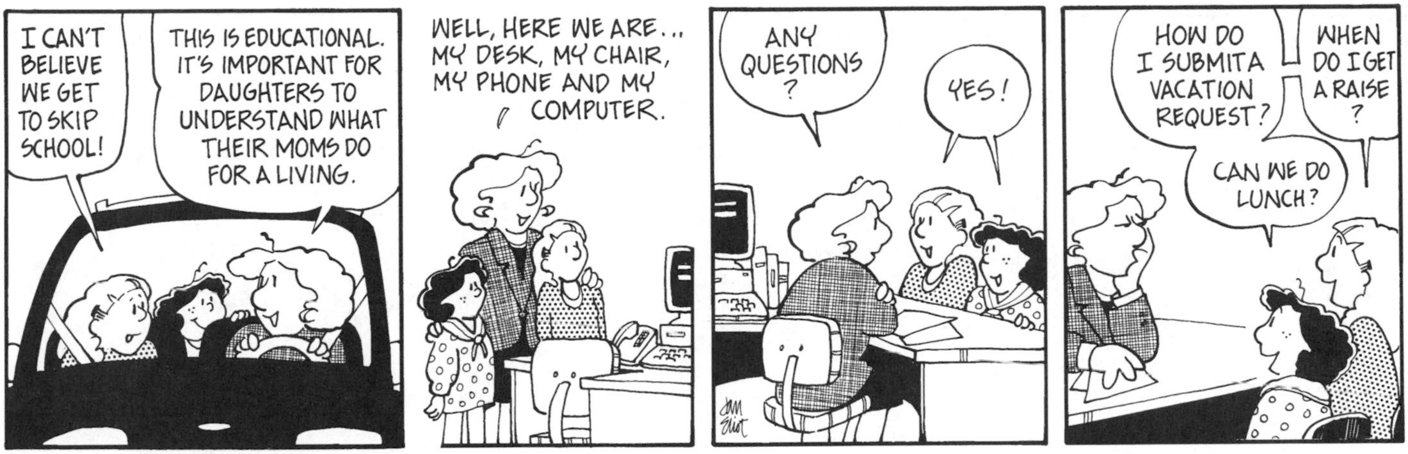
I CAN'T BELIEVE WE GET TO SKIP SCHOOL!
THIS IS EDUCATIONAL. IT'S IMPORTANT FOR DAUGHTERS TO UNDERSTAND WHAT THEIR MOMS DO FOR A LIVING.
WELL, HERE WE ARE... MY DESK, MY CHAIR, MY PHONE AND MY COMPUTER.
ANY QUESTIONS?
YES!
HOW DO I SUBMIT A VACATION REQUEST?
WHEN DO I GET A RAISE?
CAN WE DO LUNCH?

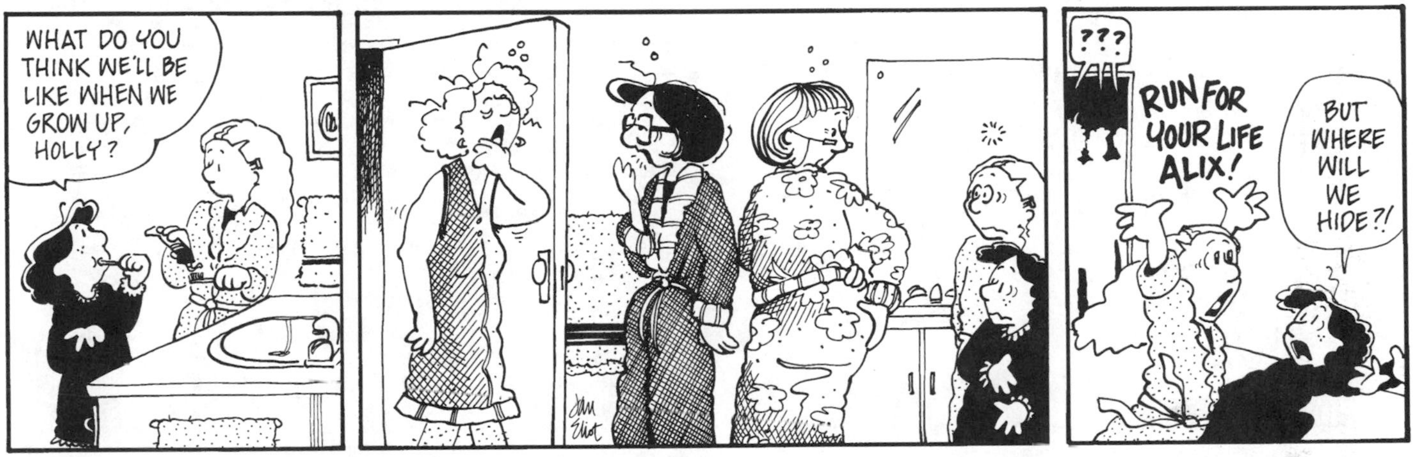
WHAT DO YOU THINK WE'LL BE LIKE WHEN WE GROW UP, HOLLY?
???
RUN FOR YOUR LIFE ALIX!
BUT WHERE WILL WE HIDE?!

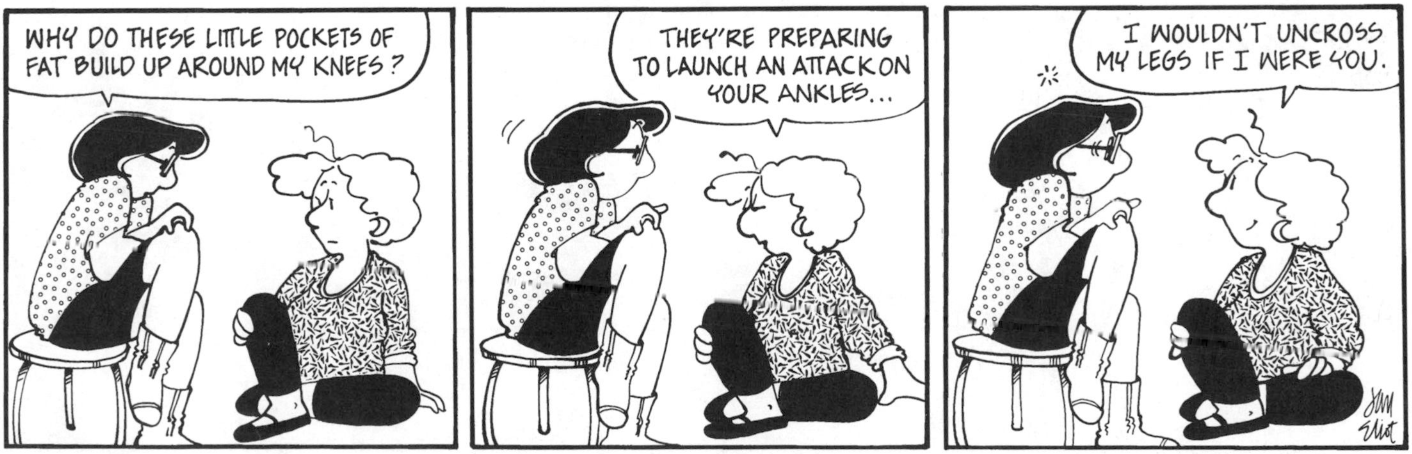
WHY DO THESE LITTLE POCKETS OF FAT BUILD UP AROUND MY KNEES?
THEY'RE PREPARING TO LAUNCH AN ATTACK ON YOUR ANKLES...
I WOULDN'T UNCROSS MY LEGS IF I WERE YOU.

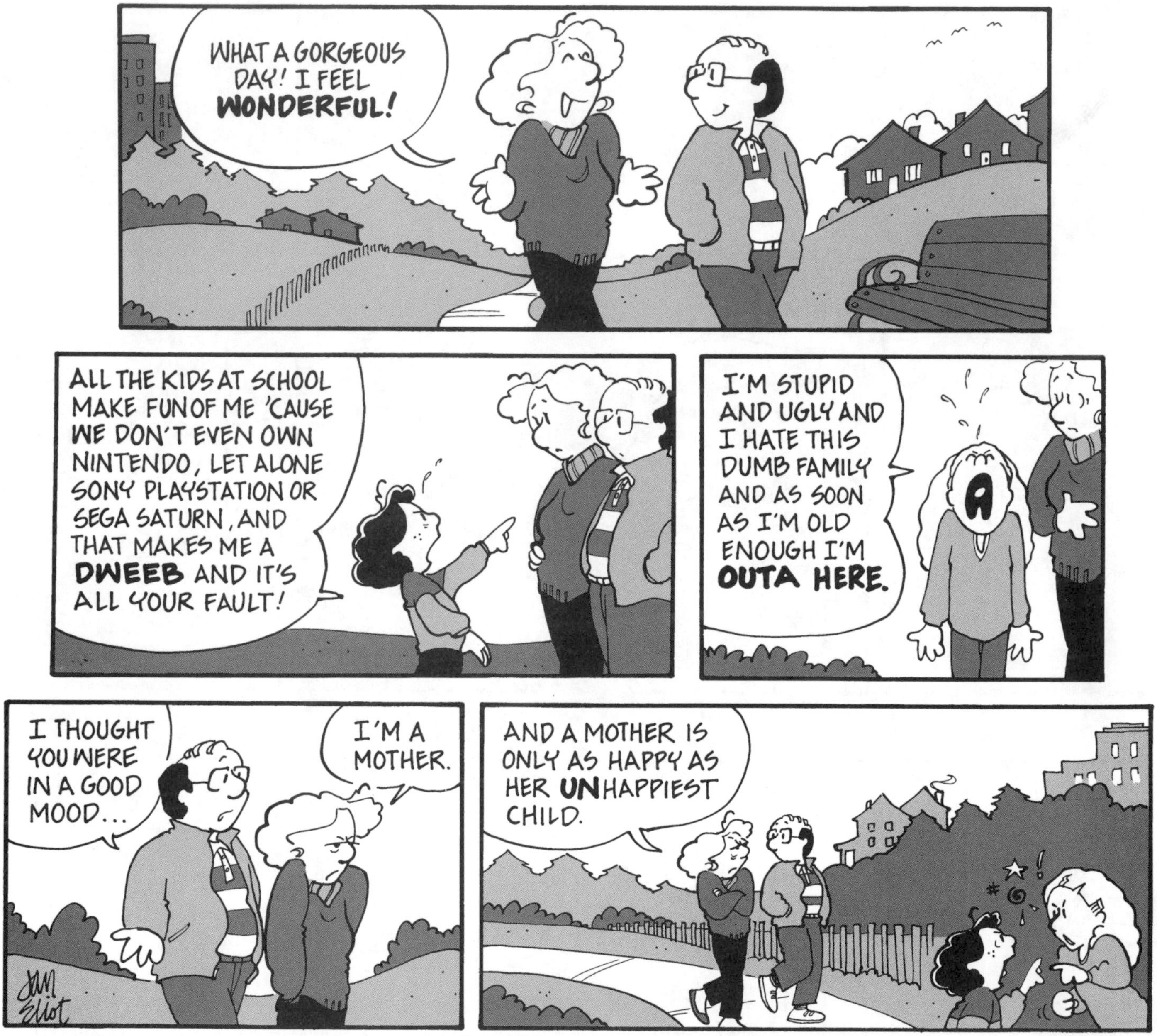
WHAT A GORGEOUS DAY! I FEEL WONDERFUL!
ALL THE KIDS AT SCHOOL MAKE FUN OF ME 'CAUSE WE DON'T EVEN OWN NINTENDO, LET ALONE SONY PLAYSTATION OR SEGA SATURN, AND THAT MAKES ME A DWEEB AND IT'S ALL YOUR FAULT!
I'M STUPID AND UGLY AND I HATE THIS DUMB FAMILY AND AS SOON AS I'M OLD ENOUGH I'M OUTA HERE.
I THOUGHT YOU WERE IN A GOOD MOOD...
I'M A MOTHER.
AND A MOTHER IS ONLY AS HAPPY AS HER UNHAPPIEST CHILD.

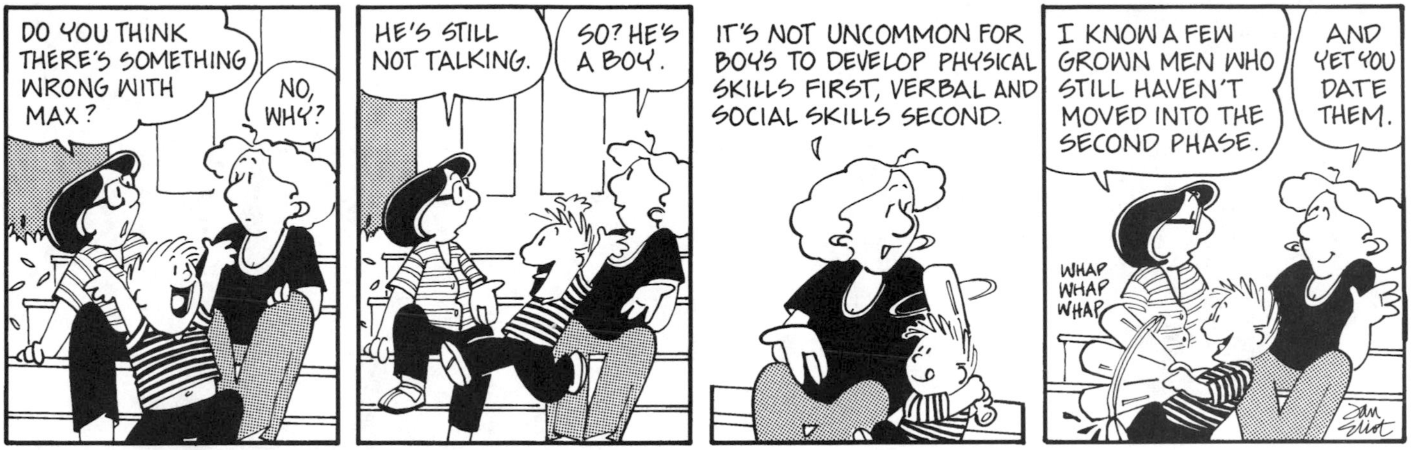
DO YOU THINK THERE'S SOMETHING WRONG WITH MAX?
NO, WHY?
HE'S STILL NOT TALKING.
SO? HE'S A BOY.
IT'S NOT UNCOMMON FOR BOYS TO DEVELOP PHYSICAL SKILLS FIRST, VERBAL AND SOCIAL SKILLS SECOND.
WHAP WHAP WHAP
I KNOW A FEW GROWN MEN WHO STILL HAVEN'T MOVED INTO THE SECOND PHASE.
AND YET YOU DATE THEM.

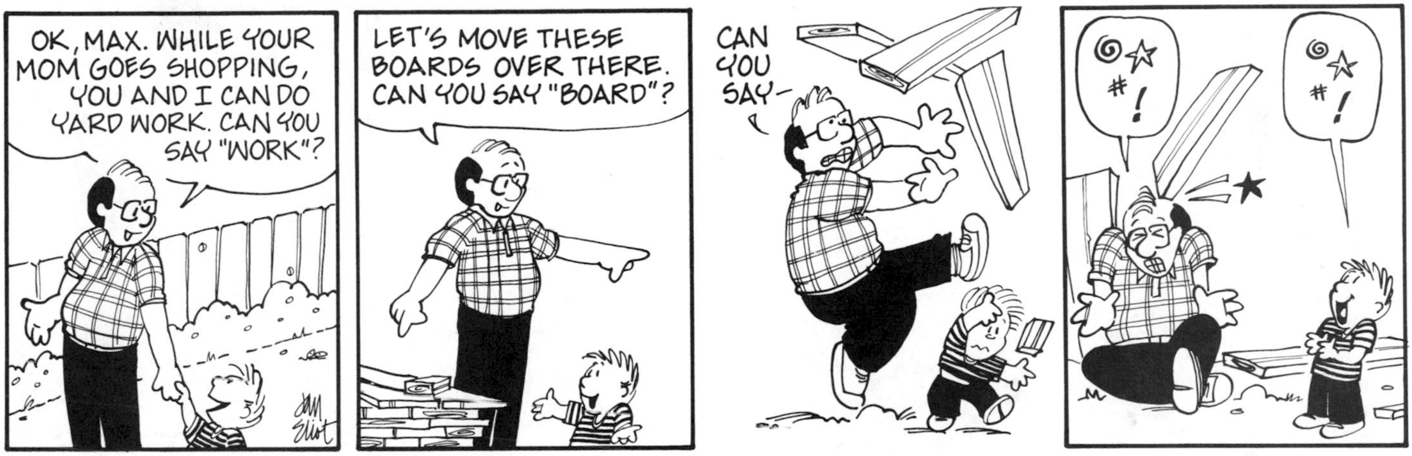
OK, MAX. WHILE YOUR MOM GOES SHOPPING, YOU AND I CAN DO YARD WORK. CAN YOU SAY "WORK"?
LET'S MOVE THESE BOARDS OVER THERE. CAN YOU SAY "BOARD"?
CAN YOU SAY—
!
!

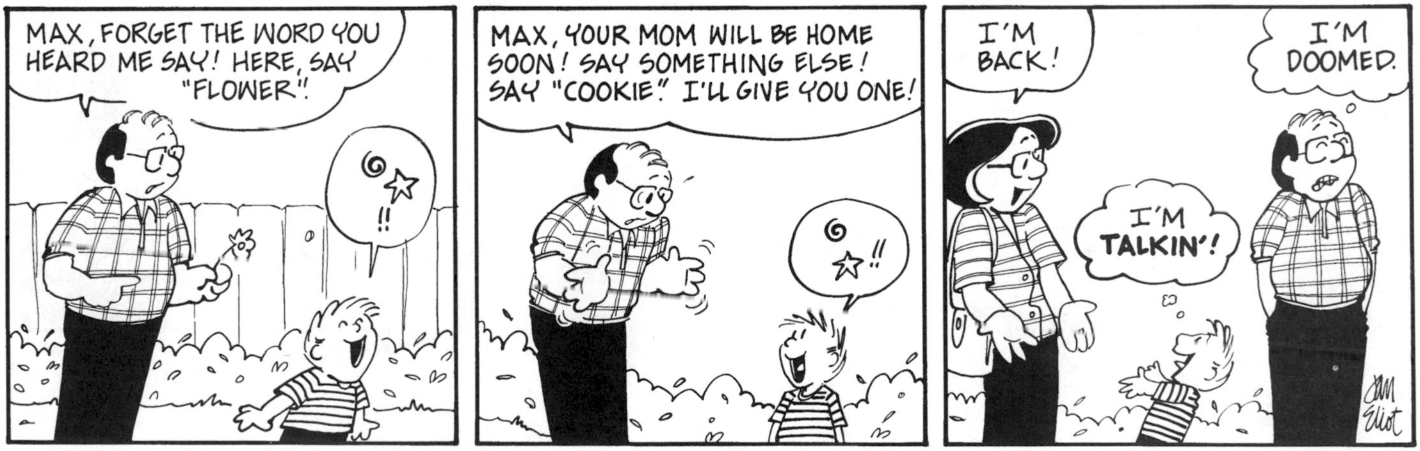
MAX, FORGET THE WORD YOU HEARD ME SAY! HERE, SAY "FLOWER".
!!
MAX, YOUR MOM WILL BE HOME SOON! SAY SOMETHING ELSE! SAY "COOKIE." I'LL GIVE YOU ONE!
!!
I'M BACK!
I'M DOOMED.
I'M **TALKIN'!**

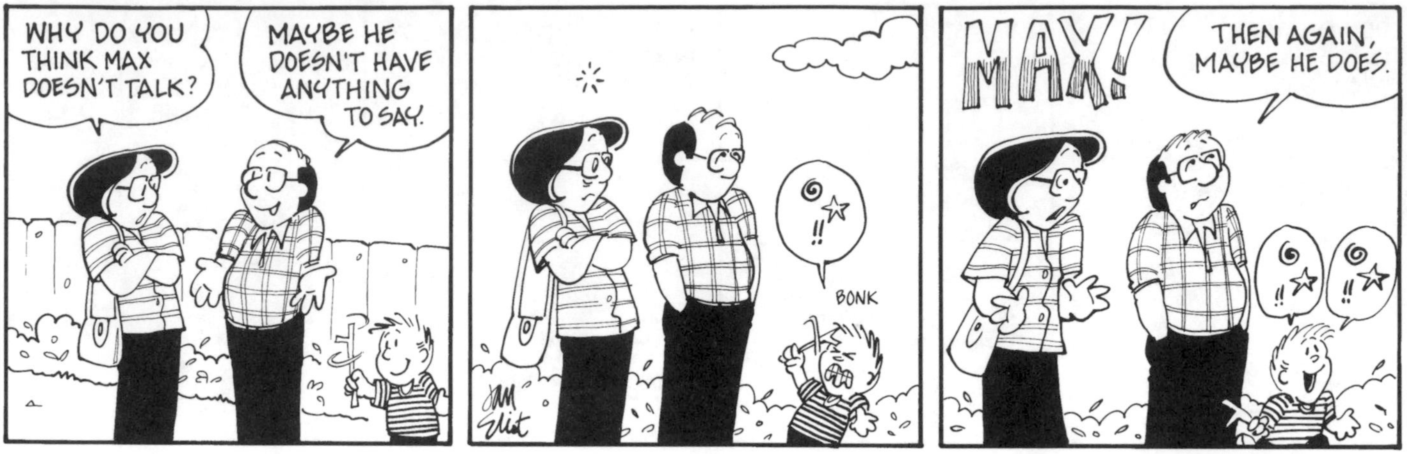
WHY DO YOU THINK MAX DOESN'T TALK?
MAYBE HE DOESN'T HAVE ANYTHING TO SAY.
!!
BONK
MAX!
THEN AGAIN, MAYBE HE DOES.
!!
!!

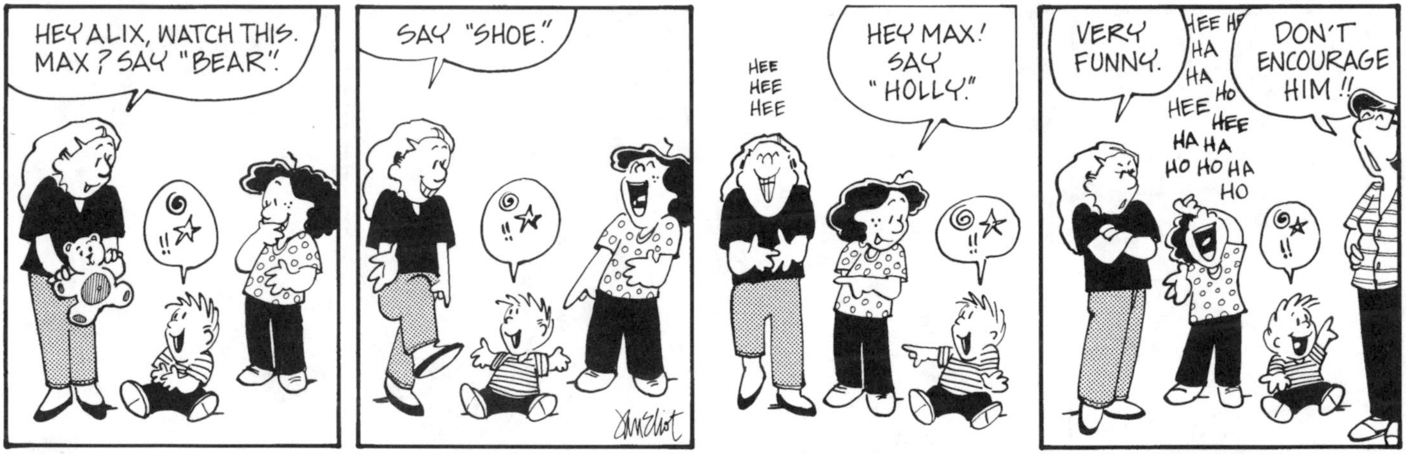
HEY ALIX, WATCH THIS. MAX? SAY "BEAR".
!!
SAY "SHOE."
!!
HEE HEE HEE
HEY MAX! SAY "HOLLY."
!!
VERY FUNNY.
HEE HA HA HEE HO HEE HA HA HO HO HA HO
DON'T ENCOURAGE HIM!!
!!

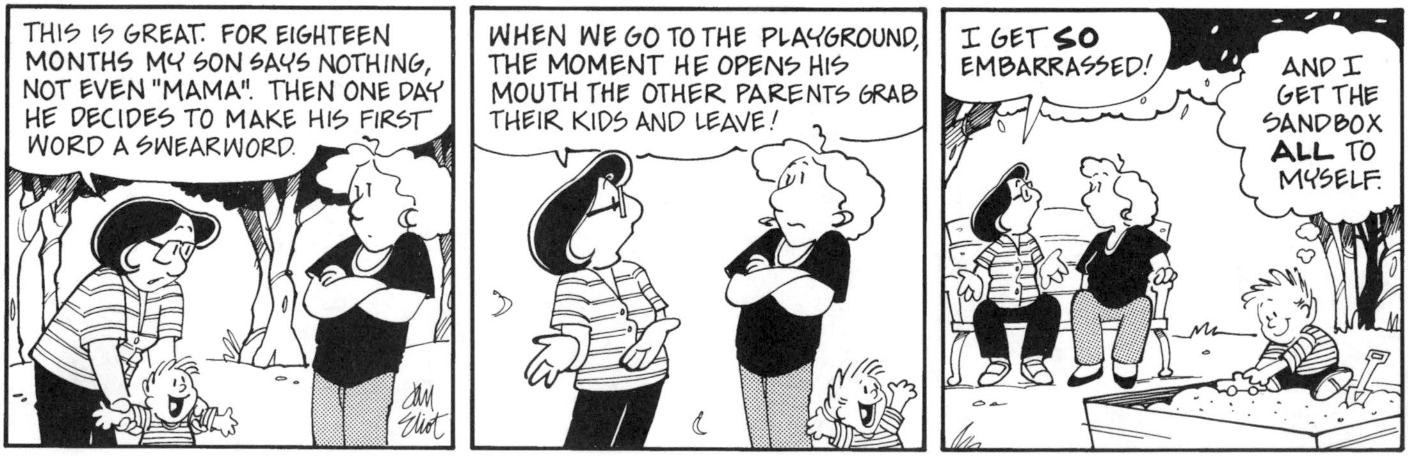
THIS IS GREAT. FOR EIGHTEEN MONTHS MY SON SAYS NOTHING, NOT EVEN "MAMA". THEN ONE DAY HE DECIDES TO MAKE HIS FIRST WORD A SWEARWORD.
WHEN WE GO TO THE PLAYGROUND, THE MOMENT HE OPENS HIS MOUTH THE OTHER PARENTS GRAB THEIR KIDS AND LEAVE!
I GET SO EMBARRASSED!
AND I GET THE SANDBOX ALL TO MYSELF.

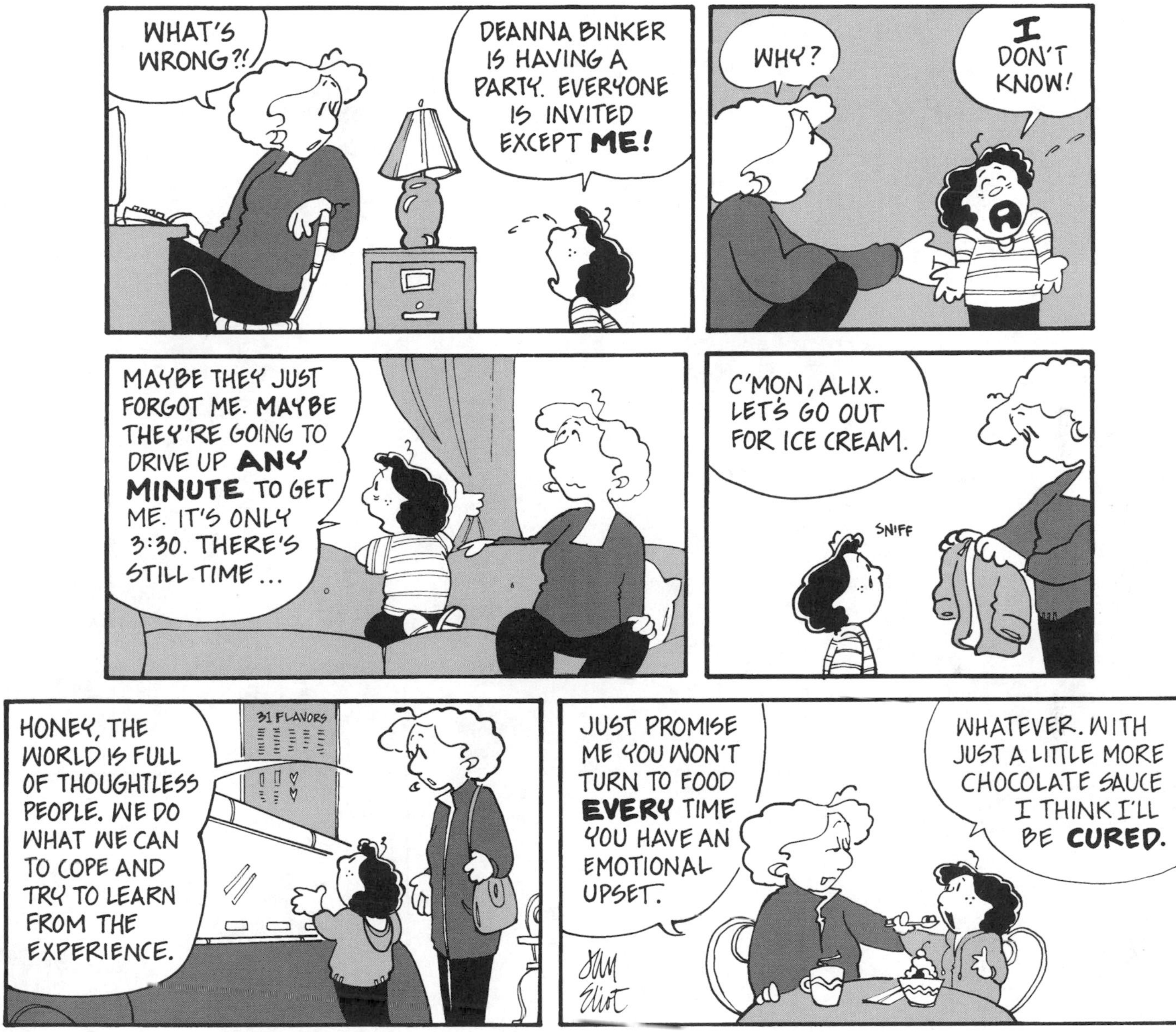

WHAT'S WRONG?!
DEANNA BINKER IS HAVING A PARTY. EVERYONE IS INVITED EXCEPT **ME!**
WHY?
I DON'T KNOW!
MAYBE THEY JUST FORGOT ME. **MAYBE** THEY'RE GOING TO DRIVE UP **ANY MINUTE** TO GET ME. IT'S ONLY 3:30. THERE'S STILL TIME ...
C'MON, ALIX. LET'S GO OUT FOR ICE CREAM.
SNIFF
31 FLAVORS
HONEY, THE WORLD IS FULL OF THOUGHTLESS PEOPLE. WE DO WHAT WE CAN TO COPE AND TRY TO LEARN FROM THE EXPERIENCE.
JUST PROMISE ME YOU WON'T TURN TO FOOD **EVERY** TIME YOU HAVE AN EMOTIONAL UPSET.
WHATEVER. WITH JUST A LITTLE MORE CHOCOLATE SAUCE I THINK I'LL BE **CURED**.

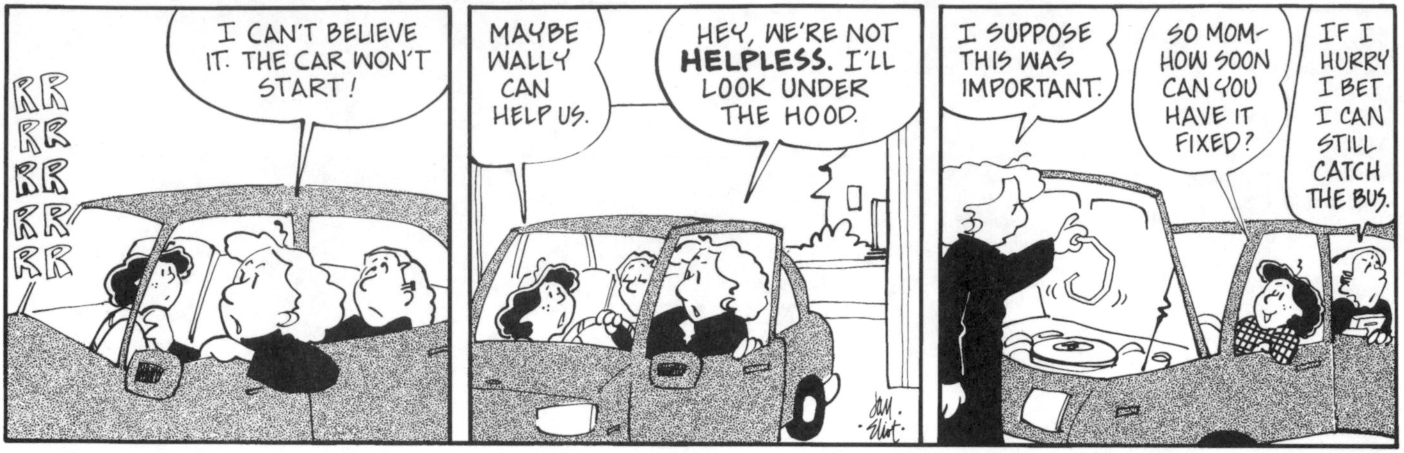
RR RR RR RR RR
I CAN'T BELIEVE IT. THE CAR WON'T START!
MAYBE WALLY CAN HELP US.
HEY, WE'RE NOT **HELPLESS.** I'LL LOOK UNDER THE HOOD.
I SUPPOSE THIS WAS IMPORTANT.
SO MOM- HOW SOON CAN YOU HAVE IT FIXED?
IF I HURRY I BET I CAN STILL CATCH THE BUS.

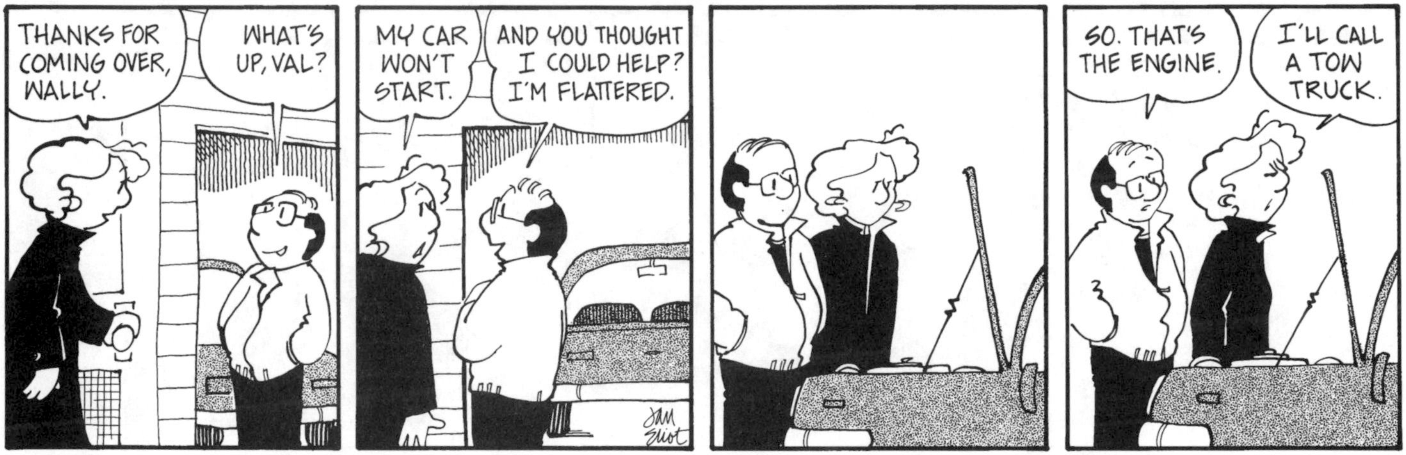
THANKS FOR COMING OVER, WALLY.
WHAT'S UP, VAL?
MY CAR WON'T START.
AND YOU THOUGHT I COULD HELP? I'M FLATTERED.
SO. THAT'S THE ENGINE.
I'LL CALL A TOW TRUCK.

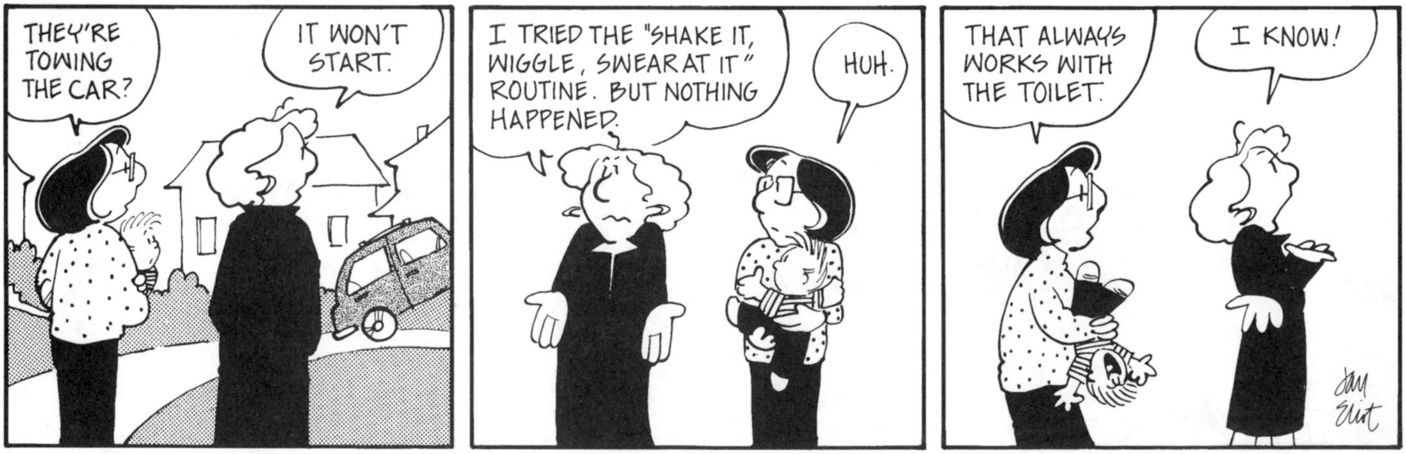
THEY'RE TOWING THE CAR?
IT WON'T START.
I TRIED THE "SHAKE IT, WIGGLE, SWEAR AT IT" ROUTINE. BUT NOTHING HAPPENED.
HUH.
THAT ALWAYS WORKS WITH THE TOILET.
I KNOW!

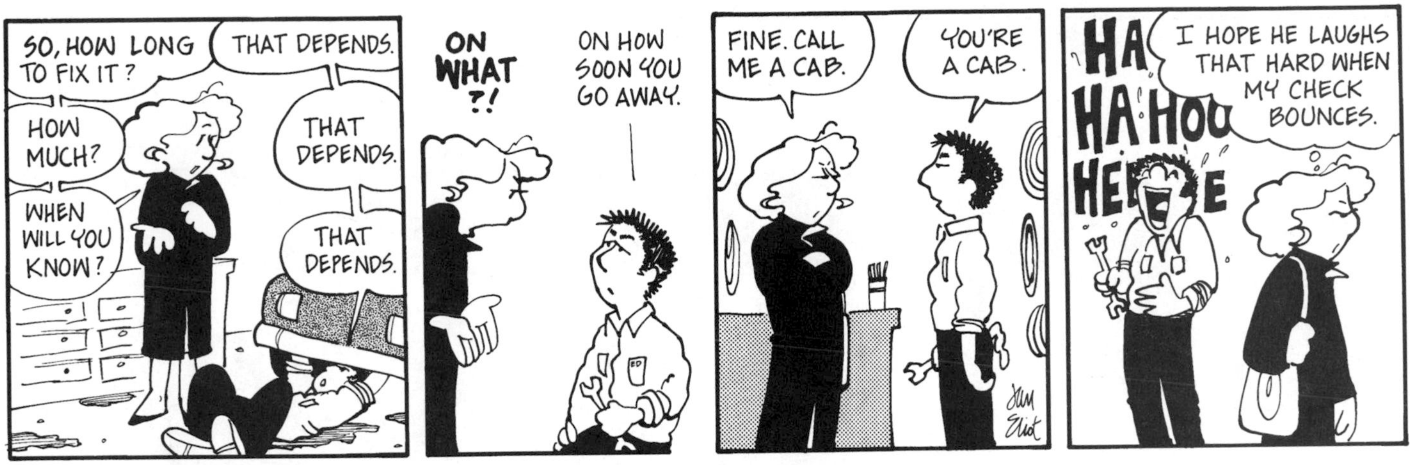
SO, HOW LONG TO FIX IT?
THAT DEPENDS.
HOW MUCH?
THAT DEPENDS.
WHEN WILL YOU KNOW?
THAT DEPENDS.
ON WHAT ?!
ON HOW SOON YOU GO AWAY.
FINE. CALL ME A CAB.
YOU'RE A CAB.
HA
HA HOO
HE E
I HOPE HE LAUGHS THAT HARD WHEN MY CHECK BOUNCES.

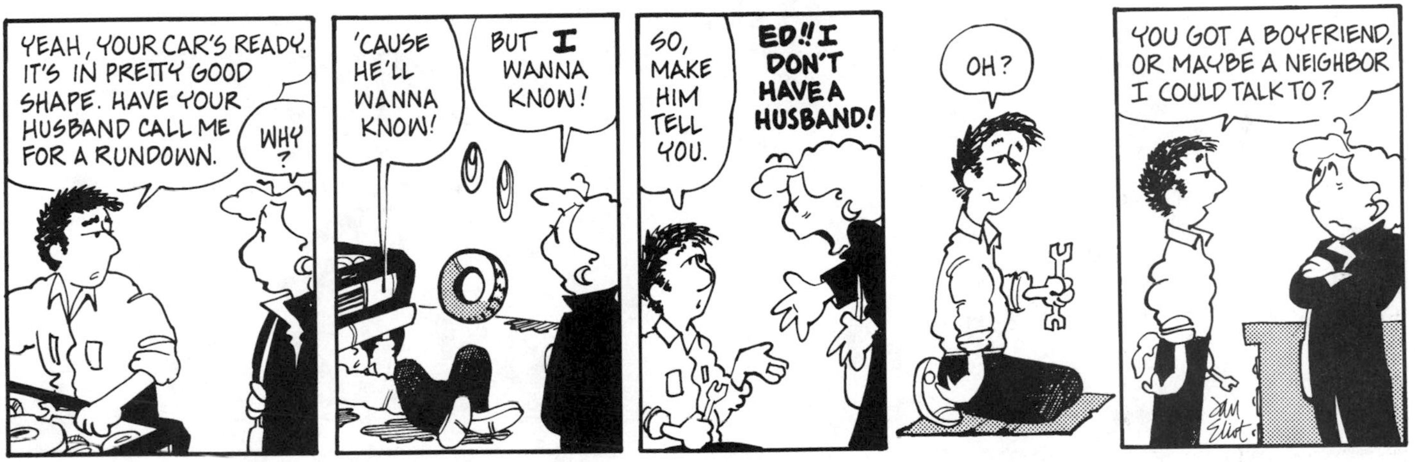
YEAH, YOUR CAR'S READY. IT'S IN PRETTY GOOD SHAPE. HAVE YOUR HUSBAND CALL ME FOR A RUNDOWN.
WHY?
'CAUSE HE'LL WANNA KNOW!
BUT I WANNA KNOW!
SO, MAKE HIM TELL YOU.
ED!! I DON'T HAVE A HUSBAND!
OH?
YOU GOT A BOYFRIEND, OR MAYBE A NEIGHBOR I COULD TALK TO?

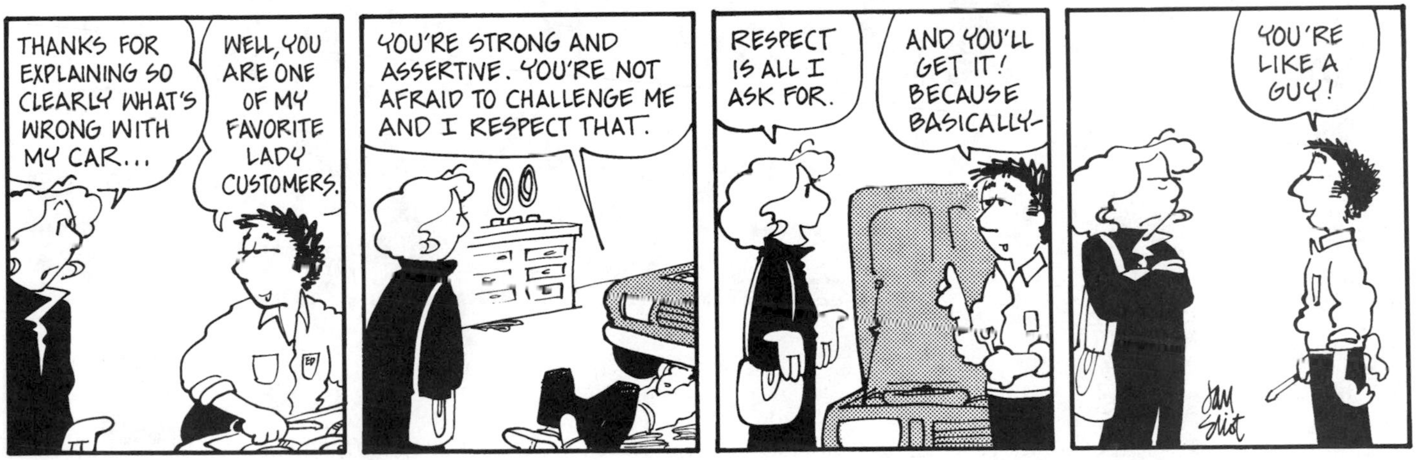
THANKS FOR EXPLAINING SO CLEARLY WHAT'S WRONG WITH MY CAR...
WELL, YOU ARE ONE OF MY FAVORITE LADY CUSTOMERS.
YOU'RE STRONG AND ASSERTIVE. YOU'RE NOT AFRAID TO CHALLENGE ME AND I RESPECT THAT.
RESPECT IS ALL I ASK FOR.
AND YOU'LL GET IT! BECAUSE BASICALLY-
YOU'RE LIKE A GUY!

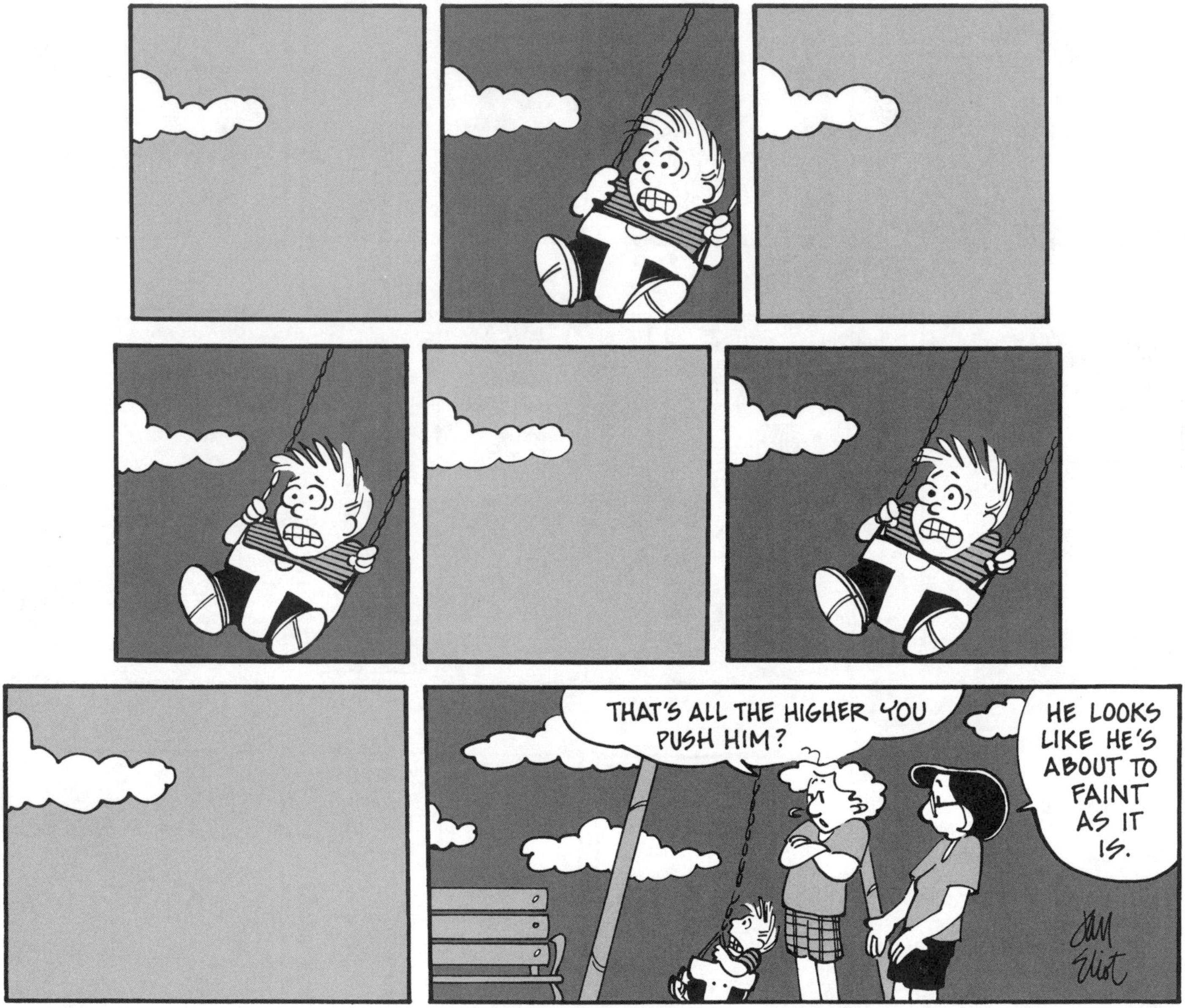
THAT'S ALL THE HIGHER YOU PUSH HIM?
HE LOOKS LIKE HE'S ABOUT TO FAINT AS IT IS.
Jan Eliot

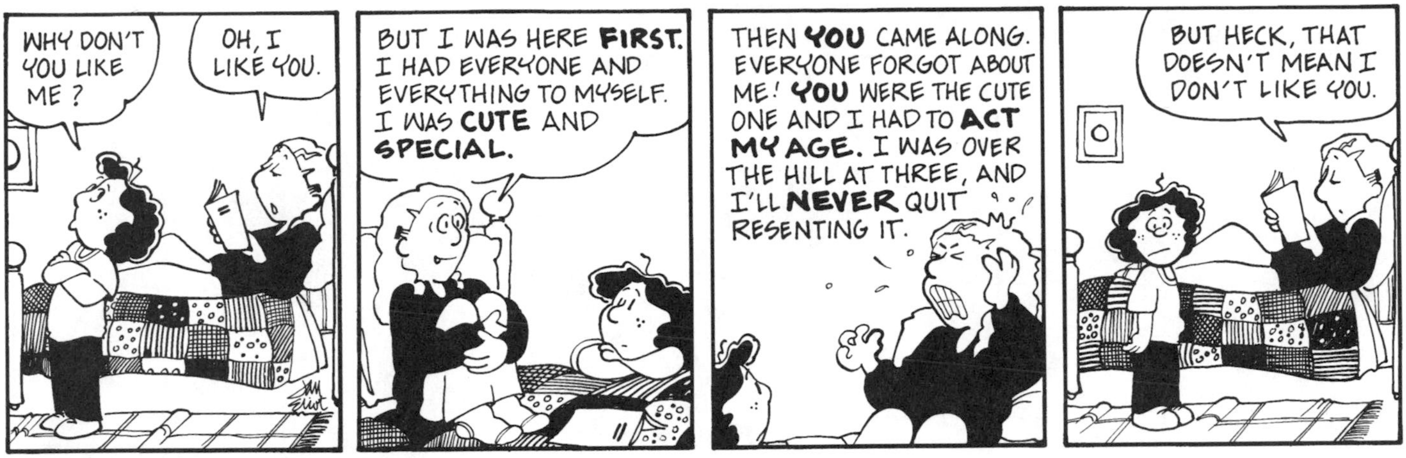
WHY DON'T YOU LIKE ME?
OH, I LIKE YOU.
BUT I WAS HERE FIRST. I HAD EVERYONE AND EVERYTHING TO MYSELF. I WAS CUTE AND SPECIAL.
THEN YOU CAME ALONG. EVERYONE FORGOT ABOUT ME! YOU WERE THE CUTE ONE AND I HAD TO ACT MY AGE. I WAS OVER THE HILL AT THREE, AND I'LL NEVER QUIT RESENTING IT.
BUT HECK, THAT DOESN'T MEAN I DON'T LIKE YOU.

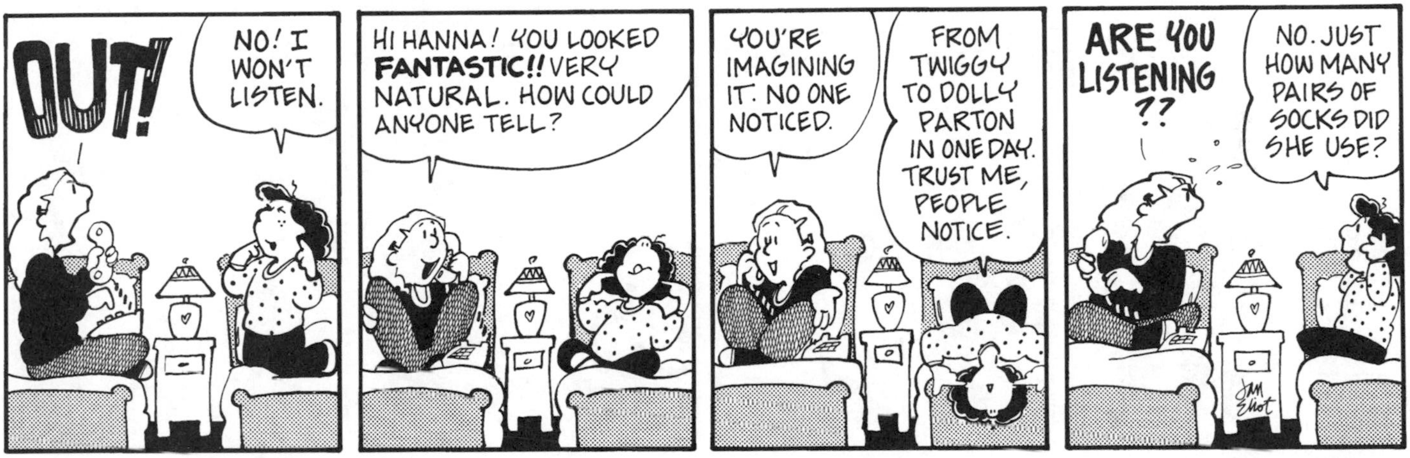
OUT!
NO! I WON'T LISTEN.
HI HANNA! YOU LOOKED FANTASTIC!! VERY NATURAL. HOW COULD ANYONE TELL?
YOU'RE IMAGINING IT. NO ONE NOTICED.
FROM TWIGGY TO DOLLY PARTON IN ONE DAY. TRUST ME, PEOPLE NOTICE.
ARE YOU LISTENING ??
NO. JUST HOW MANY PAIRS OF SOCKS DID SHE USE?

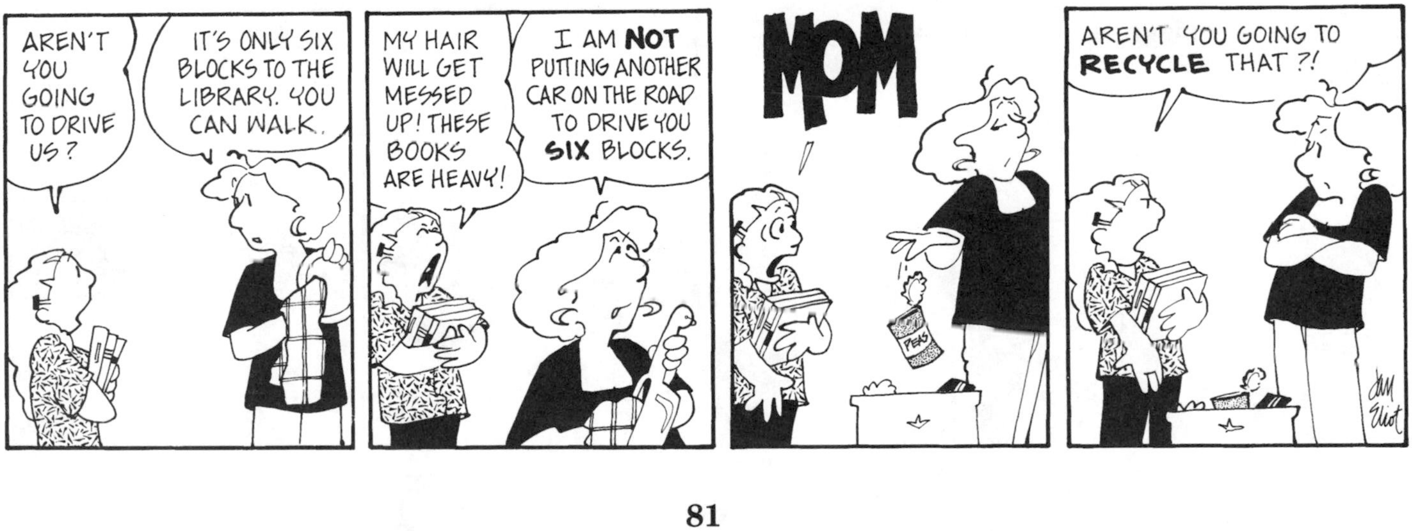
AREN'T YOU GOING TO DRIVE US?
IT'S ONLY SIX BLOCKS TO THE LIBRARY. YOU CAN WALK.
MY HAIR WILL GET MESSED UP! THESE BOOKS ARE HEAVY!
I AM NOT PUTTING ANOTHER CAR ON THE ROAD TO DRIVE YOU SIX BLOCKS.
MOM
PEAS
AREN'T YOU GOING TO RECYCLE THAT?!

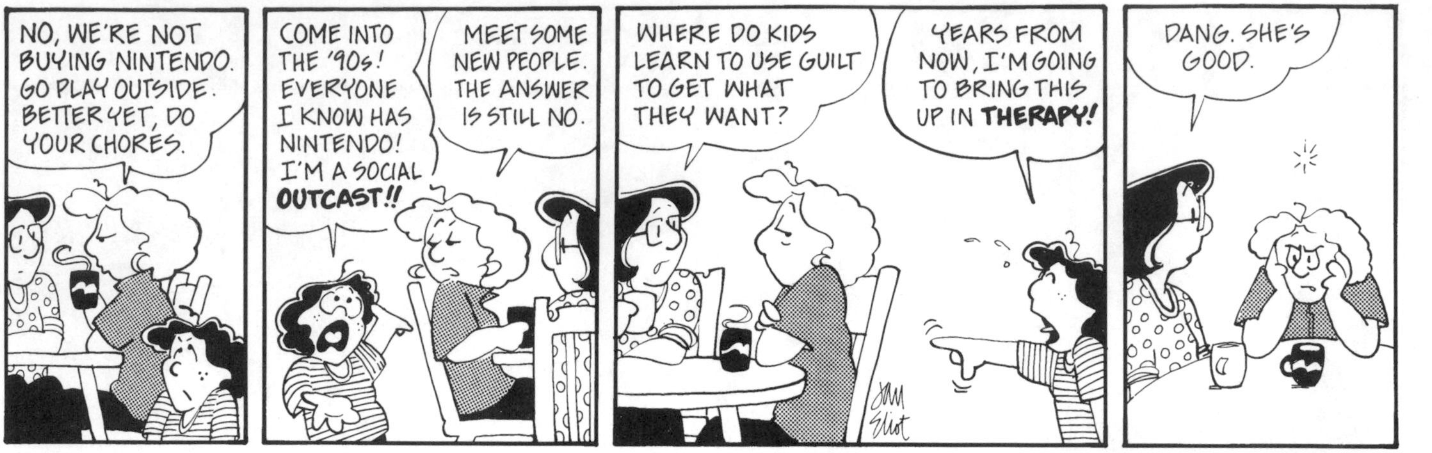
NO, WE'RE NOT BUYING NINTENDO. GO PLAY OUTSIDE. BETTER YET, DO YOUR CHORES.
COME INTO THE '90s! EVERYONE I KNOW HAS NINTENDO! I'M A SOCIAL OUTCAST!!
MEET SOME NEW PEOPLE. THE ANSWER IS STILL NO.
WHERE DO KIDS LEARN TO USE GUILT TO GET WHAT THEY WANT?
YEARS FROM NOW, I'M GOING TO BRING THIS UP IN THERAPY!
DANG. SHE'S GOOD.

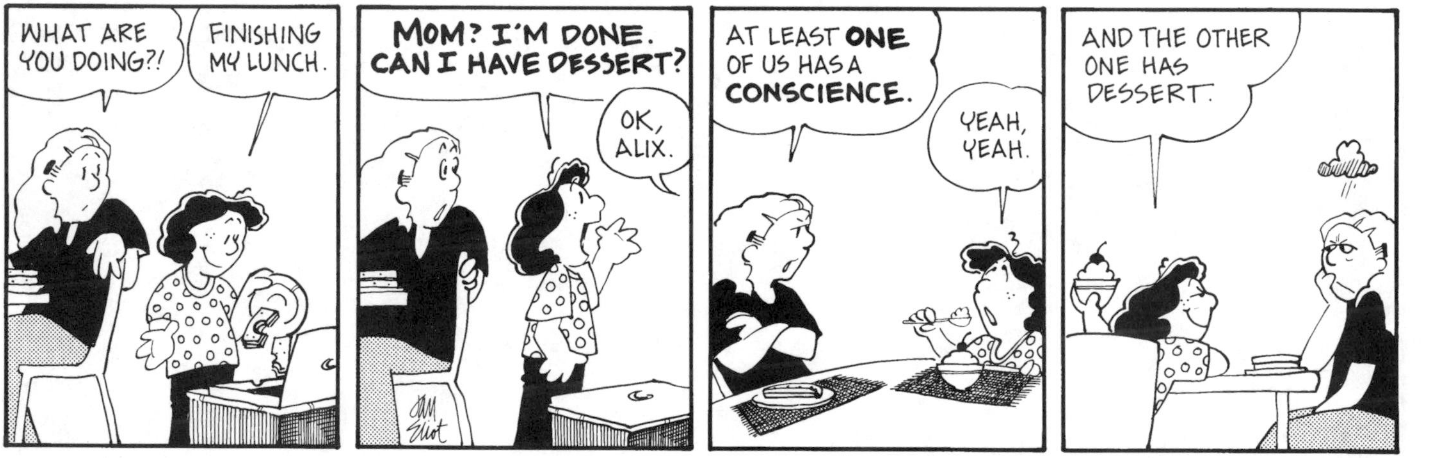
WHAT ARE YOU DOING?!
FINISHING MY LUNCH.
MOM? I'M DONE. CAN I HAVE DESSERT?
OK, ALIX.
AT LEAST ONE OF US HAS A CONSCIENCE.
YEAH, YEAH.
AND THE OTHER ONE HAS DESSERT.

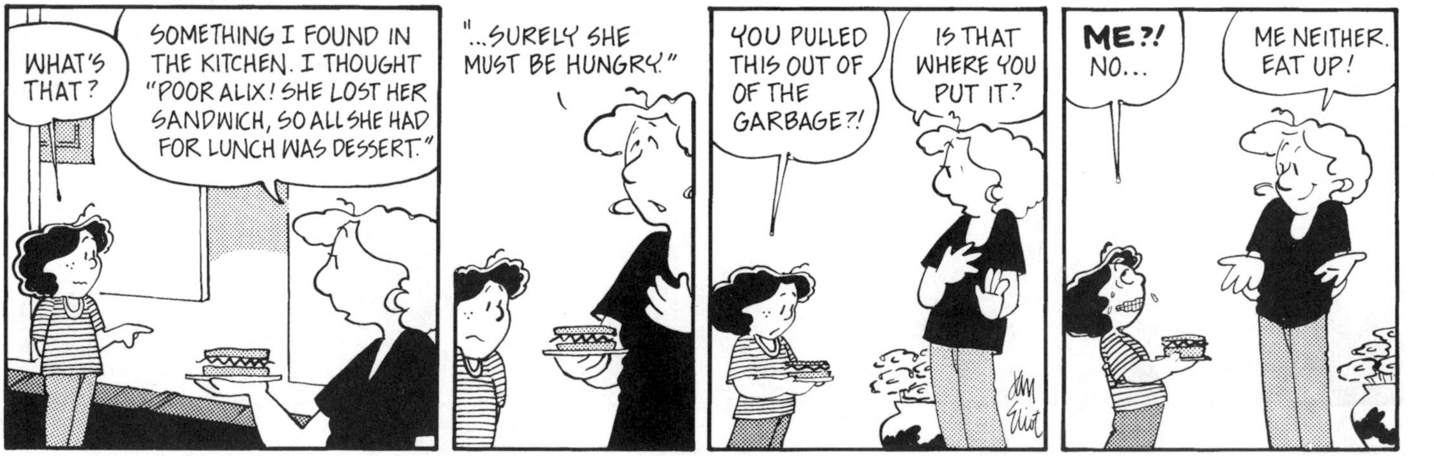
WHAT'S THAT?
SOMETHING I FOUND IN THE KITCHEN. I THOUGHT "POOR ALIX! SHE LOST HER SANDWICH, SO ALL SHE HAD FOR LUNCH WAS DESSERT."
"...SURELY SHE MUST BE HUNGRY."
YOU PULLED THIS OUT OF OF THE GARBAGE?!
IS THAT WHERE YOU PUT IT?
ME?! NO...
ME NEITHER. EAT UP!

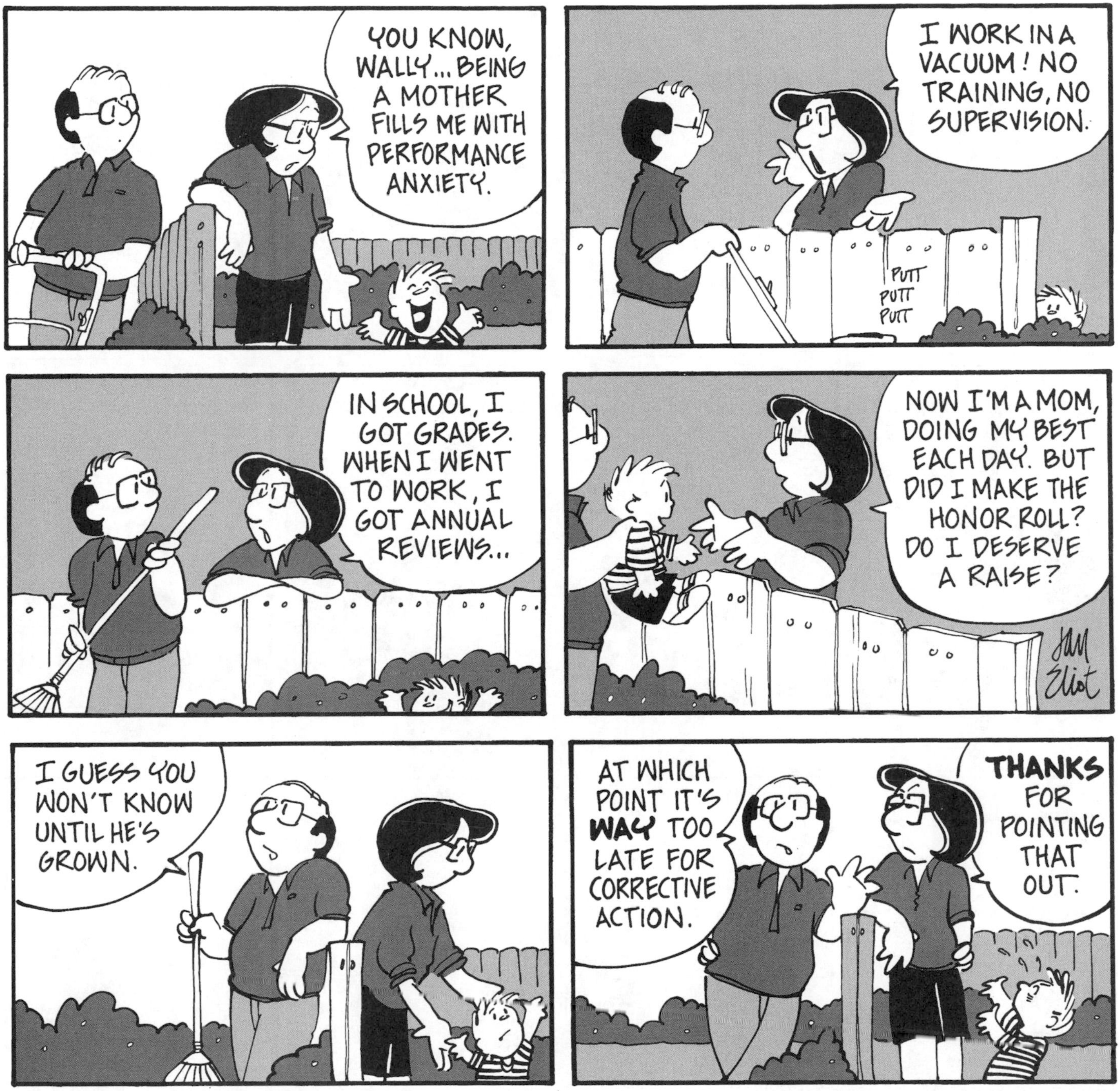
YOU KNOW, WALLY... BEING A MOTHER FILLS ME WITH PERFORMANCE ANXIETY.
I WORK IN A VACUUM! NO TRAINING, NO SUPERVISION.
PUTT PUTT PUTT
IN SCHOOL, I GOT GRADES. WHEN I WENT TO WORK, I GOT ANNUAL REVIEWS...
NOW I'M A MOM, DOING MY BEST EACH DAY. BUT DID I MAKE THE HONOR ROLL? DO I DESERVE A RAISE?
Jan Eliot
I GUESS YOU WON'T KNOW UNTIL HE'S GROWN.
AT WHICH POINT IT'S WAY TOO LATE FOR CORRECTIVE ACTION.
THANKS FOR POINTING THAT OUT.

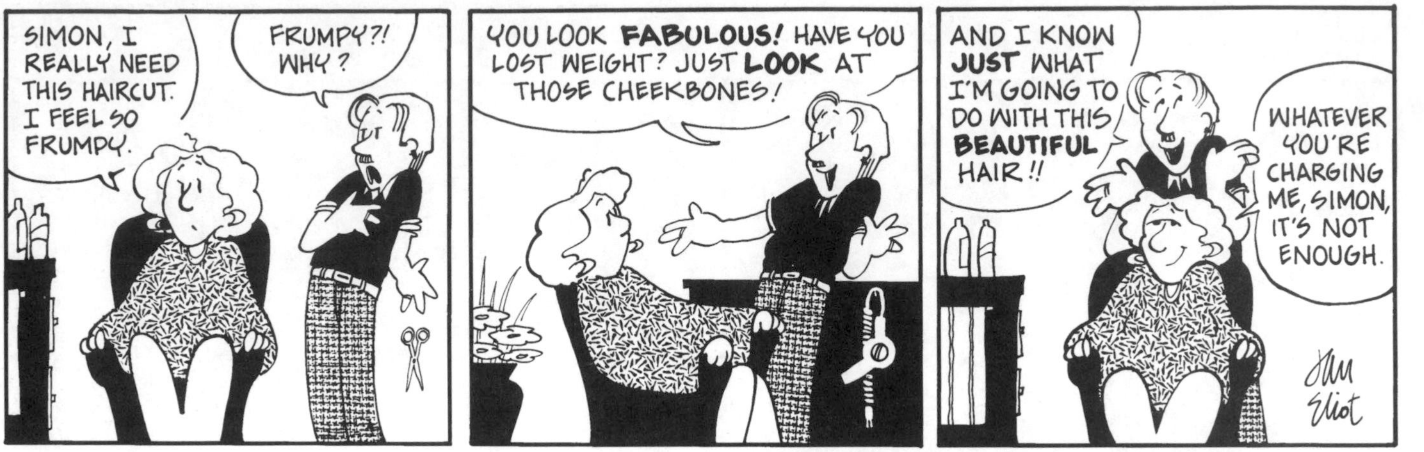
SIMON, I REALLY NEED THIS HAIRCUT. I FEEL SO FRUMPY.
FRUMPY?! WHY?
YOU LOOK **FABULOUS!** HAVE YOU LOST WEIGHT? JUST **LOOK** AT THOSE CHEEKBONES!
AND I KNOW **JUST** WHAT I'M GOING TO DO WITH THIS **BEAUTIFUL** HAIR!!
WHATEVER YOU'RE CHARGING ME, SIMON, IT'S NOT ENOUGH.

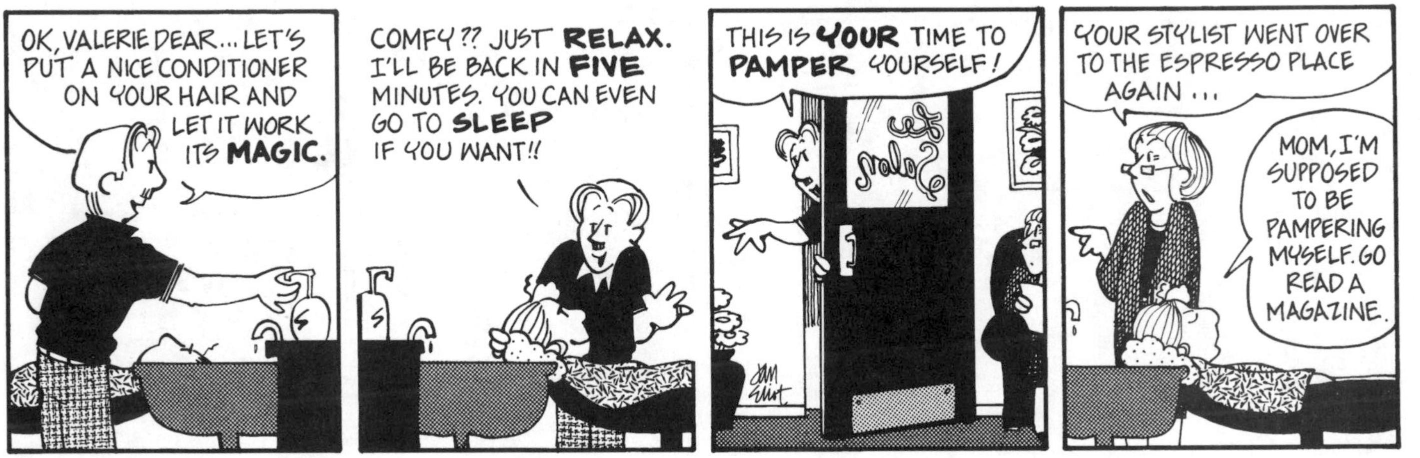
OK, VALERIE DEAR... LET'S PUT A NICE CONDITIONER ON YOUR HAIR AND LET IT WORK ITS **MAGIC.**
COMFY?? JUST **RELAX.** I'LL BE BACK IN **FIVE** MINUTES. YOU CAN EVEN GO TO **SLEEP** IF YOU WANT!!
THIS IS **YOUR** TIME TO **PAMPER** YOURSELF!
YOUR STYLIST WENT OVER TO THE ESPRESSO PLACE AGAIN ...
MOM, I'M SUPPOSED TO BE PAMPERING MYSELF. GO READ A MAGAZINE.

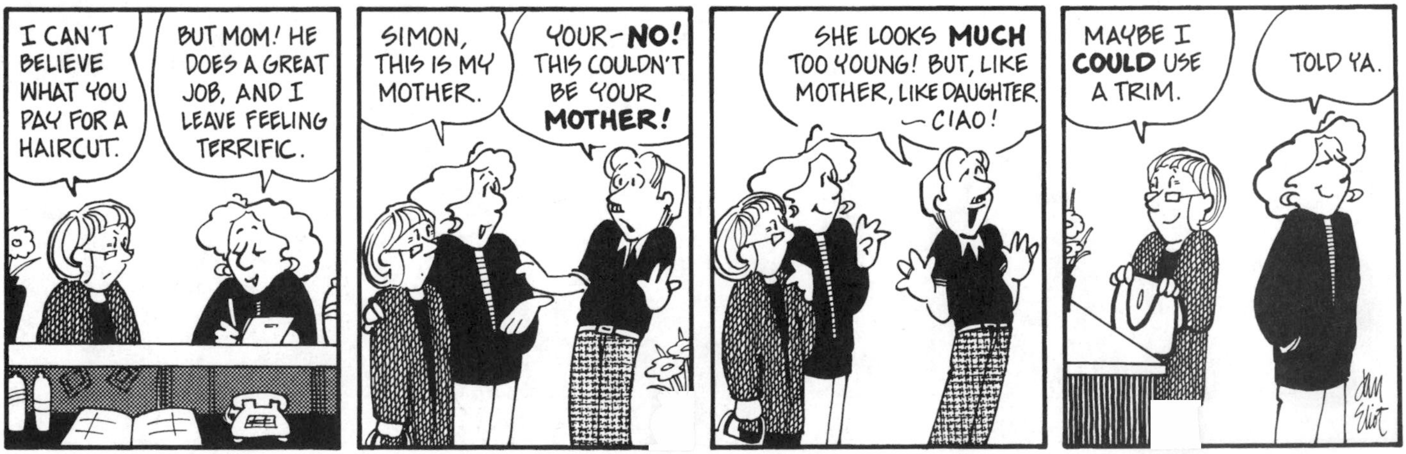
I CAN'T BELIEVE WHAT YOU PAY FOR A HAIRCUT.
BUT MOM! HE DOES A GREAT JOB, AND I LEAVE FEELING TERRIFIC.
SIMON, THIS IS MY MOTHER.
YOUR-**NO!** THIS COULDN'T BE YOUR **MOTHER!**
SHE LOOKS **MUCH** TOO YOUNG! BUT, LIKE MOTHER, LIKE DAUGHTER. —CIAO!
MAYBE I **COULD** USE A TRIM.
TOLD YA.

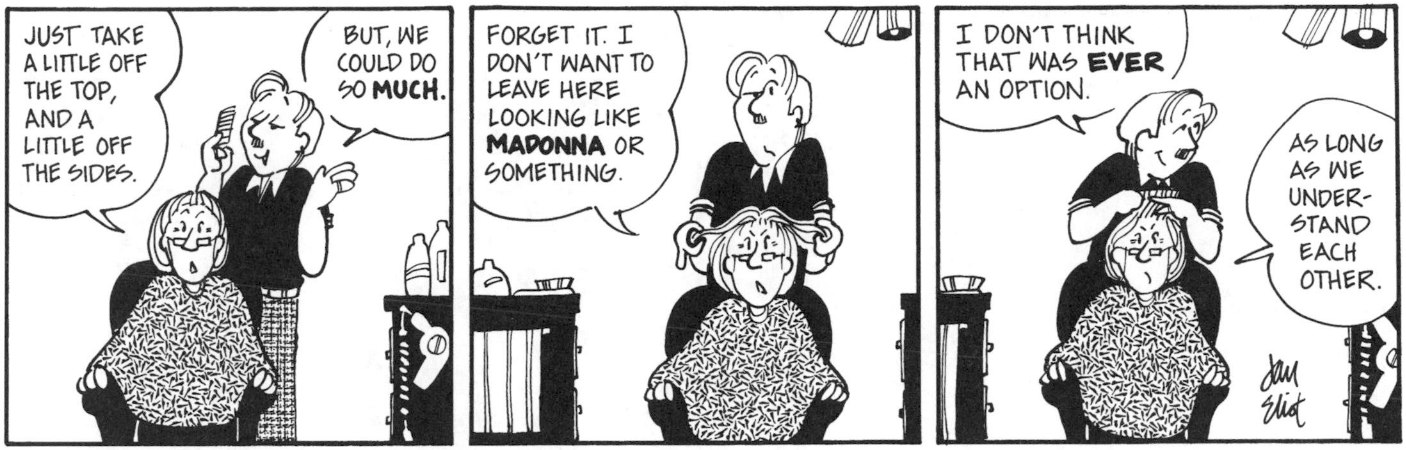
JUST TAKE A LITTLE OFF THE TOP, AND A LITTLE OFF THE SIDES.
BUT, WE COULD DO SO **MUCH**.
FORGET IT. I DON'T WANT TO LEAVE HERE LOOKING LIKE **MADONNA** OR SOMETHING.
I DON'T THINK THAT WAS **EVER** AN OPTION.
AS LONG AS WE UNDER-STAND EACH OTHER.
Jan Eliot

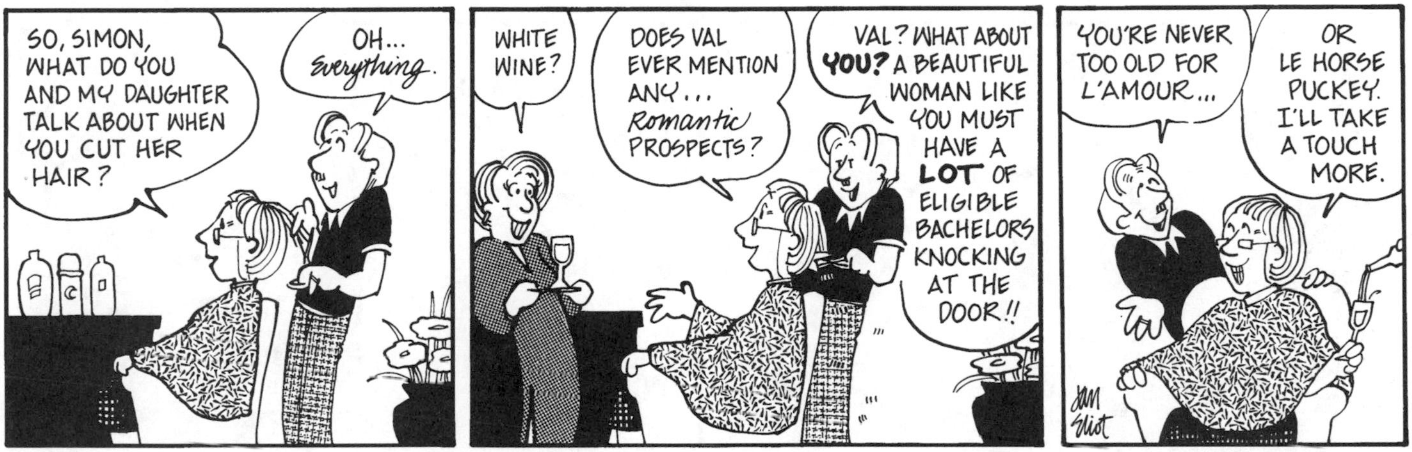
SO, SIMON, WHAT DO YOU AND MY DAUGHTER TALK ABOUT WHEN YOU CUT HER HAIR?
OH... *Everything*.
WHITE WINE?
DOES VAL EVER MENTION ANY... *Romantic* PROSPECTS?
VAL? WHAT ABOUT **YOU?** A BEAUTIFUL WOMAN LIKE YOU MUST HAVE A **LOT** OF ELIGIBLE BACHELORS KNOCKING AT THE DOOR!!
YOU'RE NEVER TOO OLD FOR L'AMOUR...
OR LE HORSE PUCKEY. I'LL TAKE A TOUCH MORE.
Jan Eliot

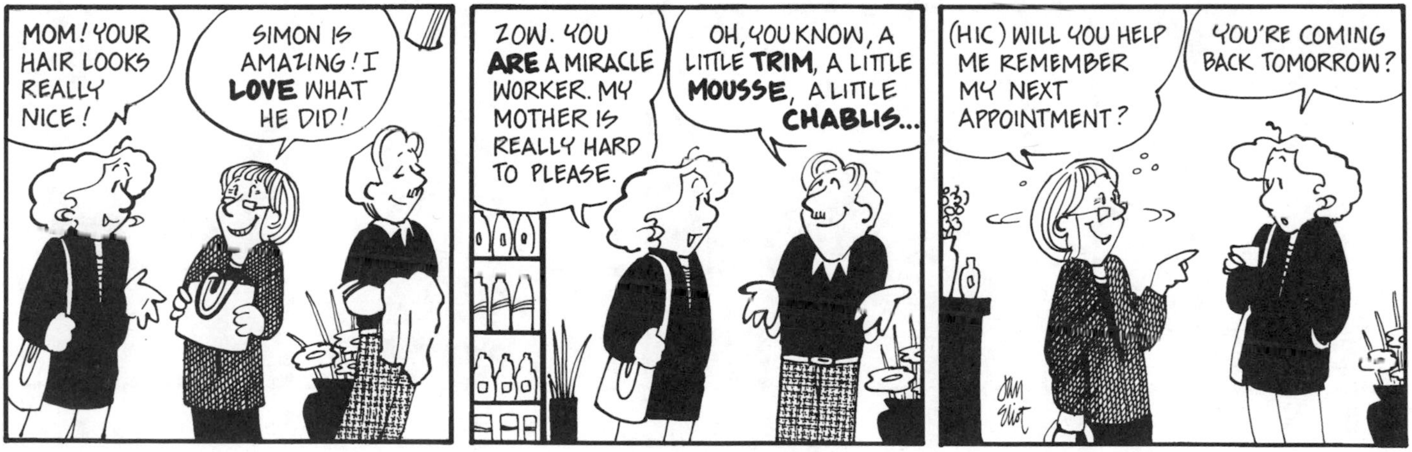
MOM! YOUR HAIR LOOKS REALLY NICE!
SIMON IS AMAZING! I **LOVE** WHAT HE DID!
ZOW. YOU **ARE** A MIRACLE WORKER. MY MOTHER IS REALLY HARD TO PLEASE.
OH, YOU KNOW, A LITTLE **TRIM**, A LITTLE **MOUSSE**, A LITTLE **CHABLIS...**
(HIC) WILL YOU HELP ME REMEMBER MY NEXT APPOINTMENT?
YOU'RE COMING BACK TOMORROW?
Jan Eliot

I'M THINKING OF GETTING RID OF THIS...
PAT PAT
YOU'RE CONSIDERING PLASTIC SURGERY?
MAYBE.
I CAN'T BELIEVE YOU! YOU LOOK EXACTLY AS YOU **SHOULD** LOOK!!
DON'T BUY INTO THE AGEIST ATTITUDES OF MADISON AVENUE! **EMBRACE** YOUR BAGS AND WRINKLES AS MEDALS OF HONOR FROM A LIFE WELL-LIVED!
THAT'S EASY FOR YOU TO SAY, DEAR. YOU'RE AGING QUITE NICELY.
YOU THINK I'M **AGING**?
Jan Eliot

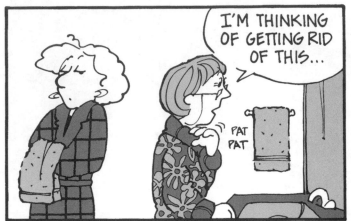

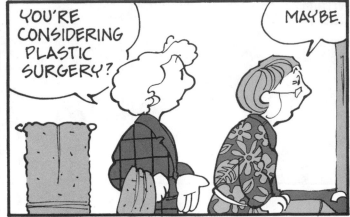

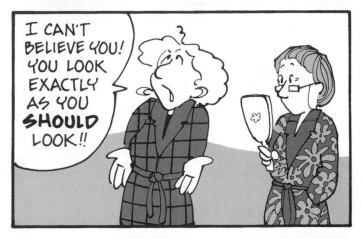

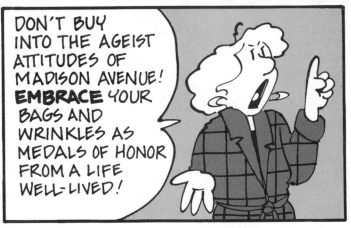

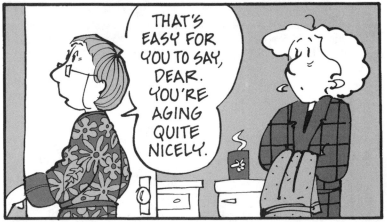

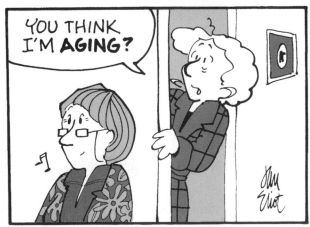

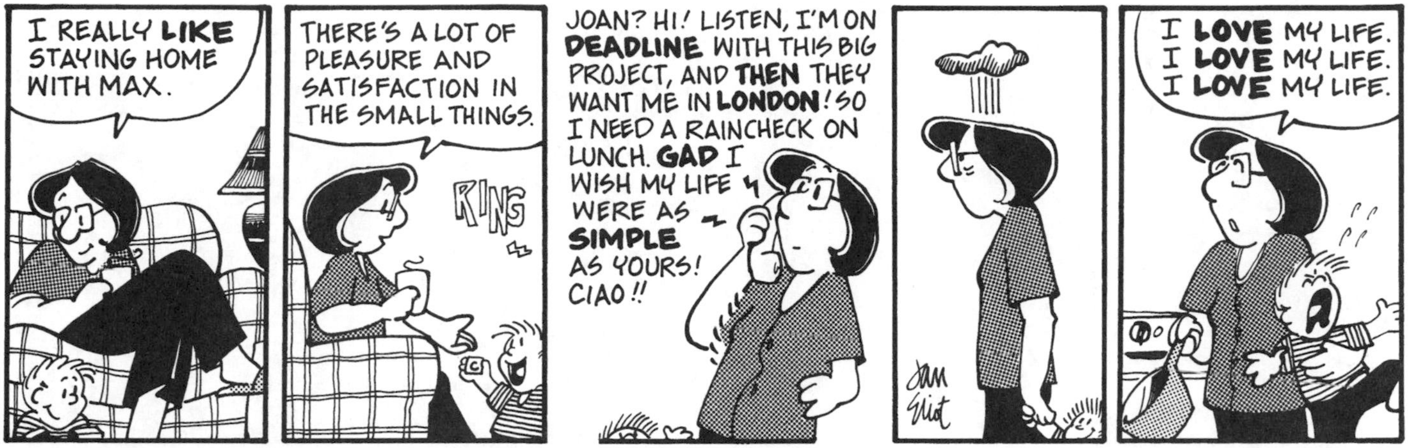
I REALLY **LIKE** STAYING HOME WITH MAX.
THERE'S A LOT OF PLEASURE AND SATISFACTION IN THE SMALL THINGS.
RING
JOAN? HI! LISTEN, I'M ON **DEADLINE** WITH THIS BIG PROJECT, AND **THEN** THEY WANT ME IN **LONDON**! SO I NEED A RAINCHECK ON LUNCH. **GAD** I WISH MY LIFE WERE AS **SIMPLE** AS YOURS! CIAO!!
I **LOVE** MY LIFE. I **LOVE** MY LIFE. I **LOVE** MY LIFE.

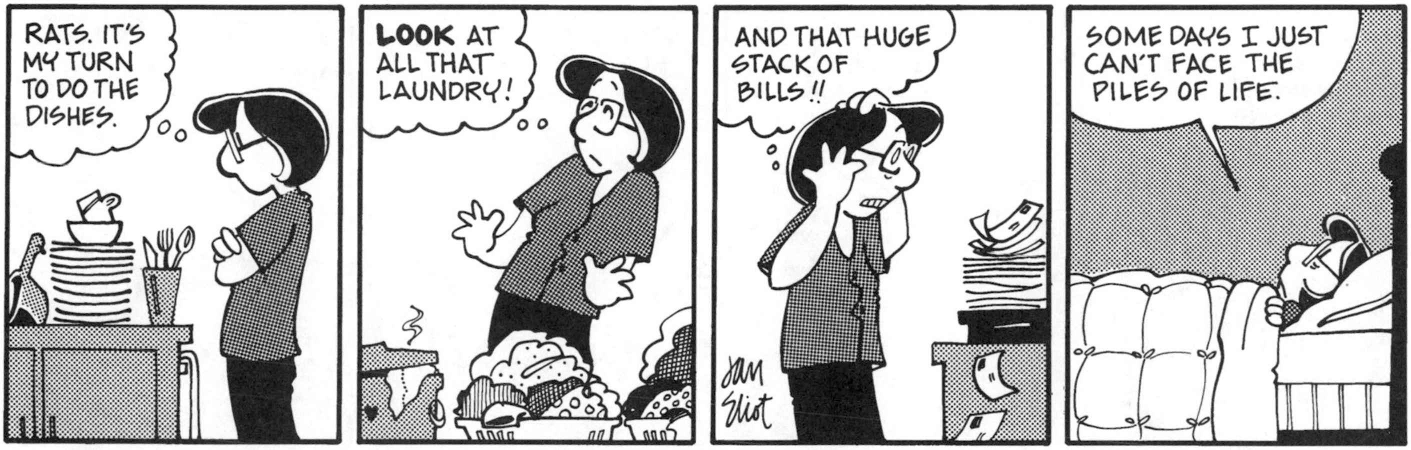
RATS. IT'S MY TURN TO DO THE DISHES.
LOOK AT ALL THAT LAUNDRY!
AND THAT HUGE STACK OF BILLS!!
SOME DAYS I JUST CAN'T FACE THE PILES OF LIFE.

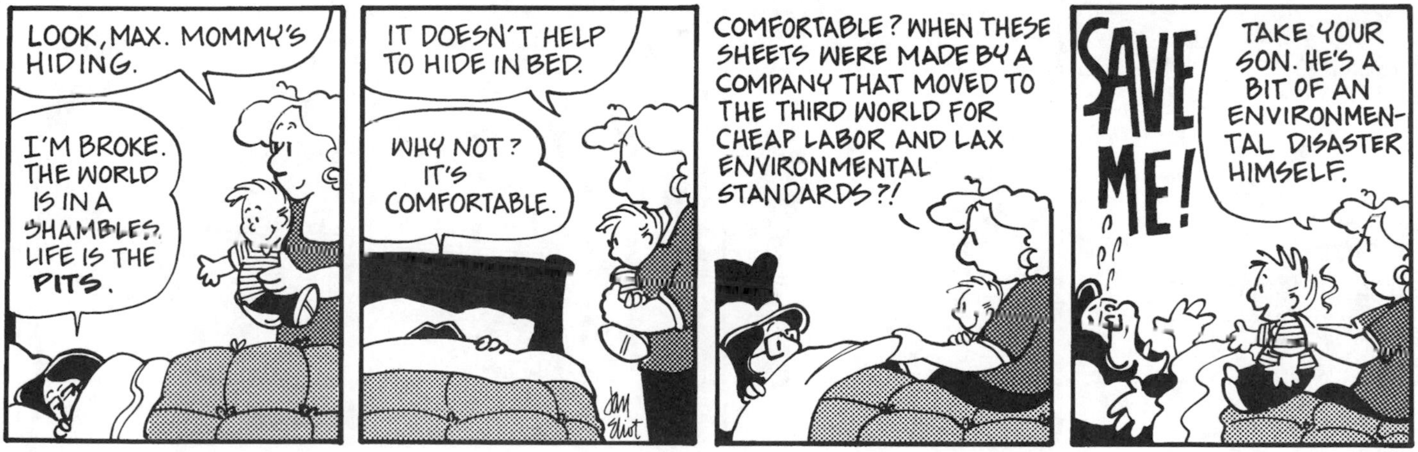
LOOK, MAX. MOMMY'S HIDING.
I'M BROKE. THE WORLD IS IN A SHAMBLES. LIFE IS THE **PITS**.
IT DOESN'T HELP TO HIDE IN BED.
WHY NOT? IT'S COMFORTABLE.
COMFORTABLE? WHEN THESE SHEETS WERE MADE BY A COMPANY THAT MOVED TO THE THIRD WORLD FOR CHEAP LABOR AND LAX ENVIRONMENTAL STANDARDS?!
SAVE ME!
TAKE YOUR SON. HE'S A BIT OF AN ENVIRONMENTAL DISASTER HIMSELF.

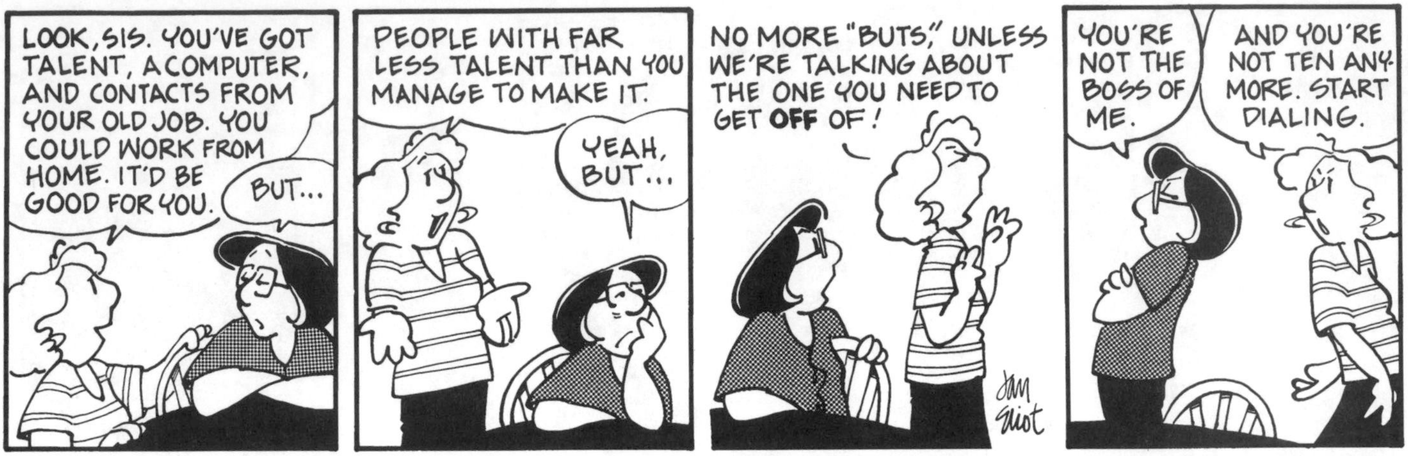
LOOK, SIS. YOU'VE GOT TALENT, A COMPUTER, AND CONTACTS FROM YOUR OLD JOB. YOU COULD WORK FROM HOME. IT'D BE GOOD FOR YOU.
BUT...
PEOPLE WITH FAR LESS TALENT THAN YOU MANAGE TO MAKE IT.
YEAH, BUT...
NO MORE "BUTS," UNLESS WE'RE TALKING ABOUT THE ONE YOU NEED TO GET **OFF** OF!
YOU'RE NOT THE BOSS OF ME.
AND YOU'RE NOT TEN ANYMORE. START DIALING.

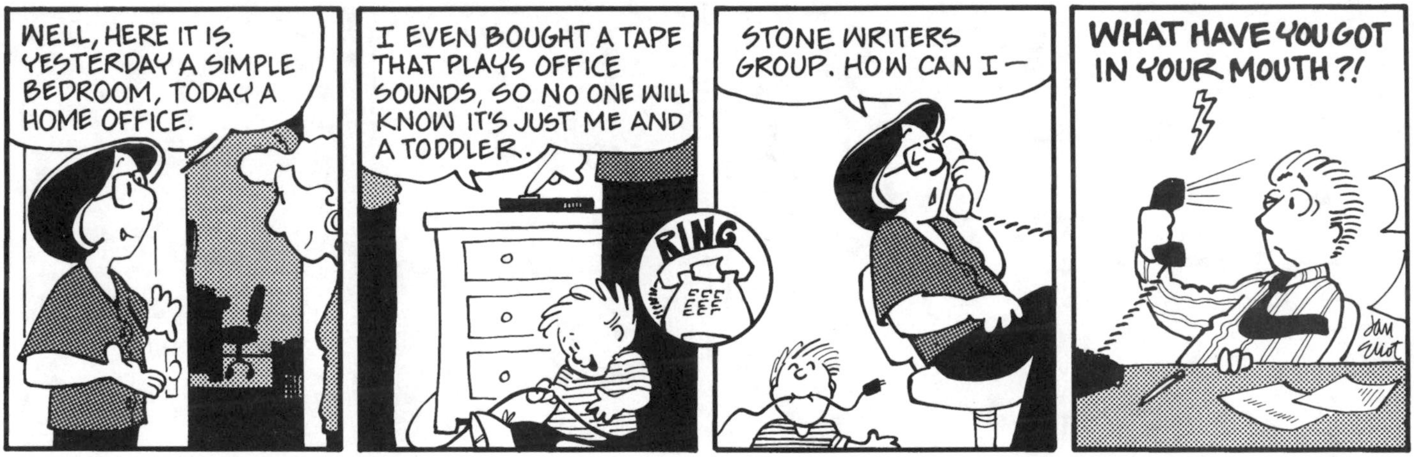
WELL, HERE IT IS. YESTERDAY A SIMPLE BEDROOM, TODAY A HOME OFFICE.
I EVEN BOUGHT A TAPE THAT PLAYS OFFICE SOUNDS, SO NO ONE WILL KNOW IT'S JUST ME AND A TODDLER.
RING
STONE WRITERS GROUP. HOW CAN I—
WHAT HAVE YOU GOT IN YOUR MOUTH?!

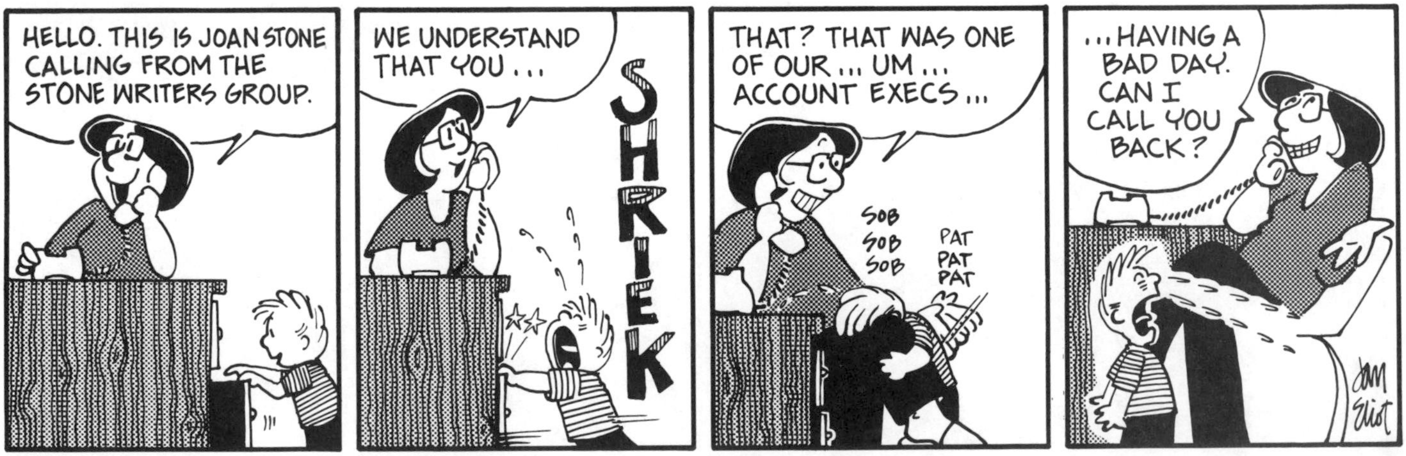
HELLO. THIS IS JOAN STONE CALLING FROM THE STONE WRITERS GROUP.
WE UNDERSTAND THAT YOU...
SHRIEK
THAT? THAT WAS ONE OF OUR... UM... ACCOUNT EXECS...
SOB SOB SOB
PAT PAT PAT
...HAVING A BAD DAY. CAN I CALL YOU BACK?

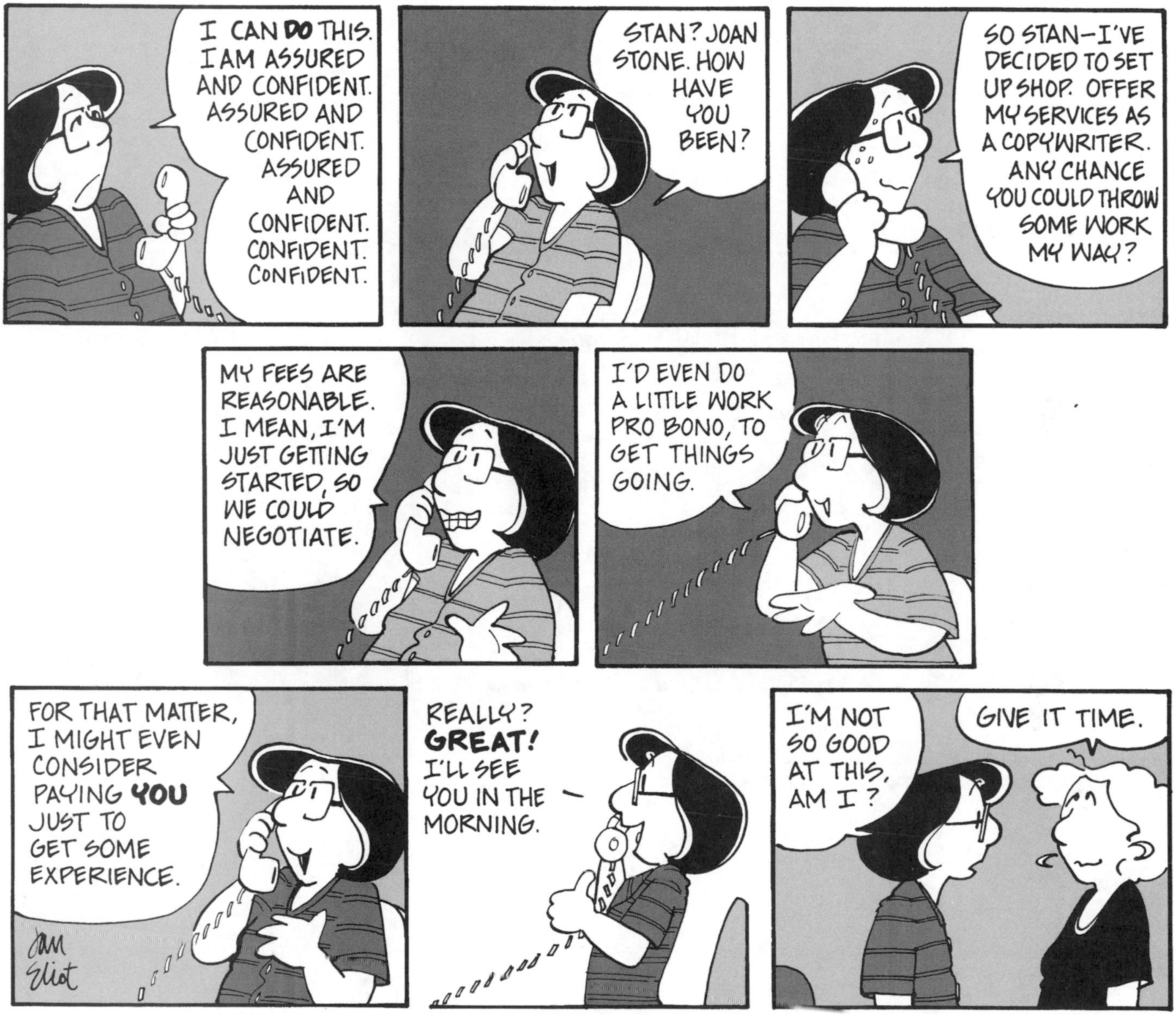
I CAN DO THIS. I AM ASSURED AND CONFIDENT. ASSURED AND CONFIDENT. ASSURED AND CONFIDENT. CONFIDENT. CONFIDENT.
STAN? JOAN STONE. HOW HAVE YOU BEEN?
SO STAN—I'VE DECIDED TO SET UP SHOP. OFFER MY SERVICES AS A COPYWRITER. ANY CHANCE YOU COULD THROW SOME WORK MY WAY?
MY FEES ARE REASONABLE. I MEAN, I'M JUST GETTING STARTED, SO WE COULD NEGOTIATE.
I'D EVEN DO A LITTLE WORK PRO BONO, TO GET THINGS GOING.
FOR THAT MATTER, I MIGHT EVEN CONSIDER PAYING YOU JUST TO GET SOME EXPERIENCE.
Jan Eliot
REALLY? GREAT! I'LL SEE YOU IN THE MORNING.
I'M NOT SO GOOD AT THIS, AM I?
GIVE IT TIME.

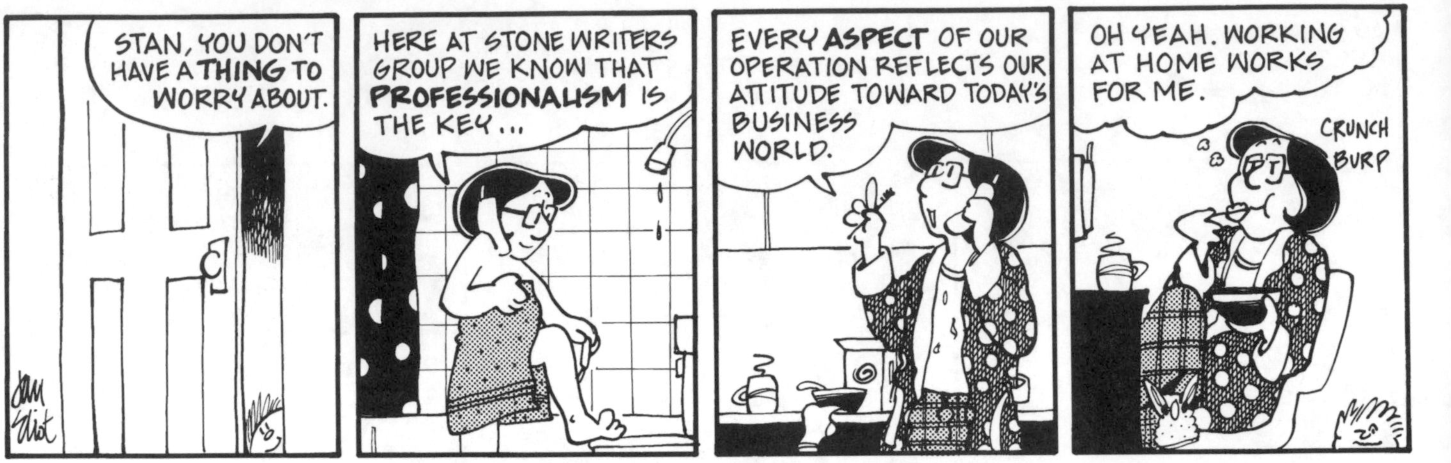
STAN, YOU DON'T HAVE A **THING** TO WORRY ABOUT.
HERE AT STONE WRITERS GROUP WE KNOW THAT **PROFESSIONALISM** IS THE KEY...
EVERY **ASPECT** OF OUR OPERATION REFLECTS OUR ATTITUDE TOWARD TODAY'S BUSINESS WORLD.
OH YEAH. WORKING AT HOME WORKS FOR ME.
CRUNCH
BURP

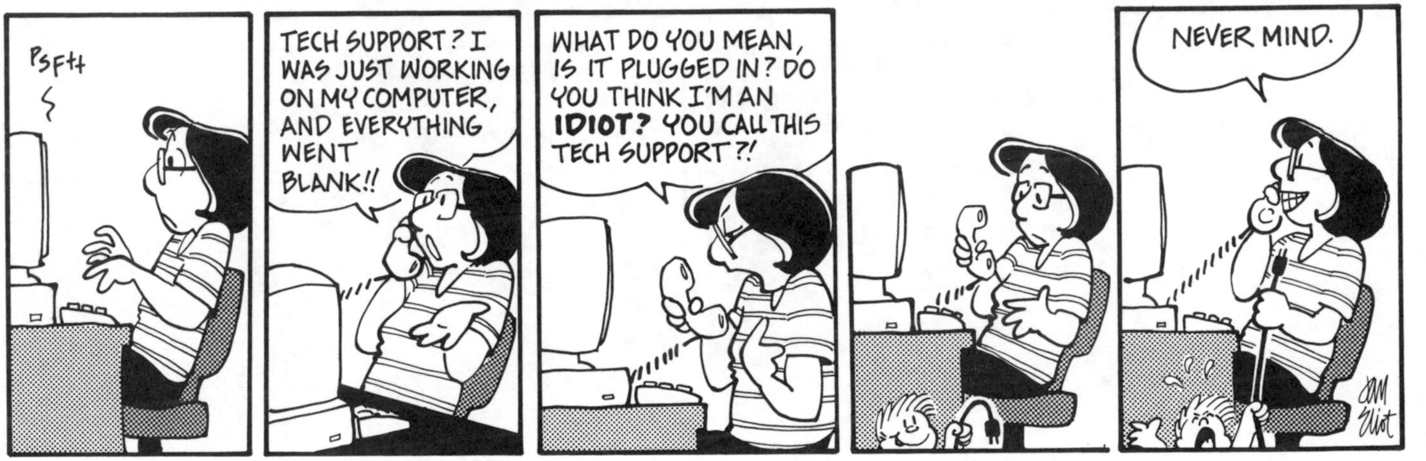
PSFTT
TECH SUPPORT? I WAS JUST WORKING ON MY COMPUTER, AND EVERYTHING WENT BLANK!!
WHAT DO YOU MEAN, IS IT PLUGGED IN? DO YOU THINK I'M AN **IDIOT?** YOU CALL THIS TECH SUPPORT?!
NEVER MIND.

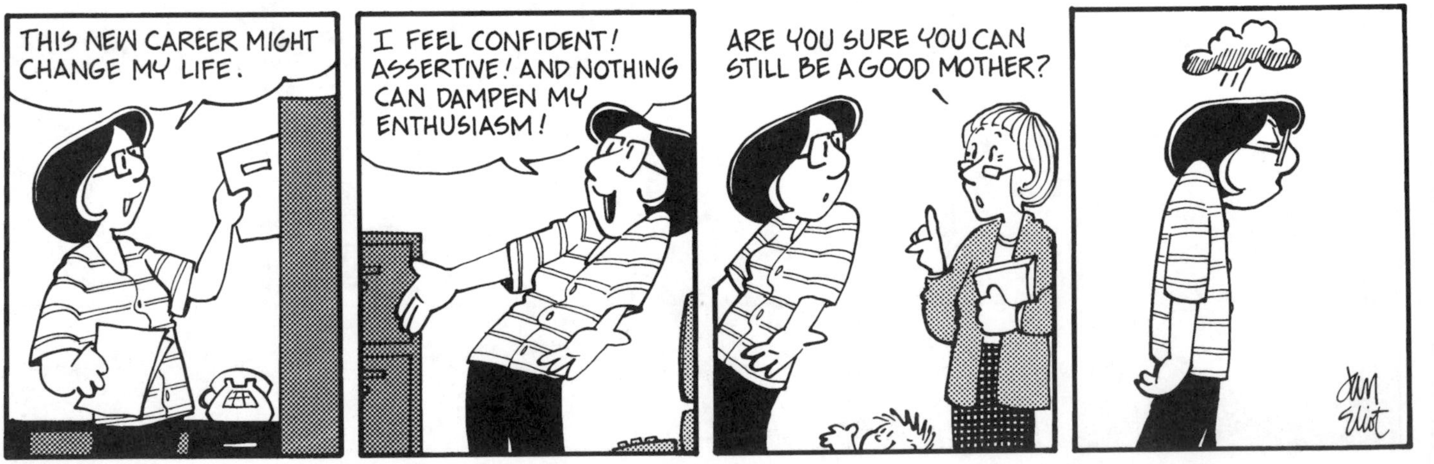
THIS NEW CAREER MIGHT CHANGE MY LIFE.
I FEEL CONFIDENT! ASSERTIVE! AND NOTHING CAN DAMPEN MY ENTHUSIASM!
ARE YOU SURE YOU CAN STILL BE A GOOD MOTHER?

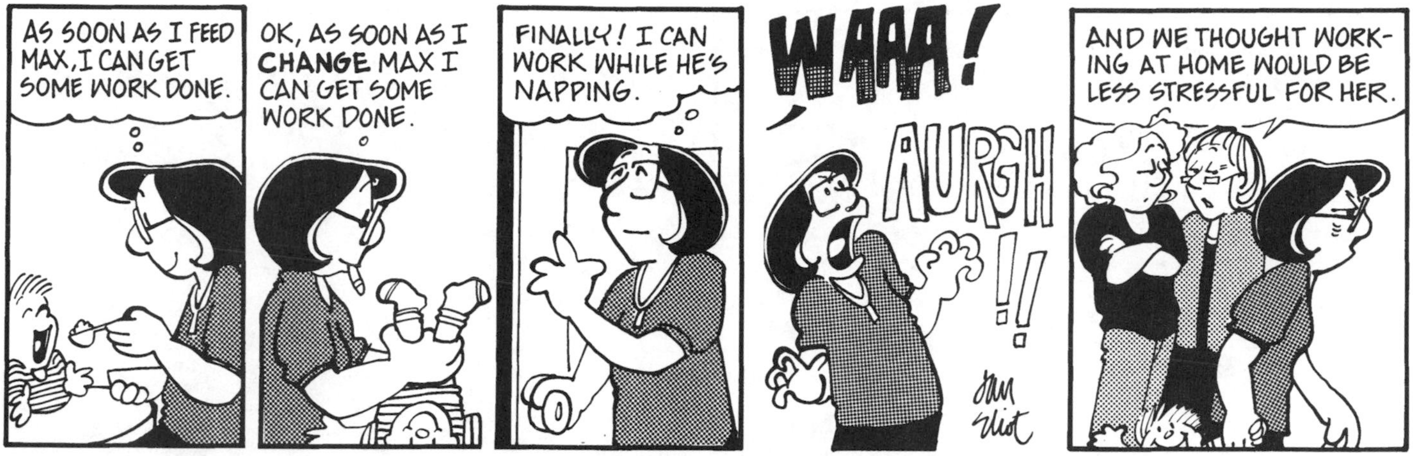
AS SOON AS I FEED MAX, I CAN GET SOME WORK DONE.
OK, AS SOON AS I CHANGE MAX I CAN GET SOME WORK DONE.
FINALLY! I CAN WORK WHILE HE'S NAPPING.
WAAA!
AURGH!!
AND WE THOUGHT WORKING AT HOME WOULD BE LESS STRESSFUL FOR HER.
Jan Eliot

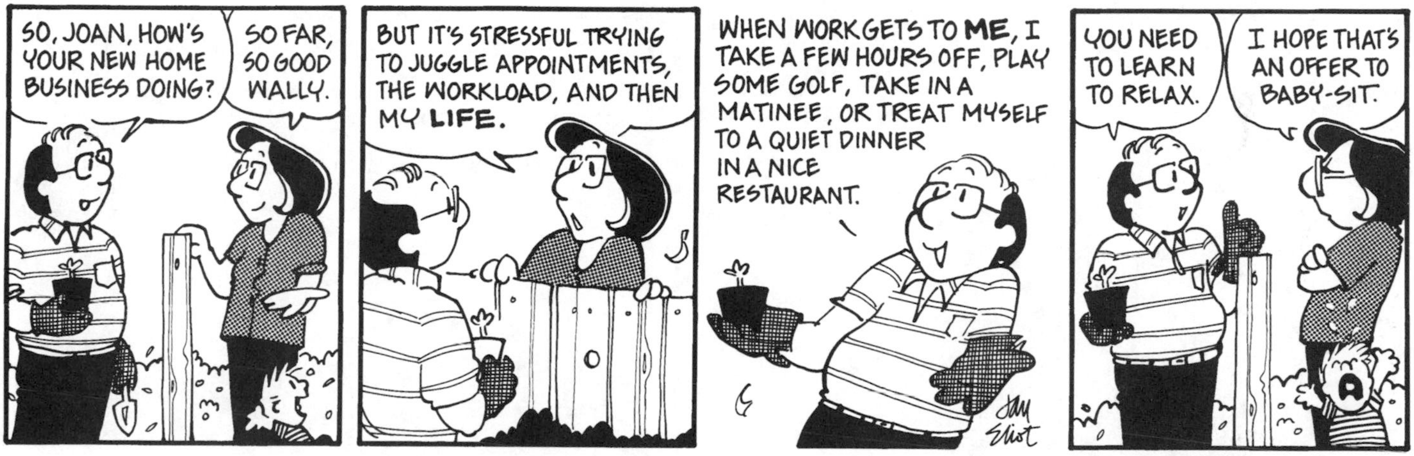
SO, JOAN, HOW'S YOUR NEW HOME BUSINESS DOING?
SO FAR, SO GOOD WALLY.
BUT IT'S STRESSFUL TRYING TO JUGGLE APPOINTMENTS, THE WORKLOAD, AND THEN MY LIFE.
WHEN WORK GETS TO ME, I TAKE A FEW HOURS OFF, PLAY SOME GOLF, TAKE IN A MATINEE, OR TREAT MYSELF TO A QUIET DINNER IN A NICE RESTAURANT.
YOU NEED TO LEARN TO RELAX.
I HOPE THAT'S AN OFFER TO BABY-SIT.
Jan Eliot

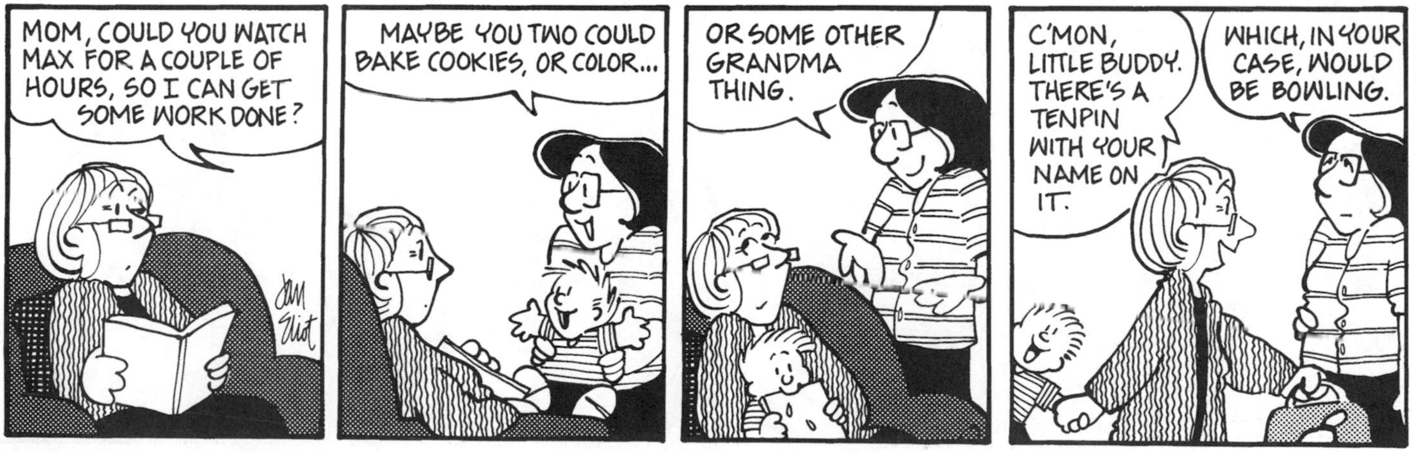
MOM, COULD YOU WATCH MAX FOR A COUPLE OF HOURS, SO I CAN GET SOME WORK DONE?
MAYBE YOU TWO COULD BAKE COOKIES, OR COLOR...
OR SOME OTHER GRANDMA THING.
C'MON, LITTLE BUDDY. THERE'S A TENPIN WITH YOUR NAME ON IT.
WHICH, IN YOUR CASE, WOULD BE BOWLING.
Jan Eliot

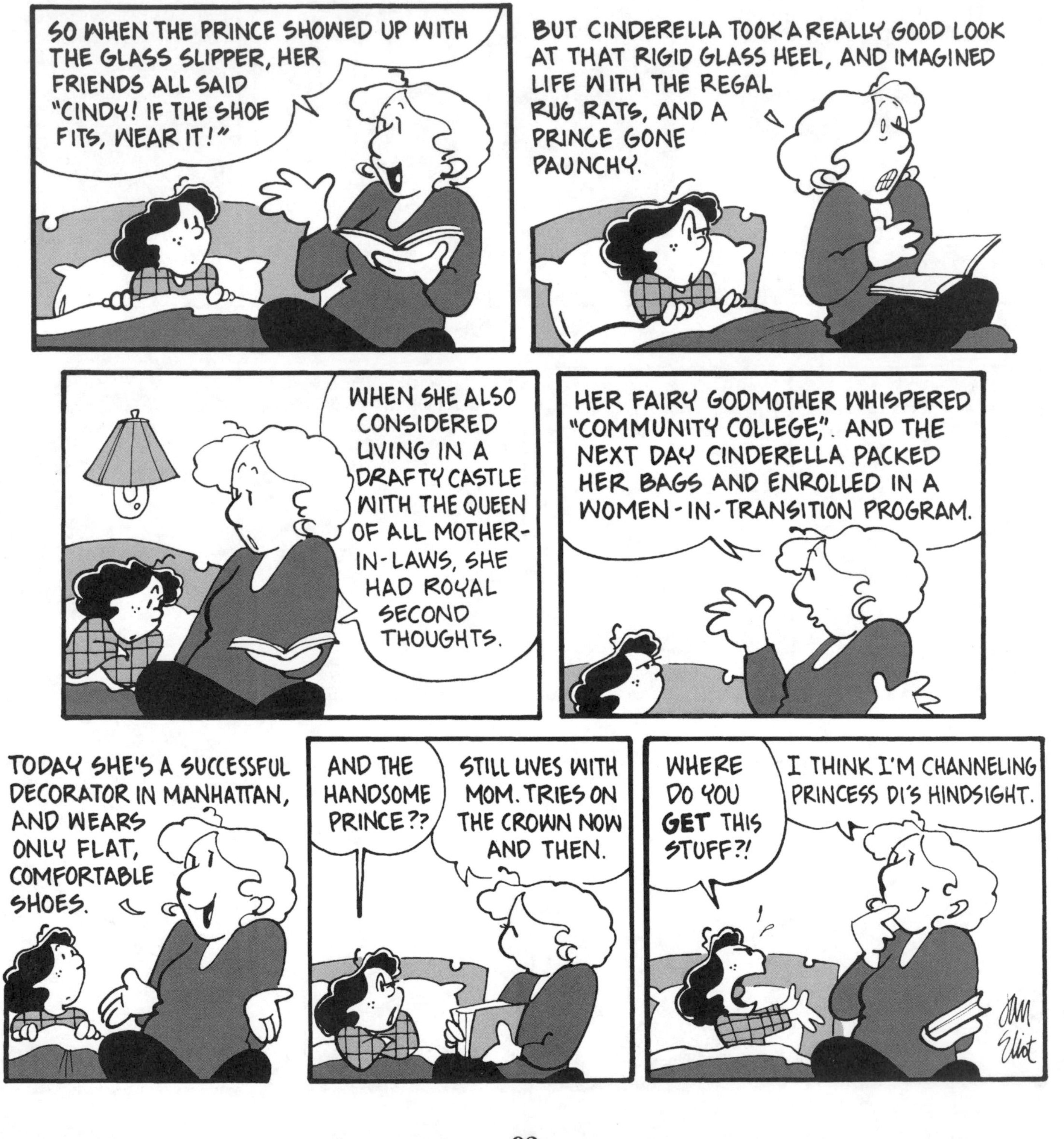
SO WHEN THE PRINCE SHOWED UP WITH THE GLASS SLIPPER, HER FRIENDS ALL SAID "CINDY! IF THE SHOE FITS, WEAR IT!"
BUT CINDERELLA TOOK A REALLY GOOD LOOK AT THAT RIGID GLASS HEEL, AND IMAGINED LIFE WITH THE REGAL RUG RATS, AND A PRINCE GONE PAUNCHY.
WHEN SHE ALSO CONSIDERED LIVING IN A DRAFTY CASTLE WITH THE QUEEN OF ALL MOTHER-IN-LAWS, SHE HAD ROYAL SECOND THOUGHTS.
HER FAIRY GODMOTHER WHISPERED "COMMUNITY COLLEGE,". AND THE NEXT DAY CINDERELLA PACKED HER BAGS AND ENROLLED IN A WOMEN-IN-TRANSITION PROGRAM.
TODAY SHE'S A SUCCESSFUL DECORATOR IN MANHATTAN, AND WEARS ONLY FLAT, COMFORTABLE SHOES.
AND THE HANDSOME PRINCE??
STILL LIVES WITH MOM. TRIES ON THE CROWN NOW AND THEN.
WHERE DO YOU **GET** THIS STUFF?!
I THINK I'M CHANNELING PRINCESS DI'S HINDSIGHT.
JAN ELIOT

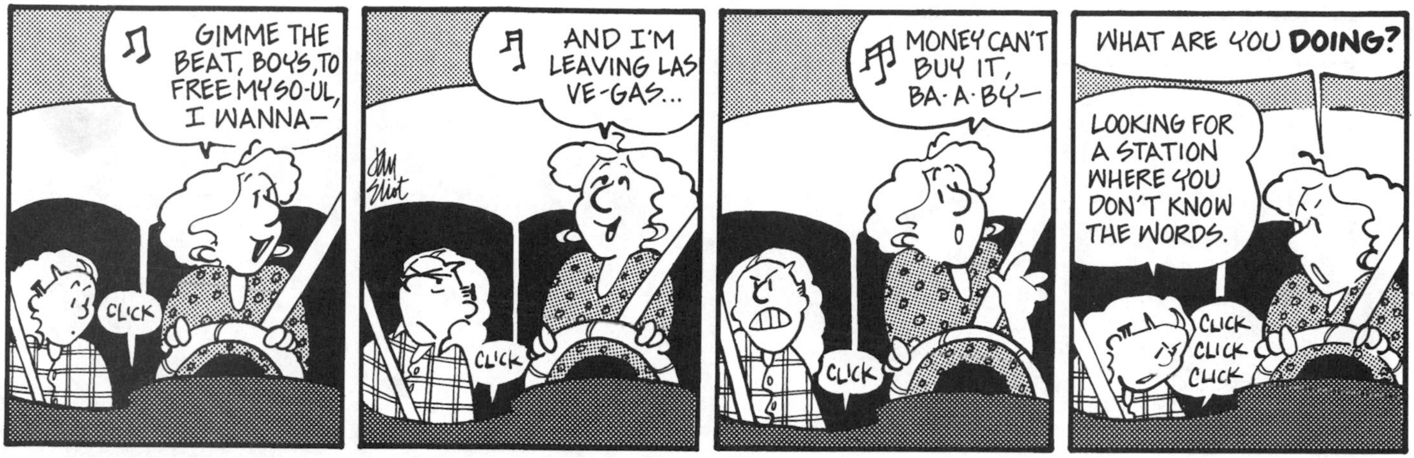
♫ GIMME THE BEAT, BOYS, TO FREE MY SO-UL, I WANNA—
CLICK
♫ AND I'M LEAVING LAS VE-GAS...
CLICK
♫ MONEY CAN'T BUY IT, BA-A-BY—
CLICK
WHAT ARE YOU **DOING?**
LOOKING FOR A STATION WHERE YOU DON'T KNOW THE WORDS.
CLICK CLICK CLICK

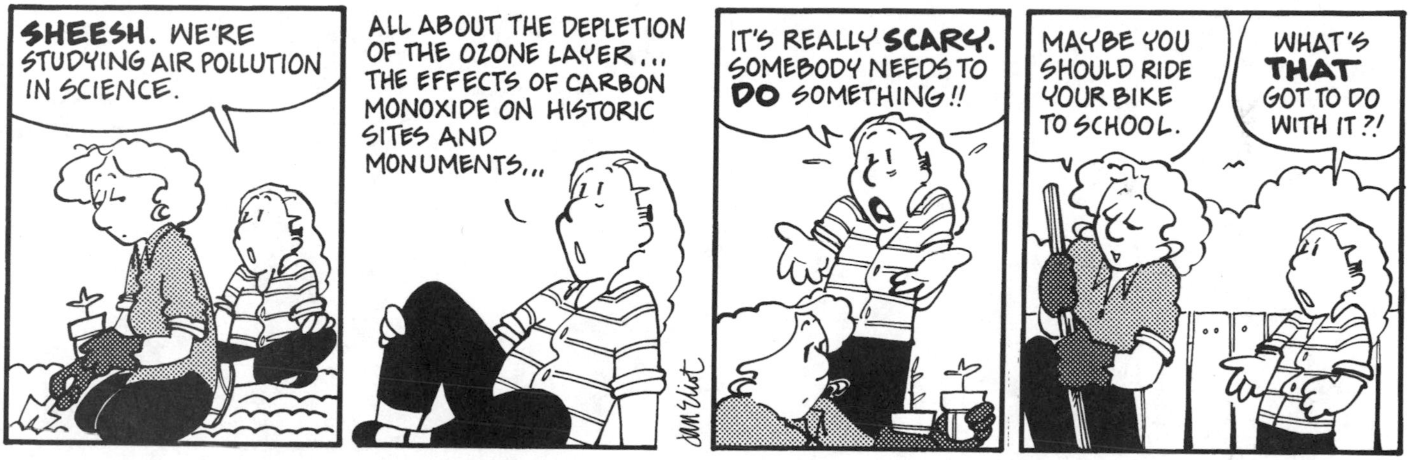
SHEESH. WE'RE STUDYING AIR POLLUTION IN SCIENCE.
ALL ABOUT THE DEPLETION OF THE OZONE LAYER... THE EFFECTS OF CARBON MONOXIDE ON HISTORIC SITES AND MONUMENTS...
IT'S REALLY **SCARY.** SOMEBODY NEEDS TO **DO** SOMETHING!!
MAYBE YOU SHOULD RIDE YOUR BIKE TO SCHOOL.
WHAT'S **THAT** GOT TO DO WITH IT?!

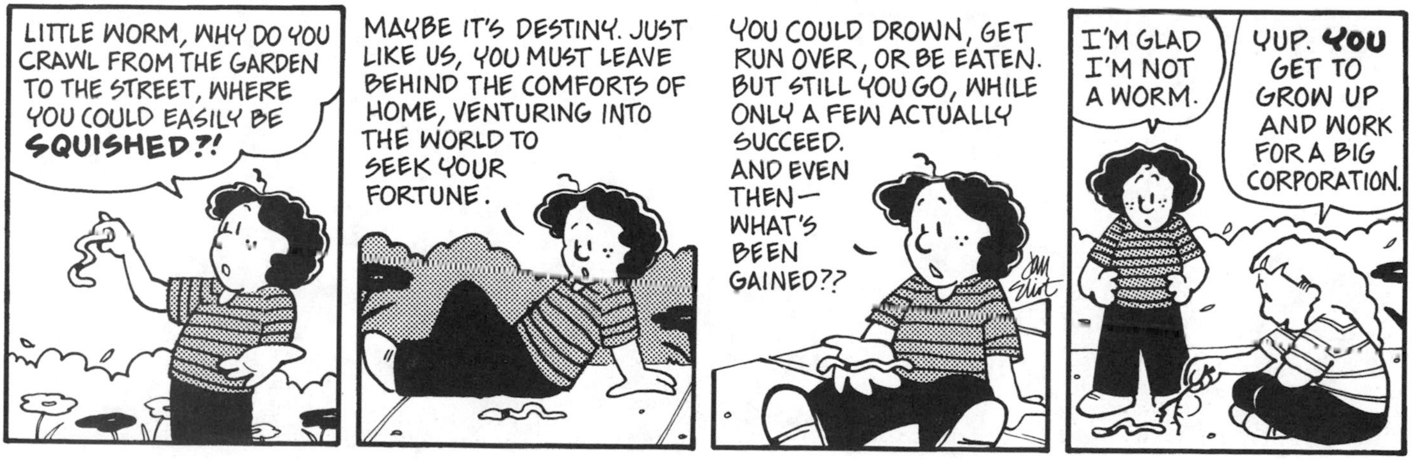
LITTLE WORM, WHY DO YOU CRAWL FROM THE GARDEN TO THE STREET, WHERE YOU COULD EASILY BE **SQUISHED?!**
MAYBE IT'S DESTINY. JUST LIKE US, YOU MUST LEAVE BEHIND THE COMFORTS OF HOME, VENTURING INTO THE WORLD TO SEEK YOUR FORTUNE.
YOU COULD DROWN, GET RUN OVER, OR BE EATEN. BUT STILL YOU GO, WHILE ONLY A FEW ACTUALLY SUCCEED.
AND EVEN THEN— WHAT'S BEEN GAINED??
I'M GLAD I'M NOT A WORM.
YUP. **YOU** GET TO GROW UP AND WORK FOR A BIG CORPORATION.

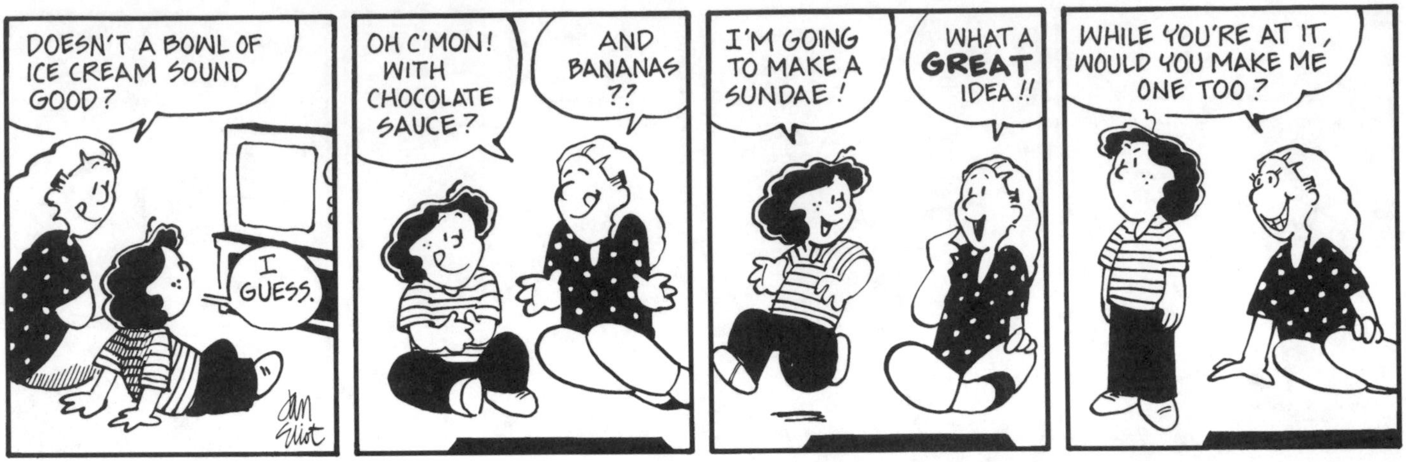
DOESN'T A BOWL OF ICE CREAM SOUND GOOD?
I GUESS.
OH C'MON! WITH CHOCOLATE SAUCE?
AND BANANAS ??
I'M GOING TO MAKE A SUNDAE!
WHAT A **GREAT** IDEA!!
WHILE YOU'RE AT IT, WOULD YOU MAKE ME ONE TOO?

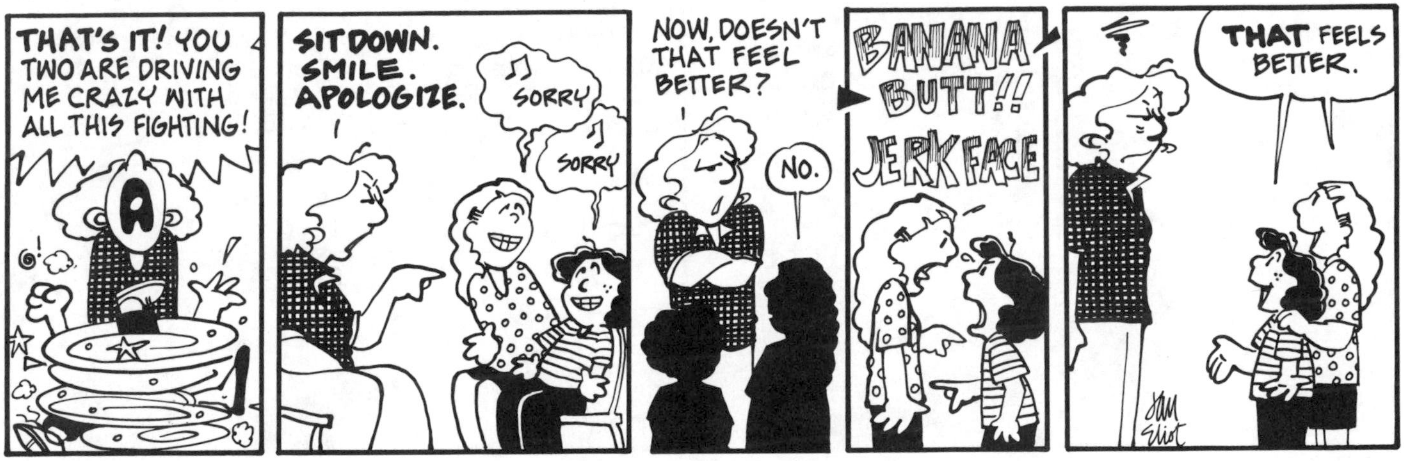
THAT'S IT! YOU TWO ARE DRIVING ME CRAZY WITH ALL THIS FIGHTING!
SIT DOWN. SMILE. APOLOGIZE.
♪ SORRY
♪ SORRY
NOW, DOESN'T THAT FEEL BETTER?
NO.
BANANA BUTT!!
JERK FACE
THAT FEELS BETTER.

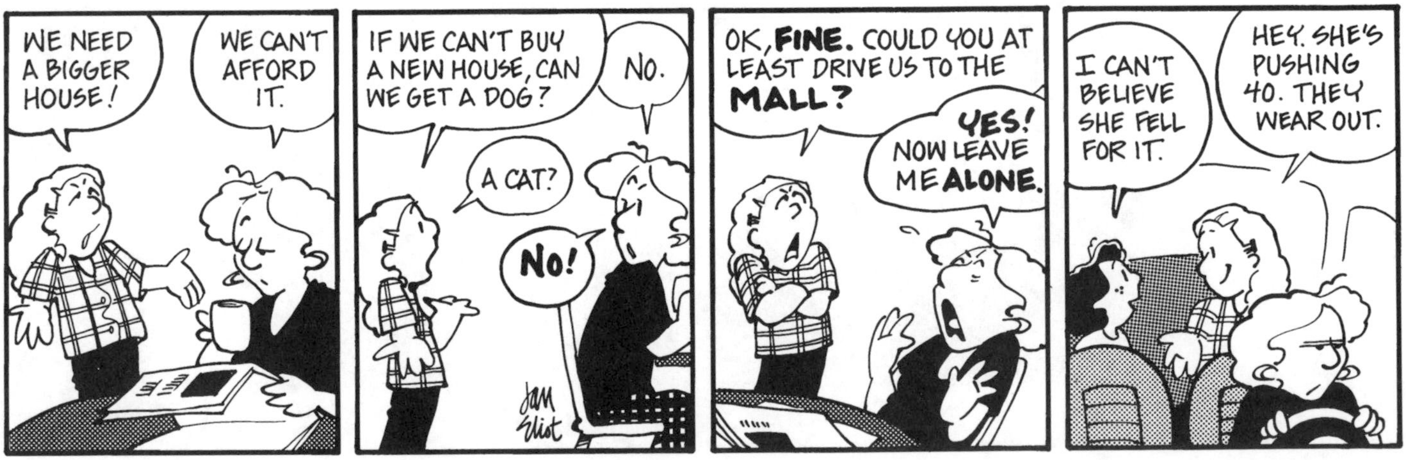
WE NEED A BIGGER HOUSE!
WE CAN'T AFFORD IT.
IF WE CAN'T BUY A NEW HOUSE, CAN WE GET A DOG?
NO.
A CAT?
No!
OK, **FINE.** COULD YOU AT LEAST DRIVE US TO THE **MALL?**
YES! NOW LEAVE ME **ALONE.**
I CAN'T BELIEVE SHE FELL FOR IT.
HEY. SHE'S PUSHING 40. THEY WEAR OUT.

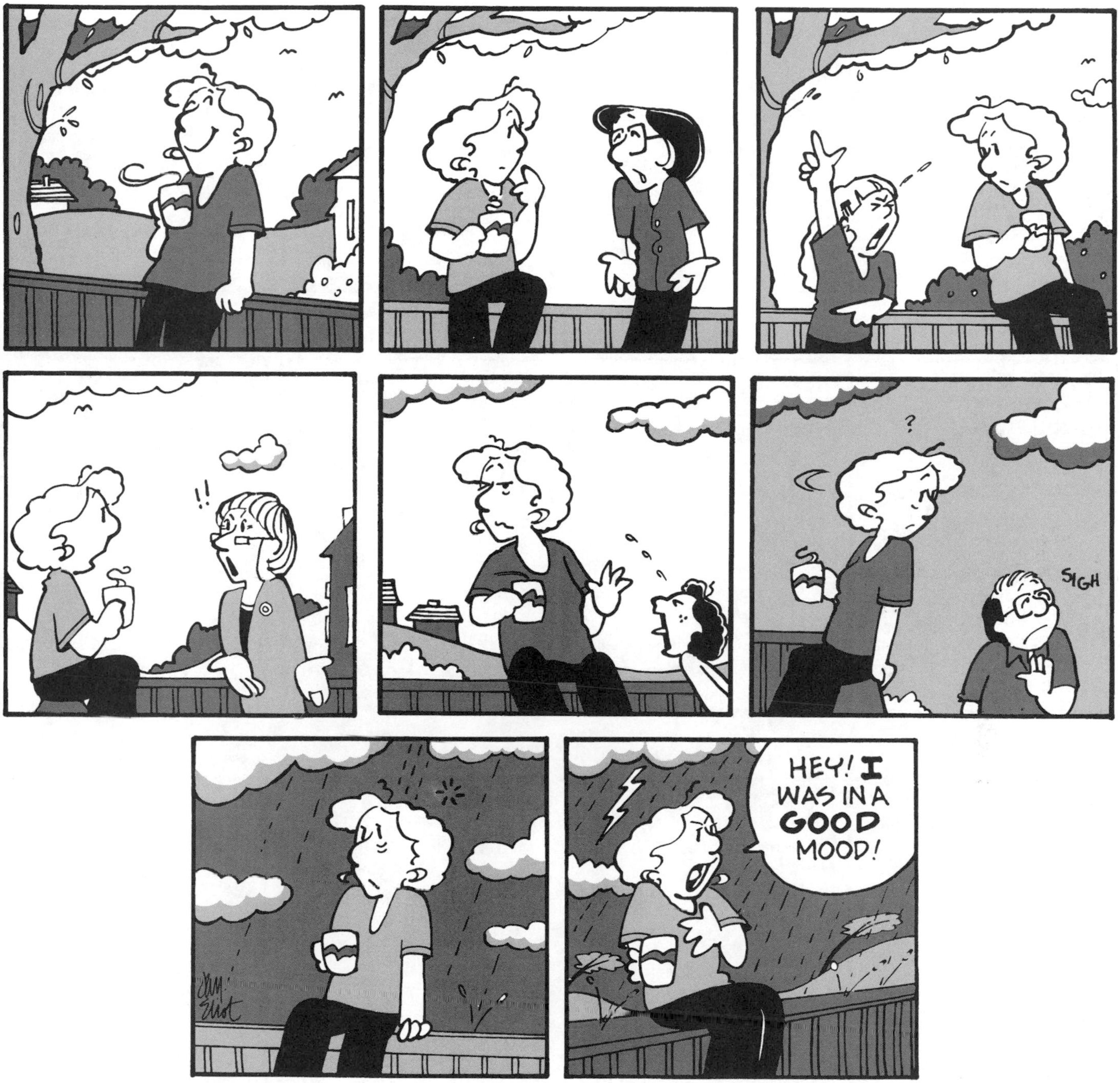
!!
?
SIGH
HEY! I WAS IN A GOOD MOOD!

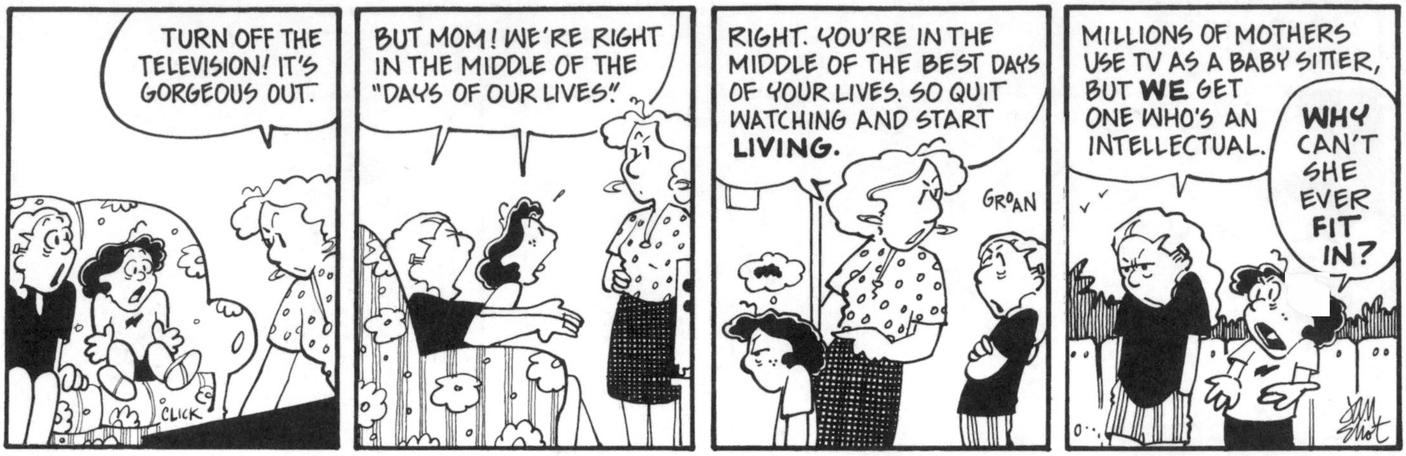
TURN OFF THE TELEVISION! IT'S GORGEOUS OUT.
CLICK
BUT MOM! WE'RE RIGHT IN THE MIDDLE OF THE "DAYS OF OUR LIVES!"
RIGHT. YOU'RE IN THE MIDDLE OF THE BEST DAYS OF YOUR LIVES. SO QUIT WATCHING AND START **LIVING.**
GROAN
MILLIONS OF MOTHERS USE TV AS A BABY SITTER, BUT **WE** GET ONE WHO'S AN INTELLECTUAL.
WHY CAN'T SHE EVER **FIT IN?**

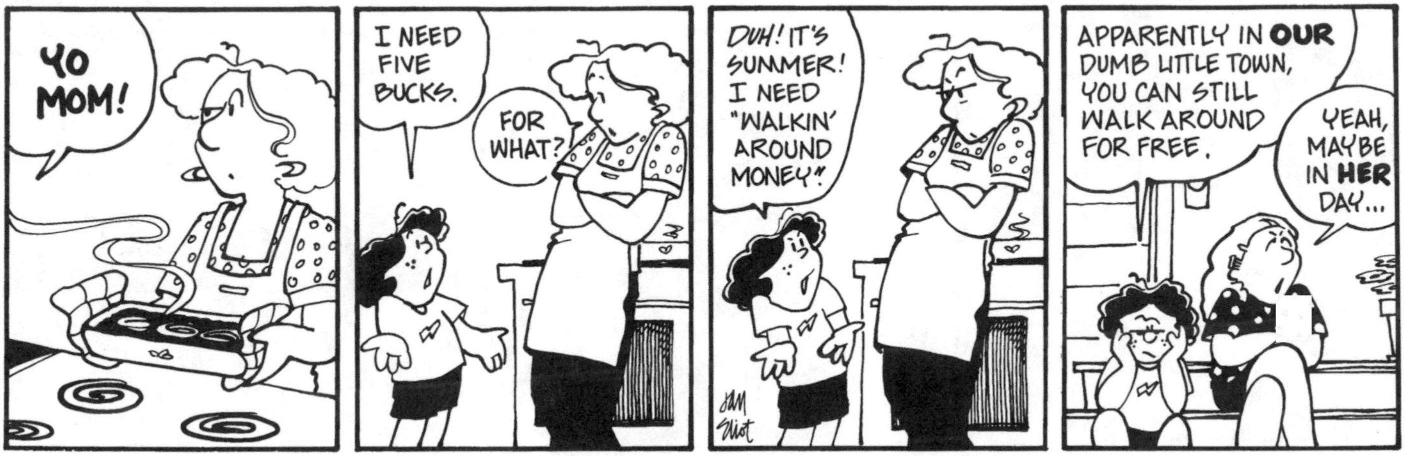
YO MOM!
I NEED FIVE BUCKS.
FOR WHAT?
DUH! IT'S SUMMER! I NEED "WALKIN' AROUND MONEY"!
APPARENTLY IN **OUR** DUMB LITTLE TOWN, YOU CAN STILL WALK AROUND FOR FREE.
YEAH, MAYBE IN **HER** DAY...

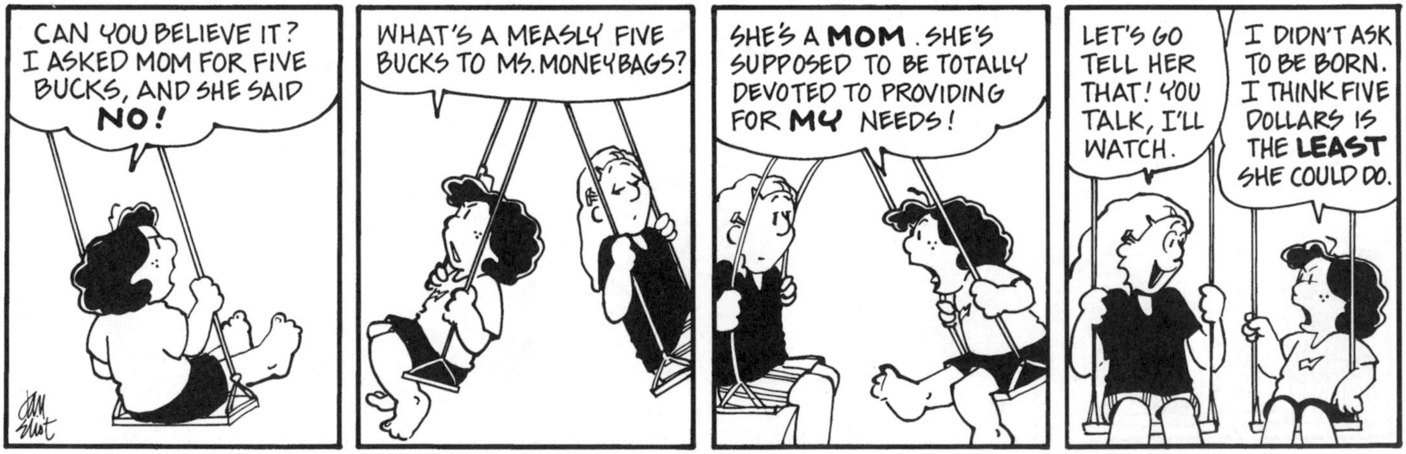
CAN YOU BELIEVE IT? I ASKED MOM FOR FIVE BUCKS, AND SHE SAID **NO!**
WHAT'S A MEASLY FIVE BUCKS TO MS. MONEYBAGS?
SHE'S A **MOM**. SHE'S SUPPOSED TO BE TOTALLY DEVOTED TO PROVIDING FOR **MY** NEEDS!
LET'S GO TELL HER THAT! YOU TALK, I'LL WATCH.
I DIDN'T ASK TO BE BORN. I THINK FIVE DOLLARS IS THE **LEAST** SHE COULD DO.

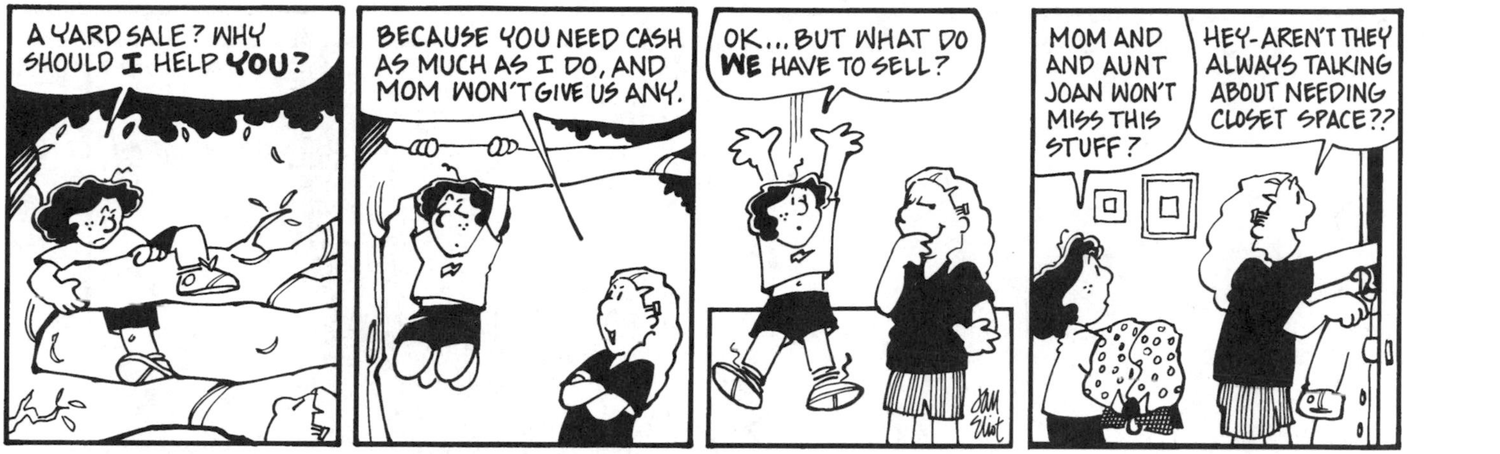
A YARD SALE? WHY SHOULD I HELP YOU?
BECAUSE YOU NEED CASH AS MUCH AS I DO, AND MOM WON'T GIVE US ANY.
OK... BUT WHAT DO WE HAVE TO SELL?
MOM AND AND AUNT JOAN WON'T MISS THIS STUFF?
HEY- AREN'T THEY ALWAYS TALKING ABOUT NEEDING CLOSET SPACE??

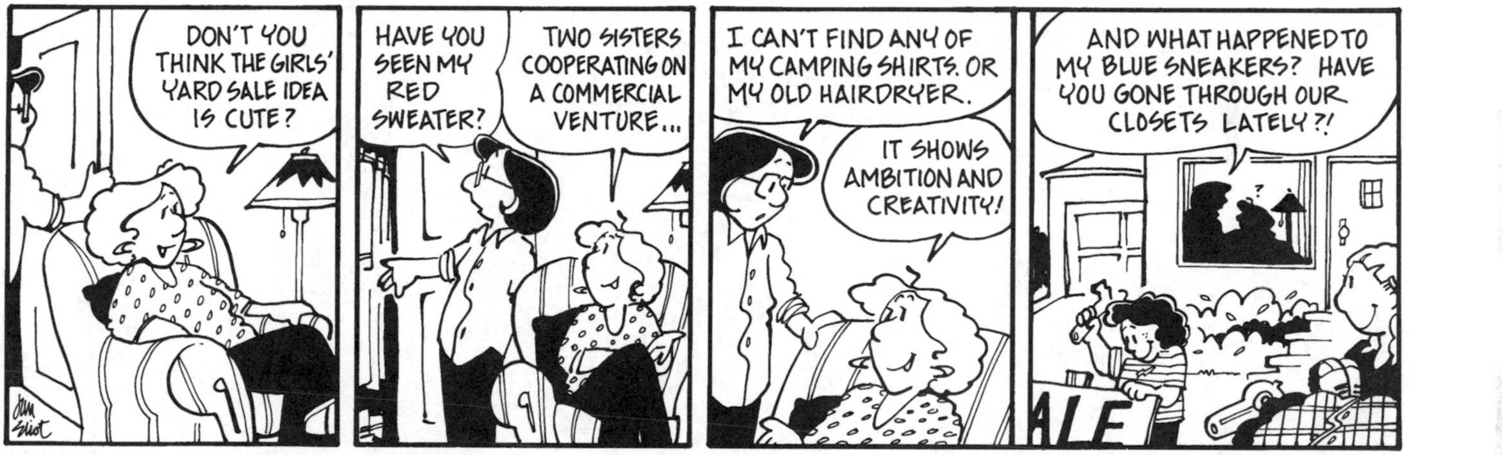
DON'T YOU THINK THE GIRLS' YARD SALE IDEA IS CUTE?
HAVE YOU SEEN MY RED SWEATER?
TWO SISTERS COOPERATING ON A COMMERCIAL VENTURE...
I CAN'T FIND ANY OF MY CAMPING SHIRTS. OR MY OLD HAIRDRYER.
IT SHOWS AMBITION AND CREATIVITY!
AND WHAT HAPPENED TO MY BLUE SNEAKERS? HAVE YOU GONE THROUGH OUR CLOSETS LATELY?!
ALE

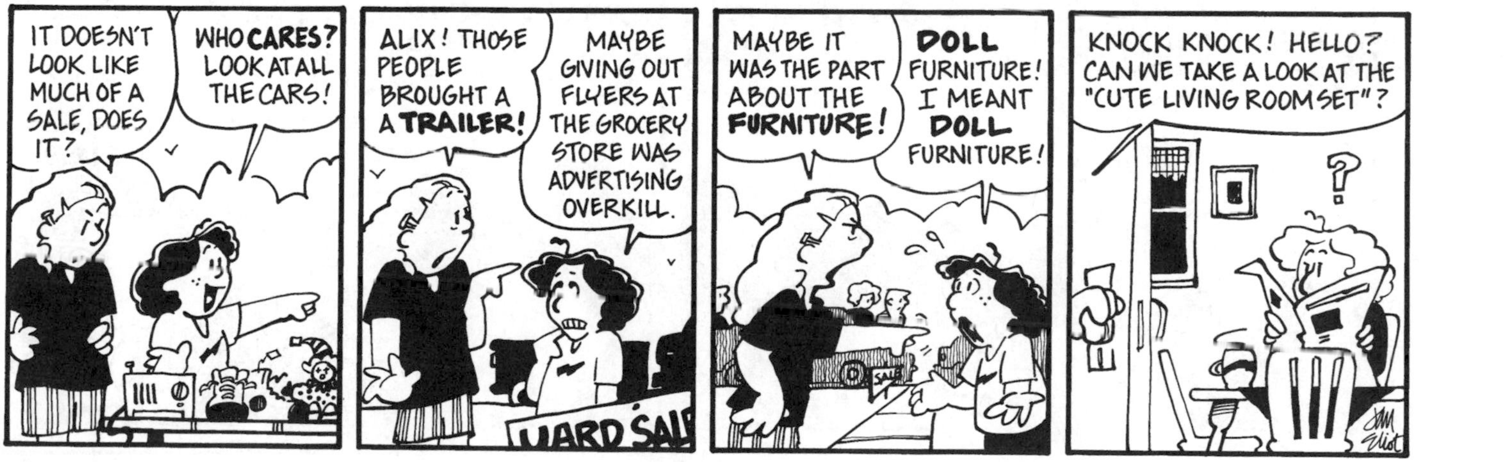
IT DOESN'T LOOK LIKE MUCH OF A SALE, DOES IT?
WHO CARES? LOOK AT ALL THE CARS!
ALIX! THOSE PEOPLE BROUGHT A A TRAILER!
MAYBE GIVING OUT FLYERS AT THE GROCERY STORE WAS ADVERTISING OVERKILL.
YARD SALE
MAYBE IT WAS THE PART ABOUT THE FURNITURE!
DOLL FURNITURE! I MEANT DOLL FURNITURE!
KNOCK KNOCK! HELLO? CAN WE TAKE A LOOK AT THE "CUTE LIVING ROOM SET"?
?

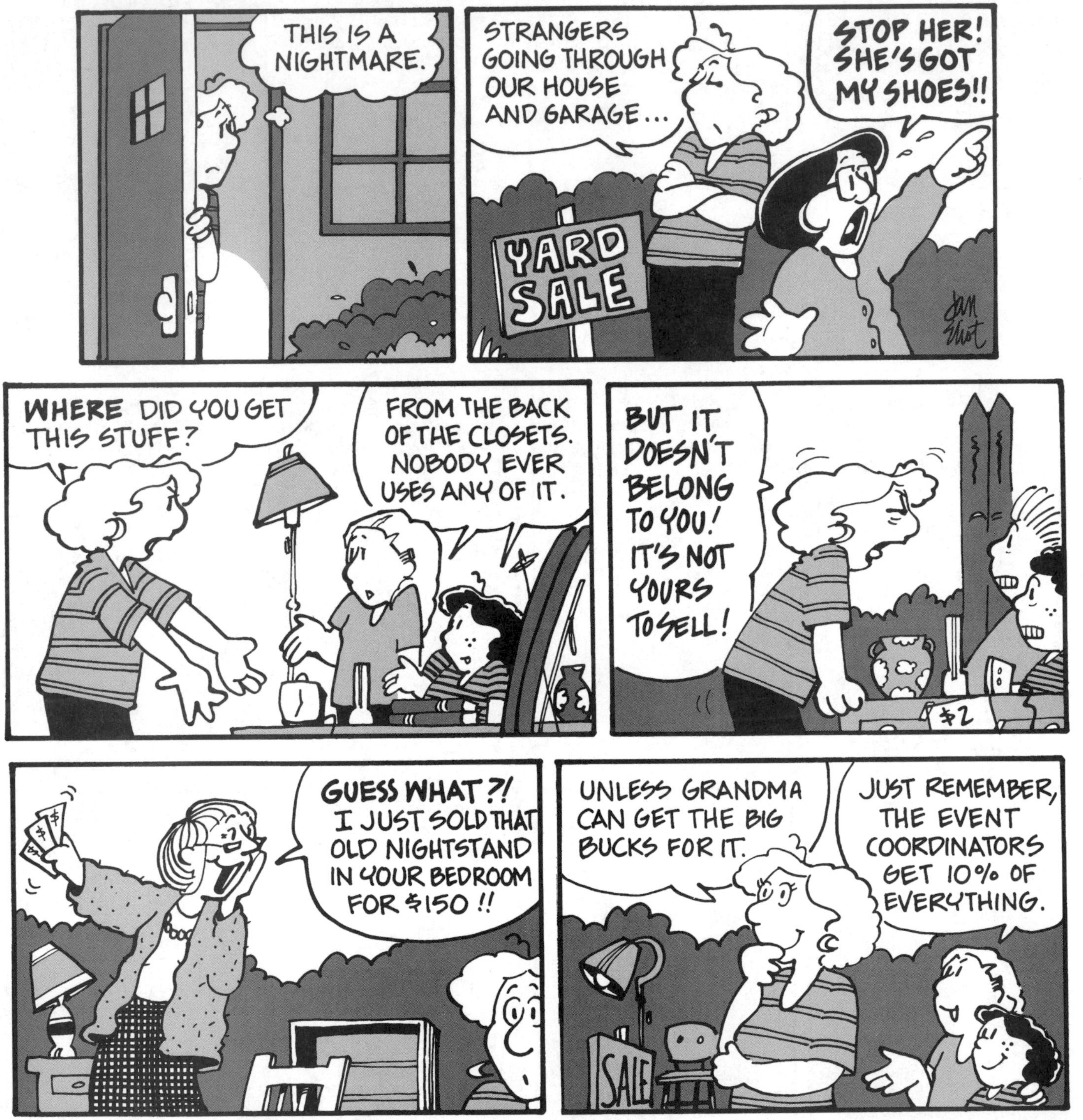
THIS IS A NIGHTMARE.
STRANGERS GOING THROUGH OUR HOUSE AND GARAGE...
STOP HER! SHE'S GOT MY SHOES!!
YARD SALE
WHERE DID YOU GET THIS STUFF?
FROM THE BACK OF THE CLOSETS. NOBODY EVER USES ANY OF IT.
BUT IT DOESN'T BELONG TO YOU! IT'S NOT YOURS TO SELL!
$2
GUESS WHAT?! I JUST SOLD THAT OLD NIGHTSTAND IN YOUR BEDROOM FOR $150 !!
UNLESS GRANDMA CAN GET THE BIG BUCKS FOR IT.
JUST REMEMBER, THE EVENT COORDINATORS GET 10% OF EVERYTHING.
SALE

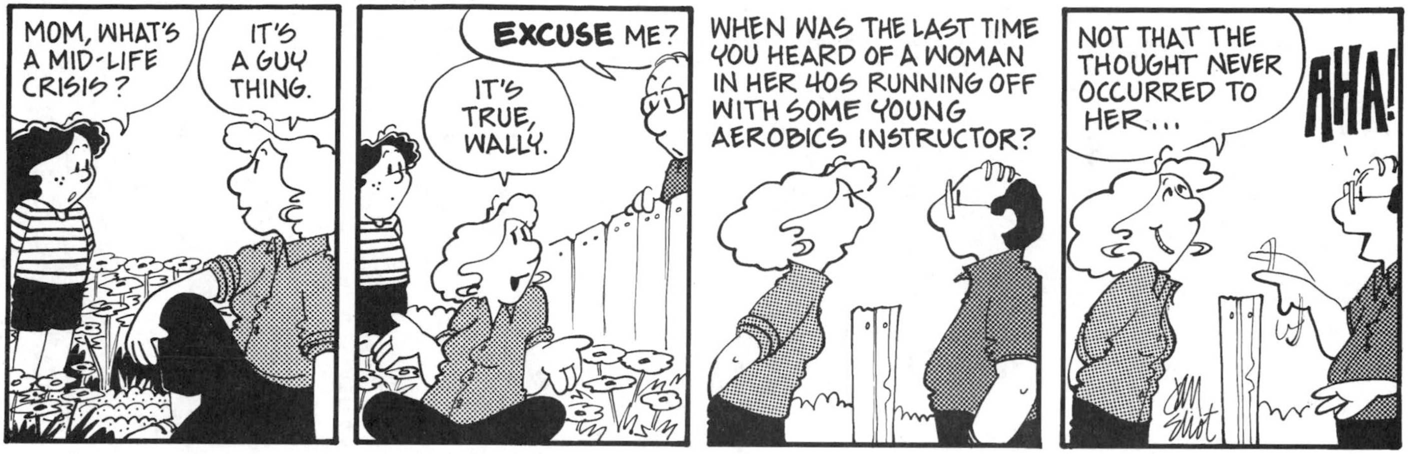
MOM, WHAT'S A MID-LIFE CRISIS?
IT'S A GUY THING.
EXCUSE ME?
IT'S TRUE, WALLY.
WHEN WAS THE LAST TIME YOU HEARD OF A WOMAN IN HER 40S RUNNING OFF WITH SOME YOUNG AEROBICS INSTRUCTOR?
NOT THAT THE THOUGHT NEVER OCCURRED TO HER...
AHA!

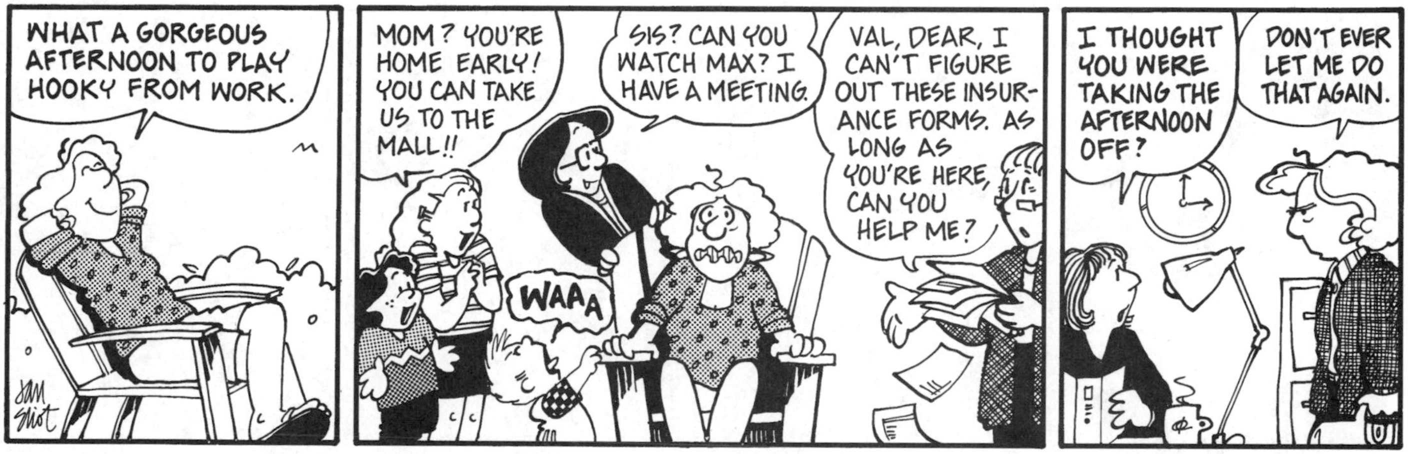
WHAT A GORGEOUS AFTERNOON TO PLAY HOOKY FROM WORK.
MOM? YOU'RE HOME EARLY! YOU CAN TAKE US TO THE MALL!!
SIS? CAN YOU WATCH MAX? I HAVE A MEETING.
VAL, DEAR, I CAN'T FIGURE OUT THESE INSUR-ANCE FORMS. AS LONG AS YOU'RE HERE, CAN YOU HELP ME?
WAAA
I THOUGHT YOU WERE TAKING THE AFTERNOON OFF?
DON'T EVER LET ME DO THAT AGAIN.

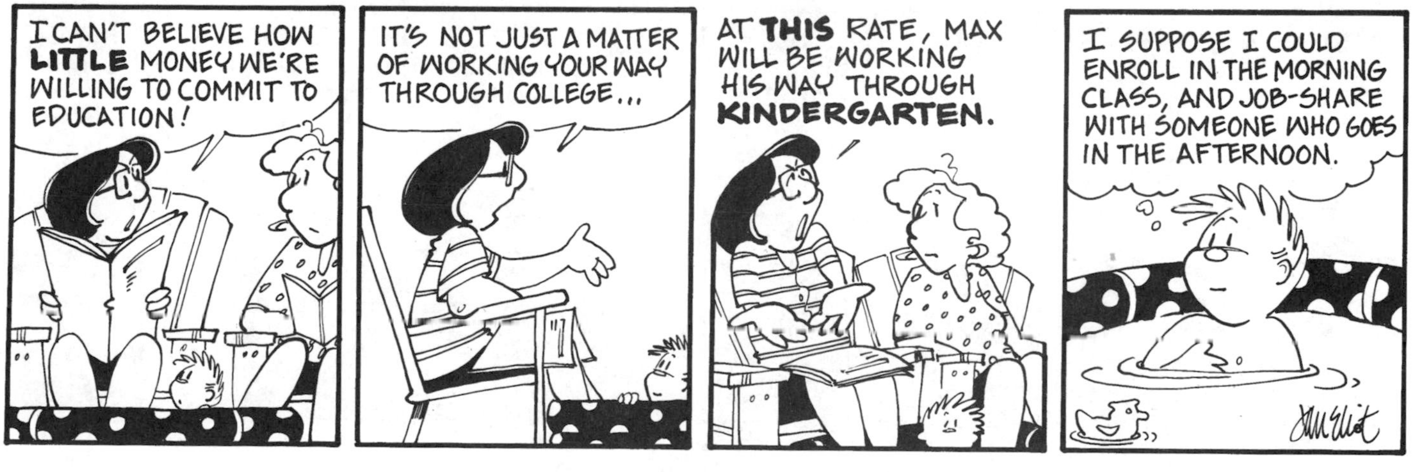
I CAN'T BELIEVE HOW LITTLE MONEY WE'RE WILLING TO COMMIT TO EDUCATION!
IT'S NOT JUST A MATTER OF WORKING YOUR WAY THROUGH COLLEGE...
AT THIS RATE, MAX WILL BE WORKING HIS WAY THROUGH KINDERGARTEN.
I SUPPOSE I COULD ENROLL IN THE MORNING CLASS, AND JOB-SHARE WITH SOMEONE WHO GOES IN THE AFTERNOON.

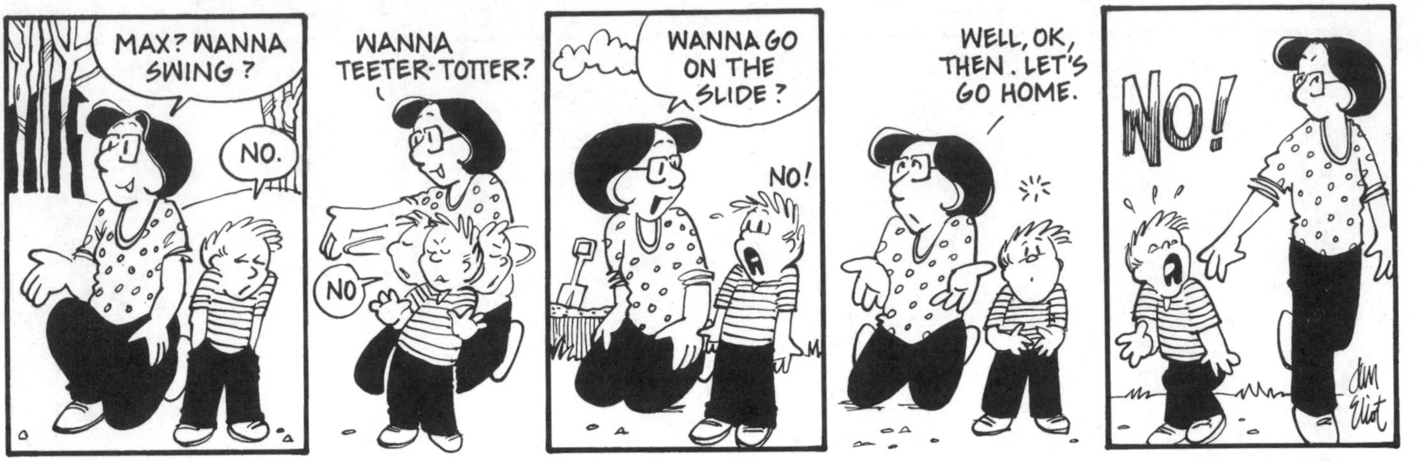
MAX? WANNA SWING?
NO.
WANNA TEETER-TOTTER?
NO
WANNA GO ON THE SLIDE?
NO!
WELL, OK, THEN. LET'S GO HOME.
NO!

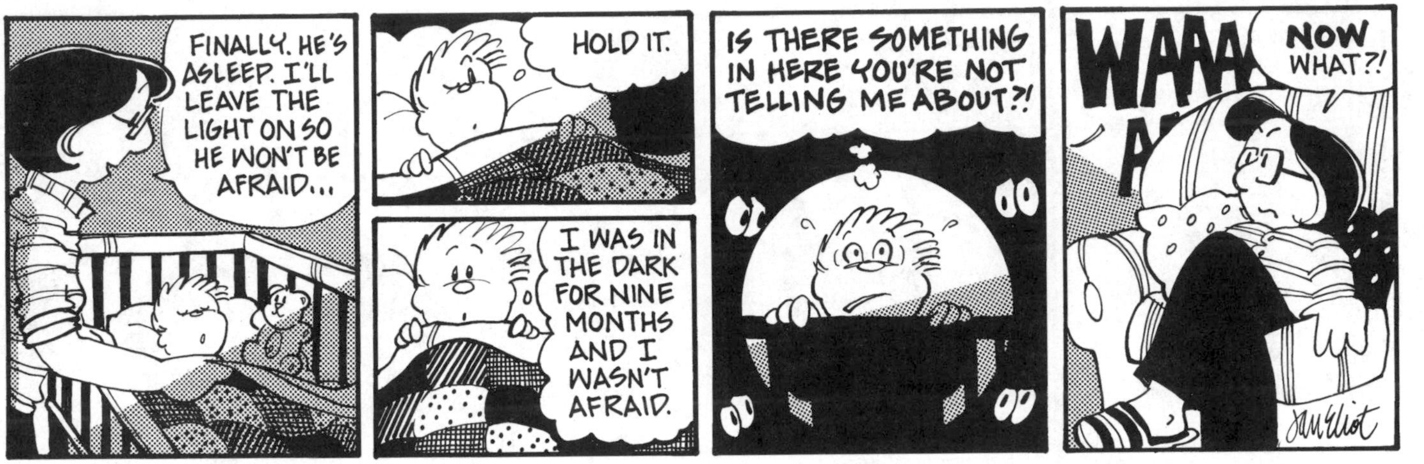
FINALLY. HE'S ASLEEP. I'LL LEAVE THE LIGHT ON SO HE WON'T BE AFRAID...
HOLD IT.
I WAS IN THE DARK FOR NINE MONTHS AND I WASN'T AFRAID.
IS THERE SOMETHING IN HERE YOU'RE NOT TELLING ME ABOUT?!
NOW WHAT?!

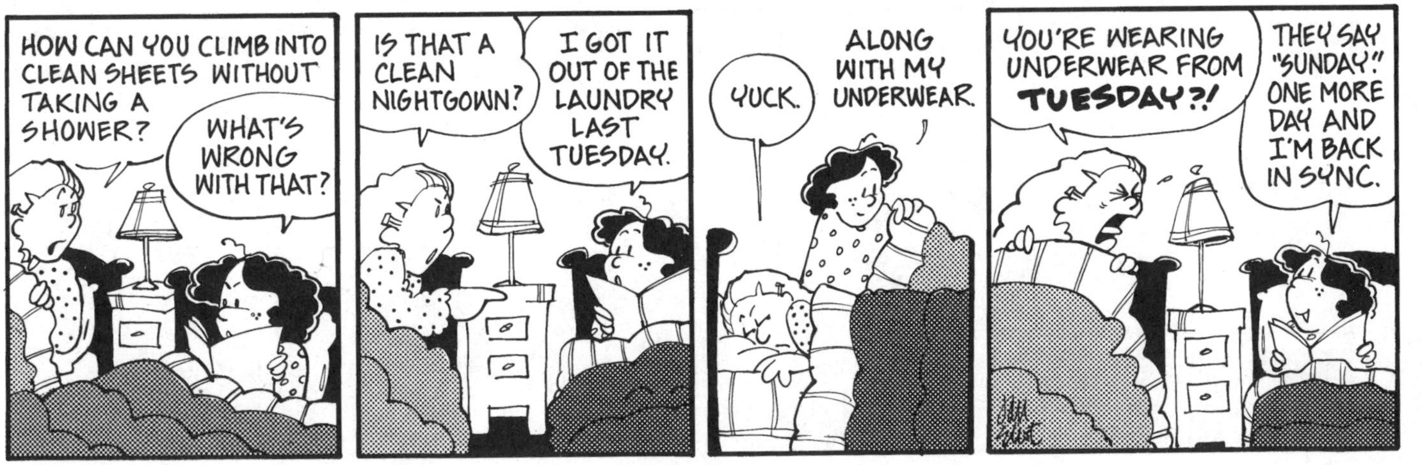
HOW CAN YOU CLIMB INTO CLEAN SHEETS WITHOUT TAKING A SHOWER?
WHAT'S WRONG WITH THAT?
IS THAT A CLEAN NIGHTGOWN?
I GOT IT OUT OF THE LAUNDRY LAST TUESDAY.
YUCK.
ALONG WITH MY UNDERWEAR.
YOU'RE WEARING UNDERWEAR FROM TUESDAY?!
THEY SAY "SUNDAY." ONE MORE DAY AND I'M BACK IN SYNC.

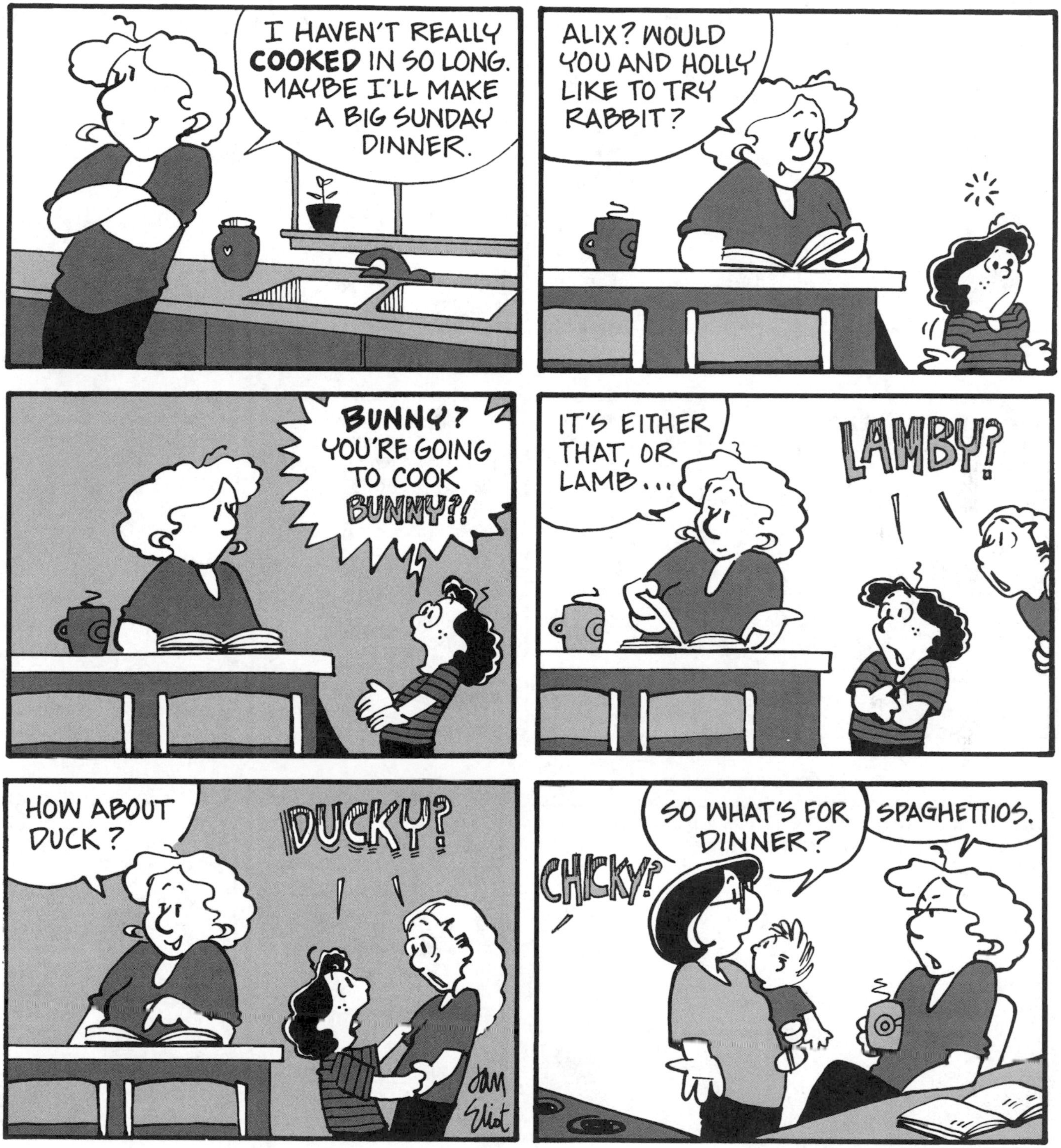
I HAVEN'T REALLY **COOKED** IN SO LONG. MAYBE I'LL MAKE A BIG SUNDAY DINNER.
ALIX? WOULD YOU AND HOLLY LIKE TO TRY RABBIT?
BUNNY? YOU'RE GOING TO COOK BUNNY?!
IT'S EITHER THAT, OR LAMB...
LAMBY?
HOW ABOUT DUCK?
DUCKY?
CHICKY?
SO WHAT'S FOR DINNER?
SPAGHETTIOS.
Jan Eliot

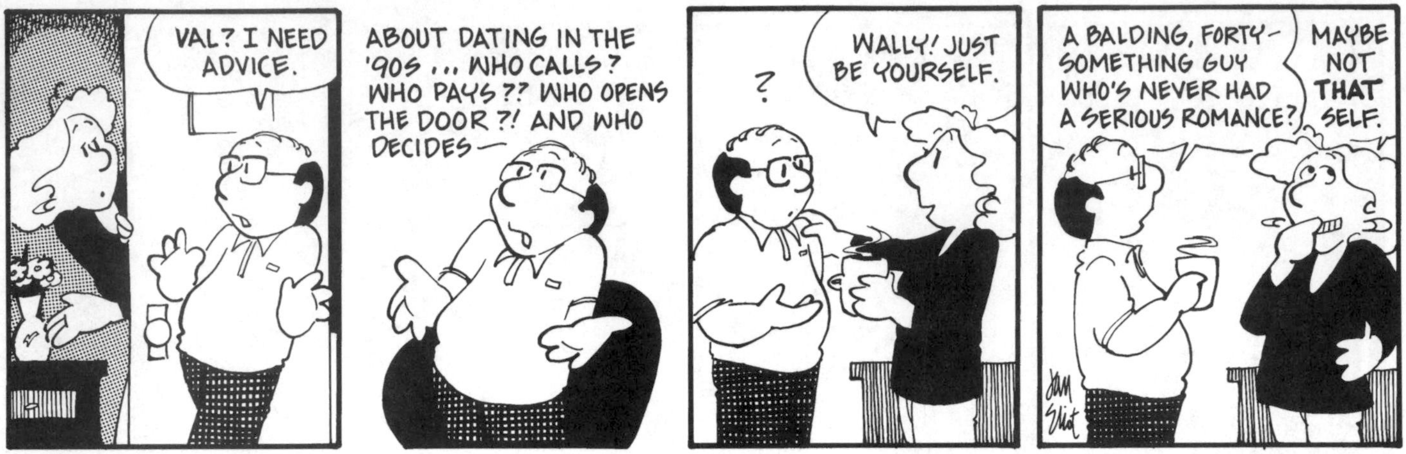
VAL? I NEED ADVICE.
ABOUT DATING IN THE '90S ... WHO CALLS? WHO PAYS?? WHO OPENS THE DOOR?! AND WHO DECIDES—
?
WALLY! JUST BE YOURSELF.
A BALDING, FORTY-SOMETHING GUY WHO'S NEVER HAD A SERIOUS ROMANCE?
MAYBE NOT THAT SELF.

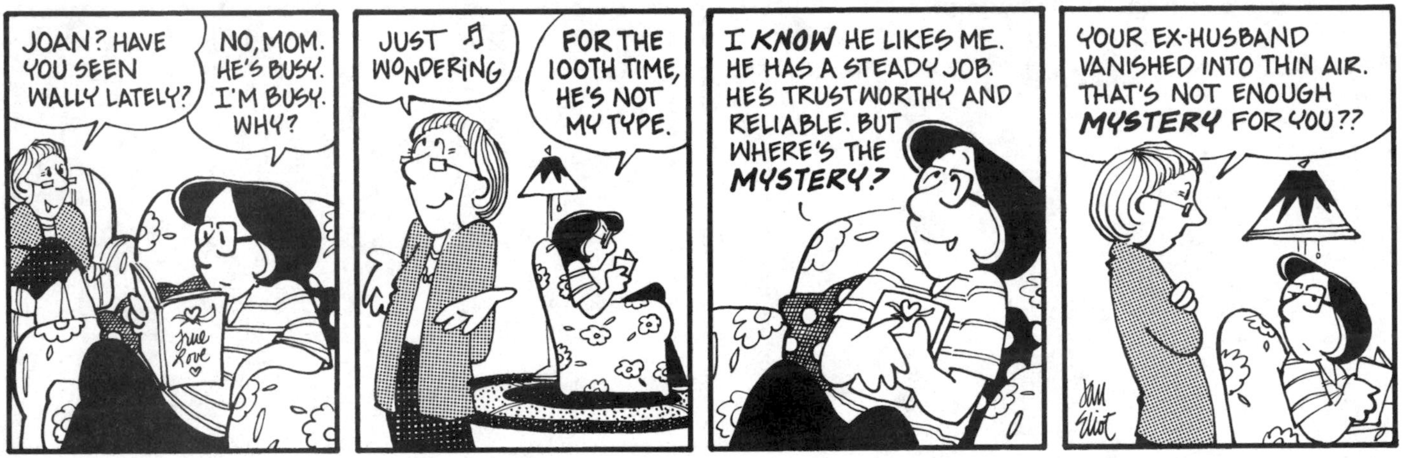
JOAN? HAVE YOU SEEN WALLY LATELY?
NO, MOM. HE'S BUSY. I'M BUSY. WHY?
JUST WONDERING ♫
FOR THE 100TH TIME, HE'S NOT MY TYPE.
True Love
I KNOW HE LIKES ME. HE HAS A STEADY JOB. HE'S TRUSTWORTHY AND RELIABLE. BUT WHERE'S THE MYSTERY?
YOUR EX-HUSBAND VANISHED INTO THIN AIR. THAT'S NOT ENOUGH MYSTERY FOR YOU??

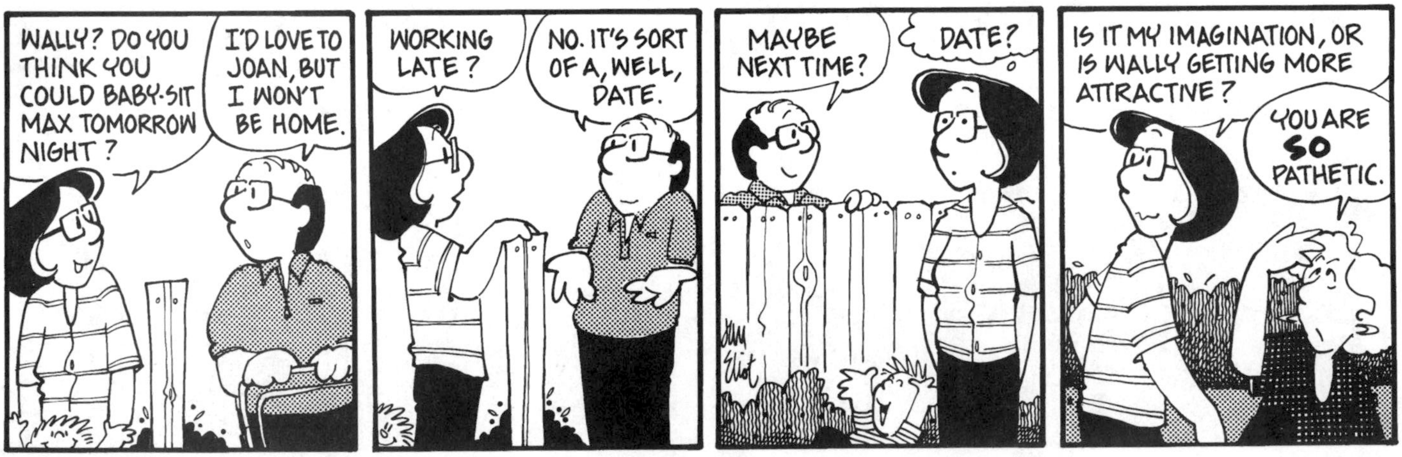
WALLY? DO YOU THINK YOU COULD BABY-SIT MAX TOMORROW NIGHT?
I'D LOVE TO JOAN, BUT I WON'T BE HOME.
WORKING LATE?
NO. IT'S SORT OF A, WELL, DATE.
MAYBE NEXT TIME?
DATE?
IS IT MY IMAGINATION, OR IS WALLY GETTING MORE ATTRACTIVE?
YOU ARE SO PATHETIC.

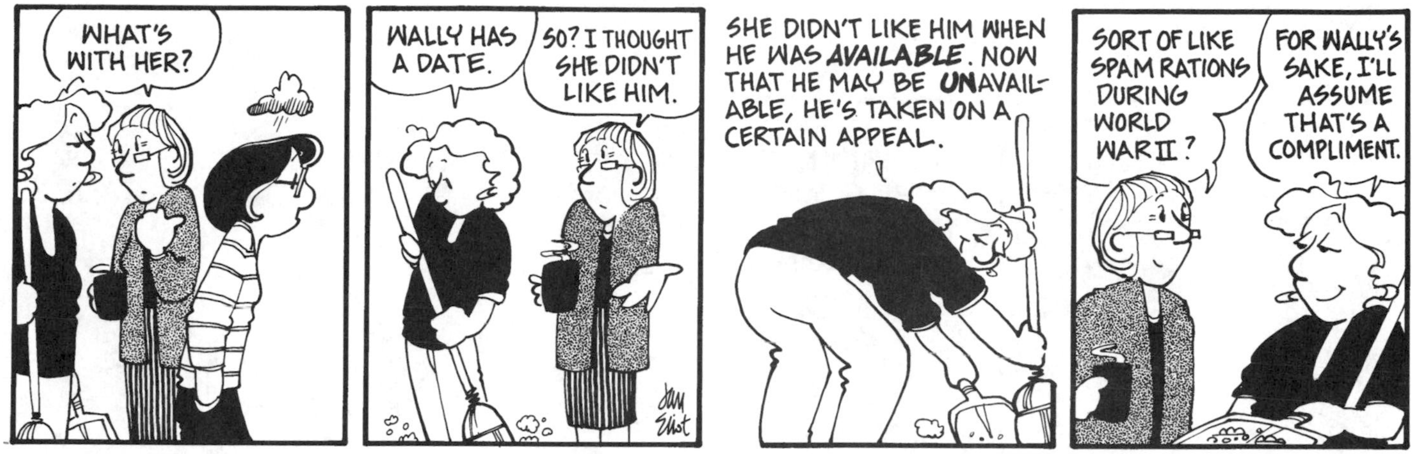
WHAT'S WITH HER?
WALLY HAS A DATE.
SO? I THOUGHT SHE DIDN'T LIKE HIM.
SHE DIDN'T LIKE HIM WHEN HE WAS AVAILABLE. NOW THAT HE MAY BE UNAVAILABLE, HE'S TAKEN ON A CERTAIN APPEAL.
SORT OF LIKE SPAM RATIONS DURING WORLD WAR II?
FOR WALLY'S SAKE, I'LL ASSUME THAT'S A COMPLIMENT.

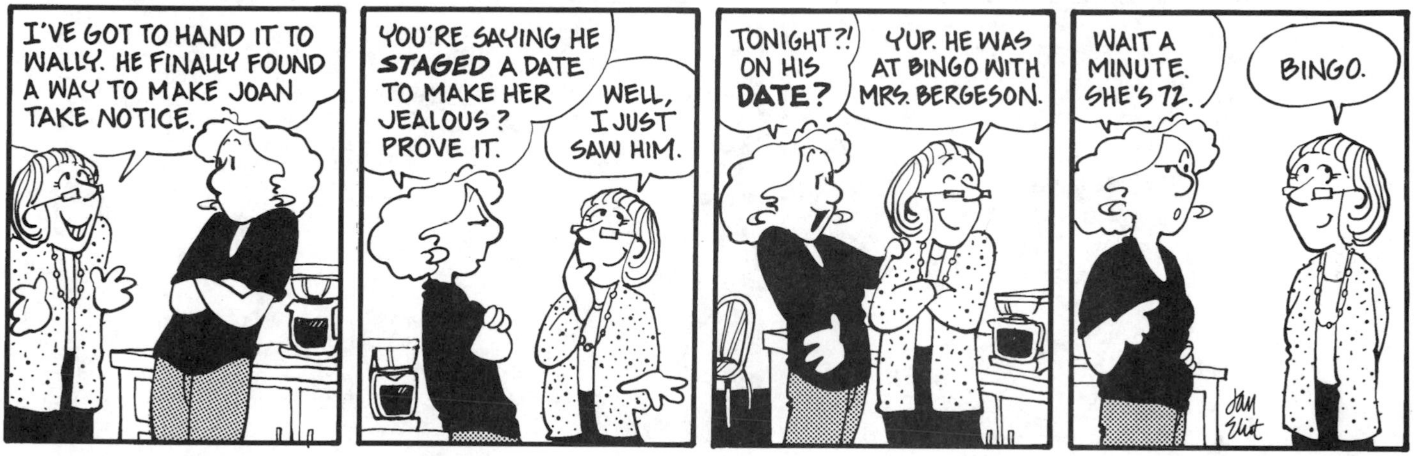
I'VE GOT TO HAND IT TO WALLY. HE FINALLY FOUND A WAY TO MAKE JOAN TAKE NOTICE.
YOU'RE SAYING HE STAGED A DATE TO MAKE HER JEALOUS? PROVE IT.
WELL, I JUST SAW HIM.
TONIGHT?! ON HIS DATE?
YUP. HE WAS AT BINGO WITH MRS. BERGESON.
WAIT A MINUTE. SHE'S 72.
BINGO.

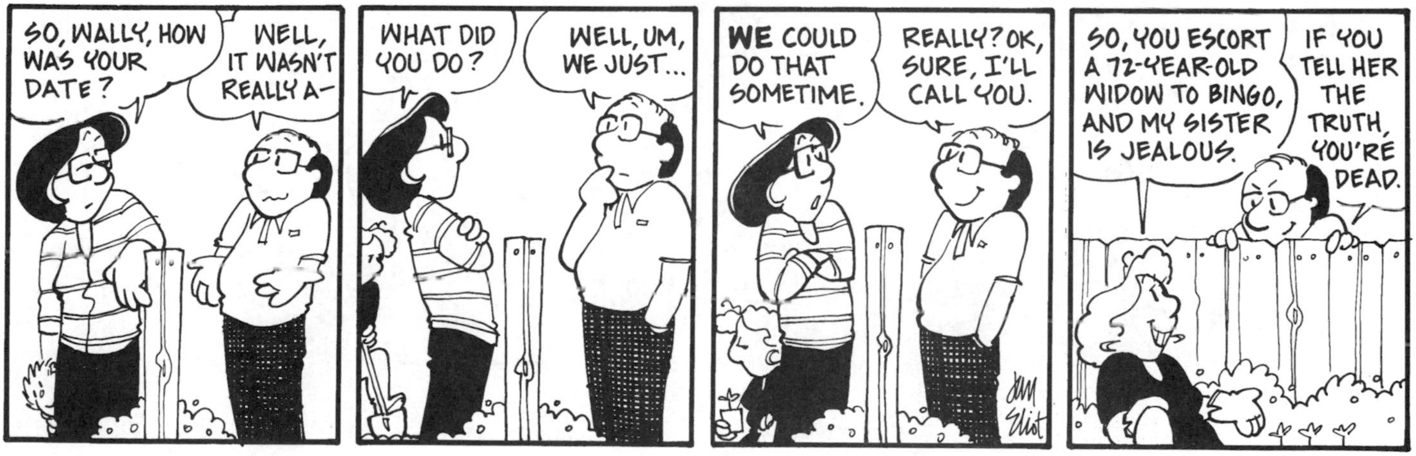
SO, WALLY, HOW WAS YOUR DATE?
WELL, IT WASN'T REALLY A-
WHAT DID YOU DO?
WELL, UM, WE JUST...
WE COULD DO THAT SOMETIME.
REALLY? OK, SURE, I'LL CALL YOU.
SO, YOU ESCORT A 72-YEAR-OLD WIDOW TO BINGO, AND MY SISTER IS JEALOUS.
IF YOU TELL HER THE TRUTH, YOU'RE DEAD.

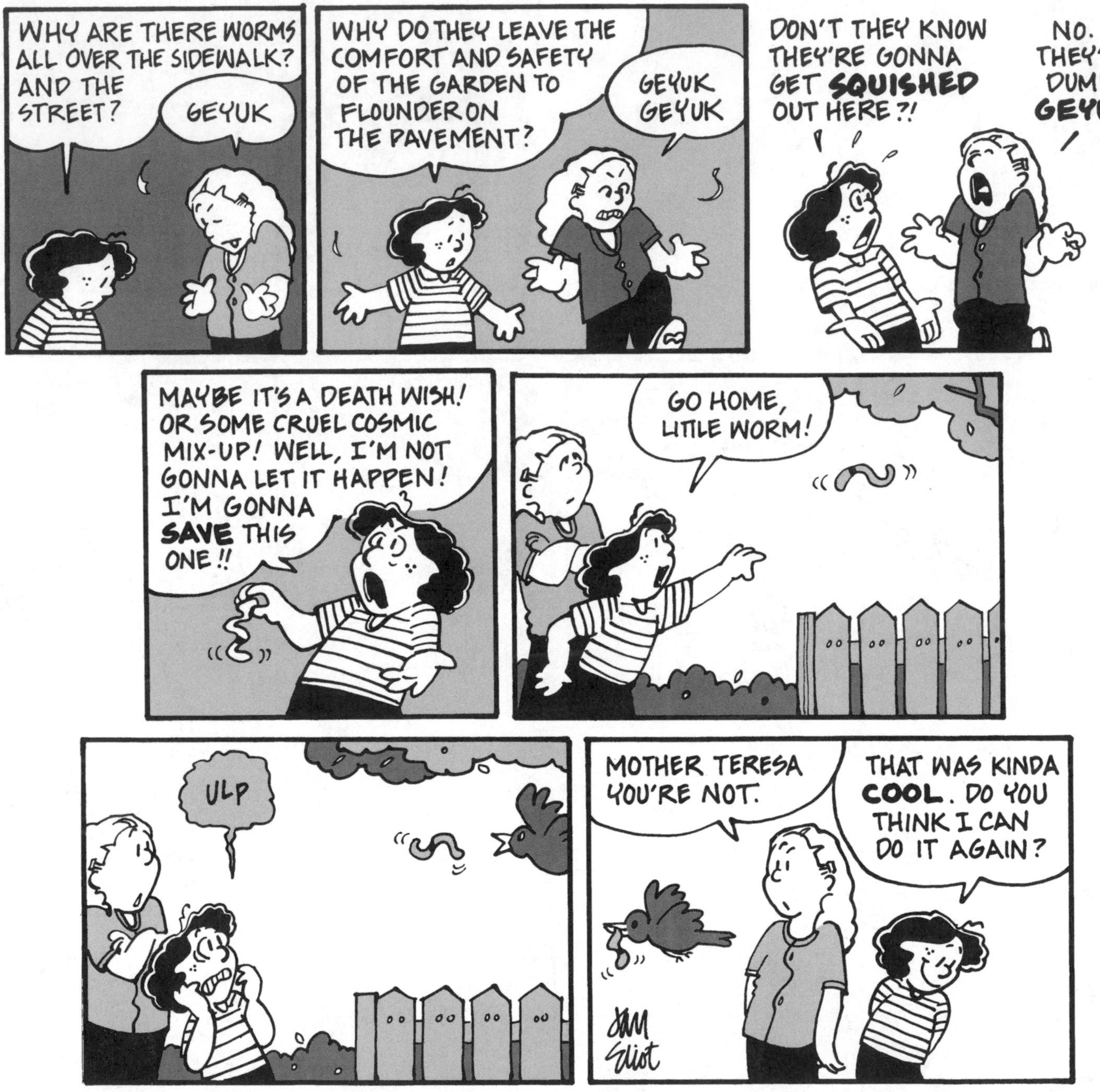
WHY ARE THERE WORMS ALL OVER THE SIDEWALK? AND THE STREET?
GEYUK
WHY DO THEY LEAVE THE COMFORT AND SAFETY OF THE GARDEN TO FLOUNDER ON THE PAVEMENT?
GEYUK GEYUK
DON'T THEY KNOW THEY'RE GONNA GET **SQUISHED** OUT HERE?!
NO. THEY'RE DUMB. **GEYUK.**
MAYBE IT'S A DEATH WISH! OR SOME CRUEL COSMIC MIX-UP! WELL, I'M NOT GONNA LET IT HAPPEN! I'M GONNA **SAVE** THIS ONE!!
GO HOME, LITTLE WORM!
ULP
MOTHER TERESA YOU'RE NOT.
THAT WAS KINDA **COOL**. DO YOU THINK I CAN DO IT AGAIN?
JAN Eliot

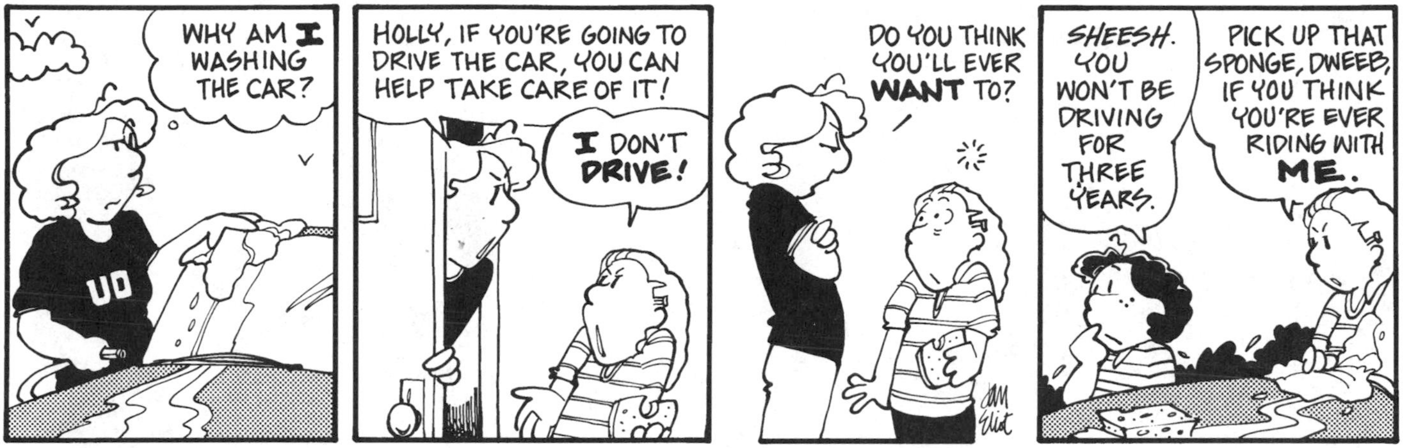
WHY AM I WASHING THE CAR?
HOLLY, IF YOU'RE GOING TO DRIVE THE CAR, YOU CAN HELP TAKE CARE OF IT!
I DON'T DRIVE!
DO YOU THINK YOU'LL EVER WANT TO?
SHEESH. YOU WON'T BE DRIVING FOR THREE YEARS.
PICK UP THAT SPONGE, DWEEB, IF YOU THINK YOU'RE EVER RIDING WITH ME.

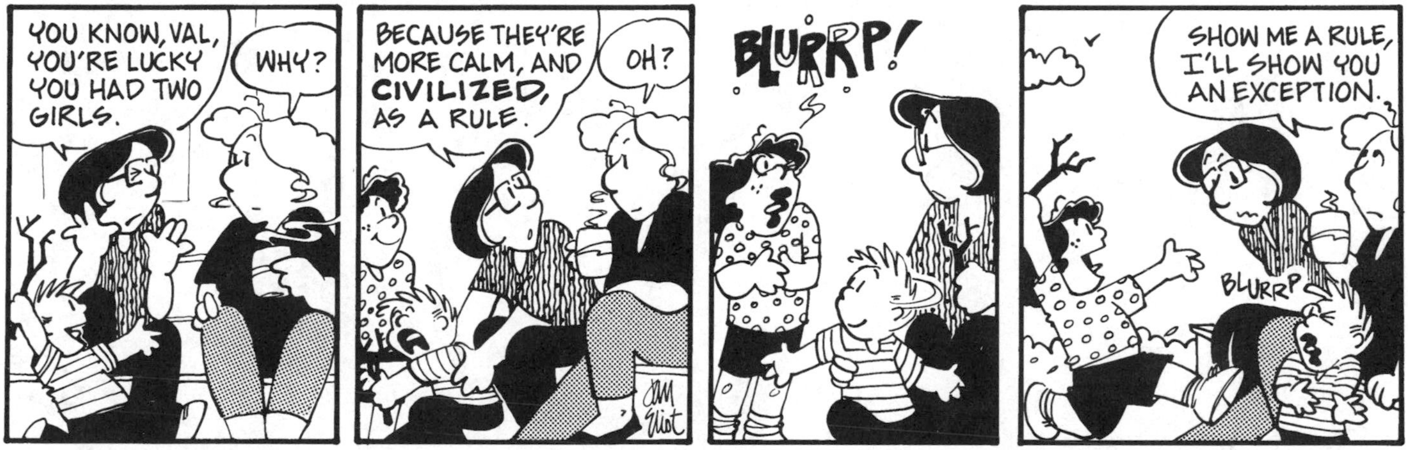
YOU KNOW, VAL, YOU'RE LUCKY YOU HAD TWO GIRLS.
WHY?
BECAUSE THEY'RE MORE CALM, AND CIVILIZED, AS A RULE.
OH?
BLURRP!
SHOW ME A RULE, I'LL SHOW YOU AN EXCEPTION.
BLURRP

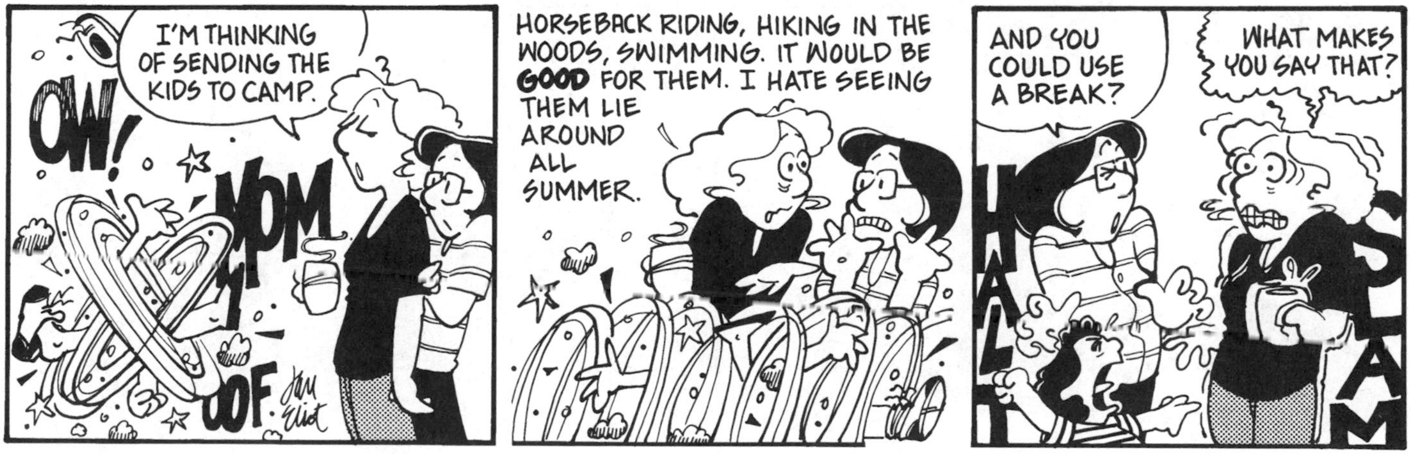
I'M THINKING OF SENDING THE KIDS TO CAMP.
OW!
MOM
OOF.
HORSEBACK RIDING, HIKING IN THE WOODS, SWIMMING. IT WOULD BE GOOD FOR THEM. I HATE SEEING THEM LIE AROUND ALL SUMMER.
AND YOU COULD USE A BREAK?
WHAT MAKES YOU SAY THAT?
WHAL
SLAM

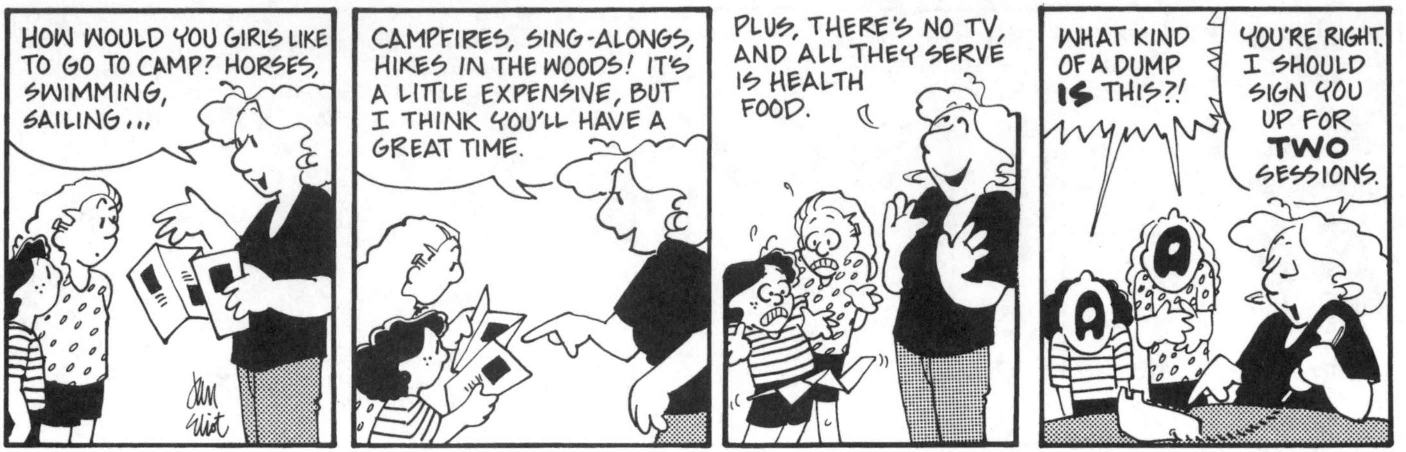
HOW WOULD YOU GIRLS LIKE TO GO TO CAMP? HORSES, SWIMMING, SAILING...
CAMPFIRES, SING-ALONGS, HIKES IN THE WOODS! IT'S A LITTLE EXPENSIVE, BUT I THINK YOU'LL HAVE A GREAT TIME.
PLUS, THERE'S NO TV, AND ALL THEY SERVE IS HEALTH FOOD.
WHAT KIND OF A DUMP **IS** THIS?!
YOU'RE RIGHT. I SHOULD SIGN YOU UP FOR **TWO** SESSIONS.

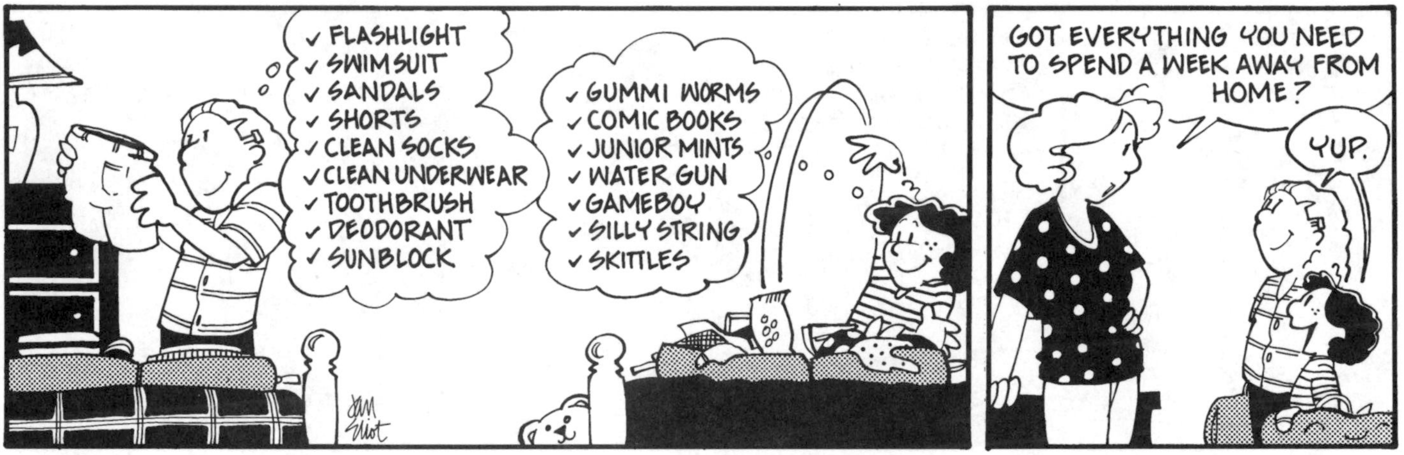
✓ FLASHLIGHT
✓ SWIMSUIT
✓ SANDALS
✓ SHORTS
✓ CLEAN SOCKS
✓ CLEAN UNDERWEAR
✓ TOOTHBRUSH
✓ DEODORANT
✓ SUNBLOCK
✓ GUMMI WORMS
✓ COMIC BOOKS
✓ JUNIOR MINTS
✓ WATER GUN
✓ GAMEBOY
✓ SILLY STRING
✓ SKITTLES
GOT EVERYTHING YOU NEED TO SPEND A WEEK AWAY FROM HOME?
YUP.

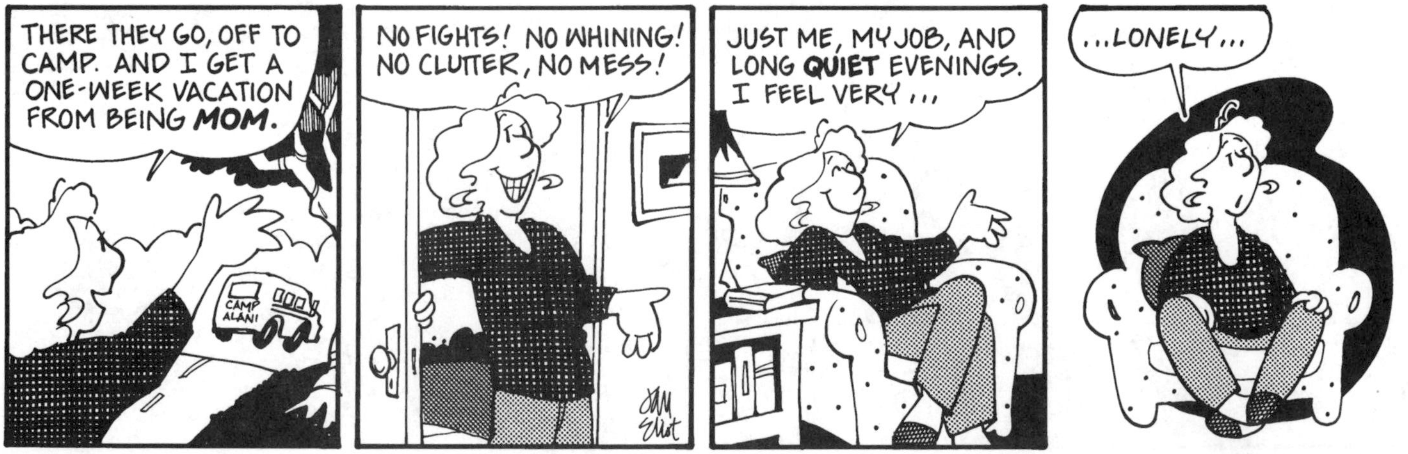
THERE THEY GO, OFF TO CAMP. AND I GET A ONE-WEEK VACATION FROM BEING **MOM**.
CAMP ALANI
NO FIGHTS! NO WHINING! NO CLUTTER, NO MESS!
JUST ME, MY JOB, AND LONG **QUIET** EVENINGS. I FEEL VERY...
...LONELY...

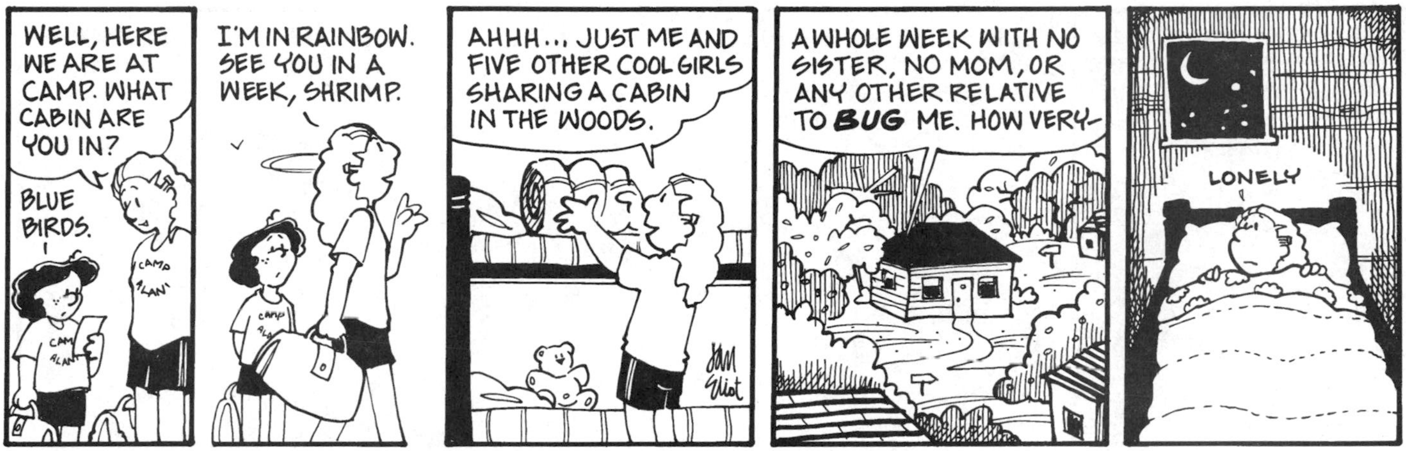
WELL, HERE WE ARE AT CAMP. WHAT CABIN ARE YOU IN?
BLUE BIRDS.
I'M IN RAINBOW. SEE YOU IN A WEEK, SHRIMP.
AHHH... JUST ME AND FIVE OTHER COOL GIRLS SHARING A CABIN IN THE WOODS.
A WHOLE WEEK WITH NO SISTER, NO MOM, OR ANY OTHER RELATIVE TO BUG ME. HOW VERY-
LONELY

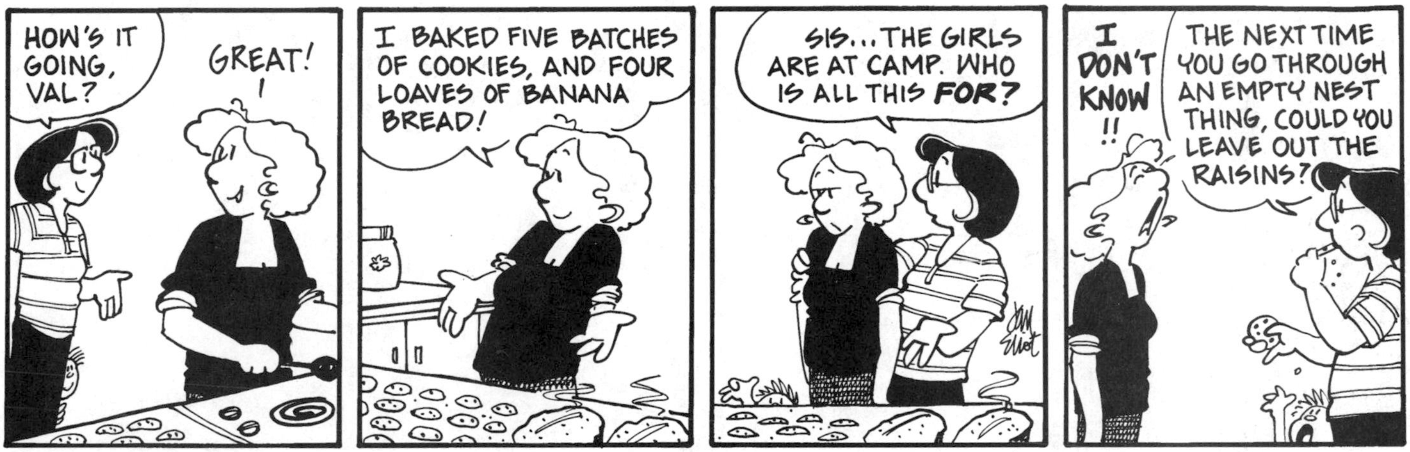
HOW'S IT GOING, VAL?
GREAT!
I BAKED FIVE BATCHES OF COOKIES, AND FOUR LOAVES OF BANANA BREAD!
SIS... THE GIRLS ARE AT CAMP. WHO IS ALL THIS FOR?
I DON'T KNOW !!
THE NEXT TIME YOU GO THROUGH AN EMPTY NEST THING, COULD YOU LEAVE OUT THE RAISINS?

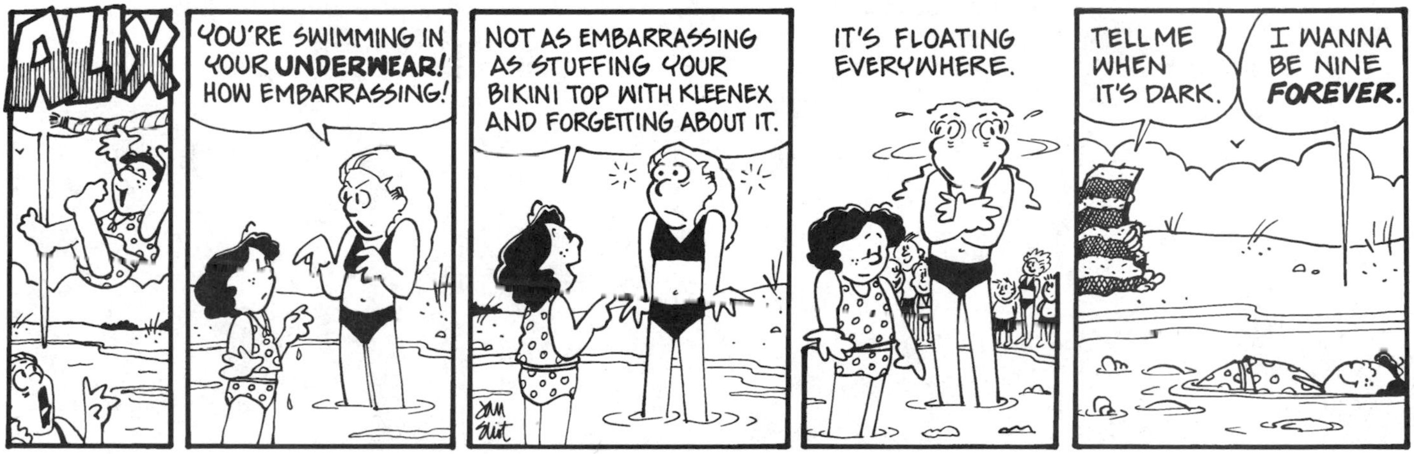
YOU'RE SWIMMING IN YOUR UNDERWEAR! HOW EMBARRASSING!
NOT AS EMBARRASSING AS STUFFING YOUR BIKINI TOP WITH KLEENEX AND FORGETTING ABOUT IT.
IT'S FLOATING EVERYWHERE.
TELL ME WHEN IT'S DARK.
I WANNA BE NINE FOREVER.

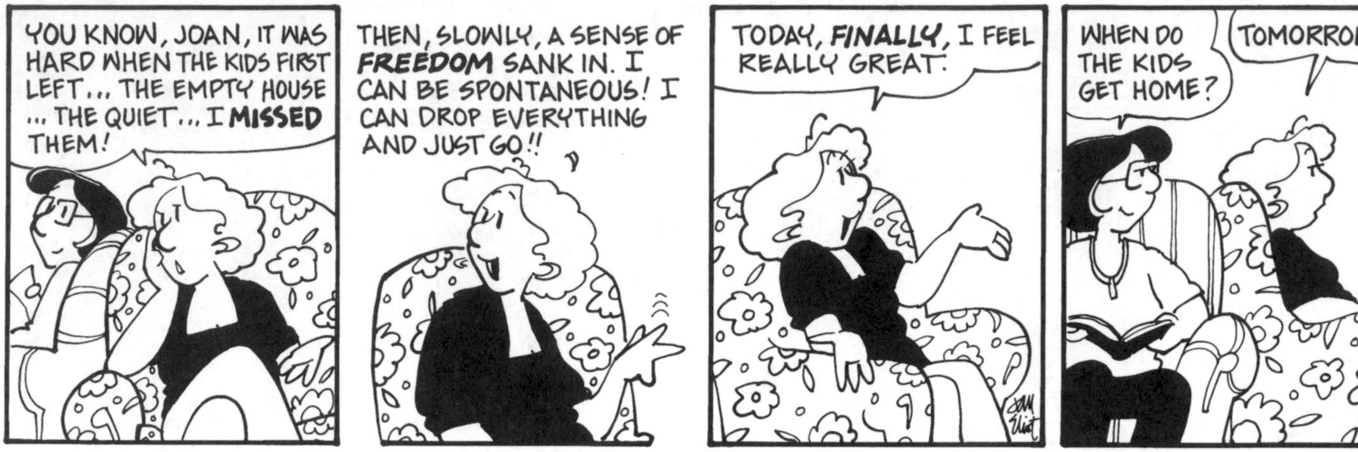
YOU KNOW, JOAN, IT WAS HARD WHEN THE KIDS FIRST LEFT... THE EMPTY HOUSE ... THE QUIET... I **MISSED** THEM!
THEN, SLOWLY, A SENSE OF ***FREEDOM*** SANK IN. I CAN BE SPONTANEOUS! I CAN DROP EVERYTHING AND JUST GO!!
TODAY, ***FINALLY***, I FEEL REALLY GREAT.
WHEN DO THE KIDS GET HOME?
TOMORROW.

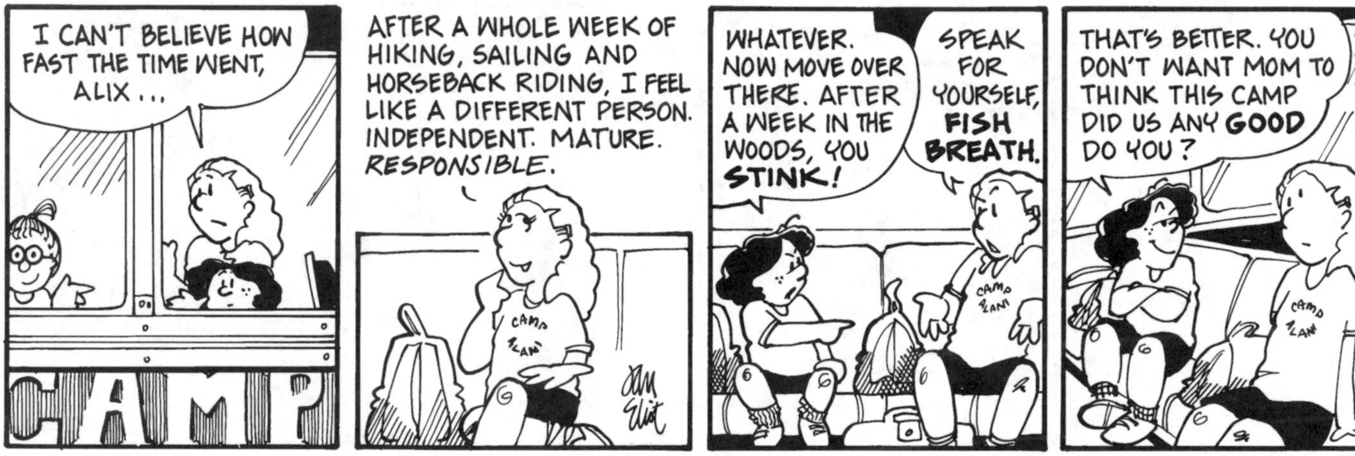
I CAN'T BELIEVE HOW FAST THE TIME WENT, ALIX...
CAMP
AFTER A WHOLE WEEK OF HIKING, SAILING AND HORSEBACK RIDING, I FEEL LIKE A DIFFERENT PERSON. INDEPENDENT. MATURE. *RESPONSIBLE.*
WHATEVER. NOW MOVE OVER THERE. AFTER A WEEK IN THE WOODS, YOU **STINK!**
SPEAK FOR YOURSELF, **FISH BREATH.**
THAT'S BETTER. YOU DON'T WANT MOM TO THINK THIS CAMP DID US ANY **GOOD** DO YOU?

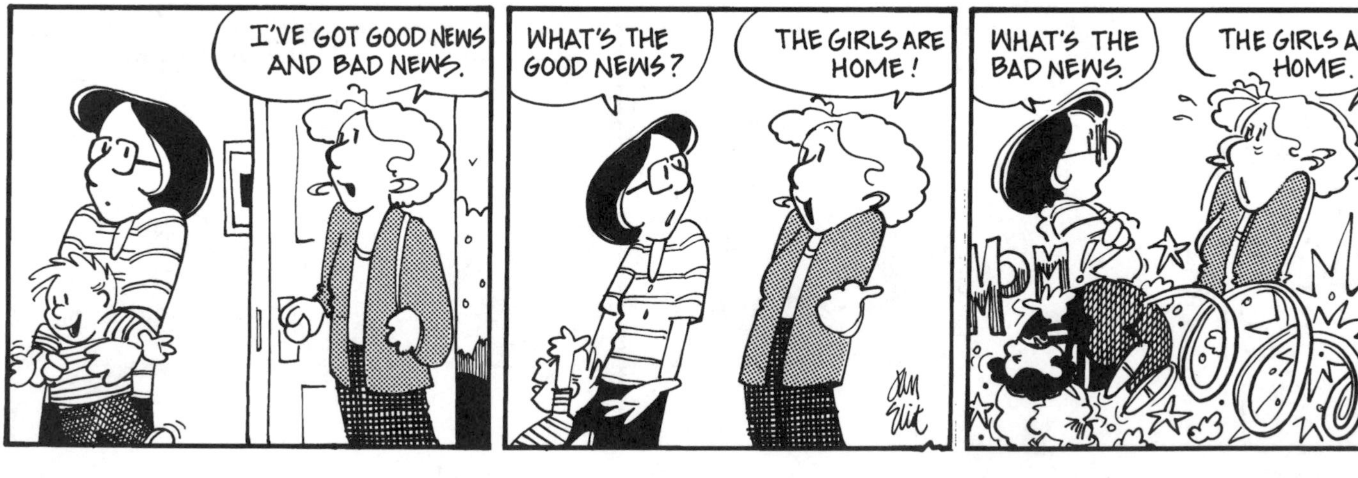
I'VE GOT GOOD NEWS AND BAD NEWS.
WHAT'S THE GOOD NEWS?
THE GIRLS ARE HOME!
WHAT'S THE BAD NEWS.
THE GIRLS ARE HOME.
MOM!

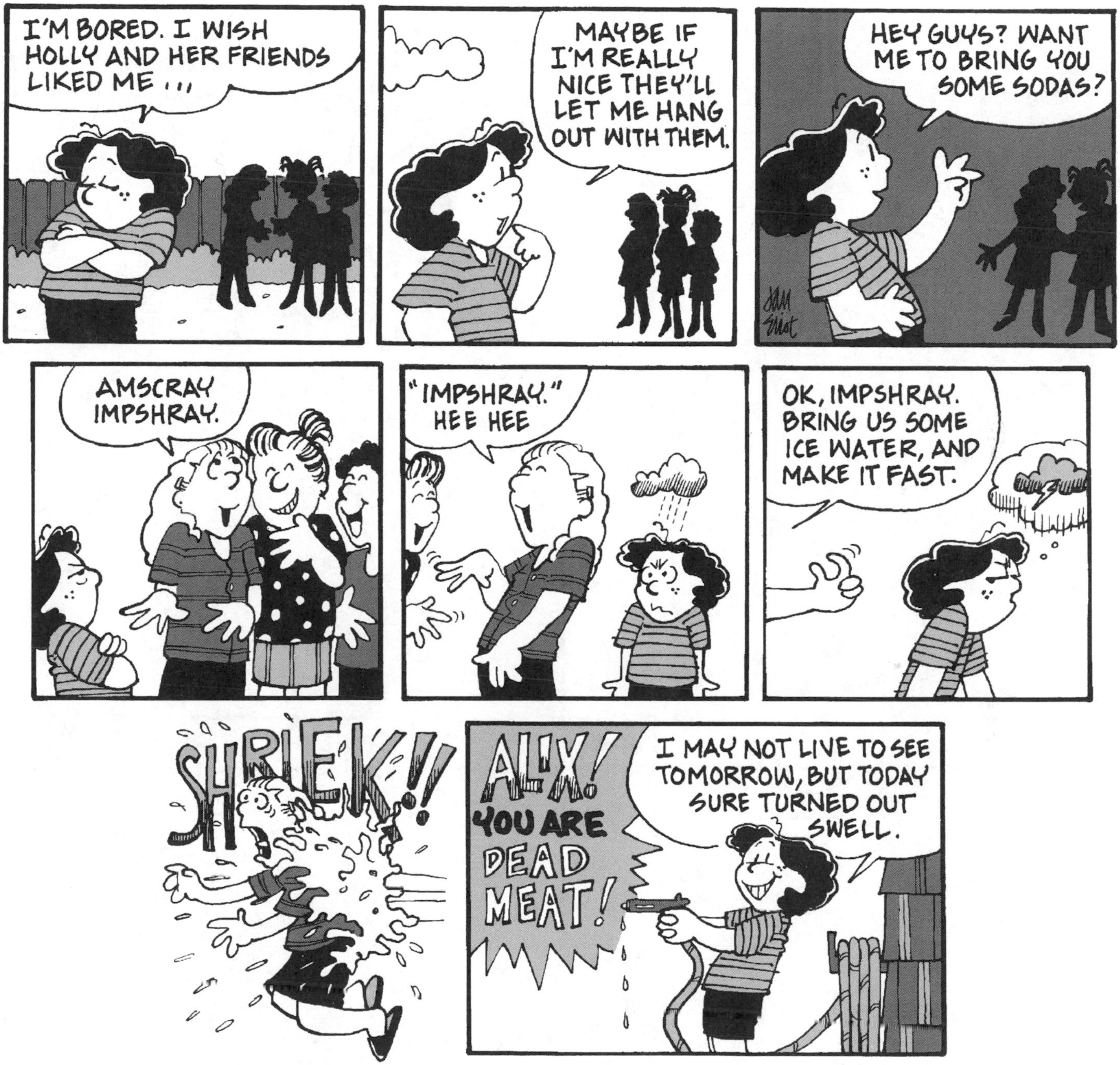

I'M BORED. I WISH HOLLY AND HER FRIENDS LIKED ME ...
MAYBE IF I'M REALLY NICE THEY'LL LET ME HANG OUT WITH THEM.
HEY GUYS? WANT ME TO BRING YOU SOME SODAS?
AMSCRAY IMPSHRAY.
"IMPSHRAY." HEE HEE
OK, IMPSHRAY. BRING US SOME ICE WATER, AND MAKE IT FAST.
SHRIEK!!
ALIX! YOU ARE DEAD MEAT!
I MAY NOT LIVE TO SEE TOMORROW, BUT TODAY SURE TURNED OUT SWELL.

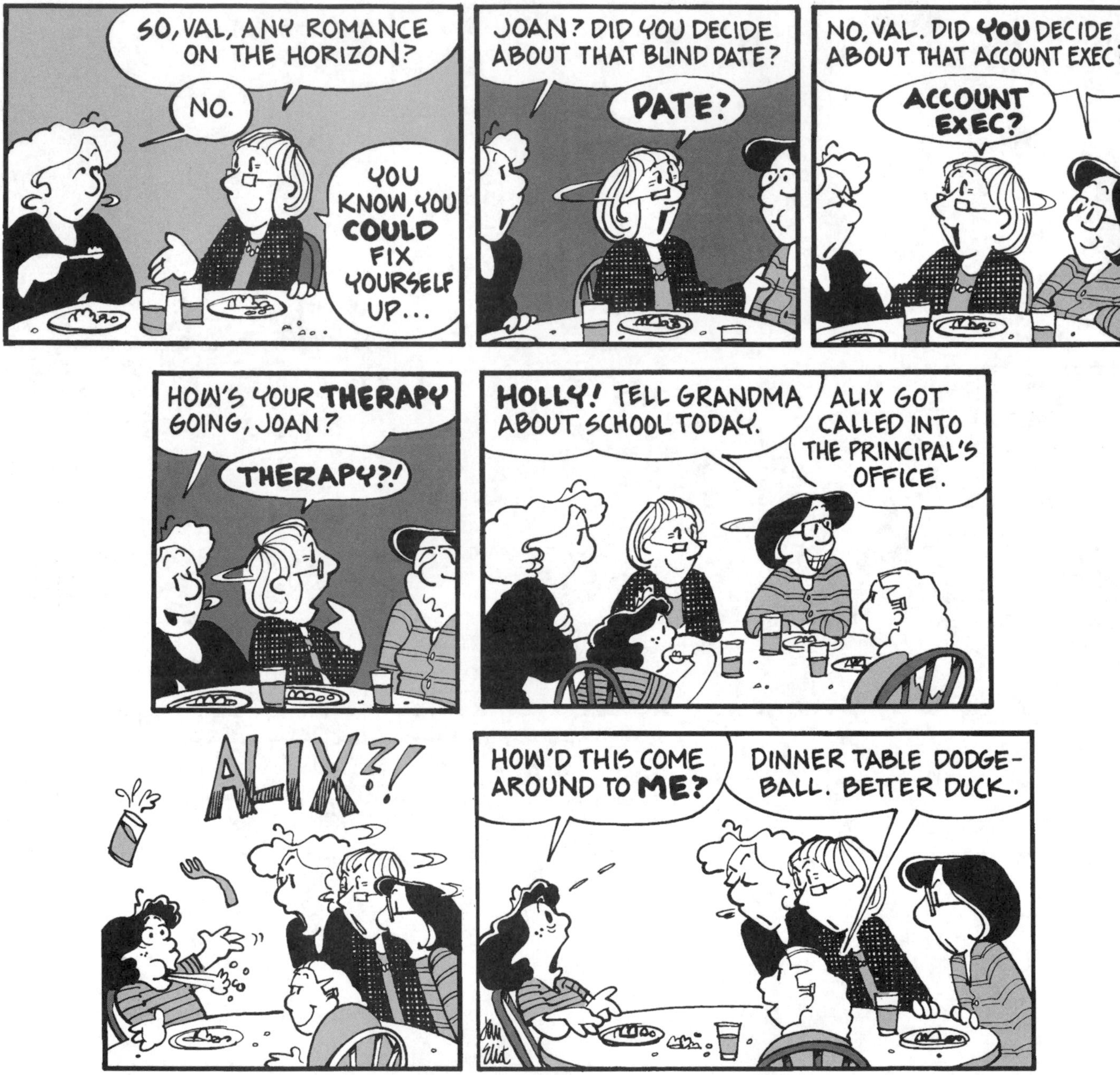
SO, VAL, ANY ROMANCE ON THE HORIZON?
NO.
YOU KNOW, YOU **COULD** FIX YOURSELF UP...
JOAN? DID YOU DECIDE ABOUT THAT BLIND DATE?
DATE?
NO, VAL. DID **YOU** DECIDE ABOUT THAT ACCOUNT EXEC?
ACCOUNT EXEC?
HOW'S YOUR **THERAPY** GOING, JOAN?
THERAPY?!
HOLLY! TELL GRANDMA ABOUT SCHOOL TODAY.
ALIX GOT CALLED INTO THE PRINCIPAL'S OFFICE.
ALIX?!
HOW'D THIS COME AROUND TO **ME?**
DINNER TABLE DODGE-BALL. BETTER DUCK.

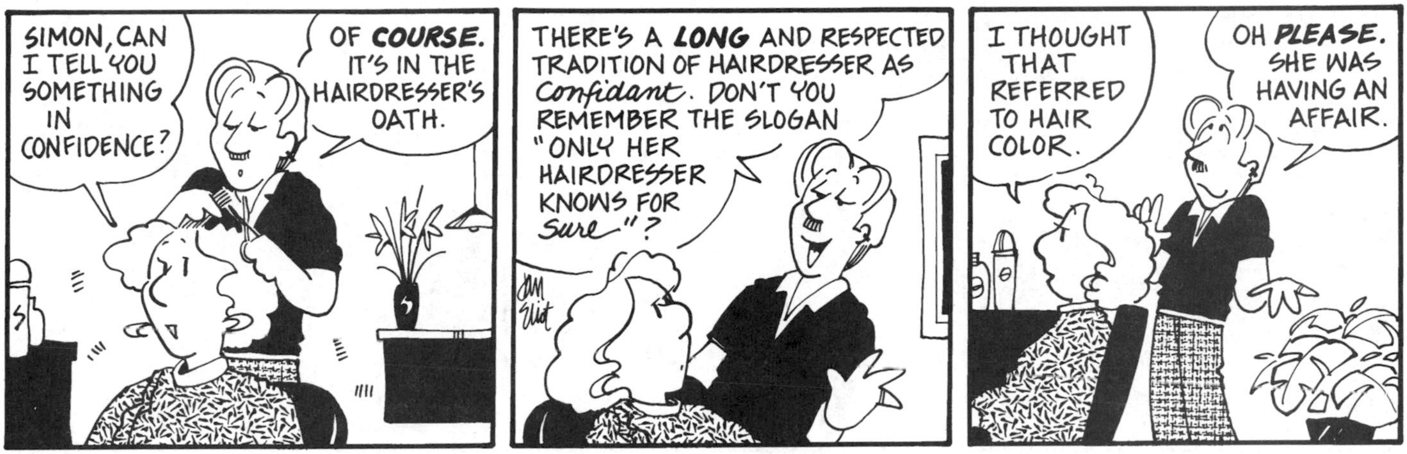
SIMON, CAN I TELL YOU SOMETHING IN CONFIDENCE?
OF COURSE. IT'S IN THE HAIRDRESSER'S OATH.
THERE'S A LONG AND RESPECTED TRADITION OF HAIRDRESSER AS Confidant. DON'T YOU REMEMBER THE SLOGAN "ONLY HER HAIRDRESSER KNOWS FOR Sure"?
I THOUGHT THAT REFERRED TO HAIR COLOR.
OH PLEASE. SHE WAS HAVING AN AFFAIR.

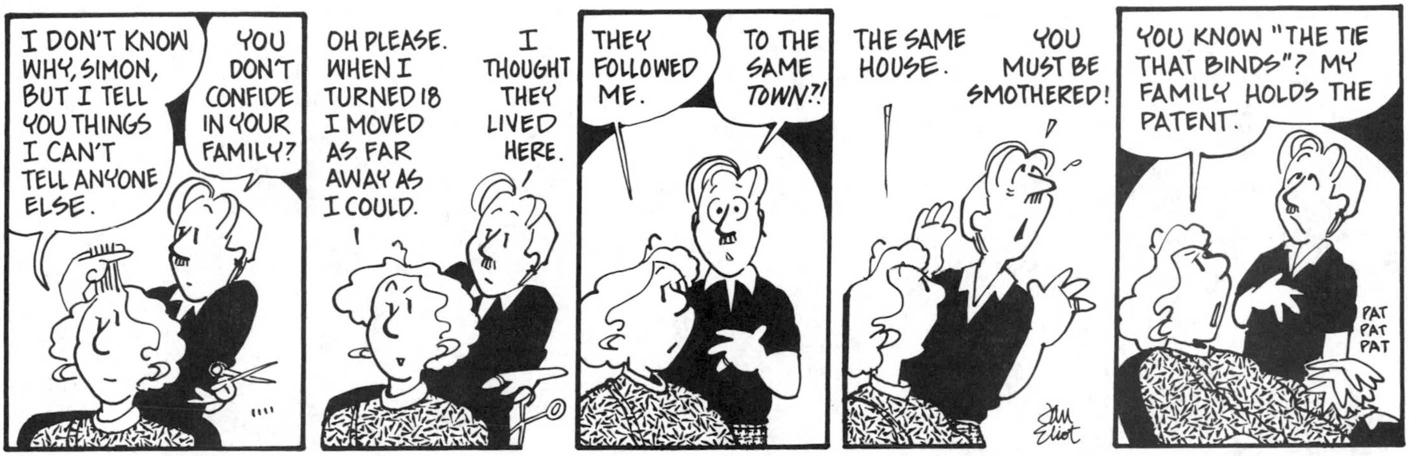
I DON'T KNOW WHY, SIMON, BUT I TELL YOU THINGS I CAN'T TELL ANYONE ELSE.
YOU DON'T CONFIDE IN YOUR FAMILY?
OH PLEASE. WHEN I TURNED 18 I MOVED AS FAR AWAY AS I COULD.
I THOUGHT THEY LIVED HERE.
THEY FOLLOWED ME.
TO THE SAME TOWN?!
THE SAME HOUSE.
YOU MUST BE SMOTHERED!
YOU KNOW "THE TIE THAT BINDS"? MY FAMILY HOLDS THE PATENT.
PAT PAT PAT

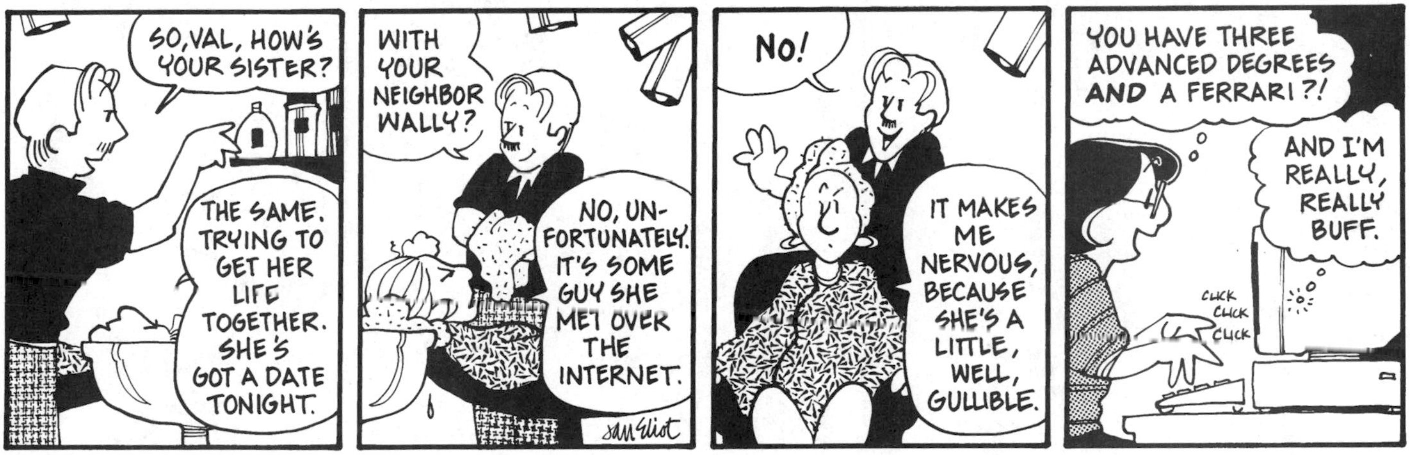
SO, VAL, HOW'S YOUR SISTER?
THE SAME. TRYING TO GET HER LIFE TOGETHER. SHE'S GOT A DATE TONIGHT.
WITH YOUR NEIGHBOR WALLY?
NO, UN-FORTUNATELY. IT'S SOME GUY SHE MET OVER THE INTERNET.
NO!
IT MAKES ME NERVOUS, BECAUSE SHE'S A LITTLE, WELL, GULLIBLE.
YOU HAVE THREE ADVANCED DEGREES AND A FERRARI?!
AND I'M REALLY, REALLY BUFF.
CLICK CLICK CLICK

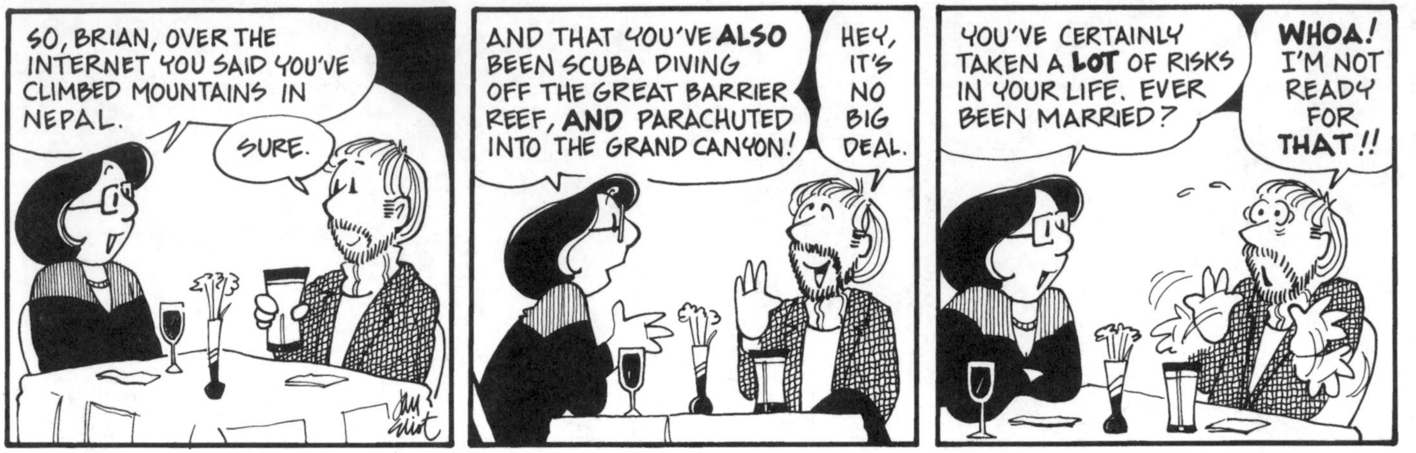
SO, BRIAN, OVER THE INTERNET YOU SAID YOU'VE CLIMBED MOUNTAINS IN NEPAL.
SURE.
AND THAT YOU'VE ALSO BEEN SCUBA DIVING OFF THE GREAT BARRIER REEF, AND PARACHUTED INTO THE GRAND CANYON!
HEY, IT'S NO BIG DEAL.
YOU'VE CERTAINLY TAKEN A LOT OF RISKS IN YOUR LIFE. EVER BEEN MARRIED?
WHOA! I'M NOT READY FOR THAT!!

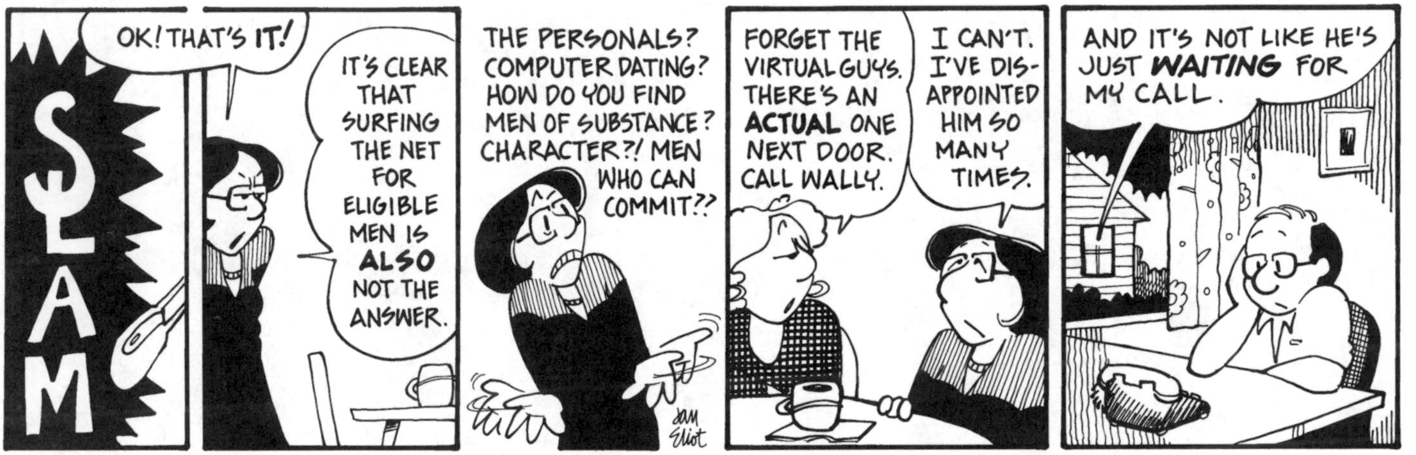
SLAM
OK! THAT'S IT!
IT'S CLEAR THAT SURFING THE NET FOR ELIGIBLE MEN IS ALSO NOT THE ANSWER.
THE PERSONALS? COMPUTER DATING? HOW DO YOU FIND MEN OF SUBSTANCE? CHARACTER?! MEN WHO CAN COMMIT??
FORGET THE VIRTUAL GUYS. THERE'S AN ACTUAL ONE NEXT DOOR. CALL WALLY.
I CAN'T. I'VE DISAPPOINTED HIM SO MANY TIMES.
AND IT'S NOT LIKE HE'S JUST WAITING FOR MY CALL.

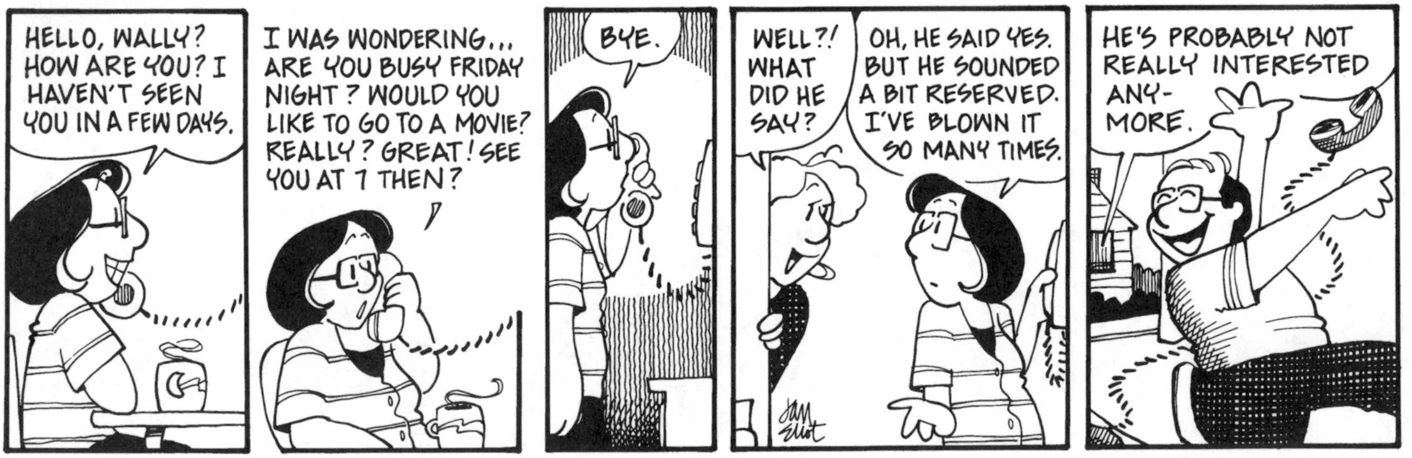
HELLO, WALLY? HOW ARE YOU? I HAVEN'T SEEN YOU IN A FEW DAYS.
I WAS WONDERING... ARE YOU BUSY FRIDAY NIGHT? WOULD YOU LIKE TO GO TO A MOVIE? REALLY? GREAT! SEE YOU AT 7 THEN?
BYE.
WELL?! WHAT DID HE SAY?
OH, HE SAID YES. BUT HE SOUNDED A BIT RESERVED. I'VE BLOWN IT SO MANY TIMES.
HE'S PROBABLY NOT REALLY INTERESTED ANYMORE.

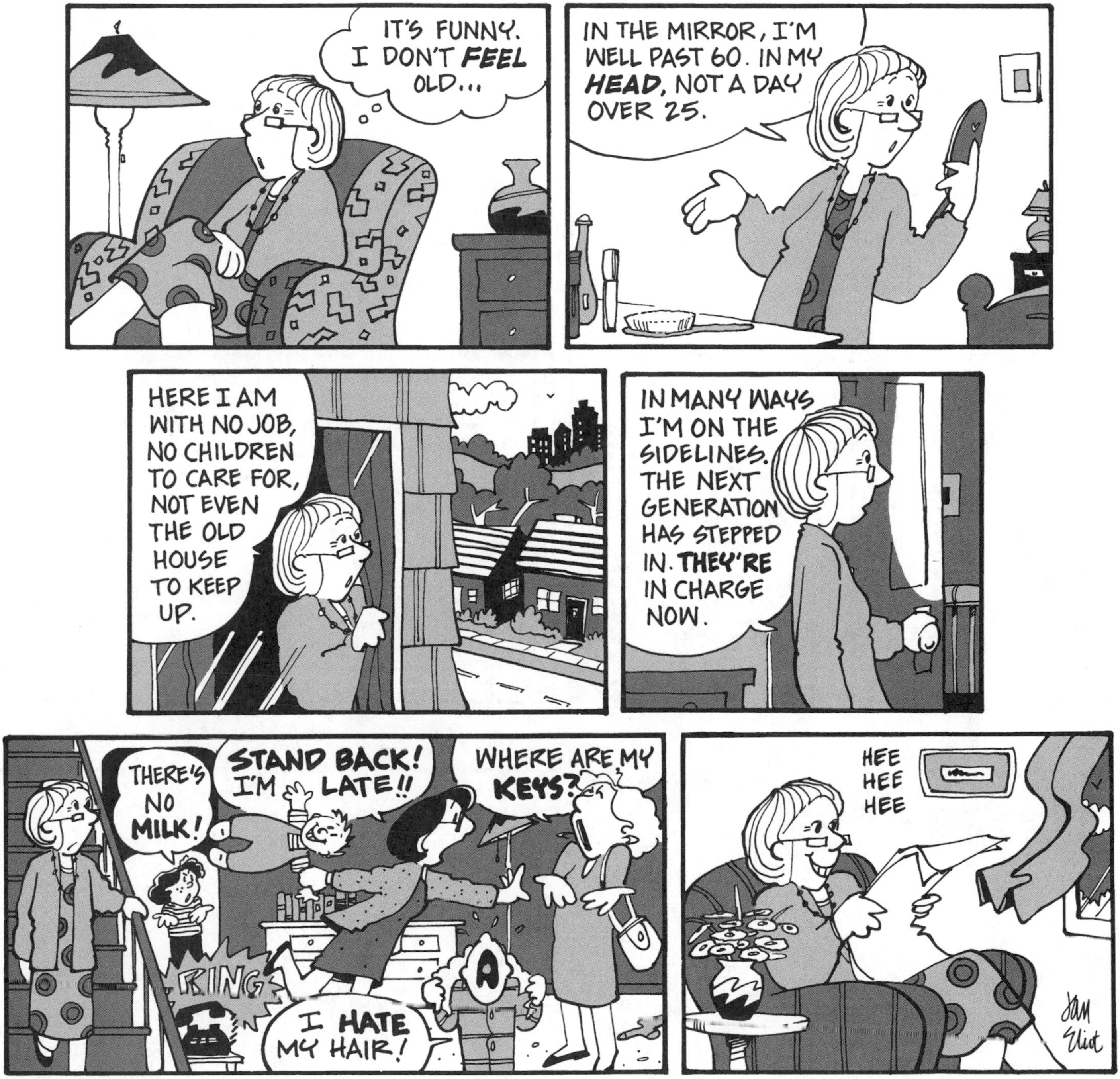
IT'S FUNNY. I DON'T **FEEL** OLD...
IN THE MIRROR, I'M WELL PAST 60. IN MY **HEAD**, NOT A DAY OVER 25.
HERE I AM WITH NO JOB, NO CHILDREN TO CARE FOR, NOT EVEN THE OLD HOUSE TO KEEP UP.
IN MANY WAYS I'M ON THE SIDELINES. THE NEXT GENERATION HAS STEPPED IN. **THEY'RE** IN CHARGE NOW.
THERE'S NO **MILK**!
STAND BACK! I'M LATE!!
WHERE ARE MY **KEYS**?
RING
I **HATE** MY HAIR!
HEE HEE HEE
JAN Eliot

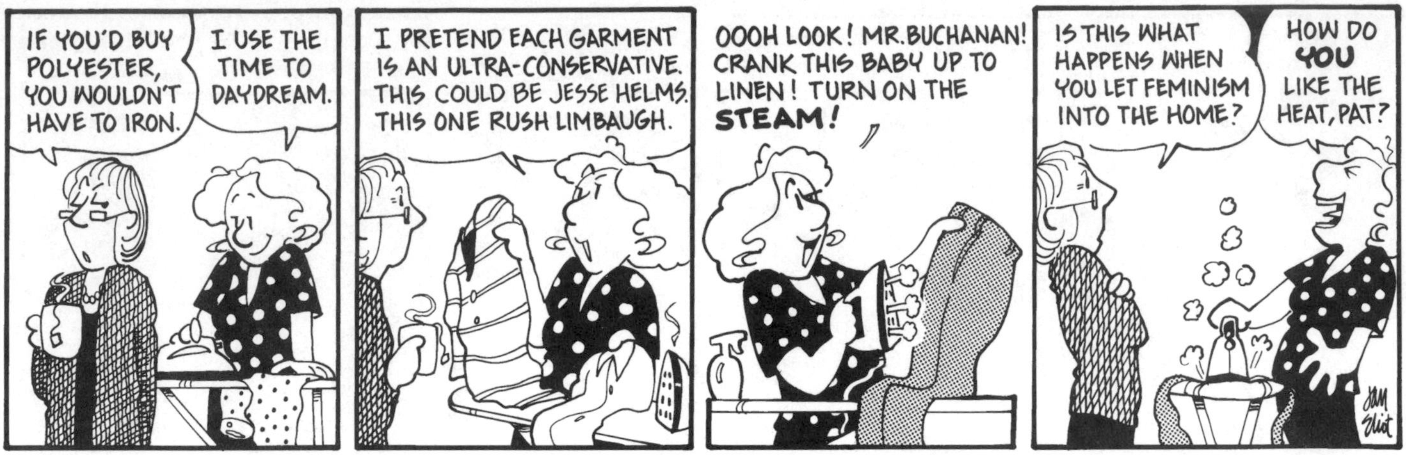
IF YOU'D BUY POLYESTER, YOU WOULDN'T HAVE TO IRON.
I USE THE TIME TO DAYDREAM.
I PRETEND EACH GARMENT IS AN ULTRA-CONSERVATIVE. THIS COULD BE JESSE HELMS. THIS ONE RUSH LIMBAUGH.
OOOH LOOK! MR. BUCHANAN! CRANK THIS BABY UP TO LINEN! TURN ON THE **STEAM**!
IS THIS WHAT HAPPENS WHEN YOU LET FEMINISM INTO THE HOME?
HOW DO **YOU** LIKE THE HEAT, PAT?
JAN Eliot

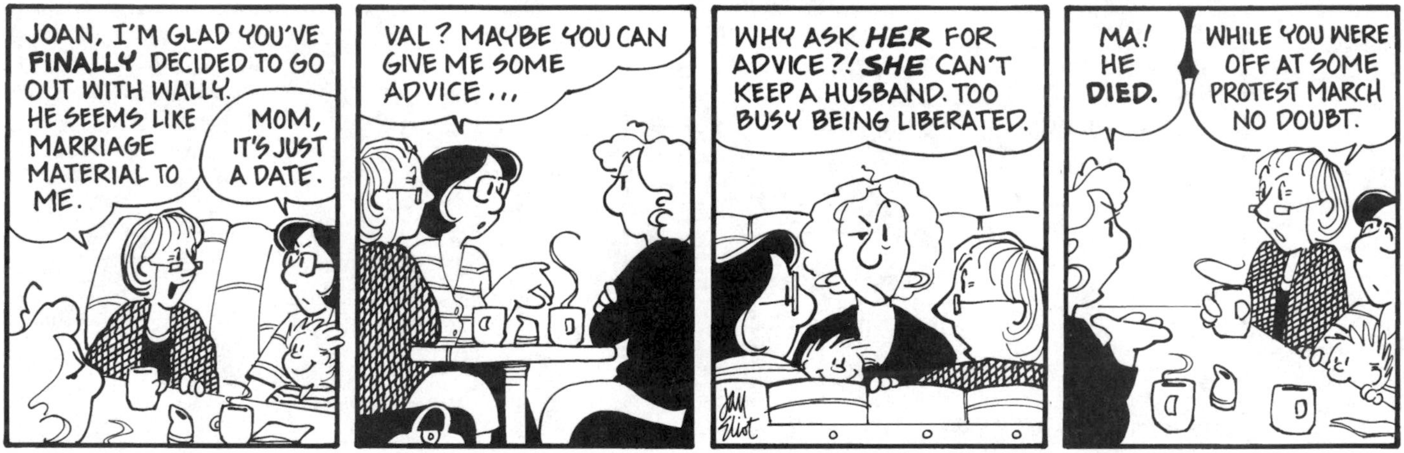
JOAN, I'M GLAD YOU'VE **FINALLY** DECIDED TO GO OUT WITH WALLY. HE SEEMS LIKE MARRIAGE MATERIAL TO ME.
MOM, IT'S JUST A DATE.
VAL? MAYBE YOU CAN GIVE ME SOME ADVICE...
WHY ASK **HER** FOR ADVICE?! **SHE** CAN'T KEEP A HUSBAND. TOO BUSY BEING LIBERATED.
JAN Eliot
MA! HE **DIED.**
WHILE YOU WERE OFF AT SOME PROTEST MARCH NO DOUBT.

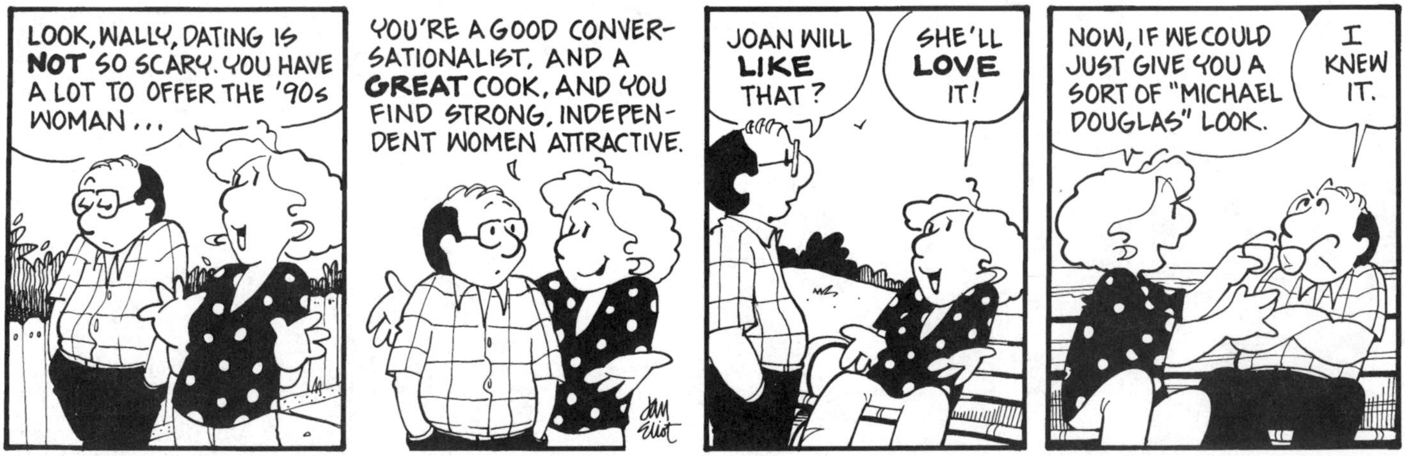
LOOK, WALLY, DATING IS **NOT** SO SCARY. YOU HAVE A LOT TO OFFER THE '90s WOMAN...
YOU'RE A GOOD CONVERSATIONALIST, AND A **GREAT** COOK, AND YOU FIND STRONG, INDEPENDENT WOMEN ATTRACTIVE.
JAN Eliot
JOAN WILL **LIKE** THAT?
SHE'LL **LOVE** IT!
NOW, IF WE COULD JUST GIVE YOU A SORT OF "MICHAEL DOUGLAS" LOOK.
I KNEW IT.

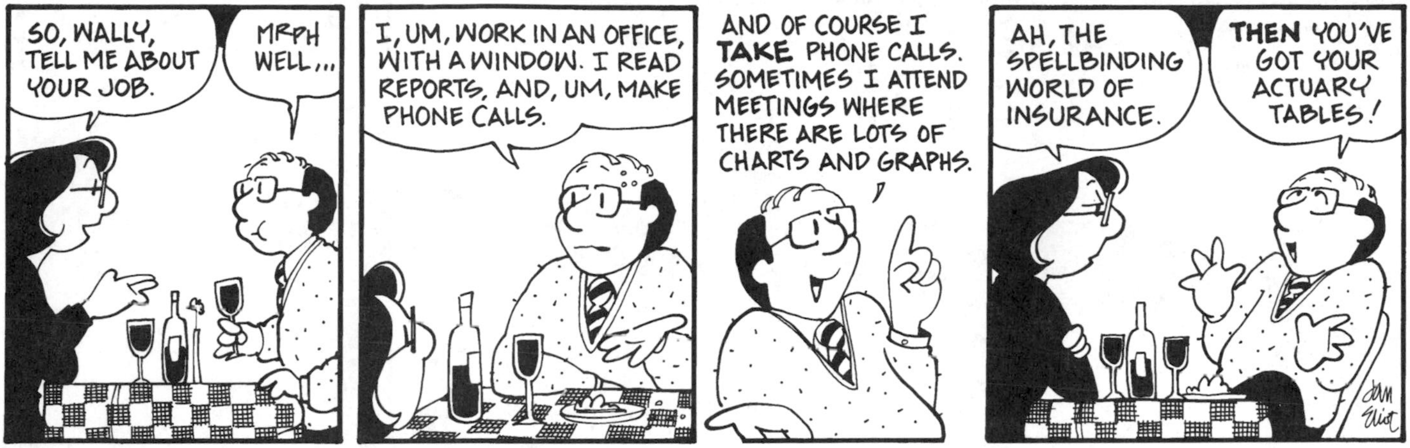
SO, WALLY, TELL ME ABOUT YOUR JOB.
MRPH WELL,..
I, UM, WORK IN AN OFFICE, WITH A WINDOW. I READ REPORTS, AND, UM, MAKE PHONE CALLS.
AND OF COURSE I TAKE PHONE CALLS. SOMETIMES I ATTEND MEETINGS WHERE THERE ARE LOTS OF CHARTS AND GRAPHS.
AH, THE SPELLBINDING WORLD OF INSURANCE.
THEN YOU'VE GOT YOUR ACTUARY TABLES!

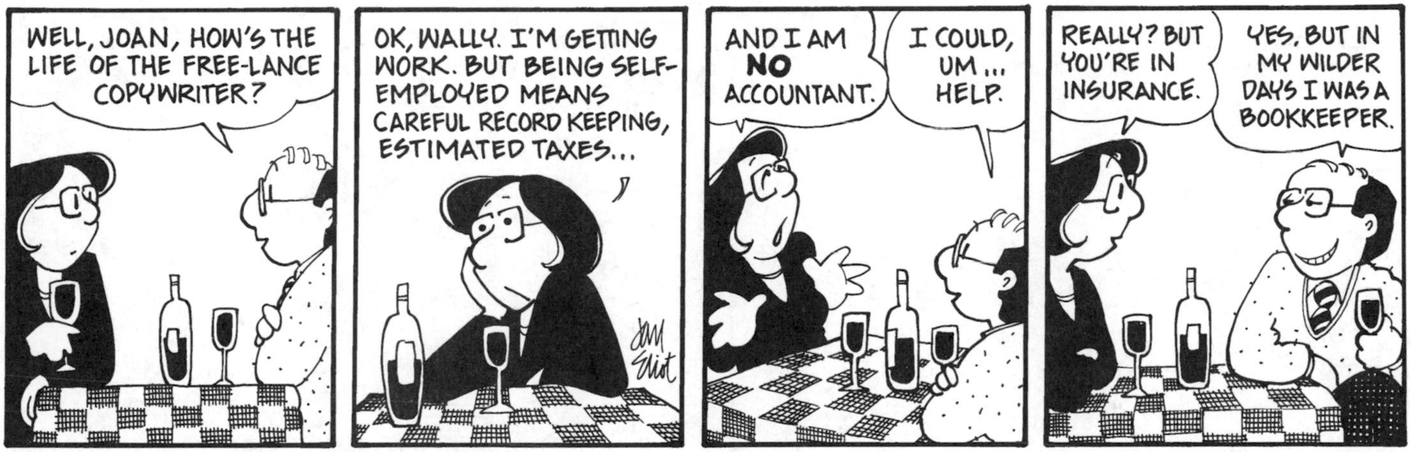
WELL, JOAN, HOW'S THE LIFE OF THE FREE-LANCE COPYWRITER?
OK, WALLY. I'M GETTING WORK. BUT BEING SELF-EMPLOYED MEANS CAREFUL RECORD KEEPING, ESTIMATED TAXES...
AND I AM NO ACCOUNTANT.
I COULD, UM... HELP.
REALLY? BUT YOU'RE IN INSURANCE.
YES, BUT IN MY WILDER DAYS I WAS A BOOKKEEPER.

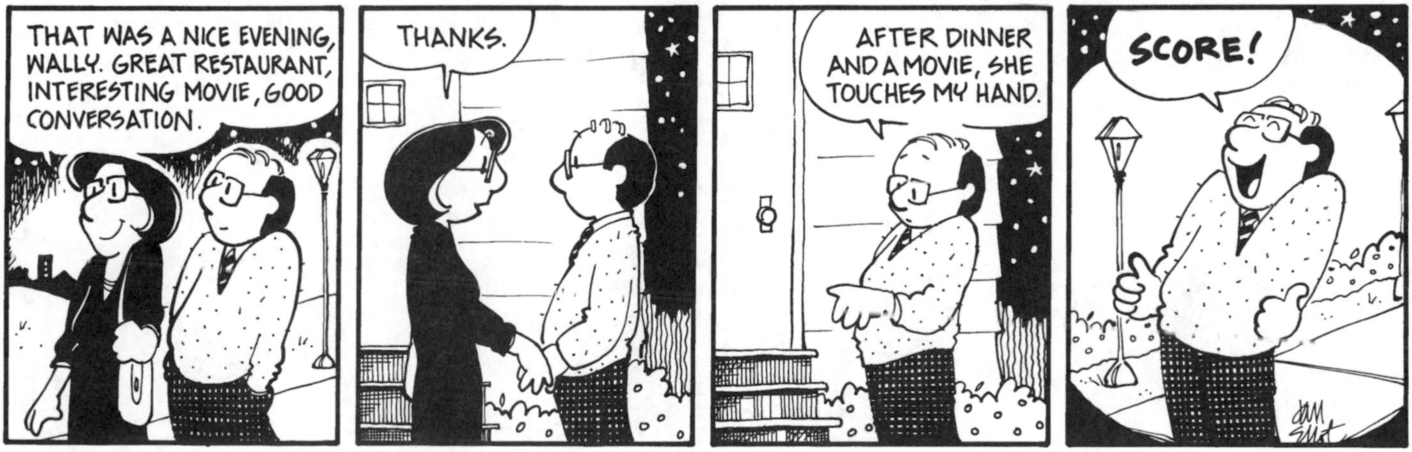
THAT WAS A NICE EVENING, WALLY. GREAT RESTAURANT, INTERESTING MOVIE, GOOD CONVERSATION.
THANKS.
AFTER DINNER AND A MOVIE, SHE TOUCHES MY HAND.
SCORE!

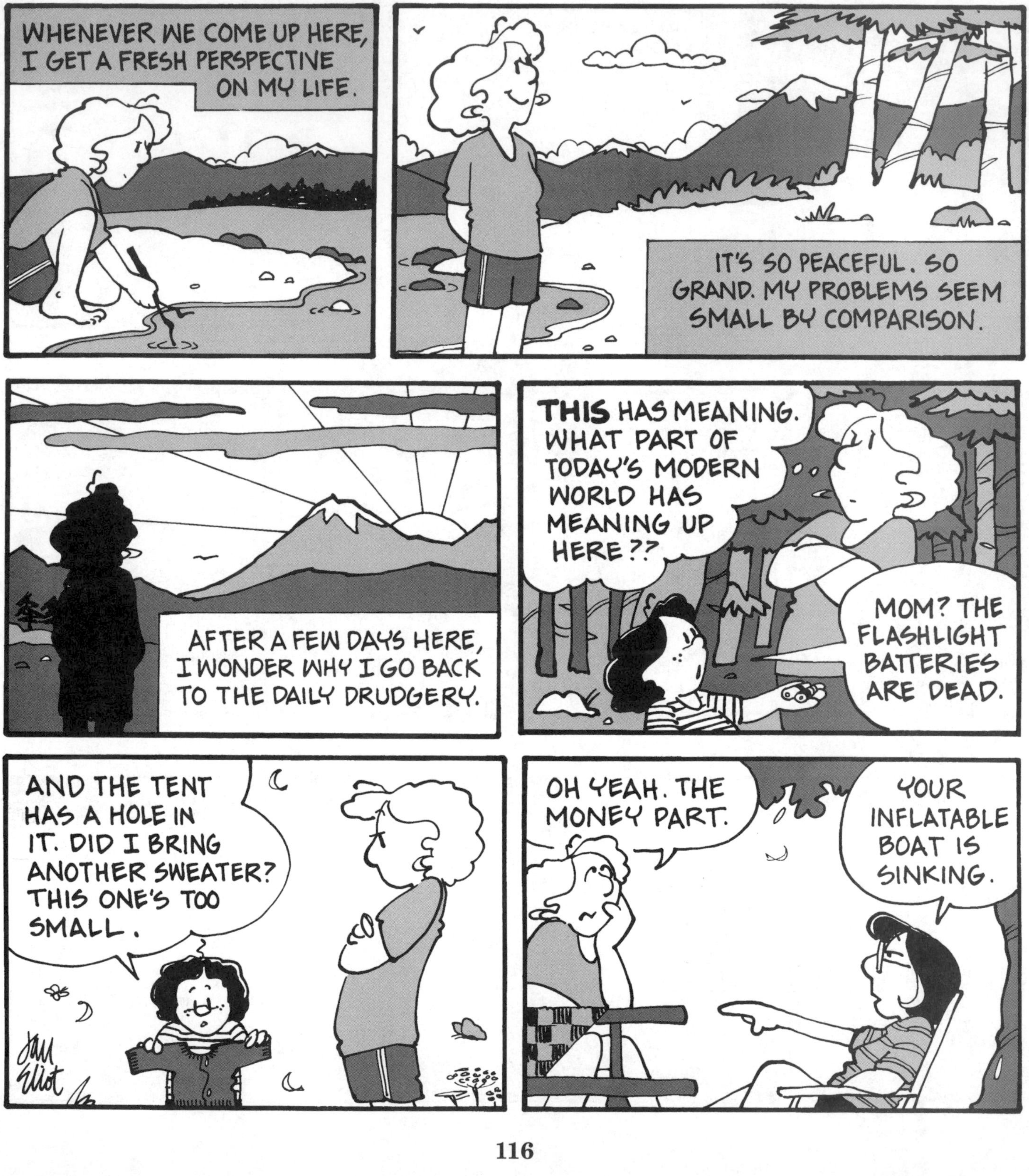
WHENEVER WE COME UP HERE, I GET A FRESH PERSPECTIVE ON MY LIFE.
IT'S SO PEACEFUL. SO GRAND. MY PROBLEMS SEEM SMALL BY COMPARISON.
AFTER A FEW DAYS HERE, I WONDER WHY I GO BACK TO THE DAILY DRUDGERY.
THIS HAS MEANING. WHAT PART OF TODAY'S MODERN WORLD HAS MEANING UP HERE??
MOM? THE FLASHLIGHT BATTERIES ARE DEAD.
AND THE TENT HAS A HOLE IN IT. DID I BRING ANOTHER SWEATER? THIS ONE'S TOO SMALL.
OH YEAH. THE MONEY PART.
YOUR INFLATABLE BOAT IS SINKING.

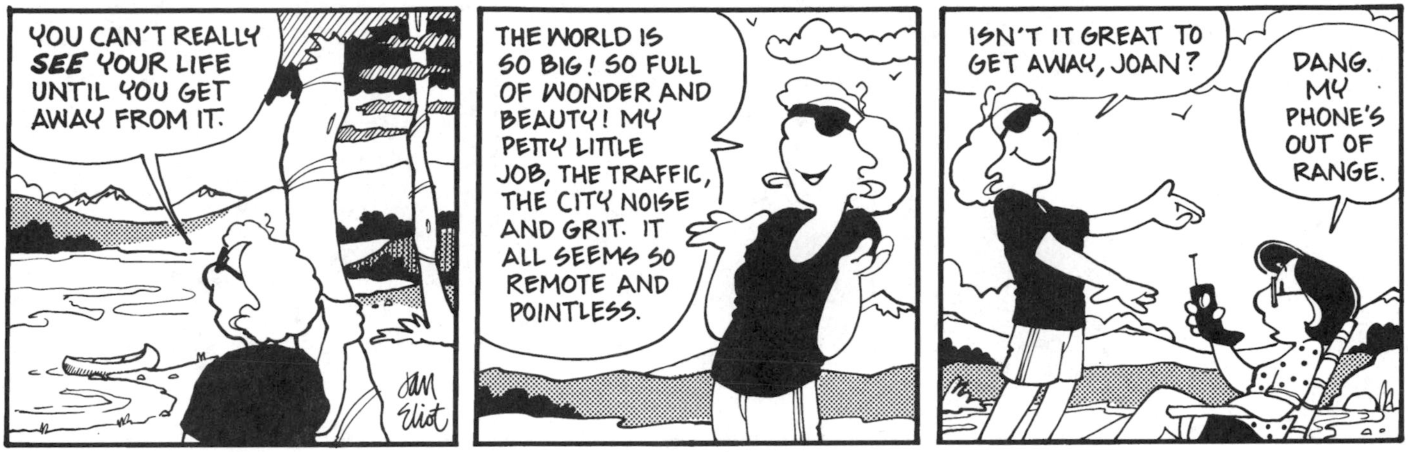
YOU CAN'T REALLY **SEE** YOUR LIFE UNTIL YOU GET AWAY FROM IT.
THE WORLD IS SO BIG! SO FULL OF WONDER AND BEAUTY! MY PETTY LITTLE JOB, THE TRAFFIC, THE CITY NOISE AND GRIT. IT ALL SEEMS SO REMOTE AND POINTLESS.
ISN'T IT GREAT TO GET AWAY, JOAN?
DANG. MY PHONE'S OUT OF RANGE.
JAN Eliot

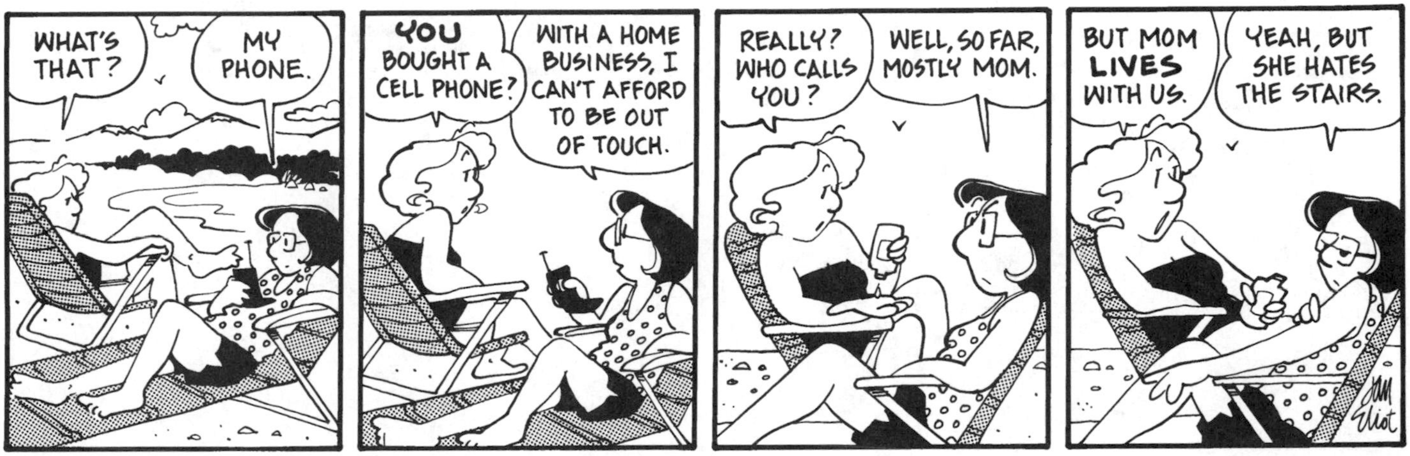
WHAT'S THAT?
MY PHONE.
YOU BOUGHT A CELL PHONE?
WITH A HOME BUSINESS, I CAN'T AFFORD TO BE OUT OF TOUCH.
REALLY? WHO CALLS YOU?
WELL, SO FAR, MOSTLY MOM.
BUT MOM **LIVES** WITH US.
YEAH, BUT SHE HATES THE STAIRS.
JAN Eliot

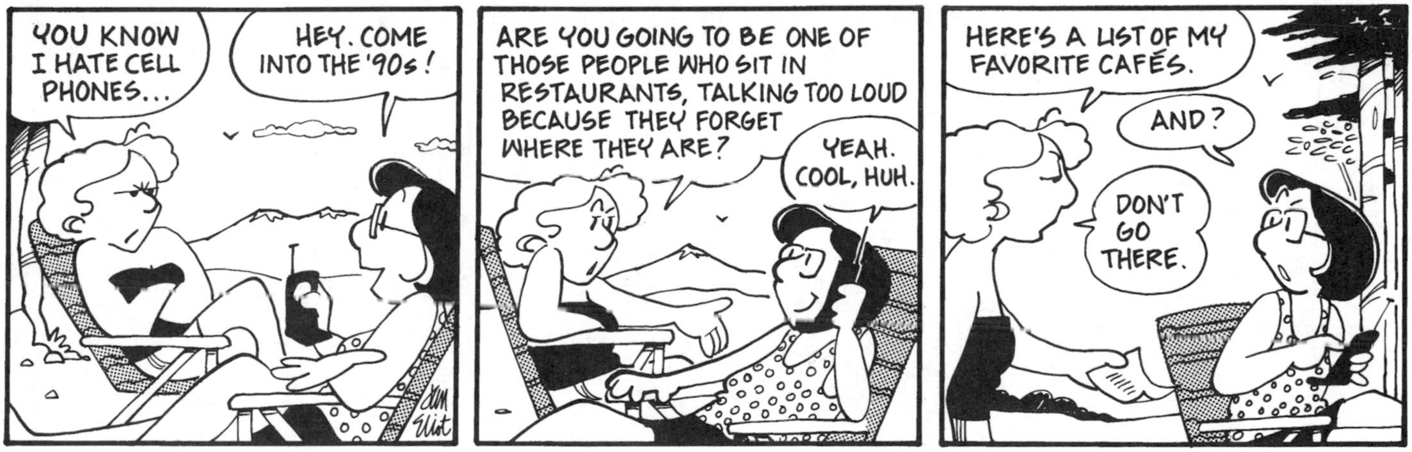
YOU KNOW I HATE CELL PHONES...
HEY. COME INTO THE '90s!
JAN Eliot
ARE YOU GOING TO BE ONE OF THOSE PEOPLE WHO SIT IN RESTAURANTS, TALKING TOO LOUD BECAUSE THEY FORGET WHERE THEY ARE?
YEAH. COOL, HUH.
HERE'S A LIST OF MY FAVORITE CAFÉS.
AND?
DON'T GO THERE.

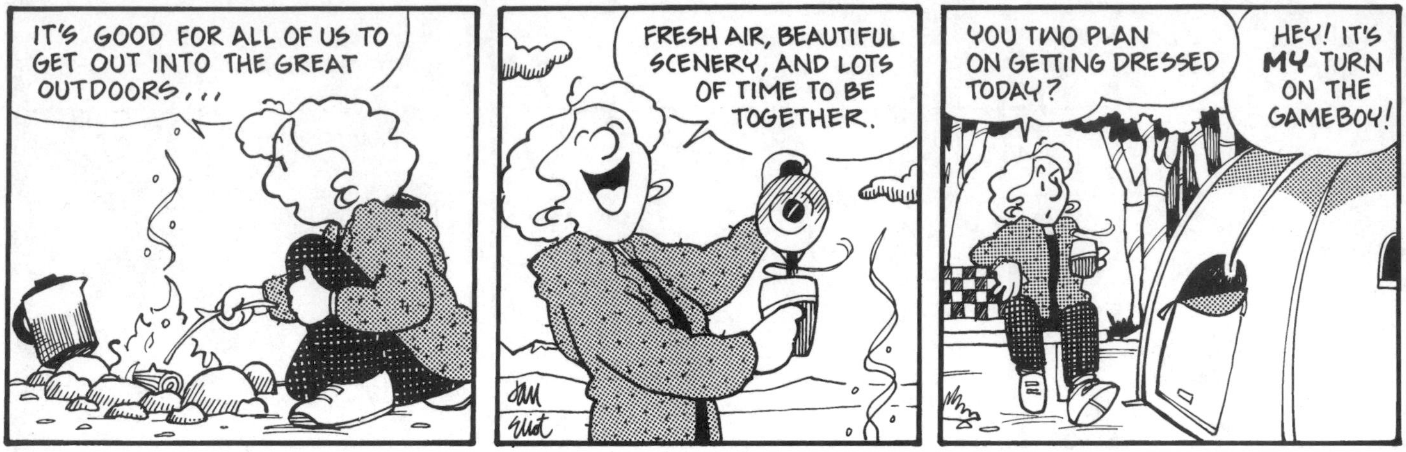
IT'S GOOD FOR ALL OF US TO GET OUT INTO THE GREAT OUTDOORS...
FRESH AIR, BEAUTIFUL SCENERY, AND LOTS OF TIME TO BE TOGETHER.
YOU TWO PLAN ON GETTING DRESSED TODAY?
HEY! IT'S MY TURN ON THE GAMEBOY!

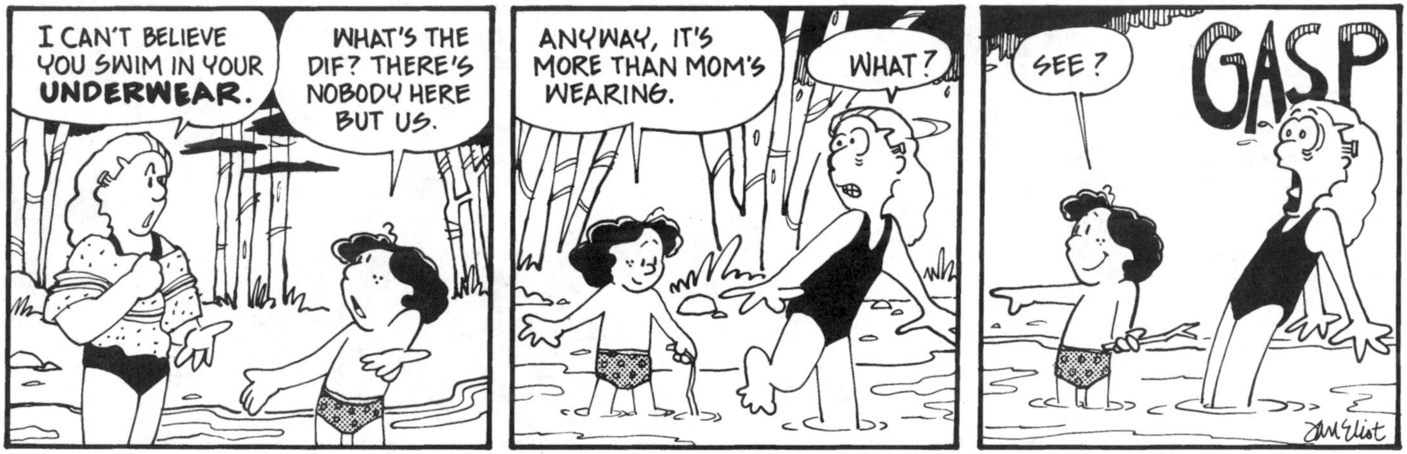
I CAN'T BELIEVE YOU SWIM IN YOUR UNDERWEAR.
WHAT'S THE DIF? THERE'S NOBODY HERE BUT US.
ANYWAY, IT'S MORE THAN MOM'S WEARING.
WHAT?
SEE?
GASP

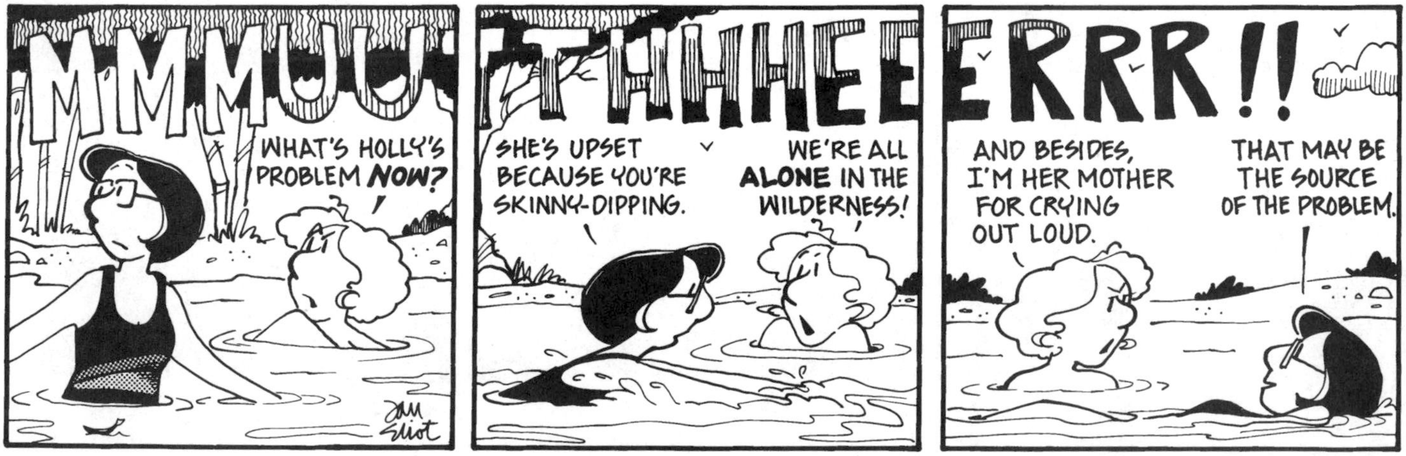
MMMUUTTHHHEEERRR!!
WHAT'S HOLLY'S PROBLEM NOW?
SHE'S UPSET BECAUSE YOU'RE SKINNY-DIPPING.
WE'RE ALL ALONE IN THE WILDERNESS!
AND BESIDES, I'M HER MOTHER FOR CRYING OUT LOUD.
THAT MAY BE THE SOURCE OF THE PROBLEM.

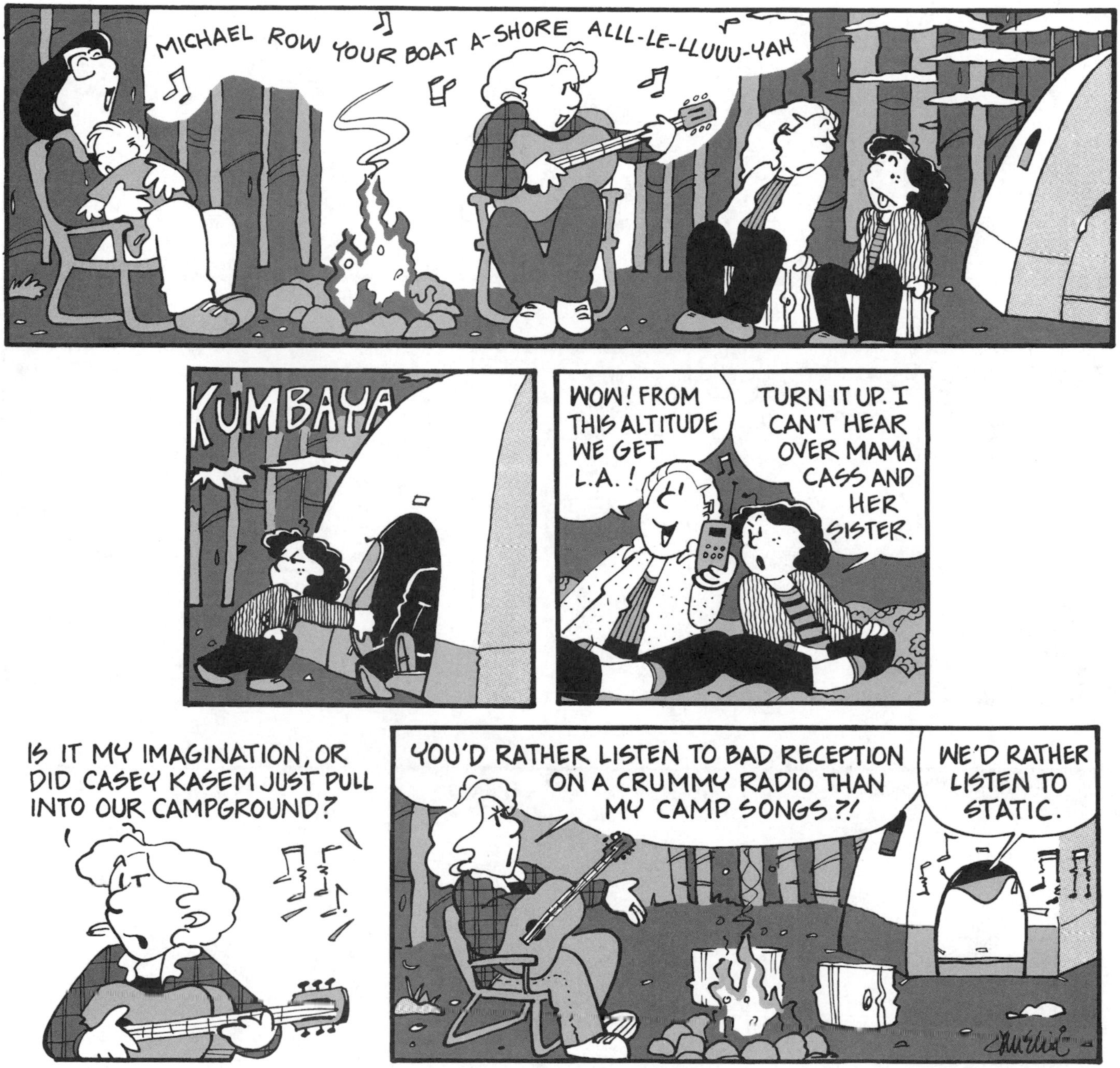
MICHAEL ROW YOUR BOAT A-SHORE ALLL-LE-LLUUU-YAH
KUMBAYA
WOW! FROM THIS ALTITUDE WE GET L.A.!
TURN IT UP. I CAN'T HEAR OVER MAMA CASS AND HER SISTER.
IS IT MY IMAGINATION, OR DID CASEY KASEM JUST PULL INTO OUR CAMPGROUND?
YOU'D RATHER LISTEN TO BAD RECEPTION ON A CRUMMY RADIO THAN MY CAMP SONGS?!
WE'D RATHER LISTEN TO STATIC.

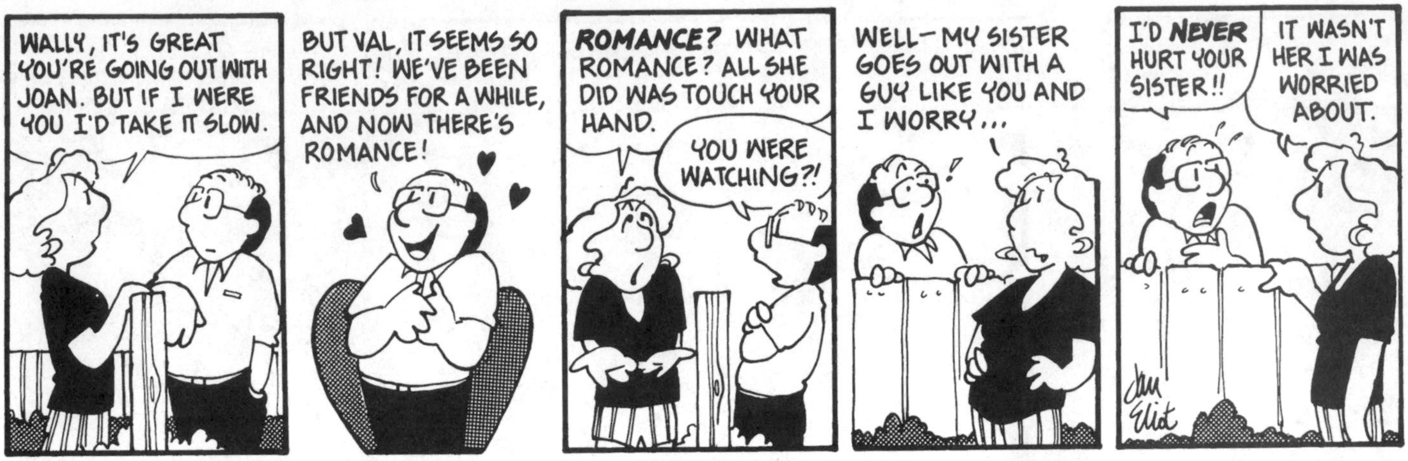
WALLY, IT'S GREAT YOU'RE GOING OUT WITH JOAN. BUT IF I WERE YOU I'D TAKE IT SLOW.
BUT VAL, IT SEEMS SO RIGHT! WE'VE BEEN FRIENDS FOR A WHILE, AND NOW THERE'S ROMANCE!
ROMANCE? WHAT ROMANCE? ALL SHE DID WAS TOUCH YOUR HAND.
YOU WERE WATCHING?!
WELL– MY SISTER GOES OUT WITH A GUY LIKE YOU AND I WORRY...
I'D NEVER HURT YOUR SISTER!!
IT WASN'T HER I WAS WORRIED ABOUT.

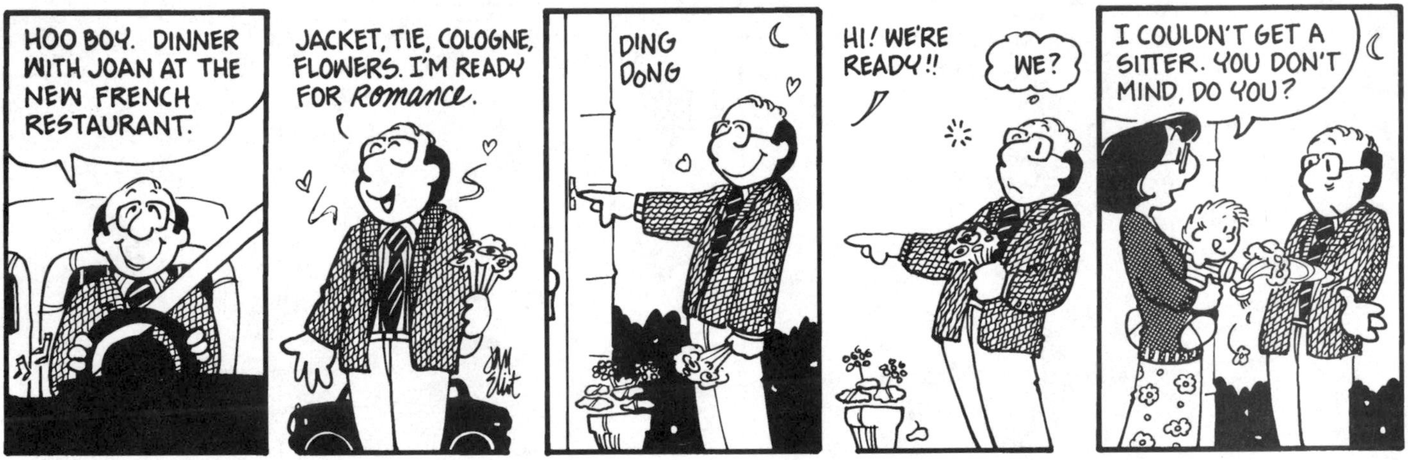
HOO BOY. DINNER WITH JOAN AT THE NEW FRENCH RESTAURANT.
JACKET, TIE, COLOGNE, FLOWERS. I'M READY FOR Romance.
DING DONG
HI! WE'RE READY!!
WE?
I COULDN'T GET A SITTER. YOU DON'T MIND, DO YOU?

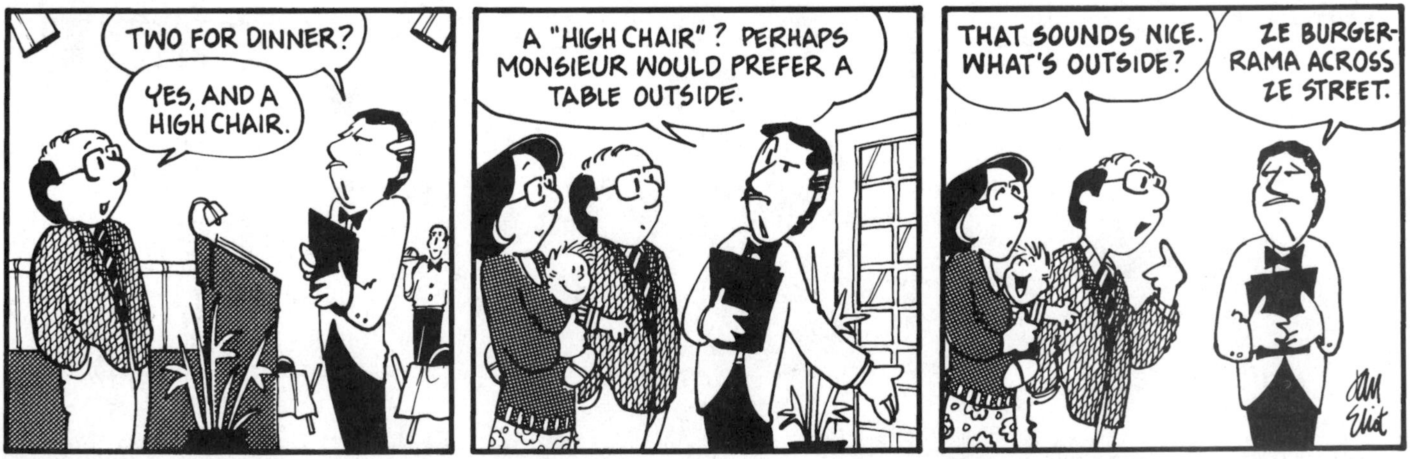
TWO FOR DINNER?
YES, AND A HIGH CHAIR.
A "HIGH CHAIR"? PERHAPS MONSIEUR WOULD PREFER A TABLE OUTSIDE.
THAT SOUNDS NICE. WHAT'S OUTSIDE?
ZE BURGER-RAMA ACROSS ZE STREET.

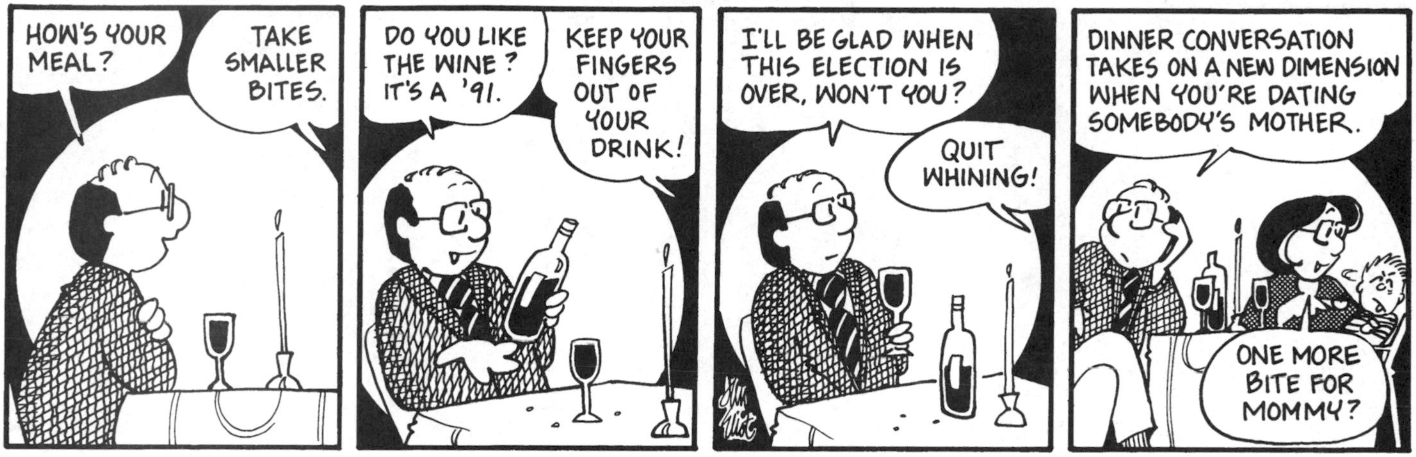
HOW'S YOUR MEAL?
TAKE SMALLER BITES.
DO YOU LIKE THE WINE? IT'S A '91.
KEEP YOUR FINGERS OUT OF YOUR DRINK!
I'LL BE GLAD WHEN THIS ELECTION IS OVER, WON'T YOU?
QUIT WHINING!
DINNER CONVERSATION TAKES ON A NEW DIMENSION WHEN YOU'RE DATING SOMEBODY'S MOTHER.
ONE MORE BITE FOR MOMMY?

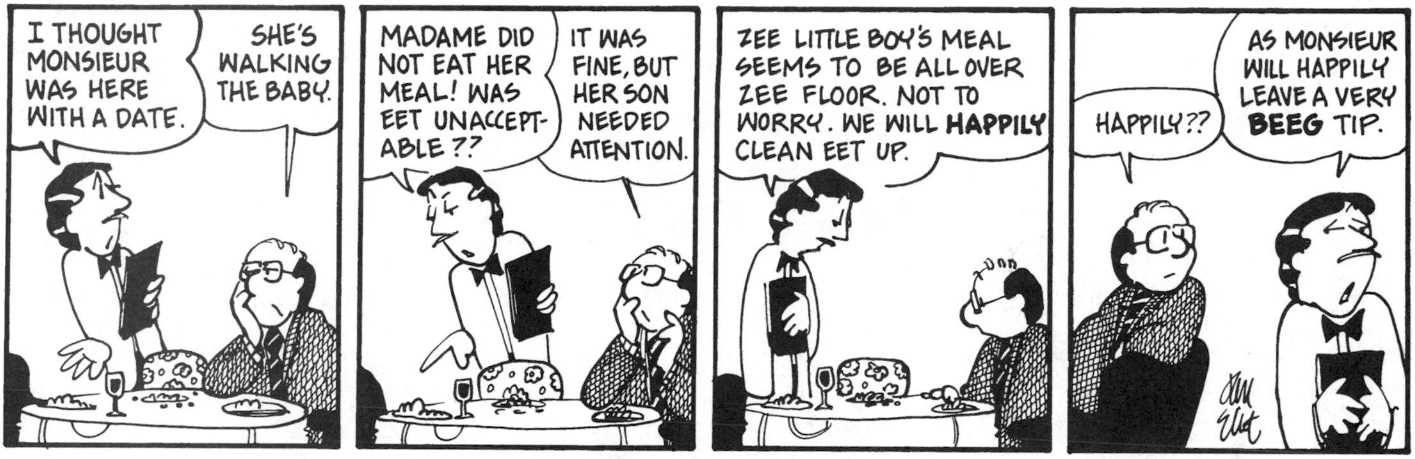
I THOUGHT MONSIEUR WAS HERE WITH A DATE.
SHE'S WALKING THE BABY.
MADAME DID NOT EAT HER MEAL! WAS EET UNACCEPTABLE??
IT WAS FINE, BUT HER SON NEEDED ATTENTION.
ZEE LITTLE BOY'S MEAL SEEMS TO BE ALL OVER ZEE FLOOR. NOT TO WORRY. WE WILL HAPPILY CLEAN EET UP.
HAPPILY??
AS MONSIEUR WILL HAPPILY LEAVE A VERY BEEG TIP.

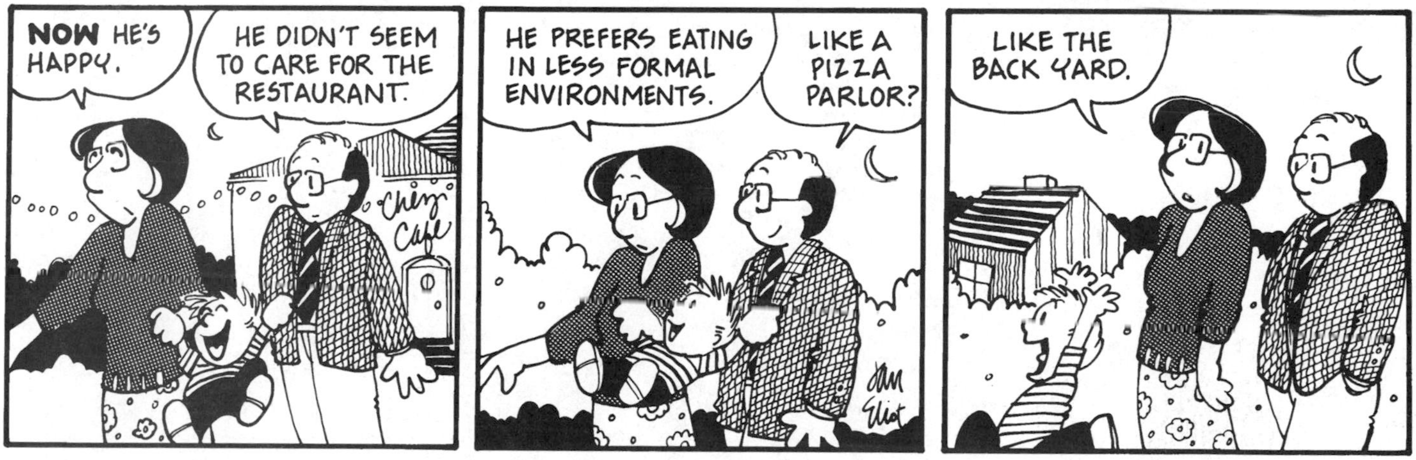
NOW HE'S HAPPY.
HE DIDN'T SEEM TO CARE FOR THE RESTAURANT.
Chez Café
HE PREFERS EATING IN LESS FORMAL ENVIRONMENTS.
LIKE A PIZZA PARLOR?
LIKE THE BACK YARD.

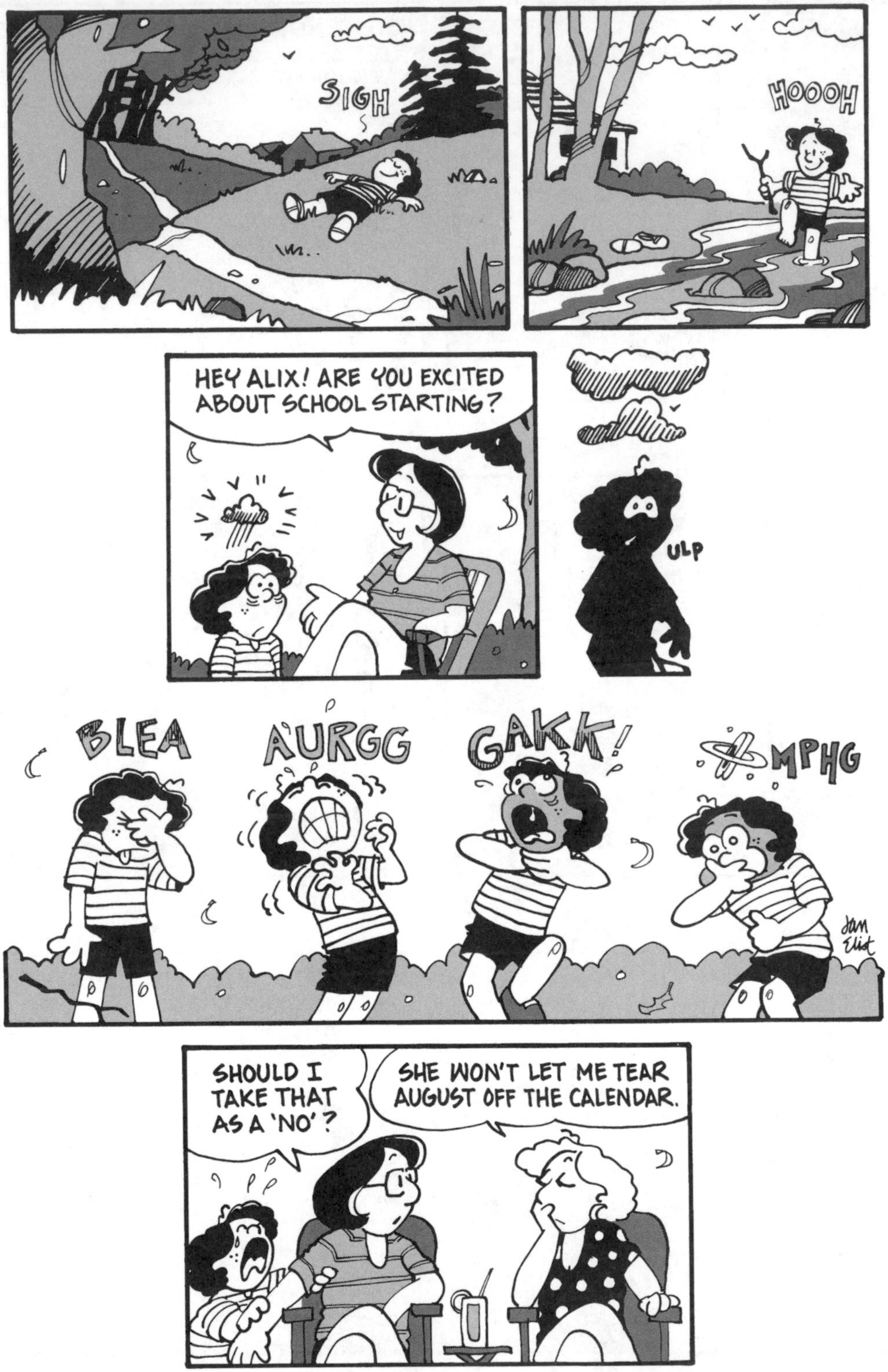

SIGH
HOOOH
HEY ALIX! ARE YOU EXCITED ABOUT SCHOOL STARTING?
ULP
BLEA
AURGG
GAKK!
MPHG
SHOULD I TAKE THAT AS A 'NO'?
SHE WON'T LET ME TEAR AUGUST OFF THE CALENDAR.

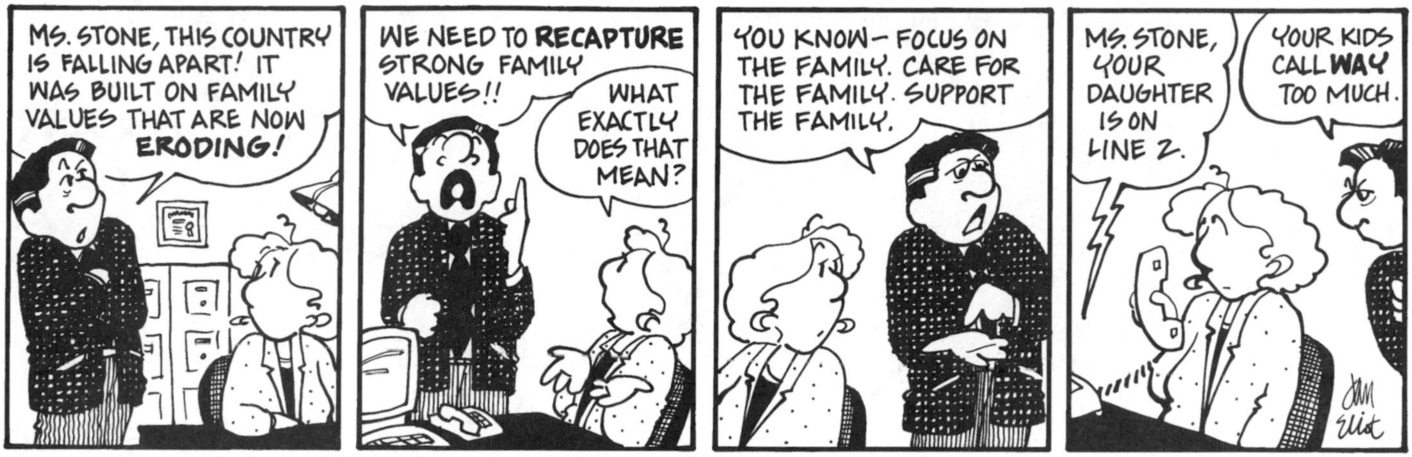
MS. STONE, THIS COUNTRY IS FALLING APART! IT WAS BUILT ON FAMILY VALUES THAT ARE NOW **ERODING!**
WE NEED TO **RECAPTURE** STRONG FAMILY VALUES!!
WHAT EXACTLY DOES THAT MEAN?
YOU KNOW— FOCUS ON THE FAMILY. CARE FOR THE FAMILY. SUPPORT THE FAMILY.
MS. STONE, YOUR DAUGHTER IS ON LINE 2.
YOUR KIDS CALL **WAY** TOO MUCH.

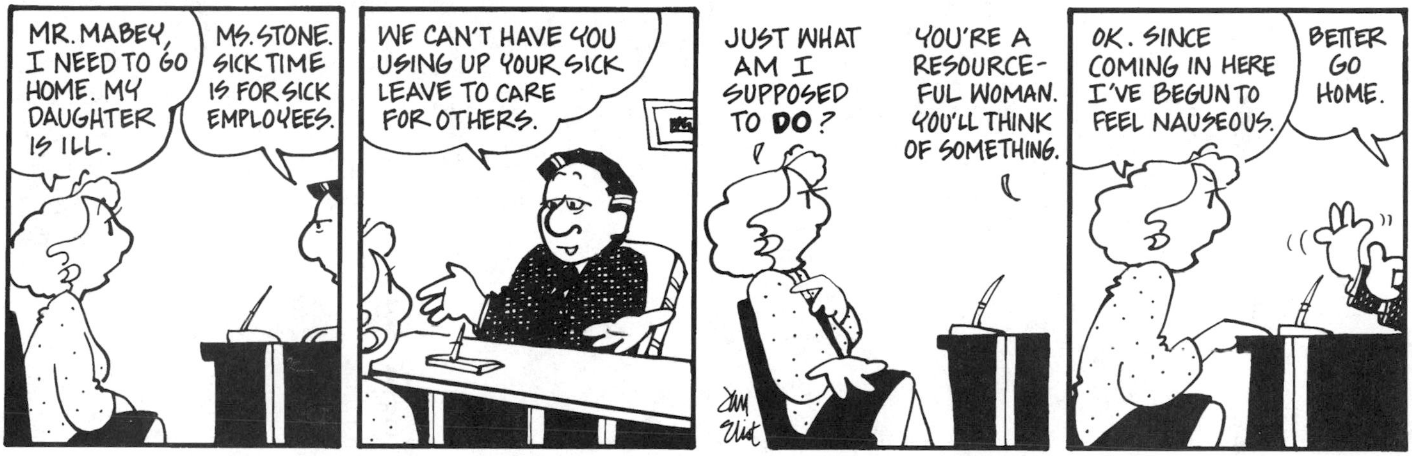
MR. MABEY, I NEED TO GO HOME. MY DAUGHTER IS ILL.
MS. STONE. SICK TIME IS FOR SICK EMPLOYEES.
WE CAN'T HAVE YOU USING UP YOUR SICK LEAVE TO CARE FOR OTHERS.
JUST WHAT AM I SUPPOSED TO **DO**?
YOU'RE A RESOURCE-FUL WOMAN. YOU'LL THINK OF SOMETHING.
OK. SINCE COMING IN HERE I'VE BEGUN TO FEEL NAUSEOUS.
BETTER GO HOME.

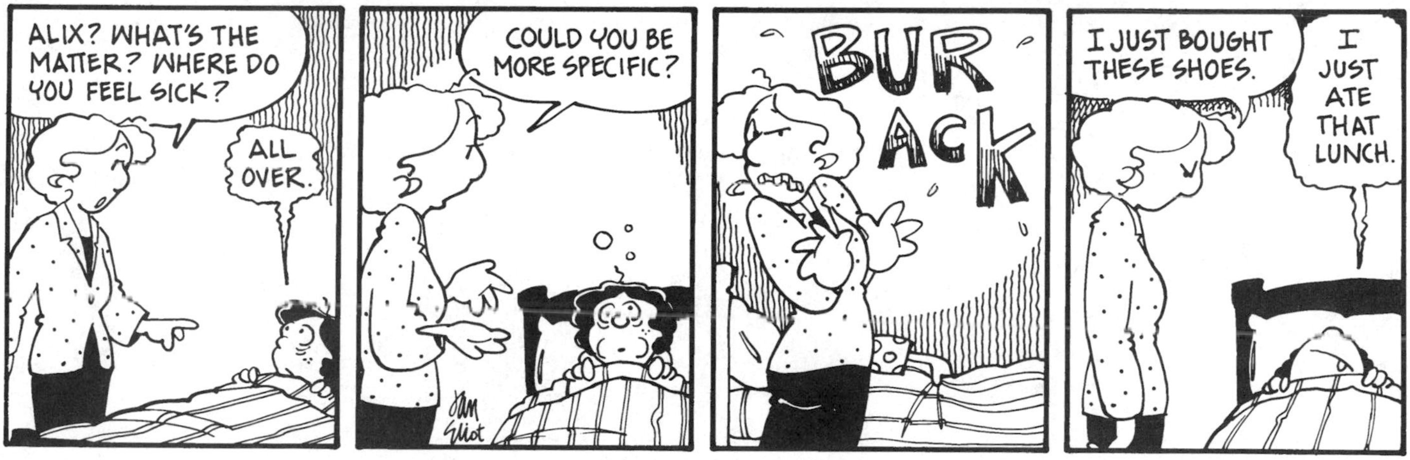
ALIX? WHAT'S THE MATTER? WHERE DO YOU FEEL SICK?
ALL OVER.
COULD YOU BE MORE SPECIFIC?
BUR ACK
I JUST BOUGHT THESE SHOES.
I JUST ATE THAT LUNCH.

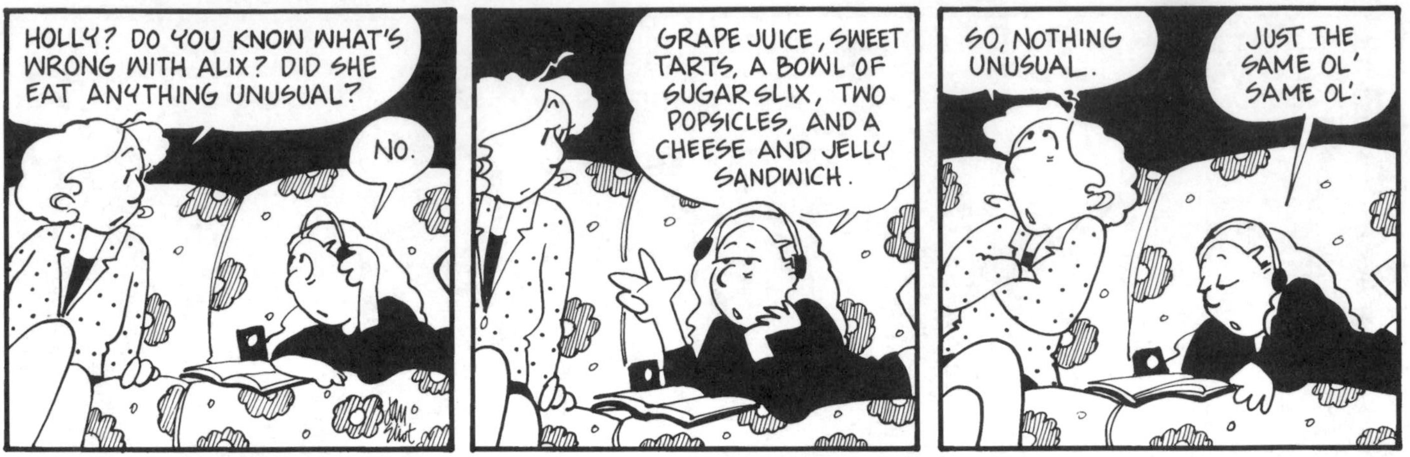
HOLLY? DO YOU KNOW WHAT'S WRONG WITH ALIX? DID SHE EAT ANYTHING UNUSUAL?
NO.
GRAPE JUICE, SWEET TARTS, A BOWL OF SUGAR SLIX, TWO POPSICLES, AND A CHEESE AND JELLY SANDWICH.
SO, NOTHING UNUSUAL.
JUST THE SAME OL' SAME OL'.

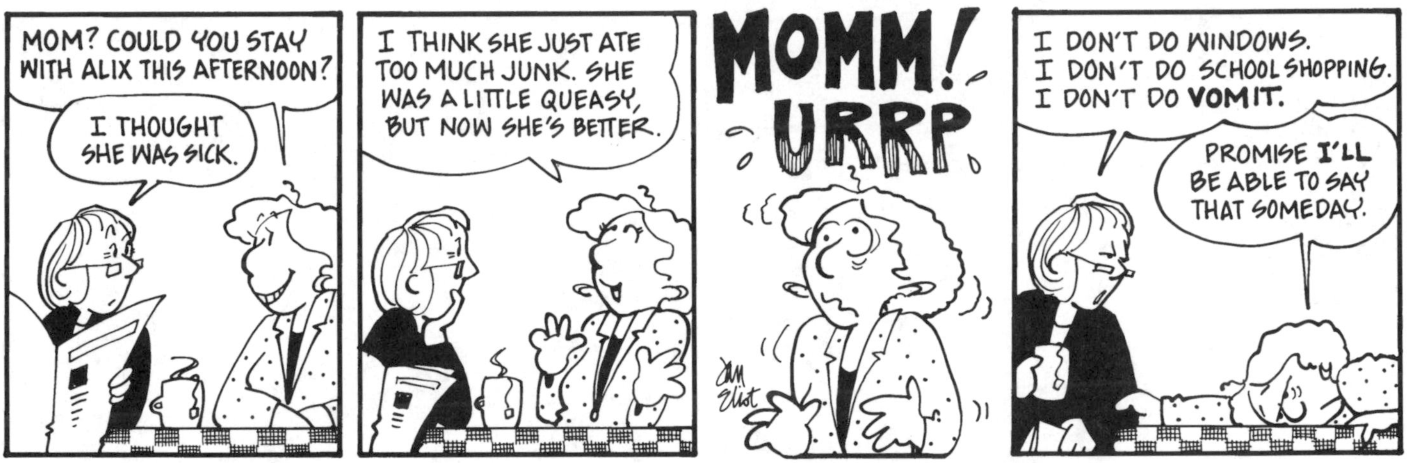
MOM? COULD YOU STAY WITH ALIX THIS AFTERNOON?
I THOUGHT SHE WAS SICK.
I THINK SHE JUST ATE TOO MUCH JUNK. SHE WAS A LITTLE QUEASY, BUT NOW SHE'S BETTER.
MOMM!
URRP
I DON'T DO WINDOWS. I DON'T DO SCHOOL SHOPPING. I DON'T DO **VOMIT.**
PROMISE **I'LL** BE ABLE TO SAY THAT SOMEDAY.

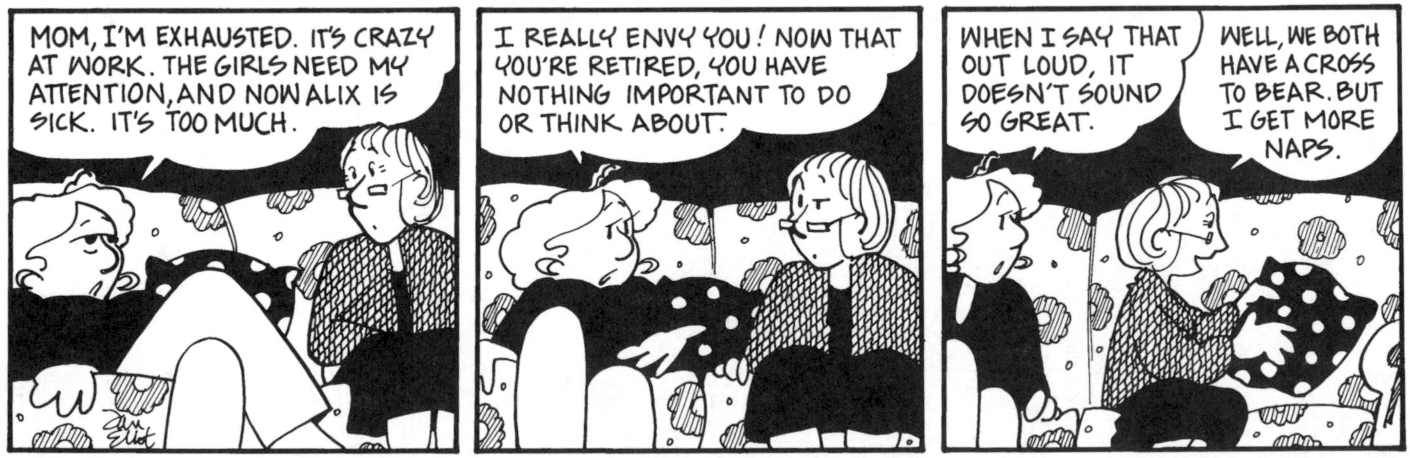
MOM, I'M EXHAUSTED. IT'S CRAZY AT WORK. THE GIRLS NEED MY ATTENTION, AND NOW ALIX IS SICK. IT'S TOO MUCH.
I REALLY ENVY YOU! NOW THAT YOU'RE RETIRED, YOU HAVE NOTHING IMPORTANT TO DO OR THINK ABOUT.
WHEN I SAY THAT OUT LOUD, IT DOESN'T SOUND SO GREAT.
WELL, WE BOTH HAVE A CROSS TO BEAR. BUT I GET MORE NAPS.

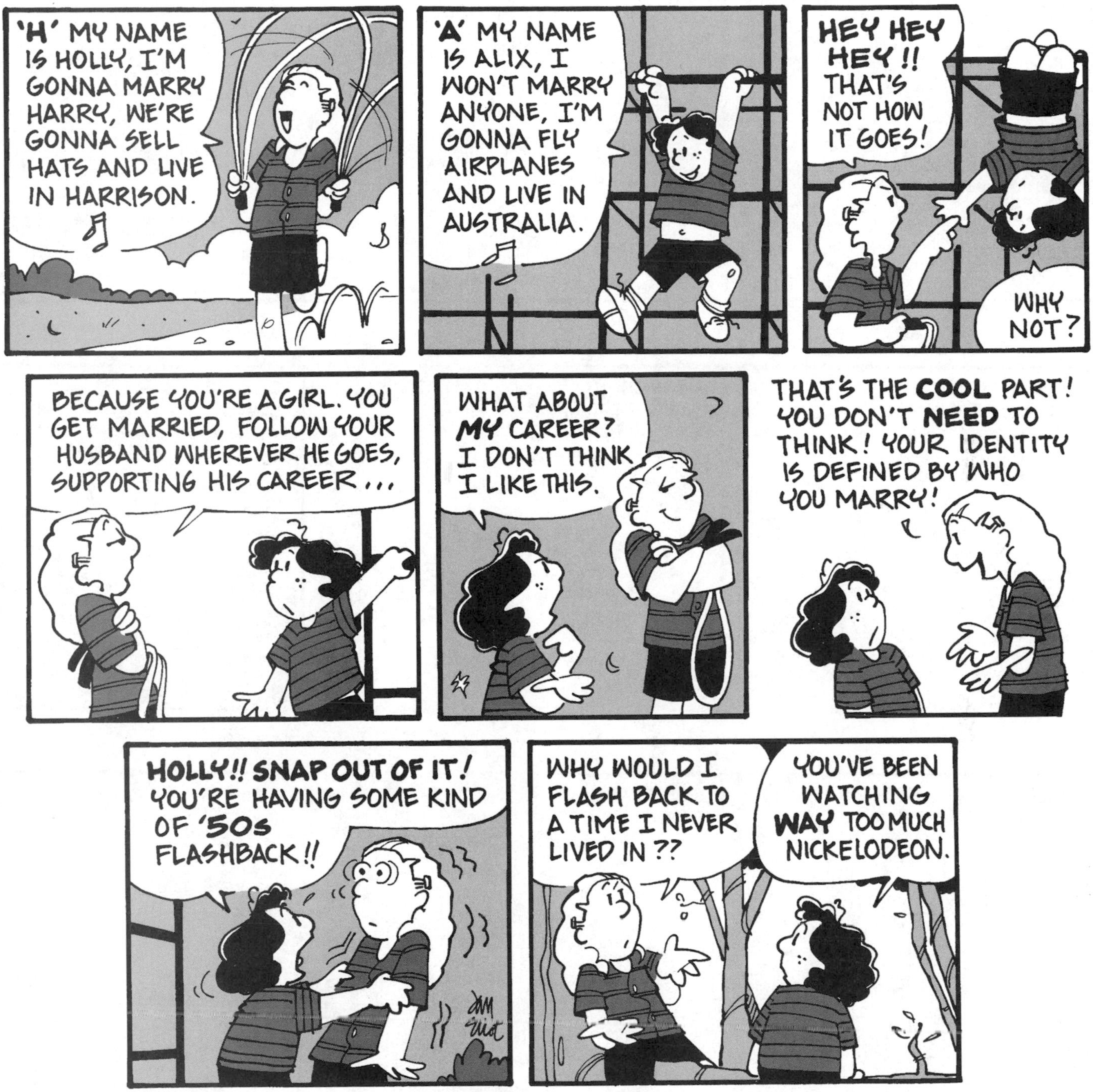
'H' MY NAME IS HOLLY, I'M GONNA MARRY HARRY, WE'RE GONNA SELL HATS AND LIVE IN HARRISON.
'A' MY NAME IS ALIX, I WON'T MARRY ANYONE, I'M GONNA FLY AIRPLANES AND LIVE IN AUSTRALIA.
HEY HEY HEY!! THAT'S NOT HOW IT GOES!
WHY NOT?
BECAUSE YOU'RE A GIRL. YOU GET MARRIED, FOLLOW YOUR HUSBAND WHEREVER HE GOES, SUPPORTING HIS CAREER...
WHAT ABOUT MY CAREER? I DON'T THINK I LIKE THIS.
THAT'S THE COOL PART! YOU DON'T NEED TO THINK! YOUR IDENTITY IS DEFINED BY WHO YOU MARRY!
HOLLY!! SNAP OUT OF IT! YOU'RE HAVING SOME KIND OF '50s FLASHBACK!!
WHY WOULD I FLASH BACK TO A TIME I NEVER LIVED IN??
YOU'VE BEEN WATCHING WAY TOO MUCH NICKELODEON.

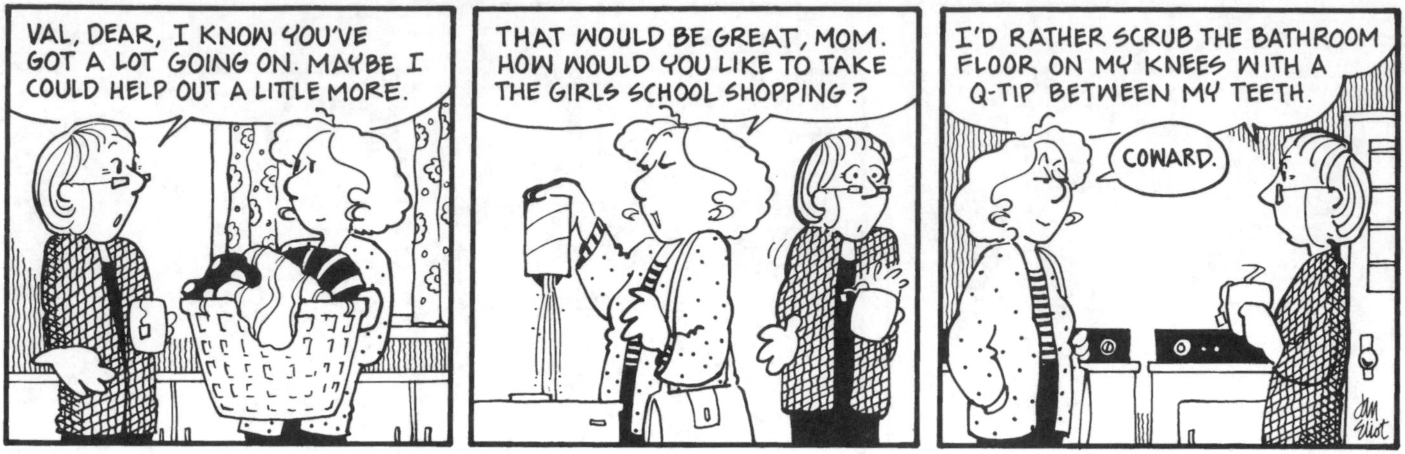
VAL, DEAR, I KNOW YOU'VE GOT A LOT GOING ON. MAYBE I COULD HELP OUT A LITTLE MORE.
THAT WOULD BE GREAT, MOM. HOW WOULD YOU LIKE TO TAKE THE GIRLS SCHOOL SHOPPING?
I'D RATHER SCRUB THE BATHROOM FLOOR ON MY KNEES WITH A Q-TIP BETWEEN MY TEETH.
COWARD.

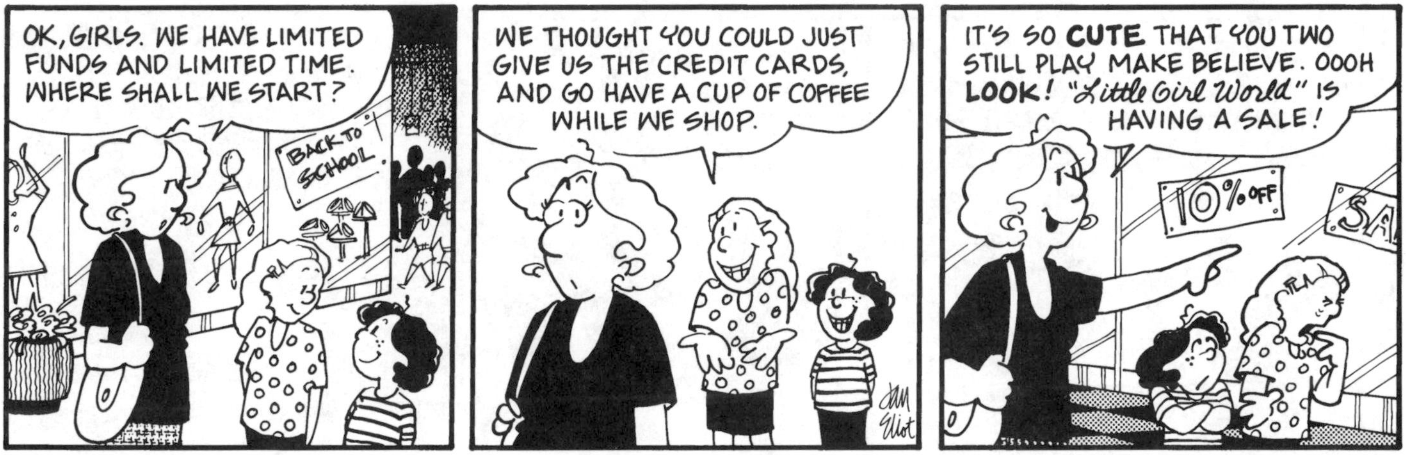
OK, GIRLS. WE HAVE LIMITED FUNDS AND LIMITED TIME. WHERE SHALL WE START?
BACK TO SCHOOL
WE THOUGHT YOU COULD JUST GIVE US THE CREDIT CARDS, AND GO HAVE A CUP OF COFFEE WHILE WE SHOP.
IT'S SO CUTE THAT YOU TWO STILL PLAY MAKE BELIEVE. OOOH LOOK! "Little Girl World" IS HAVING A SALE!
10% OFF

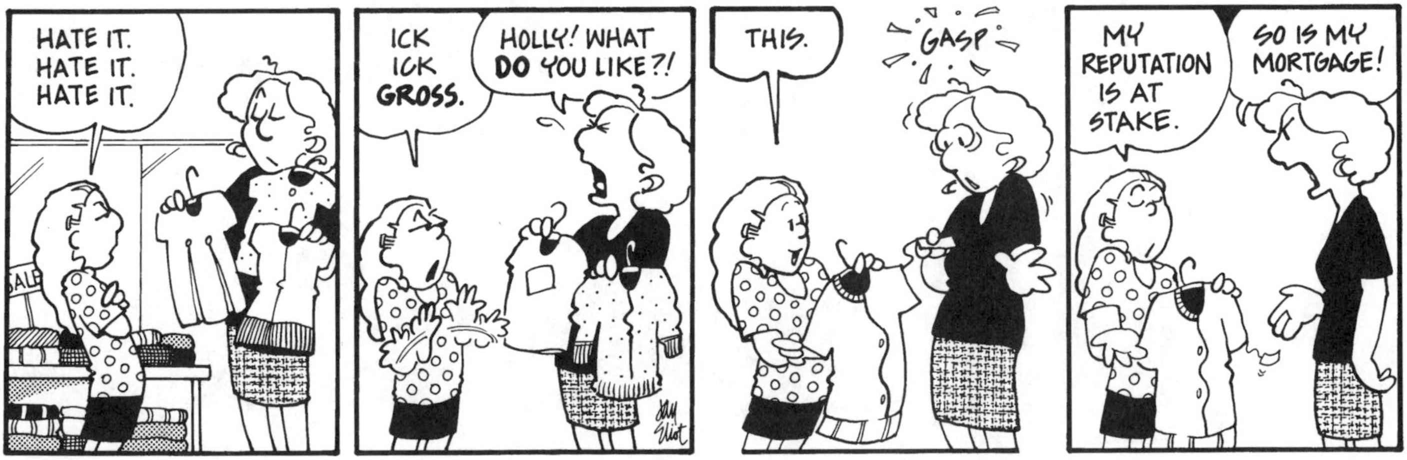
HATE IT. HATE IT. HATE IT.
ICK ICK GROSS.
HOLLY! WHAT DO YOU LIKE?!
THIS.
GASP
MY REPUTATION IS AT STAKE.
SO IS MY MORTGAGE!

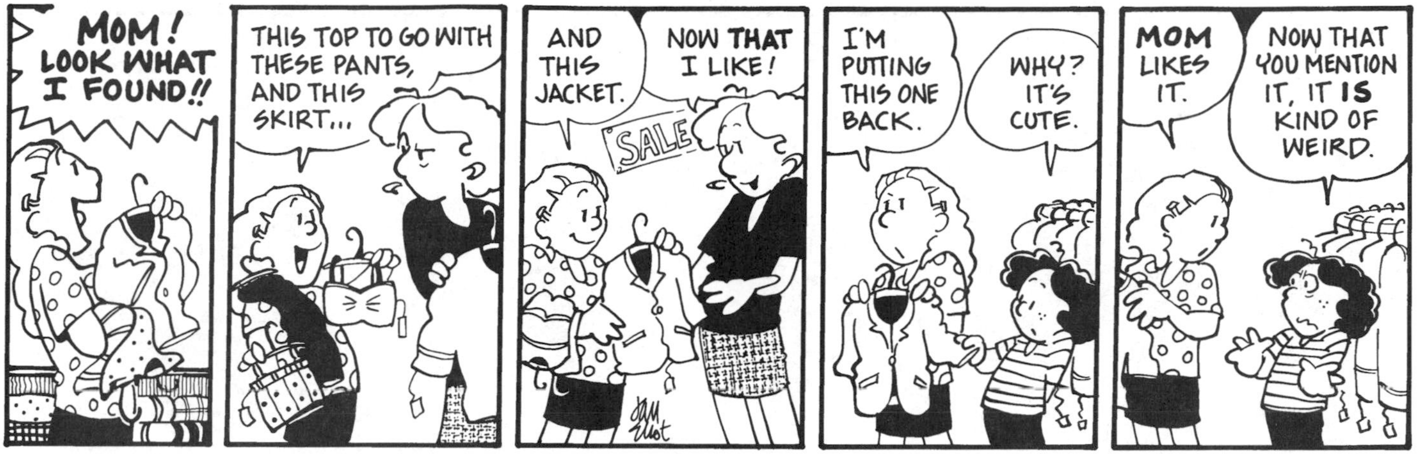
MOM! LOOK WHAT I FOUND!!
THIS TOP TO GO WITH THESE PANTS, AND THIS SKIRT...
AND THIS JACKET.
NOW THAT I LIKE!
SALE
I'M PUTTING THIS ONE BACK.
WHY? IT'S CUTE.
MOM LIKES IT.
NOW THAT YOU MENTION IT, IT IS KIND OF WEIRD.

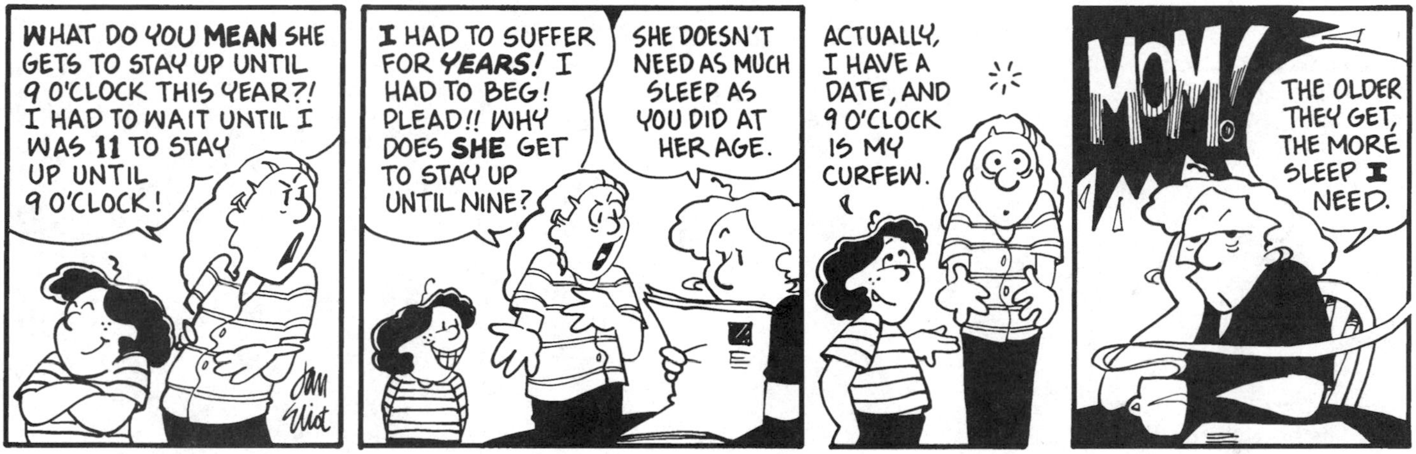
WHAT DO YOU MEAN SHE GETS TO STAY UP UNTIL 9 O'CLOCK THIS YEAR?! I HAD TO WAIT UNTIL I WAS 11 TO STAY UP UNTIL 9 O'CLOCK!
I HAD TO SUFFER FOR YEARS! I HAD TO BEG! PLEAD!! WHY DOES SHE GET TO STAY UP UNTIL NINE?
SHE DOESN'T NEED AS MUCH SLEEP AS YOU DID AT HER AGE.
ACTUALLY, I HAVE A DATE, AND 9 O'CLOCK IS MY CURFEW.
MOM!
THE OLDER THEY GET, THE MORE SLEEP I NEED.

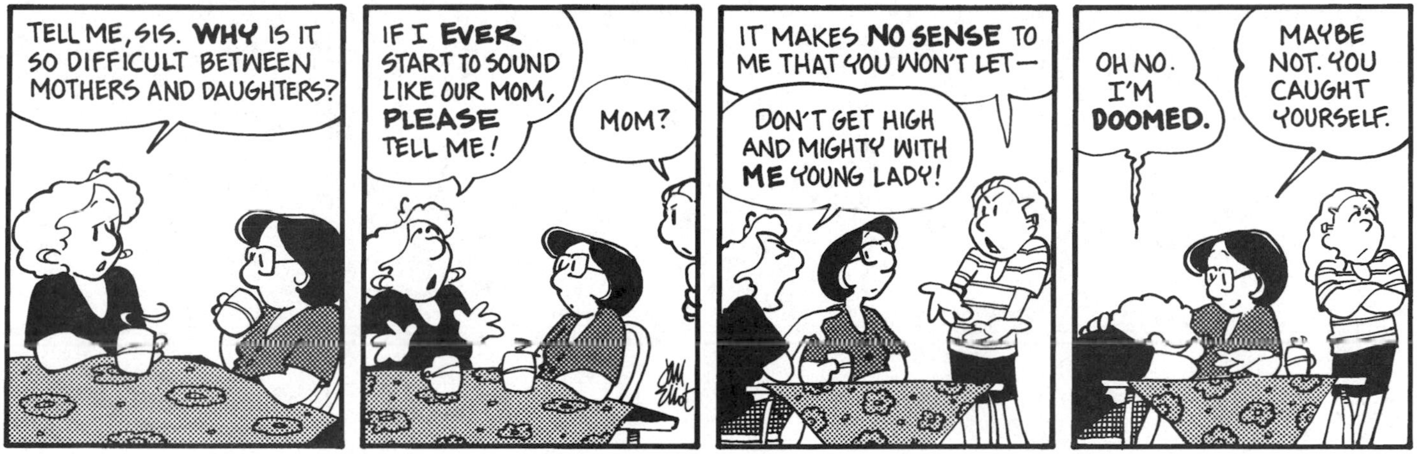
TELL ME, SIS. WHY IS IT SO DIFFICULT BETWEEN MOTHERS AND DAUGHTERS?
IF I EVER START TO SOUND LIKE OUR MOM, PLEASE TELL ME!
MOM?
IT MAKES NO SENSE TO ME THAT YOU WON'T LET—
DON'T GET HIGH AND MIGHTY WITH ME YOUNG LADY!
OH NO. I'M DOOMED.
MAYBE NOT. YOU CAUGHT YOURSELF.

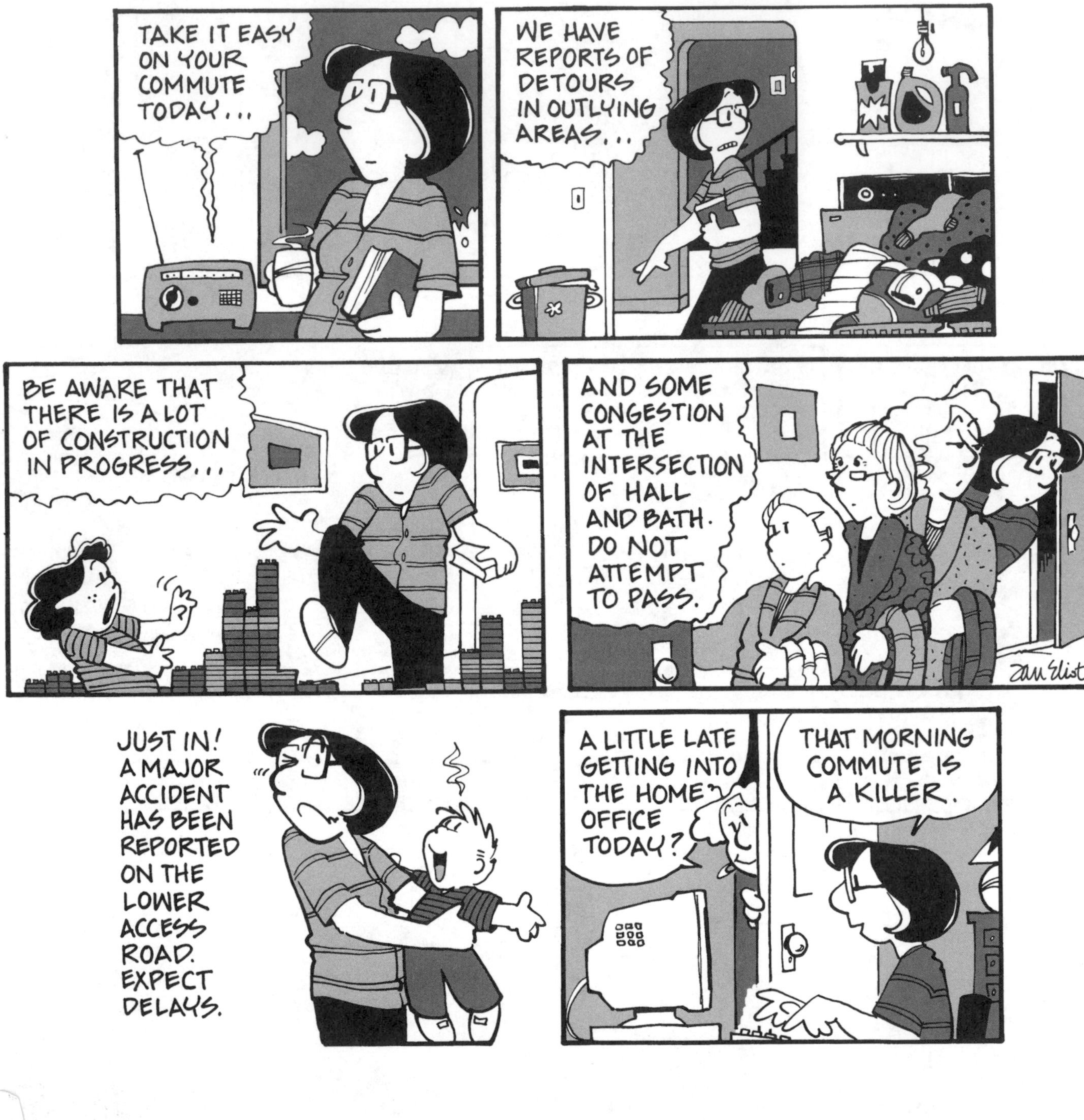
TAKE IT EASY ON YOUR COMMUTE TODAY...
WE HAVE REPORTS OF DETOURS IN OUTLYING AREAS...
BE AWARE THAT THERE IS A LOT OF CONSTRUCTION IN PROGRESS...
AND SOME CONGESTION AT THE INTERSECTION OF HALL AND BATH. DO NOT ATTEMPT TO PASS.
JUST IN! A MAJOR ACCIDENT HAS BEEN REPORTED ON THE LOWER ACCESS ROAD. EXPECT DELAYS.
A LITTLE LATE GETTING INTO THE HOME OFFICE TODAY?
THAT MORNING COMMUTE IS A KILLER.